'In Empathy as Competence, Johann Steinberger, rooting his work in intersubjectivity, resonance, and mentalization theory, understands and portrays empathy not just as a talent, but as a skill. Equally important, Steinberger presents the method he has devised to teach this crucial skill. The practice of empathy, in other words, does not necessarily require that the student of empathy already be gifted in this respect, which means that Steinberger's method, Affect Resonance Therapy, can be very widely taught. In taking this step, and doing the research to establish it, Steinberger broadens the empirical demonstration of psychoanalytic conceptualizations in a way that serves as a model for all such work, and simultaneously offers not only mental health professionals, but all healthcare workers, and even practitioners in other fields, such as education, a means of meaningfully contextualizing the understanding of persons.'

Donnel B. Stern, Ph.D., William Alanson White Institute, New York, U.S.A

'We have known for decades that the relationship, as perceived by the patient, is key to outcomes in psychotherapy. We also grasp the contributions of the therapist's capacity for empathy to that relationship. But are we constrained to select trainees with higher innate capacity for empathy, or can it be taught? Johann Steinberger has made a significant step in the project outlined in this book to answer this question. He is a major contributor to the recent move towards unpacking the tools, interventions, and therapist qualities that matter, by showing us how to go about increasing one of these– empathy. Kudos to Dr. Steinberger for this excellent book.'

Stewart Kiritz, PhD, Clinical Assistant Professor, Department of Psychiatry and Human Behavior, The Warren Alpert Medical School of Brown University, Clinical Assistant Professor Emeritus, Department of Psychiatry and Behavioral Sciences, Stanford Medical School, California, U.S.A.

An Intersubjective Mentalization-Based Primer

This book explores how Affect Resonance Training (ART), as developed by the Viennese psychotherapist Johann Steinberger, offers students and trainees in psychosocial professions the opportunity to develop competence in empathy, allowing them to better understand themselves and others.

Based on concepts of empathy, resonance, and mentalization, this innovative mode of teaching offers effective tools and training for empathetic understanding. This book presents clear instructions for its application in the classroom, summarizing several years of intensive institutional practice. The book also outlines the program's rich theoretical background and documents its empirical effectiveness.

With clear instruction on the use of ART and clinical insights on how increased empathy is effective in therapeutic settings, this book is essential reading for psychoanalysts, psychotherapists, and others across the psychosocial professions.

Dr. Johann Steinberger is a Founding Faculty Member of the academy for Affect Resonance Therapy (A.R.T.) Vienna, Austria; teaches; consults; and offers study groups for health care workers (nursing stuff, psychotherapists, psychologists, teachers, pedagogues, and medical professionals). He works in private practice and at the Forensic Outpatient Clinic Vienna, Austria.

An Intersubjective Mentalization-Based Primer

Empathy as Competence

Johann Steinberger

Translated by
Brían Hanrahan

Routledge
Taylor & Francis Group
LONDON AND NEW YORK

Designed cover image: Sarah Guttenberger, 2023

First published
by Routledge
4 Park Square, Milton Park, Abingdon, Oxon OX14 4RN

and by Routledge
605 Third Avenue, New York, NY 10158

Routledge is an imprint of the Taylor & Francis Group, an informa business

First English edition published 2026

First German edition published by Psychosozial-Verlag 2021

Johann Steinberger: Empathie als Kompetenz. Ein intersubjektives, mentalisierungsgestütztes Pädagogikkonzept © Johann Steinberger/ Psychosozial-Verlag, Gießen, 2021, www.psychosozialverlag.de

First English edition published by Routledge 2026

Library of Congress Cataloging-in-Publication Data
A catalog record has been requested for this book

ISBN: 978-1-032-77496-1 (hbk)
ISBN: 978-1-032-77493-0 (pbk)
ISBN: 978-1-003-48344-1 (ebk)

DOI: 10.4324/9781003483441

Typeset in Optima
by Taylor & Francis Books

To Claudia, Sarah, Angelika, Talis, Maris

Contents

Illustrations

Figures

Tables

Foreword

Our social fabric and well-being depend on the essential care provided by healthcare workers. As I write these words, the global population is struggling with the effects of the coronavirus. We are in the grips of a pandemic and healthcare workers are as susceptible to the virus and its associated anxieties as the patients they treat. The pressures they face are enormous. Societal expectations of healthcare workers, and the responsibilities they experience, create a constant emotional burden, even as they work to relieve the physical suffering of the individual patients under their care.

In his important new book, the psychotherapist and educator Johann Steinberger demonstrates that our emotional well-being is manifestly complex and always exists in relationship with other people. The emotional lives of healthcare workers, or of anyone else for that matter, can only be understood if we appreciate the social contexts that bind us together as human beings. We are all fundamentally emotional and social in nature. This basic precept raises some important questions: How do healthcare workers relate to the humanity of their patients, or to their own emotional experience? How might a greater emotional awareness improve not only patient care, but also the lives of healthcare workers themselves? And what kind of educative process can instil emotional understanding, given the prevailing emphasis on cognitive knowledge and biomedical research?

The societal crises we face today, from pandemics and rapid climate change to repressive and authoritarian regimes, surely provide good reason to attend to our emotions. This book asks us to engage with our emotions and recognize how they manifest themselves in our everyday and professional lives. But this is neither easy nor straightforward to do. We often do not know what we are feeling, and our current system of medical education neglects the centrality of emotional life. Steinberger demonstrates that in order to achieve emotional awareness and possibilities for emotional regulation, we need first to understand how we interact with others and the world around us. To this end, he lays out a carefully planned and practiced program of training that teaches us to reflect on and understand emotionality – to mentalize our emotions – and thus, to learn from and deepen our emotional lives.

Empathy as Competence is a thoroughly and wonderfully interdisciplinary book. It is both scholarly and highly readable, a work that combines history and theory, with evidence-based practice and training models that draw upon ongoing qualitative and quantitative research. Above all, this book seeks to render psychoanalytic ideas relevant for the present, and to invigorate an approach to medical and therapeutic education that moves beyond cognition and embraces the reality of our emotions, in all their richness and complexity.

This book is both an introduction to an essential training course in the emotions and a vital reminder of the importance of psychoanalysis at a time when psychotherapy is increasingly dominated by cognitive and behavioural approaches. Steinberger provides a wide-ranging and rigorous introduction to an essential body of psychodynamic theory and practice, from mentalization to intersubjectivity and relational psychoanalysis. In this sense, the book's purpose is twofold: to provide a new and specific emotion-focused model of education for healthcare workers called *Affektresonanztraining*, or ART; and to outline a contemporary and cutting-edge psychodynamic perspective on emotional life and well-being.

Steinberger's work will resonate with readers in myriad ways. As a university professor, teaching in the Faculties of Education and Psychiatry, and as a practicing psychoanalyst with hospital experience, Steinberger's book brought home for me the challenges and opportunities we face today. How do we think and practice, be it as healthcare workers in today's medical system, or as individual clinicians interacting with our patients? For example, young psychiatrists are increasingly educated only in the biomedical model and receive limited exposure to therapeutic forms of patient care. The important but often outdated psychodynamic models that once held sway in psychiatry have been overturned in favour of psychopharmacology, a formal diagnostic process and biomedical research. The patient, who was long defined as the one who suffers, has been increasingly transformed into a medical object that can be measured and assessed. As a result of these changes, today's psychiatrists-in-training are often ill prepared to understand the emotional dynamic of the healing relationship with their patients. Nor are they prepared to understand their own emotional lives or how the emotions shape what they perceive, understand and do with their patients.

How can today's educative system prepare healthcare workers to appreciate the empathic process or their emotional relationship with their patients? For Steinberger, the solution to this dilemma is clear:

> New perspectives are needed in the education of upcoming generations, moving away from cognitive meaning and towards developing psychological meanings and new forms of psychological understanding. We attach great importance to technical progress and the pursuit of change in cognitive experience. We attach less importance to our psychological development and thus stick with outdated development models. Our explanations of violent phenomena and of gender roles and their meaning still await further development. The creative basis for future generations will be found in attitude and in psychological understanding.

When we empathize with another person, we may relate differently to them depending on how we perceive and understand the patient's pain or suffering (see Luhrmann, 2000). When psychiatrists are schooled in diagnosing and prescribing in a biomedical setting, they learn to see their patients in terms of categories of illness, defined by specific brain functions and psychological symptoms. But what of their patient's lived experience, the way that an illness is felt or can shape the trajectory of life? In order to understand and empathize with a patient's lived experience, it is necessary to move beyond categories, functions, and symptoms, to grasp the experience of suffering at the heart of their struggle. This requires a different kind of relationship. It requires seeing the patient as a person, someone who is more alike than different. Empathy, the ability to think, see, or feel oneself into the place of the other, plays a crucial role in this humanizing process.

The traditional medical model, with its emphasis on universalization and objectification, tends to neglect our embeddedness in the social world. As Steinberger points out, the consequences are far reaching: "Our current understanding of science detaches itself from the actual person, attempting to present their thoughts and theories as something independent of time and place". In response, Steinberger develops an educative model that seeks to foster awareness and appreciation of the social and cultural contexts that shape emotional life. It is essential to understand human experience in the contexts in which it takes place (Frie & Coburn, 2011). This is particularly relevant for understanding emotions. Viewed from a developmental lens, patterns of emotional interaction between a child and its caregivers unfold in specific sociocultural contexts and historical trajectories and give rise to interpersonal frameworks and implicit meanings that shape subsequent emotional experiences. Viewed from a contemporary psychodynamic perspective, our emotional lives are a central dimension of all human experience and fundamentally relational and sociocultural in nature.

Steinberger's book seeks to overcome and question the overarching contemporary emphasis on cognition. In the process, it teaches us how to engage with new and different forms of emotional awareness. *Empathy as Competence* is written to help professionals concerned with the crucial task of training tomorrow's healthcare workers. This book is equally relevant to practicing therapists and students because it provides an essential guide to a growing and important body of work on mentalization. Clear and comprehensive, reaching the expert and novice alike, Steinberger's careful and sensitive study is both necessary and inspiring.

Roger Frie, PhD, PsyD, R.Psych, Professor of Education, Simon Fraser University, Affiliate Professor of Psychiatry, University of British Columbia, Vancouver, Canada

References

Frie, R. & Coburn, W.J. (Eds.). (2011). *Persons in Context: The Challenge of Individuality in Theory and Practice*. New York: Routledge.
Luhrmann, T.M. (2000). *Of Two Minds: An Anthropologist Looks at American Psychiatry*. New York: Vintage.

Preface

It is a great pleasure for me to present our training project to an English-speaking audience.

As I write this, the world is in a post-pandemic period, in a climate crisis, and wars are showing us the fragility of the world around us and the importance of becoming a cooperative community to face all these challenges. Empathy and cooperation are important keys to meeting these challenges.

Our training project has evolved and the Academy for Affect-Resonance-Therapy (A.R.T.) has been founded, where the focus of knowledge transfer is on encounter skills.

A committed group of young people carry the knowledge of A.R.T. out into society. They support people whose emotional world are shattered, advise colleagues who work in a difficult social field, and pass on their knowledge in various forms of teaching at different training institutes in lectures and seminars.

I would like to thank Nadine Weisz, Mariam Dominguez-Ramirez, Miriam Arp, Dominik Seyer, Markus Wallner, and Benjamin Herbrik. Wolfgang Berner and Roger Frie have been very helpful with their advice and wisdom. I would also like to thank Laura Stahman, Cherie Villano, and Stewart Kiritz for their intellectual exchange and patient listening. Thank you to Christoph Sulyok for his thoughts.

Brian Hanrahan translated the text from German into English with his subtle sense of language.

To my old friends who are there for me in all situations: Leo Forsthofer and Manfred Stattler.

Donnel Stern and Kate Hawes at Routledge deserve a huge thank you for making this book a reality. I would like to thank the Routledge production team, led by Deepika Batra, for their dedication to the book process.

I am grateful to all the people who have come into contact with me, whether as students, patients, or colleagues, all of whom have in common that I have learned something about myself from them.

Acknowledgments

Me tomó cuatro años pintar como Rafael, pero me llevó toda una vida aprender a dibujar como un niño. (It took me four years to learn to paint like Raphael, but a whole lifetime to learn to draw like a child.)

Pablo Picasso (in Fernández Mínguez, 2019, p. 161)

As I write these lines, the world is in a fragile condition, in the grip of a virus which is profoundly disrupting our usual patterns of understanding. Many of the students the reader will meet in this book are now working in the hospital wards, outpatient clinics, and other health facilities which are taking responsibility for our well-being. Thanks to modern technologies of communication, some of these students look out at me from my computer screen, overworked and with tired faces. Metaphors of war, metaphors of helplessness, make an appearance, connecting to me the overwhelming demands from outside. Here with me, in the calm encounter, many experience feelings of guilt that they are not with colleagues on the "frontline." Out there, the prevailing feeling is one of community with colleagues; fear is transformed into action, and courage becomes a synonym for endurance. The fear of quarantine for family members and health workers is everywhere: the fear of being locked up in your home, in a nursing home, etc., banished from action to a state of stagnation. The fear of being taken away from one's own significance, from the actions taken on the ward, the fear of being hurled into the absolute existence of one's own self, determined and signified by feelings of fear, helplessness and rage. Loneliness gives birth to our existence in all its aspects, the absence of the other determines their presence.

The protagonists of this book are patients and students; their immersion in the shared encounter in a meaningful process for us, conveying to us the meaning of being. All of this shared living and shared activity made it possible to create a space of fulfilling identity. I am grateful to all of my committed students, with their great drive to discover: grateful for having found myself in their midst.

The book presents a project which began in autumn 2010: we were a small, constantly changing group, starting into a new mode of teaching with spaces for reflection. Quite a number of people were involved in establishing, developing, and maintaining the project, with a core group involved since the beginning.

Throughout all this time, Hubert Streif has given us the possibilities of a home: as Director of the School of Health and Nursing at the Penzing Campus, he has defended the project against all adversities, as well as being the person responsible for financing our joint project. He gave everyone involved the confidence that our work would take place within a meaningful overall educational concept.

Ewa Zemann and Gerlinde Zöchling were early advocates of our project and helped greatly in its early days, encouraging our small teaching group (three people), keeping destructive critical voices away from group leaders. Ewa always kept a thoughtful eye on the process of development, as well as designing our questionnaire and, along with Claudia Gundacker, handling our research data.

We are grateful to Angelika Guttenberger and Wolfgang Sieberth, who led the first groups: they planted the seeds and tended to the early growth of our work; our thanks for their courage in experimentation and reflection, even in this delicate initial phase. Later group leaders included Georg Totzauer, with his spontaneous and creative group moderation, who introduced new design-dynamic moments, and Claudia Gundacker, who contributed much, including her scientific expertise. It was she who made us aware of the Giessen test. I am very grateful to all four leaders for breathing life into this project. Later, Gerhard Schossmeier joined our group, developing the first two semesters of our six-year project, with a focus on self-awareness. He also brought Gerhard Sprinzel on board, to further develop self-awareness elements. It was Gerhard Schossmaier's creativity with language which gave us the name Affect Resonance Training (ART), an artistic way of describing what we do.

Five group leaders have forged new paths and have been indispensable components of our process, their comings and goings reflecting the dynamic, fluid process itself. Gisela Hajek has been an integral part of managing and developing the groups for many years now.

Tanja Stroblmayr has been in charge of editing and fine-tuning the text; I was kindly accompanied in publication by Jana Motzet of Psychosozial-Verlag. I am grateful to Brit Haslinger for her support, helping me to frame the texts within a comprehensible language of scientific interdisciplinarity through intellectual conversation and an understanding of linguistic meaning as a process of "digestion."

Thomas Stephenson prompted me to think about the importance of relational thinkers in the psychodynamic field. Martin Jandl lent support via benevolent emails. To serve as witness to my actions and thus to recognize my generative embeddedness: this was the responsibility of Wilhelm Burian.

Roger Frie provides a foreword, for which I am very grateful: I have gained inspiration and insight from Roger since meeting him at a conference in 2018 and reading his book Not in my Family: German Memory and Responsibility after the Holocaust.

Renate Steinberger is responsible for the book's wonderful photographs. Sarah Guttenberger provided the image for the cover.

I owe great gratitude to the family from which I come, in which unfolds the life of handing on, and which one also chooses, as a family in which one works.

There are many other names which are not listed here, to whom I am deeply grateful for their role in my development: those who accompanied me, who inspired me greatly, who believed in me.

1 Introduction

All forms of training in psychosocial fields regard social competency as an essential basic requirement.[1] In the last two decades, the idea of educational qualifications has changed from imparting or acquiring "knowledge" to the imparting or learning of "competencies". But how can we define the competencies and skills needed for life and work? And what is meant by professionalism, when it comes to teaching or learning the kind of social skills expected in every psychosocial field of activity? These questions are often addressed with terms that are not particularly precise: they are described in terms of an ability to establish "sustainable relationships" or hold a "relieving" conversation. If one presses these terms more closely, they reveal themselves to have as many meanings as they do users.

We have a clear sense of how to impart "knowledge", how to render it reproducible and verifiable. Explicit knowledge can be communicated well in the form of language. In contrast, when learning implicit knowledge or social skills, terms like "personality" are used, terms which denote a complex web of implicit and explicit perception, understandings, and possibilities of communicative action. Depending on the situation, these possibilities can lead to helpful interventions (Buchholz, 2008). The capacity for social skills is closely linked to the personality of the intervening person. These skills thus begin with the skill of being able to represent or define personality. Personality can be posited or described as the role behaviour which defines me, or as the expectations placed on me by others. But in the spirit of Wittgenstein, competency as role attribution only works when one person demonstrates behaviour which is interpreted by another as competent action. The concept of "competence" is thus simply a more highly-structured, metaphor-like word, which can only be characterized in terms of action, followed by external attribution. We see something similar with the meanings assigned to the word "social". We always need a level of action, which we then "insert" into a describable construct, so as to translate it into action or to use it as an implicit construct to guide action. All epistemological theories agree that perception and processing, taking place in implicit or unconscious form, are crucial for developing the competencies and expertise needed to understand and resolve difficult social situations. When we give

DOI: 10.4324/9781003483441-1

meaning to what we recognize, we do so within a given situation. Perceiving something always means taking something into ourselves, whereby we deduce a whole from implicit and discrete pieces of information within our brain (Neuweg, 2004). Building on previous experience, our implicit knowledge primarily begins from individual elements we perceive, which emerge as affects and are then transformed into an image (Krause, 2005). A sort of back-and-forth goes on between background consciousness and focal consciousness (Kahl-Popp, 2004, 2009, 2011, 2015). Polanyi assumes an implicit triad which people use to cope with situations by focusing on their experiences and their already assimilated knowledge (Neuweg, 2004). The three elements of the triad are, first, the subject; second, a listening-inward; and third, the simultaneously anticipatory and imaginative purpose which exists outside the self. What this means is that we cope with situations where we encounter others by permitting ourselves to exist in a condition of not-knowing and not-understanding. This in turn enables us to adopt an attitude of affinitive self-organization. In short, we can say that social competency is a process of learning and implementation, which is in turn based on a process of perception.

Starting from this fundamental idea, I have developed an overall approach to instruction, based on the training of perception. This approach found its first practical application in the training of psychiatric nurses. The training course for these nurses lasts six semesters, divided into theoretical and practical blocks. The particular demands of psychiatric nursing as a job mean that students must develop the ability to deal with their own personality, as well as the capacity to work with their own and other people's feelings.

To give greater emphasis to these aspects within the training program, we put together a conceptual outline covering the whole six semesters of the nurses' training. Introspection is the focus for the first two semesters: this is taught through self-reflection conducted in small groups. In the first year, teaching thus focuses on the student becoming aware of their own needs and emotional reactions, as experienced in various life situations, as well as reflecting on the personal life narrative they associate with these situations. In the final year of training, the emphasis shifts to developing a capacity to benefit from supervision while demonstrating self-reflexive behaviour in dealings with patients and staff. By now, students should possess the ability to connect together declarative knowledge – in other words, explicit and articulable factual knowledge – in the context of specific processes.

For the second year of the training process, I have developed a particular form of "patient observation". Above all, this aims to help the student to develop and use a particular inner attitude, one characterized by relational mentalization. These two semesters focus on the student's capacity to separate out and reconnect the very different modes of perception which are needed to conduct patient observation. What is at stake here is the capacity to mentalize, based on a prior stage in which students learn to clearly assess subject-object boundaries in specific interpersonal situations.

This second year of training begins with a theory block, made up of four teaching units. This block of teaching is used to impart general ideas and theoretical background, as well as eventually to create groups of six students, groups in which they will collectively "reflect". These groups identify an opportunity for patient observation: for example in a ward or outpatient clinic, or in some other area of the social organizations in which the students are active.

The training of perception is based on two elements: the input factor and the output factor. The first part of the training focuses on students changing their inner attitude with regard to external stimuli, thus reducing their own enactment. The student finds a place from which they may observe and maintains a passive mode of behaviour. At all times, they must try to remain below the stimulus threshold of their surroundings, in this way creating a kind of "differential" within themselves. Now the student can begin to observe, opening their sensorium to the situation, allowing images to enter into them and encounter their own previous experiences, based on their seven fundamental emotions (Ekman, 2010, 2011). This in turn leads to an internalization of the images coming from outside, which can now fall on fertile ground within them. In other words, these images affect students' own internal models of attachment, leading to a process of inner transformation.

Next, the student writes up their observations in an observation record. Based on the notes they write, group discussion can now begin, focusing on how the student's reflection on the situation – their externalization of the images they had previously internalized – contributes to their understanding of interactions between people observed. Moreover, the student is also explicitly asked to write down their feelings about the scenes they have observed.

In this second part of the process, the small group discusses the written observation records. The group's own reactions to the material presented in turn become the subject matter for reflection, in a process which can lead to a better understanding of the observed patient and the scene around them. The group can consider whether its own reactions to the observation record have produced a more differentiated representation of the scene. After two semesters engaged in this work, students should be able to recognize when and how their own patterns of attachment are influencing their interpretations. They can also reflect on their own success or otherwise in creating a mentalization situation when they encounter others. Mentalization means developing the ability to understand one's own intentions and feelings, and in this way gaining a sense of others' feelings and intentions and becoming better able to communicate one's observations to others.

This three-year project aims to train students in empathy, metacognition, inner mindfulness, and emotional intelligence, which are learned as fundamental skills within the overall development of reflexive behavioural competence. In short, they develop the ability to mentalize.

1 Higher and Further Education

Many people rush into third-level education, keen to earn educational credentials. The European Commission forecasts that by 2050 at least one third of all jobs will be in the high-skill sector, with the proportion of low-skill jobs falling below 15 percent (European Commission, 2011; Al-Ani, 2013). In the coming decades, institutions of public education will not have enough places to satisfy this increasing demand for higher education. The steady reduction in education budgets also seems certain to affect the quality of higher education (Kamenetz, 2011). These forecasts suggest an urgent need for action in terms of the state funding of advanced training, which would bring with it a corresponding restructuring of the delivery of educational content. Many current theories start from the belief that our education system is very much driven by economic and political interests, and tailored to the requirements of nation states (Al-Ani, 2013; Kamenetz, 2011). From this perspective, education has always been an instrument controlled by these forces, rather than being based on a universalistic, global model (Meyer & Ramirez, 2005).

In this context, the internet appears to offer a freer space, and it is here that new educational structures and participants are beginning to emerge, including P2P (peer-to-peer) and "edupunks" (Kop, 2007; Kamenetz, 2009). Modern learning goes beyond students' capacity to self-organize; this process in turn demands a new definition of the role of the teacher. Knowledge will be generated in new, self-driven forms, including those made available by P2P structures. In future, education will be even more focused on the teacher's capacity to engage with students' self-organization: the teacher's job will be more about mentoring than imparting cognitive knowledge. Teachers are becoming something which combines aspects of both peers and "edupunks".

The term "edupunks" was coined by the blogger Jim Groom in 2008 to refer to people who acquire knowledge out of interest, without aiming for a university qualification. They are, in other words, people who acquire knowledge outside of classic university structures. The year 2001 is considered to mark the birth of edupunk technology: this was when MIT began putting free courses online (Al-Ani, 2013). "If the tools work best while the learners are in control, it is time for tutors to relinquish some power and trust their students to get on with the activity of blogs and wikis as disruptive technologies", wrote the education scholar Rita Kop (2007, p. 197f.). For Kop, self-organization and self-monitoring takes place within peer groups, suggesting that the role of teachers should be reconsidered. The social theorist Jeremy Rifkin likewise highlights the importance of learning among students; "peer to peer learning shifts the focus from the lone self to the interdependent group. Learning ceases to be an isolated experience between an authority figure and a student and is transformed into a community experience" (Rifkin, 2011, p. 246). Institutions of learning will be changed by these new demands around the imparting of knowledge. "Teaching" schools must become "learning" schools, connected through interdisciplinary research across pedagogy, sociology, technology, and psychology (Günther & Hüffel, 1999; Gelernter, 2012).

In this new educational world, the classic professorial role – lecturing from a standing position at the front of the class – will be transformed into that of a mentor, mainly focusing on personal development and the practical imparting of cognitive knowledge (Al-Ani, 2013; Nentwich, 2004). The writer David Gelernter has predicted that only the 25 best-known universities in America and Europe will survive. Scientific and technically-oriented courses of study will survive in something like their traditional form. But the more that fields of study are geared towards the imparting of cognitive knowledge, the more teaching will shift to a virtual context. He goes on to suggest that students will turn to online learning, learning directly from renowned researchers, including Nobel Prize winners (Gelernter, 2012). We will see a move away from teaching and learning in their classical form, and will thus also require a redesign of the educational encounter:

> A focus on learning activity may necessitate changes in space planning projects, calling into question the traditional design approach that focuses on the shape of the room, the efficiency of the fixed seating arrangement, the instructor location, and so on.
>
> (Barone, 2005, p. 223).

Pedagogical practice must come up with new forms of communication and teaching, so that learning can take place in and through encounters. Moreover, teaching must offer structures for these encounters, structures in which these new forms of perception can actually take place. Young people need to create their own knowledge rather than simply passively absorbing it (Barone, 2005). Michael Polanyi (1958, 1985) speaks of people as knowledge-generator, rather than passively accumulating knowledge in a linear sense (Neuweg, 2004). Universities which offer only the unidirectional imparting of knowledge will destroy creative potential. Beginning in the fall semester of 2013, the University of Wisconsin launched flexible, competency-oriented models for students in some degree programs, in this way making the programs more accessible for career changers, allowing them to advance through their course in a more self-directed way (Rollwagen, 2013). Education must enable people to understand themselves and others; it must allow them to use their understanding to create is sometimes termed *loop-reflective learning*. This will mean the end of learners and teachers as such. Nor will education ever be completed; instead, it will become a permanent, shifting process of influence and absorption (Glotz, 1998).

2 Teaching

It seems important to see the process of teaching as a skill, one which enables both learners and teachers to open up a creative, mentalizing space. The specific content to be imparted is only a secondary focus in education. We need to think of this in terms of the "lubrication" required to get a machine running. But what kind of "lubrication" is needed to teach "lubrication" itself? We can already see that imparting knowledge involves a permanent overlap of systems: this is where learning takes place. The roles of teacher and learner are deconstructed and lose significance, since "knowledge" itself is based on permanent communicational exchange. Teaching means that our inner conventions and self-certainties are gently agitated, so we can begin to deconstruct our own thinking (Kahl-Popp, 2007). The process opens a space for creative thinking, which in turn counteracts the tendency to rigidity and unproductivity.

Creativity arises when students are shown a mirroring of their actions, when they experience what teaching feels like by experiencing teachers as the recipients of *their* actions. The teacher shows the learner a work situation, while the learner shows the teacher what this situation means for her, or for both of them. In this way, they both *show* the activity of educating and teaching, in the anthropologically-grounded sense of "show" suggested by Pranger, who argues that showing is an "originary gesture" for human beings. From this perspective, it is important for teachers to focus on the ways that learners process their knowledge. In return, teachers should make their own processing available to the learners, as part of this shared process. What is at stake here is the establishment of reciprocal interdependence: this is a shifting, oscillating process, a relation which is respected as such by both parties (Pranger, 2012). However, it should be noted that if either or both parties base their teaching or learning on a sadomasochistic experience of relationships, then their introjection process will lead to the formation of the same pattern of relationship. In this case, the process of reciprocal interdependence will be deformed into a hierarchical process, one which does not correspond to our ideas of interdependence.

The creative development of learners and teachers comes about when they become aware of phenomena unfolding in the encounter between them. The creative process can be initiated by either of the two interaction partners adopting a relational mentalizing attitude, whereby they take the perspective of an "as if character" (Pranger, 2012; Fonagy et al., 2002). Their perspective is transposed to the position of an observer: in this way, it is like looking at an image through a filter, so that the image mediated is not outshone by the glare of the sun. The standpoint of the observer filters out or reduces the intense feelings within the scene, preparing a space in which to play with ascribed roles. In this way, observers can evade perspectives of right-and-wrong and black-and-white when considering a scene, and in this way gain control over any inner feelings of guilt or sadism. However, if a fundamentally sadomasochistic pattern is present, there may again be a temptation to use knowledge gained in the encounter in order to satisfy this dynamic. If the teacher's anxiety prevents them from opening up creatively and assuming the role of a learner, they will only be able to impart content, to convey methods, or to give if-then instructions. This leaves them in a highly concretizing attitude (Kahl-Popp, 2007). However, it could be possible, for example, for the supposed learner to in fact teach the teacher via her own contradiction, showing the teacher how their mobilization of their fears has led them to adhere even more closely to rules, hindering the learner from acting as a learner and from paying close attention to words as they are spoken. What is significant about this scene is that it shuts down all possibility of adopting a mentalizing attitude, so that the only reaction is to escape through the use of certain words and the rote reproduction of learned material. The learner learns that fear is to be overcome through escape or repression. Their feelings cannot be "contained" by the teacher, in Bion's sense of that term (Bion, 2001). This situation becomes even more fascinating if we consider the possibility of an element of perversion in it, in which the teacher's actions produce the satisfaction of sadomasochistic tendencies.

The object of learning is to be found within, outside, and between learners and teachers. Processes of unfolding and creativity take place within the dynamic form of the encounter (Kahl-Popp, 2007). The concept of the individual here can also be replaced by that of the group. Sünkel emphasizes that all teaching must alter the personality of the learner (Sünkel, 2002). Since the specific roles of learners and teachers only correspond to the constructed role ascribed to them, Sünkel's idea can be expanded to mean that creativity only develops within a particular space if the personality of *both* figures undergoes some change.

3 Theoretical Framework

The work outlined in this book was initially guided by and based on two separate strands of thought: first, the practical concept of infant observation, as developed by Esther Bick, and second, theories of mentalization, as conceived by Fonagy and his colleagues (Fonagy et al., 2002). The idea of mentalization forms part of the wider body of intersubjective-relational thought; the history and meaning of these relational approaches within psychoanalysis will be discussed in more detail below.

Bick was brought to the Tavistock Clinic by John Bowlby in the late 1940s in order to establish a training programme in child psychotherapy. Through her experience in Vienna, where she had completed a dissertation with Charlotte Bühler on the observation of young children, Bick recognized the value of the close observation of human interaction. To prospective child psychotherapists, she sought to impart the concept of non-verbal behaviours and of infant experience (Bick, 2009a; Freud, 1976; Rustin, 2009).

Bick's (2009a) conception of infant observation, published in 1964, has four basic elements. The first is the creation of groups of four to five candidates in child psychoanalytic training. This group makes contact with the expectant mother prior to the birth of the child, with the intention of later observing and recording her interaction with the infant. In a third step, the observation reports made in this context are anonymized and distributed to all group participants, including the group leader. Seminar participants take turns to discuss their observational record of the mother-baby interaction. The group then collaboratively reflects on the observations. In the fourth element of the training, a group member notes down a record of these reflexive discussions, so as to make it easier to refer back to particular case histories (Datler, 2009; Lazar, 2000; Bick, 2009a).

To illustrate the method, there follows a short excerpt from an observation record from a particular infant observation:

> He turns his head and looks at me, his large pupils stick to me like a magnet, they seem to suck everything in. He lets his arms hang down limply, with the fingers of his hand clutching a small blue toy car, a Mercedes A-class with a small panda sticking out from the windshield. His stomach bulges outwards, representing the outermost limit of his body. His chin hangs down. A trail of mucus runs from his nose to his upper lip. He seems to have a cold. He carefully dabs at his lip with his tongue. He continues to gaze at me, then suddenly turns away. He goes to the wall, leans against it with his side, then looks at me once more. Again he turns his head away, pressing himself even harder against the wall, as if he was snuggling up against it.
>
> (Protocol 11, Steinberger, Summer Semester 2010, Kindergarten).

At this point, the observation report is read aloud within the small group and is then discussed by the participants. As well as fostering observation and record-taking abilities, this exercise is also about training psychosocial skills, including empathy and sensitivity training (Datler, 2009; Lazar, 2000).

Criticism of this kind of infant observation has suggested that the observer is a kind of intruder in the scene, disrupting intimacy and thus altering the course of the child's development. The mother's unconscious interest in giving observers access to the scene could indicate some pathological phenomenon on her part. The observer's objectivity cannot be guaranteed, since he or she is forced to be grateful for the opportunity to observe. The student has had the experience of being an unwelcome "guest"; it will later prove difficult for them to withstand pressure from "outside" (Kahl-Popp, 2001).

This book's second theoretical approach is based on my reflections on mentalization as a developmental psychological model. The word "mentalize" was already used by Pierre Marty in the 1980s, as part of his idea of psychosomatics. Marty evaluated mentalization on three axes: depth, flexibility, and consistency (Aisenstein, 2008). Today, mentalization is more associated with the way in which Fonagy et al. (1991) have developed the concept, making connections between attachment theory, developmental psychology, and psychodynamic, cognitive-behavioural, trauma-related, and neurobiological approaches, as well theories of mind (Fonagy et al., 2002).

Fonagy and his colleagues understand mentalization as the capacity to view oneself and others as beings with both mental and emotional aspects, and, based on this self-conception, the ability to understand other people's reactions and participate in their behaviour. Mentalization is a process whereby people realize that their own perceptions of the world and the perceptions of others are mediated by the mind and are therefore mental. The capacity to mentalize can be developed through a person's experiences of attachment and relationships with others, but at the same time the ability has an impact on those attachments and relationships (Fonagy, 1998; Fonagy & Luyten, 2011; Fonagy & Target, 1995, 2002, 2003, 2011; Sieberth & Steinberger, 2013; Lackinger, 2008; Dornes, 2004; Fischer-Kern & Fonagy, 2012; Bolm, 2009, 2010; Schultz-Venrath, 2013; Allen et al., 2011; Allen, 2009).

Jeremy Holmes describes the origins of the concept of mentalization in his article "Notes on Mentalizing – Old Hat, or New Wine?" (2005). Holmes highlights four aspects of mentalization. One is drawn from cognitive psychology, with the philosophical construct of a "theory of mind" (Siegler et al., 2005). Object relations theory is another reference point, with particular focus on Bion's theories. Pierre Marty adopted the idea of operational thinking from French psychoanalysis, while the concept of an overlap between reality and fantasy is taken from Winnicott's ideas of development (Fonagy & Target, 2002; Holmes, 2005; Fischer-Kern & Fonagy, 2012).

The originality of concept of mentalization lies in its combination of quite different disciplines, including controversial and contentious ones. Developmental psychology brings together the theory of mind, attachment research, and the conclusions of psychoanalysis. Another innovation is the operationalization of mentalization through the use of the Reflective Functioning Scale, which has allowed the concept to feed into empirical research.

Since mentalization was created as a developmental idea, it can also highlight aberrant developments, contributing to explanatory models for pathological development. Ideas of mentalization tend to focus on the gradual acquisition of "knowledge" about affects (Fonagy et al., 2002, p. 171ff.). Gergely and Watson's maternal biofeedback model and the associated discovery of contingency serve as a theoretical basis for this (Gergely & Watson, 1996). A "foreign self" is seen as an aberration of normal maternal affect mirroring, which can lead to borderline personality structure (Fonagy & Target, 2002; Bateman & Fonagy, 2006).

Kernberg has made repeated criticisms of the concept of mentalization, pointing out two key problems. First, on a theoretical level, he addresses the meaning of mentalization with regard to object relations theory. Second, on the level of treatment, Kernberg questions mentalization-based intervention techniques in the context of borderline patients. He suggests that idea of a "foreign self" is inadequate because it fails to capture the patient's complex oscillation between complementary and concordant transference. The contribution of "theory of mind" to ideas of mentalization centres on the creation of a realistic representation of the other, in this way enabling empathy with the other. If this process is disturbed, as in severe personality disorders, we observe an inability to react empathically towards others. Kernberg claims that antisocial personality disorder – a severe disorder – tends to contradict this, since people suffering from this disorder are in fact capable of recognizing the needs of others. They clearly do possess a "theory of mind" about the other person; the problem is that they cannot emotionally engage with them (Kernberg, 2009).

From the perspective of psychotherapeutic treatment, the Manual on Transference-Focused Psychotherapy (TFP) (Clarkin et al., 2008) makes consistent reference to promoting patients' ability to mentalize and does not rule out psychoanalytic interpretation as a technique for understanding severe personality disorders. Mentalization-based Therapy (MBT) rejects interpretative approaches, because of the risk of re-activating traumas (Kernberg, 2011b). The concept of mentalization forms part of the TFP concept, coming into play in the first third of treatment (Kernberg, personal communication, 2012). In this context, it has been trenchantly characterized as "old wine in new bottles" (Pritz, personal communication, 2013).

4 State of Research

Various attempts have been made to render implicit knowledge learnable. This project is based on aspects of observation and perception which can form a foundation for acquiring social competency. In all social professions, the focus is on establishing a positive and emotional relationship. This project combines two fundamental strands of research. First, we will examine Esther Bick's development of infant observation; her work on this subject touches on several relevant fields. Second, we will derive developmental psychological aspects and associated insights from the idea of mentalization, then examine them in terms of their practical relevance.

4.1 Infant Observation

Infant observation has formed part of child psychotherapist training at the Tavistock Clinic since 1948. From 1960 on, it was also incorporated into training at the Institute for Psychoanalysis in London (Bick, 2009a). Having begun observing young children in Vienna in 1936, this form of observation of was further developed in London and then diffused worldwide (Datler, 2009). Isca Salzberger-Wittenberg helped to spread the idea in the German-speaking world and later succeeded Bick as the leader of the training group in the field (Salzberger-Wittenberg, 2002). The method of observation was developed in seminars over many years: observations were conducted weekly, each lasting one hour, with the student assuming a passive, well-disposed attitude, which allowed them to grasp the emotional significance of the scene unfolding in front of them. The student must maintain distance from the event, identifying a position from which they can develop evenly suspended attention. Observers must be aware of their own counter-transferential feelings. The scenes observed are later recorded in observation reports, which are discussed within the training group, including comparison with other reports (Bick, 2009a).

For Bick, precise observation forms an important part of developing a *containing* orientation towards the situation under observation. Emotional responses and primitive fears are constantly stimulated in the observer. Diem-Wille describes the observation of infants as "a training of the feelings". As a person, the observer also absorbs the emotions unfolding in the scene they observe: they thus represent a "container", in Bion's sense of the term (Diem-Wille, 2009b, p. 68f.). The primary aim of infant observation is to learn how to observe. One should not have preconceived notions in one's mind and should be aware of one's own feelings. The most important inner attitude is unknowingness and curiosity. The second important point for the observer is to make themselves available as a receptive vessel, absorbing everything from a passive standpoint, not actively interfering in the events going on around them (Israel, 2007).

The technique was further developed by Martha Harris in the 1970s, who introduced the so-called "work discussion seminar". This kind of observation and perception focuses on unconscious phenomena in work processes and within organizations. The work discussion seminar is used at the Tavistock Clinic and at Klagenfurt University, among other institutions, so that people can better recognize and understand their own actions in everyday professional life. Unconscious work processes and the interactions concealed within them are made conscious by participants' observation of themselves and the work situation; within a group context, they then further reflect on the observation report (Steinhardt & Reiter, 2009). This work discussion is an important training module in studies in psychodynamic organizational development and is currently offered at the Vienna Psychoanalytic Academy (Lazar, 2000, 2009; Datler, 2004, 2006; Messerer, 2004, 2008). There have as yet been no studies evaluating these concepts. Another field of application for this form of observation is with people in retirement and care homes (Trunkenpolz et al., 2009; Datler et al., 2012). Infant observation has also been used in neonatal intensive care units to better understand premature infants (Israel & Reißmann, 2008). A reconceptualization of "infant observation" according to Bick was also undertaken in the context of the so-called Kiel Model. This model no longer requires students to observe the mother-child dyad, but rather to conduct a triadic observation, including the presence of the father. This form of family observation is intended to enable students of psychoanalysis to grasp essential features of the psychotherapeutic relationship (Kahl-Popp, 2001).

4.2 Concepts of Mentalization

The concept of mentalization is widely used in the treatment of mental illnesses, as a preventative measure in a wide variety of institutions, and for training psychiatric doctors in mentalization-based treatment (Williams et al., 2009). It is also used in the context of psychoeducation (Haslam-Hopwood et al., 2009; Allen et al., 2011) and as a technique in educational counselling (Sadler et al., 2009). Early results in the latter context are available with reference to a project entitled "Minding the Baby". Here, a first evaluation phase measured the impact of mentalization-based intervention on a small cohort, leading to the development of a clinical manual. A long-term experimental study, in which two separate groups participate, has yet to be completed (Sadler et al., 2009). Another study undertook a comparison between mentalization-based conceptions of violence in an educational context and social-systemic understandings of the same phenomenon. Over 3,000 children took part in randomized controlled trials, conducted across several schools (Twemlow & Fonagy, 2009; Allen et al., 2011). Another application of mentalization can be seen in supervision and management (Schultz-Venrath, 2013; Doering, 2013). In 1999, a London-based research project (Bateman and Fonagy) carried out efficacy studies of mentalization used a treatment concept on 44 borderline patients. Research included two follow-up evaluations (Bolm, 2009). A BA thesis on "Mentalization and Social Competence" was written as part of a research internship at a secondary school in Vienna (Böck, 2011). Another BA thesis, supervised by Dr Stephenson, addressed "the connection between psychodrama as a psychotherapeutic method and the concept of mentalization developed by Fonagy and others, from a psychoanalytic-pedagogical perspective" (Stifter, 2012). The IPU in Berlin has hosted a project looking into psycho-dynamically oriented work. Over a period from August 2012 to December 2013, four groups of children at a childcare centre were studied under the direction of Prof. Christine Ludwig-Körner (Ludwig-Körner, 2012–2013). In addition, a study investigating interest in mentalization among prospective therapists has been carried out at the University of Klagenfurt (Taubner et al., 2014).

5 Methodological Approach

The author developed his methodological approach in the context of observing students in a three-year nursing course with a focus on psychiatry. Since the course can lead to a professional license in the psychiatric field, participants must be at least 18 years old when they begin training, requiring a methodical approach and test-based selection for adults.

The work with the nursing students takes place in the second year of training. At the beginning of the project, the subjects are given a test to record their self-image. They are then given an observation report and take a test to assess their image of the person described in the report. The two tests are repeated at the end of the second year: the resulting data is used to test hypotheses. The Giessen Test II was and is used as a form of assessing oneself and others (Beckmann & Richter, 1972; Beckmann et al., 2012a). IBM's SPSS 20 (Superior Performing Software System) is used for statistical data analysis and data management of the material collected (Raab-Steiner & Benesch, 2012; Bühl, 2012). The quantitative research approach consists of both descriptive statistical and inferential statistical data analysis.

In terms of qualitative research methods, the approach used here is that of objective hermeneutics (Oevermann, 2002). The observation reports are sequenced, then analysed in terms of content and processual meaning; the resulting interpretations are checked against further text sequences. This data is meant to allow the interpretation of individual sequences to be raised to generalization; in turn, this can be related back to a mentalizing interpretation of the students' observations (Buchholz et al., 2011; Kleemann et al., 2013; Flick, 1995; Oevermann, 2002).

5.1 Sample

There were 322,468 students in Austrian vocational schools in 2013 (BMUKK Zahlenspiegel, 2013). The nine federal states had a total of 67 nursing schools, with a total of six training centres for psychiatric nursing, located in the states of Vienna, Lower Austria, Upper Austria, Styria, and Vorarlberg. Training to become a qualified psychiatric nurse has a minimum age of 18. The training period lasts three years, with the possibility of accelerated progress if a candidate possesses appropriate pre-qualifications. With these, students can enter training in the second or third year, which can alter the age cohort of the students in any given year. Over the course of two semesters in the second year of training, mentalization-based pedagogy (MBP) or affect resonance training (ART II) is used: this involves an average of 40 students, with an average of 27 female and 13 male students. The project began in 2010 and forms part of a three-year training program with a focus on personality development. As part of this project, each student writes between ten and twelve observation reports, resulting in the production and archiving of around 400 observation reports per year. Texts are randomly selected from this set of reports and subjected to a reconstruction of their latent meaning structures.

5.2 Instruments and Material

The methods used here come from psychotherapy research. The Giessen Test II was produced on the basis of the original Giessen Test, which was developed over several years in the 1970s by a team at the Psychosomatic University Clinic in Giessen. The Giessen test is one of the few test procedures in German-speaking countries to have been developed for measuring personality traits. It belongs to the broader category of psychometric personality tests, and, within this, to tests of personality structure (Brähler et al., 2002). The test allows the subject to create an image of their self. The test is designed for adults (18 years and older) and young people (14 years and older), and is also used in carrying out assessments of other people, as well as in producing a self-image. Students conduct this kind of assessment on a specific person described in one of the observation reports. At the end of two semesters, students again complete the Giessen Test II as a means of self-assessment. The same observation report as previously is used, serving as a basis for the student's assessment of another person, whom they evaluate using the third-party evaluation part of the Giessen Test II. The data obtained in this way is processed in SPSS 24, then subjected to analysis.

Five or six patient observation reports are made available to each student per semester. The reports are prepared using interpretive social research, specifically the method of objective hermeneutics. This method, developed by Ulrich Oevermann, offers a qualitative data-evaluation method for analysing interactions. With the help of objective hermeneutics, individual reports are studied in order to decipher the objective meaning-structures which underlie subjective meanings. It is a matter of making visible these deeper levels of meaning, levels which structure and thus determine the material in its present form.

5.3 Objectives of the Study

The first part of the research brings together a number of concepts from the fields of psychoanalysis, psychotherapy, infant observation, and pedagogy, using theoretical reflection to design a training program for the learning of "social competence". Social competence is understood here as the ability to reflect and to mentalize. These skills are tested with a personality test, so we can thus draw conclusions about the training's effectiveness.

The presumption is that we will see an improvement in students' ability to reflect, although the measurement period of eight months is too short to make definitive statements about changes to students' personality structure.

Quantitative and qualitative research methods allow the effectiveness of the new ART pedagogical method to be tested and evaluated; an effectiveness study allows for the evaluation of a promising pedagogical approach. On this basis, the approach can be maintained and reinforced, or else rejected as ineffective.

Note

1 A number of scenes in the book have been altered to preserve the anonymity of people and institutions.

2 The Historical Roots and Development of Infant Observation

> I mean Negative Capability, that is, when man is capable of being in uncertainties, mysteries, doubts, without any irritable reaching after fact and reason.
>
> John Keats (1817)

Observations of children have long formed part of scientific inquiry. Charles Darwin recorded his son's development in diary entries. Freud observed his one-and-a-half-year-old grandson, describing his findings in *Beyond the Pleasure Principle* (S. Freud, 1920g; Köhler-Weisker, 1980, p. 625; Ludwig-Körner, 2015, p. 1163). Within the Viennese Psychoanalytic Association (WVP), Hermine Hug-Hellmuth had undoubted expertise in understanding the mental life of children, focusing on using observation to investigate children's sexual impulses. Beginning in 1913, Hug-Hellmuth regularly took part in meetings of the WVP and is generally considered to have been the first child analyst. She later became well-known for publishing the diary of a young girl; the document's authenticity was called into question (Mühlleitner & Reichmayr 1992; Hug-Hellmuth, 1919; Graf-Nold, 1988).

On February 1, 1937, at the suggestion of Anna Freud, a nursery was established in Vienna, where observation records were regularly made. After the Freud family moved to London, Anna Freud continued this work at the Hampstead War Nurseries. In 1951, she wrote of the work:

> The observational work itself was not governed by a prearranged plan. Emulating the analyst's attitude when observing his patient during the analytic hour, attention was kept free-floating and the material was followed up wherever it led.
>
> (A. Freud, 1951, p. 20; Köhler-Weisker, 1980, p. 627).

Participatory child observation has been an integral part of the training for child analysts at the Hampstead Clinic since 1948 (Köhler-Weisker, 1980).

Around the same time, beginning in 1923, the systematic observation of newborn babies was developed in Vienna under Charlotte Bühler. Participants in this research included, among others, Lotte Schenk-Danzinger, Hildegard Hetzer, Ilse Hellmann, Liselotte Franke, and Esther Bick. Bick, at this time

DOI: 10.4324/9781003483441-2

known by her original family name, Wander, submitted her dissertation to the University of Vienna in 1935 under Bühler's supervision. The study, entitled "Group formation in the second year of life", dealt with social relationships between two-year-olds. On the basis of her observation records, Bick attempted to draw conclusions about the children's behaviour. She later considered this observation as too technical, but would use records from this time in developing her method of infant observation. Her dissertation reproduces observation records which focus on small groups. The aim was to record the children's interactions:

> Group 13: Karl 1;7 [numeration indicates the child's age] cries – Franz 1;5 caresses him, hands him a biscuit – Karl takes one, eats, picks up breadcrumbs, gives them to Franz, says: 'well' – Franz laughs, opens his mouth – Erika 1;3 grabs Karl's rattle – Karl screams, cries – Erika continues to attack – Karl screams loudly – Franz hits Erika, screams loudly at her – Now there is a building game between Karl and Franz – Erika attacks Karl again – Karl screams – Franz pounces on Erika, screams and hits her again.
>
> (Wander [Bick], 1935, p. 75, quoted in Datler, 2009, p. 44).

Bick used this observation record to address Franz's ability to participate in Karl's suffering. She felt that a loving relationship had clearly developed between the boys, suggesting that Franz in particular has a sense of Karl's inner life and can understand his pain and what causes it, which is why he hits Erika.

Bick tried to identify similar scenes in other observation records in order to draw conclusions about repeated interactions. What is not spelled out here, however, is the significance of her own involvement in the situation. The report cited above is not just about three children, it is in fact about four people, three of whom are children and one a woman around 30. She is able to develop very clear thoughts about the children's behaviour and their mutual influence on their inner psychological processes. But she does not address possible causes or triggers for the children's behaviour (Wander [Bick], 1935, p. 40; Datler, 2009, p. 46).

Here Bick is still entirely in the tradition of *infant development research* (behavioural observation). In 1948, she made the decisive move towards infant observation, although she did not regard her observation method as a scientific one; rather, it was intended as a learning inventory, compiled for pedagogical purposes (Lazar, 2000, p. 400).

The third step in the development of this mode of understanding others was the inclusion of observers. These observers were not in the first instance active participants in a physical sense, but rather the creators of an intersubjective space which made understanding possible.

The observation reports in Bick's dissertation refer to concretely observable things and thus remain rooted in a concrete worldview. Psychological states and developments can only be inferred indirectly; they come verbally clothed, in the form of metaphors.

Bick moved to Britain in 1941. In the late 1940s, she was invited by John Bowlby to set up a child psychotherapy training course at the Tavistock Clinic. She had begun analysis with Michael Balint in 1941; in 1950 she continued her training analysis with Melanie Klein, who encouraged her to focus on the experiential world of young children. Bick established the Infant Observation Seminar, which focused on one- to two-year-old children, concentrating her observation on how children themselves experience the observed situation, thus attributing intuition to the children (Bick, 2009b, pp. 37–40; Kahl-Popp, 2001, p. 175; Datler, 2009, p. 46). Her essay "Remarks on Infant Observation in Psycho-Analytic Training" summarizes her infant observation technique (Bick, 2009a, pp. 19–36). From the 1960s on, Bick's infant observation method was included as an elective subject in psychoanalytic training. One of her students was Anton Obholzer, who recounted in an interview how intuitive Bick seemed to be towards children but how uninterested she was in the children's environment. Her interest was entirely focused on the children's inner lives; she thought that the stories they told about their families were a diversion from this task. In this, she remained entirely within the tradition of her teacher Melanie Klein (Obholzer, 2009, p. 215). Other psychotherapists who studied with Bick include Isca Salzberger-Wittenberg, Joan Symington, and Jeanne Magagna. Her successor Martha Harris served as head of training at the Tavistock Clinic until 1979. Among the therapists who trained under Harris was Ross A. Lazar.

"Mother-Baby Observation" was included in training at the Anna Freud Centre from 1962 on. The focus here was on the mother-child relationship (Ludwig-Körner, 2015, p. 1165; Diem-Wille, 2009b, p. 84). In Germany, the Kiel model of family observation was developed in the context of psychoanalytic training (Kahl-Popp, 2001, pp. 175–193). Findings from infant observation are continually incorporated into understandings of clinical phenomena in what are known as early-adulthood disorders (Lichtenberg, 1990, pp. 871–901).

1 Methods of Infant Observation

Infant observation, which normally lasted for two years, was fundamentally associated with the training of child and adolescent psychoanalysts. The small group, comprised of around six people, first discusses their approach to the observation and if possible makes contact with and establishes a relationship with a pregnant woman. Care is taken not to conduct observations in problematic family situations. In addition, the family in question should not be drawn from the observer's immediate circle of acquaintance. The ideal moment to begin observation is immediately after birth. The infant should be observed for one hour a week over the course of two years. The observation should be designed to take place during the baby's waking hours. Moreover, the observation should be integrated into a spatial and temporal continuum: in other words, the observation should take place on the same day of the week, at the same time and in the same place, as inconspicuously as possible. The observer should adopt an attitude of "evenly suspended attention", reacting in as passive and value-neutral a manner as possible (Israel, 2007; Lehner & Sengschmied, 2009, p. 120f.). Care should be taken that the observation has the smallest possible impact on normal family routines. Of course, situations do arise when action must be taken, where the observer is forced to abandon the passive stance:

> I often tell this story about my own infant observation. ...]As the summer grew warmer and the child began to walk, the doors were opened. In a place where a balcony had previously been, there was now a door which opened onto nothing ... So when that door was opened, there was a two-storey abyss. The child was already crawling, and as an observer you say to yourself: 'I can't just sit here and watch the child fall.' ... I articulated this thought, and while Mrs. Bick seemed somewhat interested, she did not discuss what could be done in practical terms.
>
> (Obholzer, 2009, p. 215f.).

There is no way to avoid interference during such a long period of observation. The scene which Obholzer cites is a very drastic one, where some response is obviously required. Here, of course, the question would arise about the meaning of the observer for the family and the open door as a jointly-constructed scene. Since the conditions in the building are a reality and the person observing is only present for one hour a week, we might also reflect on the conditions in which the unsupervised child exists, and indeed about the parents.

No notes are taken during observation. After the end of the observation session, the observer recalls the perceived images in their memory and notes them down. This observation record is then read and discussed by the group, with group members seeking to understand the observation using their own inner images, fantasies, and perceived feelings, attempting by their input to make manifest the unconscious content of the observation record. A record is kept of these group sessions, and the discussion is later re-visited on a meta-level, with an attempt made to outline the group's own processes with regard to the material presented. The group meets once a week for 90 minutes, alternating between the reading of observation records and their discussion. Time for participants to present their work with particular children should be allocated evenly, although not every observation record is read aloud, given restrictions on time (Bick, 2009a, pp. 19–36; Lazar, 2000, p. 402; Ludwig-Körner, 2015, pp. 1166f.; Kahl-Popp, 2001, p. 176).

2 The Importance of Infant Observation in Training

Infant observation allows observers to experience "how the infant's rudimentary ego-core, with its archaic fears, can develop and differentiate into a more or less stable relationship structure with its parents and siblings" (Diem-Wille, 2009b,

p. 67). Another point to note is that observers can gain "significant insights" into their psyche by the process of observing and reflecting on their perception of their own feelings (Diem-Wille, 2009b). Observation is a kind of sensitivity training and empathy training, with particular focus on phenomena associated with transference and countertransference. This also allows the observer to practice adopting a psychoanalytic attitude (Lazar, 2000, p. 408; Lehner & Sengschmied, 2009, p. 119; Maiello, 2015, pp. 51–64).

> Psychoanalytic infant observation takes place in a setting which, operating between the laboratory and the treatment room, introduces a new dimension of research and learning.
>
> (Diem-Wille, 2009b, p. 69)

Making use of their own feelings, the observer can form hypotheses about the interactions observed between baby and mother. The observer benefits greatly from the practice of observation, as he or she learns to perceive and understand the development of small children. Moreover, the capacity to manage relationship processes in the pedagogical professions can also be developed in the baby observation seminar (Lehner & Sengschmid, 2009, p. 119; Rhode, 2009, p. 104f.).

Knowledge about how one's own feelings develop, and reflection on this process, can be very helpful in treating what are known as early disorders, which manifest archaic defence mechanisms such as projective identification. For Diem-Wille (2009b, p. 71), the key question, posed in the spirit of Wilfred Bion, is: "What feelings might the patient want to evoke in me through this communication?" This question is in fact less than useful for the observer. This is because the question solely anchors need with respect to the observer, ascribing a kind of objectivity to them, in spite of their attention to their own feelings. Diem-Wille's question does not posit the observer as a person whose feelings also create a kind of reality. From Bion's point of view, reality is only constructed by the patient.

These days there is a steady flow of findings from infant observation into the fields of infant and child psychotherapy (Hirschmüller, 2015; Israel, 2015, pp. 187–202; Norman, 2015, pp. 217–244; Watillon, 2015, pp. 167–186).

3 Work Discussion

Work discussion seminars at the Tavistock Clinic were established by Martha Harris, who sought to create a group where people could reflect on their own experiences in the context of their professional activities (Harris & Bick, 1987, pp. 259–282; Steinhard & Reiter, 2008, p. 136; Harris & Bick, 2011). Work discussion is the "systematic discussion of experiences of work with small and stable groups of professional workers" (Rustin, 2008, p. 4). For Harris, it was also important to bring individuals from different professional fields together in a single group, which would have psychoanalytic thinking as its common denominator, in particular the basic assumption of an unconscious which is located in and around us. Students would bring precise observation reports from their specific work context to the group, which then served as a basis for discussion. Harris insisted that her seminars taught no techniques. She wanted to remain close to the material, giving herself over entirely to the situations described and the thoughts associated with them.

> The aim of the seminar is to sharpen perceptions and to enhance the exercise of imagination, so that a richer understanding of the personality interactions described may ensue, on the basis of evidence of motivation springing from internal unconscious.
>
> (Rustin, 2008, p. 5).

Unconscious motivations are constantly feeding into what is seen by the observer. There is therefore no such thing as pure observation.

"The work discussion model is the epitome of the application of psychoanalytic ideas" (Klauber, 2008, p. xix); this claim seems somewhat exaggerated, but it is the case that the development of the "work discussion" format has been continually enriched by several strands of psychoanalysis. Psychoanalytic ideas have always been a product of their time, and specific ideas in this context have continued to develop since the founding of the Tavistock Clinic in the 1920s. Bion, Bick, Balint, and Bowlby were four of the great thinkers associated with the Tavistock. The 1960s also saw demands emerging in society for new educational and teaching methods. This shift created a liberal basis for new developments at the Tavistock.

Bion's group work on the selection of army officers served as a considerable spur to progress, including its production of the idea of the "work group". Bion's work addressed a wide variety of group processes, and described the form of a group which could work well together. Michael Balint inspired the development of work discussion by forming groups of medical professionals who would present a case from memory, which the group used to develop their ideas. Sebastian Krämer, one of the younger Tavistock researchers, contextualized Bion's and Bowlby's ideas within the traditions of Quakerism. As a religious group, the Quakers hold "meetings": a Quaker group sits in a circle, waiting in silence until a participant begins to speak (Rustin, 2008).

The work discussion group adopted Bick's observation method, which has since been continually developed. Whereas infant observation had foregrounded the theories of Melanie Klein, the guiding principle of work discussion became the unconscious as it existed between interactants and within systems. Work discussion focuses on individuals' actions in everyday work situations and the unconscious dynamics associated with this. The emphasis was thus now placed on individual involvement in the work process, rather than on organizations, or indeed on infants and small children.

Observation reports were meant as a starting point to reflect rigorously on work situations, focusing on unconscious dynamics within the scene described. At the centre of that scene is the person doing the observation.

Like infant observation, work discussion has a three-step process:

1 Participants in a work discussion seminar observe themselves and their work situation
2 Participants write a descriptive-narrative report on interactions and work processes, as well as their own actions and thoughts
3 Participants present this observation report to the seminar, where it is discussed (Steinhardt & Reiter, 2009, p. 138).

Observation reports are written in the first person; participants choose a work situation, which they then describe. The report is meant to describe the scene as accurately as possible, including everyone participating in the scene, using a descriptive-narrative form. Copies of the report are distributed to all members of the group. The observer reads the report aloud, then group participants outline the emotions and imaginative responses which the story has prompted in them. A group report-response session usually lasts 90 minutes.

The following description of a scene in a hospital, written by a paediatric nurse, can serve as an example of a work discussion report. Juliette is a teenager who will soon undergo a difficult operation. The evening before the operation, she had wanted to watch a film with the nurse:

> Juliette [a young female patient] got up and we went to the cupboard. I asked her what type of movies she liked. She shrugged in answer. So I randomly picked video titles and suggested them to her for her selection. After a few suggestions, Juliette asked me what I wanted to watch. I told her that as long as it was not scary, I would watch it with her. We finally picked about five videos and returned to her room. Juliette chose the Rugrats to watch, and I put that in. She took her prosthetic legs off and scratched her right leg, where there was a dressing. I asked her if she was OK, and she said she was fine. We watched about 20 minutes, and then Juliette decided it was boring, so I changed it to a video of the Chipmunks.
>
> Juliette asked if she could have some fruit squash instead of plain water. She was having gut surgery, which required that she was not to have food for 24 hours and have clear fluids till 10.30 on the morning of surgery. So I double-checked with the nurse in charge and got her a cup of orange squash. In the time it took me to do that, she had decided that this movie was also boring. So we changed the video to Andre. We watched a few minutes of it, and the door buzzed …
>
> I returned to Juliette, who had put her supra-pubic catheter on free drainage as her normal routine. She was scratching her arms and

abdomen. I asked if she was OK, and she said she was a little itchy. I suggested that it was time to take her medication, but she preferred to take them a little later. So we watched the movie. Then she began a conversation.

J(ULIETTE): Is it going to hurt, what they'll do tomorrow?
N(URSE): I don't know much about the surgery but since it's on your abdomen, I think it will hurt some. But I'm sure you'll get some pain relief.
J: What is morphine?
N: It is a pain relief medicine which we can give in your mouth or via a cannula, and you can push a button, when you're in pain and receive a dose. It's called PCA, which you control.
J: What about going after?
N: Do you mean when you pass stool?
J: Yes.
N: Well, it's going to be a while before you do that, but I don't know.
J: But what do you think?
N: Well, I think it shouldn't hurt, because I don't think they are going to touch anything in that area. I think it's only going to be your stomach they touch.
J: When can I eat?
N: I think possibly the day after your surgery.
J: What! I would have been starved for two days. That's not happening. I'll eat. I don't care what anyone says. (At this moment I thought I should back-track and reassure her, since I was guessing.)
N: Well, they are going to handle your bowel, which is part of your gut, and this will affect when you can eat.
J: But this is about pooing, not eating.
N: Well, it's all linked from your mouth right to your anus.
J: You know that it is a mile long. A mile long, all in there. (She pointed to her stomach.)
N: You are right about that. How come the person who 'consented' you did not speak to you about the procedure?
J: The doctor who came was rude and nasty.
N: That's not fair on you. Listen, I'll say at handover that the surgeon needs to speak to you before the procedure, so that you can ask your questions. And one of us can be with you, if it helps.
J: OK.

Juliette asked me to get her lucky pyjamas. I did, then asked her to take her medication, as her scratching had become more frantic. She sat up and put about eight tablets into her mouth at once, took a drink, and swallowed them all?

(Bradley, 2008).

In the work discussion session devoted to this report, the group was deeply affected by the account, asking where adolescent fears found a place within the story. The conversation addressed the loss of limbs, the impossibility of any future sexual life, even the possibility of death.

If we examine the story with a focus on the nurse's contribution to opening up a space of intersubjectivity, new aspects can open up.

In choosing the film to watch, the nurse excludes fear-related themes. The patient decides to watch an American series dealing with young people's lives and concerns, with a particular focus on relationships. She makes herself comfortable, taking off her prosthetic legs. She then decides to watch a children's film which does not touch on adolescent themes of disconnection and sexuality. Juliette oscillates between themes of growing up and of being a child, in the way of a girl who must deal with these topics at her age. She asks the nurse for a juice, although we can assume that she has often known a ban on eating before operations. She would like the nurse to allow her something forbidden, who in turn has to ask and whom we also experience as a child. Here she experiences the nurse like a "sister", a peer. In the dialogue cited, she seeks out the thoughts of her "sister" and does not want a technical answer.

Juliette asks the nurse if what the "rude and nasty" man will do to her tomorrow will be painful. The nurse says she doesn't know much about it, but that the patient will be given something for the pain. When asked what happens next, the sister immediately mentions *passing* her *stool*, a phrasing phonetically very close to *birth stool*. On this question, Juliette also feels understood.

The nurse tells her it will some time before she can pass a stool, but she doesn't know for sure. But Juliette insists on hearing the nurse's own opinion. The nurse adds that *he* will not touch her there, only her stomach. The conversation then turns to food, with the girl observing that she would starve after two days without food. Given her many illnesses and operations, she is undoubtedly quite familiar with this form of fasting. Again, we can assume that a hidden language is at work in the exchange. Juliette would like to eat and not have to listen to anyone. Here, the nurse allows her own impulses to come into contact with Juliette. When Juliette reacts with greater emotion, the nurse notes a personal thought in the record: she felt she wanted to back-track on her comment. The nurse is becoming afraid of the patient's emotional state, reacting with guilt and seeking to undo what she has said. Juliette gets an answer about the treatment of her intestines and intestinal flora. She insists that for her it's about eating, about having, rather than about "pooing". She doesn't want to talk about her own defecation. The nurse reacts by telling her that everything is connected anyway, from the mouth to the anus. She avoids confrontation with the patient and reacts to doctors in the same way as the patient, without asking questions. In other words, she plays the role of the patient here and will speak for her tomorrow when she asks the surgeon questions.

The collaborative construction of reality by patient and nurse was influenced by some great fears: the fear of sexuality, and the fear of feeling and living as a woman. Both figures reacted to a threatening reality with a dissociated attitude. Both of them lived a moment of not-letting-their-feelings-live. The dialogue takes place between two women – presumably young – who cling tightly to each other, not allowing space to think about anything. This is very depressing scene if we recall that Juliette's body has been ravaged by meningitis, and that she cannot look forward to a normal sexuality. What is moving about the encounter is how this shared construction manages to avoid sexuality and the destruction done to the patient's body, a body which must ultimately be managed with medication.

4 The Observation Report

The observation report is written in retrospect. In itself, it already represents a gain in knowledge, since the abstract action of expressing things as words on paper demands a meta-level of thinking. In her introduction to the German edition of Wilfred Bion's *Learning through Experience*, Erika Krejci writes: "If the perceived object is not to be decisively distorted and damaged by the act of perception, 'subjective recording' must obviously take into account its own essence" (Erika Krejci in Bion, 1992, p. 25). In other words, when we regard the object of our analysis as a person, as our counterpart, we must always consider our own subjectivity, so as not to damage our perception of the person. We must include ourselves in our own thoughts, as the authors of the observation, which we develop within the subjectivity of our own mind. If we cannot do so, we will be unable to approach the truth, in the sense of achieving an understanding. Krejci goes on to mention Bion's proposal to address this problem:

> Bion's suggestion of developing a notation to record the *emotional experiences* of a session demonstrates how different his perspective really was. The observation record forms part of an entire cognitive process. It should reflect the facts of the case but should also be a tool, that is, it should help with the psychoanalyst's own speculative reflection.
>
> (Erika Krejci in Bion, 1992, p. 25, emphasis added).

Hermeneutic discourse begins with the writing of the observation report; during the writing, another party already exists: the person to whom the story is presented. In case studies presented more spontaneously, as for example in Balint's groups, the hermeneutic circle is set in train at the meeting of the group, with the narrative influenced within this immediate moment. Unlike infant observation, the focus is not on the baby's development, but rather on the interactions of the person who is writing the record and the encounters in which *they* are immersed. Here, that person's personal involvement in the situation forms the focus of reflection (Hartland-Rowe, 2005, p. 95;

Steinhardt & Reiter, 2009, p. 140). The observer is the person best positioned to report on their own feelings, and in this way they breathe life into the scene described, raising it from a constructivist perspective to the level of mentalizing thought (Fonagy et al., 2002; Devereux, 1973).

5 Work Discussion in the Group

In the work discussion seminar, the observation record to be discussed is handed out as a photocopy. The person who wrote the report then reads it aloud, while other group members read along, or else simply listen, allowing it to have its effect on them. Another group member keeps a record of the discussion within the group. In the manner of a Balint group, everyone in the group then expresses their thoughts on the record just read aloud (Balint, 1957). To explore unconscious phenomena in the material presented, the focus is on phenomena such as transference and countertransference (Peters, 1977, p. 54). The aim of the discussion is to sharpen awareness of participants' inner and outer worlds. Internal images, feelings, moods, and perceptions should all find expression within the discussion. The group now has two approaches to thinking available to it. First, participants take in the entire story and express their feelings about it, and then, as a second step, work their way, line by line, through the observation record. In this step it is important to stick "closely to the text" (Datler, 2003, p. 250). All statements by group participants should be summed up by the group leader, who should present a meta-view, so as to make the group's statements fruitful for the process of understanding.

As the process of understanding unfolds, the next thing to be considered is the group's own reactions, using the following question as a prompt: What do the feelings, moods, and statements within the group have to do with the case history as described? In this case, it is not simply a question of the individual statements made by group members, but also the dynamics of the group, which can express envy, empathy, etc. What Bion described as the group's *container function* allows its members to express their feelings in as uncensored a way as possible. The expression of these feelings can in turn contribute to the overall process of understanding. Just as everyone in the group is a participant and thus helps to shape the process, everyone also shapes and influences what happens in his or her work. Individual group participants can also be seen as actors in an experimental laboratory procedure: by participating in the group, individuals have the opportunity to become the makers of their own fate. These jointly-obtained insights, which combine intellectual development and affective experience, lead to an increase in empathy (Lazar, 2000, p. 408). The increase in the capacity to act is connected with the pain of being involved in a situation, and thus with one's own responsibility. In Melanie Klein's sense of the term, *development* is linked to the ability to mourn one's own finiteness and thus to achieve the depressive position. The group leader processes and refines the group's internal attitude, developing participants' ability to become increasingly aware of their own fallibility. Marta Harris referred to this attitude as the "development of negative capacity" (Lazar, 1986, p. 207). The group offers an opportunity to articulate feelings arising in relation to the material and the group's participants, thus moving all participants away from the level of action in order to achieve inner freedom. By making their own involvement and the associated feelings accessible to consciousness, participants now have the possibility of making decisions about these feelings, rather than simply *enacting* things. Harris summed up the approach in the phrase: "To become more reflective than reactive" (Martha Harris, 1977, cited in Steinhardt & Reiter, 2009, p. 143).

"Learning through experience" is what Bion called this kind of development. The work discussion seminar was intended to make participants more aware of unconscious work processes, making use of their own feelings and the statements of the group. This leads to a gain in affective knowledge.

The excerpts below, taken from an observation report, will again serve to illustrate the various forms of reflection. The focus here is on the group's reaction and on possible ways of understanding the situation described.

A teacher reports on a study session where several young people from different classes have an opportunity to study or do homework. The extracts address the tricky subject of child and adolescent sexuality in a school environment.

> When we arrive in class, things are pretty chaotic. The kids are running around like crazy. The focus is on Ines, a girl who is wearing too much make-up, with a very short skirt and tight T-shirt. She is shrieking and shouting with laughter. She seems to really enjoy being hit on by the boys. However, it seems that the boys are harassing her by physically groping her, so she runs after them and fights back. I go up to her and ask her to go to her seat. I explain to her that she knows what will happen if she doesn't clearly state that she doesn't want this to happen. I say that I can only help her if she draws a clear line between herself and the boys' behaviour. But she doesn't listen to me and continues to run around like crazy ... While I'm still standing at the door, Ines runs out of the class, pursued by two boys who want to pull down her skirt. As she runs past, she calls out to ask me when we are going to the computer room. I say, in an act of verbal desperation, that there will be consequences if they all don't get to work immediately. Ines asks caustically if I had been substituted during the Easter holidays, noting that I'm different today. I no longer understand the world, and I tell her that it is probably the other way around. I tell her that there hasn't been the kind of chaos we have seen today since the beginning of school.
>
> (Steinhardt & Reiter, 2009, p. 145f)

In response to the observation report, the seminar group first talks a lot about the excessive demands in this situation and about problems with the structures put in place by the institution. Only when the report is subjected to closer examination does the group address the scene with Ines: "Discussion becomes lively when the group reaches the part of the report which discusses Ines's behaviour". Here, see how the group initially avoids the most emotional topic in the report, and thus also evades dealing with questions of sexuality and desire in the seminar group. Only when this part of the report is examined in more detail is it possible for an affectively charged mood to emerge in the group. The subsequent report on the group discussion introduces the original observation report's author in a distanced form, as seen in the following reflection:

> As Mr. A. presents the situation, Ines is being harassed by male classmates because of her provocative clothing, but she doesn't want to admit this and isn't able to defend herself against it. In addition, she is unwilling to let teachers help her. Other teachers at the school had already tried to help her, explaining to her that she could only protect herself against such attacks if she changed how she dressed and looked for support from adults. Some participants in the seminar questioned whether Ines experienced the boys' behaviour as sexual harassment or if in fact this was exactly what she had wanted to achieve: to have them perceive her as erotic and sexually attractive. She achieves this through the type of clothing she wears, which is arousing for the boys but a provocation to the teachers. Ines doesn't seem to be in an abusive situation, but instead enjoys this sexually-tinged 'game' she is playing with the boys. In the seminar, an intense conversation develops about how students' openly-expressed sexual curiosity is experienced by teachers in everyday life at the school, and how students displaying eroticism can be very difficult for adults to endure. The situation in this case is particularly difficult, since schoolteachers find it difficult to put up with the provocative way in which the students are displaying their eroticism. Ines here is not seeking help because she feels herself to be harassed. Instead, Mr. A. and the other teachers at the school experience helplessness and unconsciously seek advice on how to deal appropriately when confronted by students' sexuality and eroticism in the context of everyday life at school.
>
> (Steinhardt & Reiter, 2009, p. 145f)

Mr. A. is depicted in the case history as a committed teacher. Two narrative strands develop, which foreground Ines and a boy named Markus. Except for two girls briefly discussed, the other students remain "faceless". Markus experiences Mr. A. as very present: the teacher demands to speak with him, although later in the story, he (Markus) reacts with aggression and experiences feelings of rejection. Ines also runs to teacher A. in the hallway, trying to show him the chase scene. The extent to which the seduction is directed at him, with Ines desiring for him to run after her, cannot be established.

The group's reactions remain very much on a concrete level, where the solution to the issue of sexuality lies in Ines's choice of clothing and taming the boys' behaviour. Ines brings the relationship with and the seduction of the teacher into the broader theme of growing up. Seduction, in which sexual desire also comes into play as a form of momentum, should not be directed towards teachers in school. Everyone in the group seems surprised at the suggestion that they should "seduce" students into participating in class, and everyone seems quite afraid when students react to this as if it meant seduction in an erotic sense. The group consensus on female sexuality is that while it is provocative, it only serves to actually provoke desire on the part of "immature" men. To address these questions in the group and offer help to teachers, the group leader's reaction to seduction in the seminar group must be addressed, as well as desire among the participants in the seminar. May I seduce another person? To what extent does eroticism play a role in this? It is possible to explore *appropriate interaction* at school via affective experience within the seminar group, but only by *actually going there,* in other words actually discussing that subject. The group found it easier to return to the subject of aggression and the difficult structural conditions of everyday life at the school (Steinhardt & Reiter, 2009, p. 149).

For teachers, there is great fear associated with viewing themselves as "seducers" and thus being seen as actually forming part of the space around young people. But sexuality can only be recognized when teachers recognize it *as sexual* and frame it into words. When students begin to notice and discuss the obvious, namely that sexuality develops in every relationship, this creates great fear, very likely in themselves, but also in the teaching staff, who are conflicted about whether they are offering education in sexual matters or in fact being overly active in drawing out the theme which could be misunderstood as only following their own sexual interests. This kind of "sexual education" often remains too concrete in matters of behaviour, instead of focusing on thought. Of course, it is particularly important to clarify that fantasy is far from action, it is better to wait than to act. Understanding only develops through repeated interchange, via both verbal and gestural interaction. As long as one is "unsure", there is a risk of inflaming unnamed emotions of shame and fear. But, on the other hand, if the subject is veiled in fear, this can encourage hasty action and thus possibly also encourage sexual activity before psychological maturity reaches the level of physical maturity.

Work discussion presents an opportunity for reflection, in the tradition of psychoanalytic supervision. However, description here is not introduced dynamically, but rather via a written narrative: as a frozen situation, a mood, a moment in time captured by the writer. When reading the observation report aloud, the author is often surprised by what they had wanted to say to the audience. Now a hermeneutic circle can begin to develop within the group, which takes the specific sketch as its starting point, something that can always be returned to, simply by looking again at the written report. Every time I read this report, new ways of seeing open up, since I always come to it with different knowledge and insights. This seems to mark the fundamental difference with the classical form of psychoanalytic supervision in which case descriptions do develop dynamically, where it is impossible to look back, since one can never step into the same river twice: *Pánta chorei kaì oudèn ménei* (Gadamer, 1990).

Observation reports very quickly began to be used in an expanded field of activities. A wide variety of age groups have now been observed with the help of this method, including children in daycare, toddlers, and school-aged children (Turner & Ingrisch, 2008; Zabini, 2009; Datler, 2003; Trunkenpolz et al., 2009).

6 Organizational Observation

The method of observation is thus now also used in fields beyond child observation, subsumed under organizational observation, and has also developed further in a number of strands (Lazar, 2009, p. 202; Obholzer, 2009, p. 213; Hinshelwood & Skogstadt, 2006; Rustin, 2008; Trunkenpolz et al., 2009).

Anton Obholzer held a leadership position at the Tavistock Clinic and repeatedly heard complaints from younger colleagues about their working environment. Their problematic workload caused him to look again at the situation and attempt to get closer to the institution's unconscious. In the 1980s, through a lengthy process which included collaboration with Isca Wittenberg and others, Obholzer developed a form of organizational observation based on the techniques of infant observation. The focus shifted here from the inner life of the infant to the external world of a workplace. In this context of opening up institutions to analysis, Robert D. Hinshelwood developed a further strand of observation-based practice, one which put particular focus on healthcare facilities. Hinshelwood put more emphasis on the description of unconscious phenomena in organizations and the burdens which could result from them. He favoured a different language of explanation, seeing himself more in terms of Menzies's research tradition (Hinshelwood & Skogstadt, 2006, pp. 29–45; Menzies, 1974, pp. 183–216).

Ross A. Lazar brought the observation method to Munich in 1979 and later to Klagenfurt, looking to use it to investigate phenomena associated with the organizational unconscious. The difficulty in observing an organization which makes itself available for analysis is how to reduce the observational flow, and thus also reduce the stimuli to which observers are subjected. In any institution, there is a great deal to see and to discover. Selecting a small part of the organization and then observing it demands a change a change of perspective in organizational understanding (Obholzer, 2009, p. 216; Datler & Trunkenpolz, 2009, p. 244).

Lazar sums up the learning objectives as follows:

> 1. As an observer of an organization, you experience the organization or institution from the inside in its everyday life, but without being integrated via a defined role structure and without being subject to objectives, responsibilities, or other restrictions.
> 2. In this way you have the opportunity to perceive the experiences of the members of the organization.
> 3. It is possible to study an organization on a non-verbal, unconscious level, in which case it is less a matter of the unconscious of individual members than it is about collective group culture, the myths and unwritten rules of how to deal with each other.
> 4. To some degree, it is also possible to trace and understand the history of the organization.
> 5. In a similar way to the family of a baby under observation, the observer of an organization can study emotional patterns in the web of developing relationships – both formal and informal – in the organization in question.
>
> (Lazar, 2009, p. 211)

As an example of organizational observation, there follows a short excerpt from the record of an introductory meeting, where a request to observe the organization is made:

> I am constantly asked to say exactly what I want to know, because 'it would be good to have a structure... then you can give a more precise answer' ... And if I want to get to know the organization, they say, it would be good to assume some specific perspectives. I then tell them that my approach is a bit different, I don't go about things in such a structured way, to which Mr. W. said: 'so chaotic!?' ... At the end of the conversation (which nonetheless lasted an hour and a quarter) Mr. B. said I should email him by the end of January, telling him everything I want to know. And the two men would then identify the right people for me to talk to.

It was not possible to carry out an observation in this particular company. From an intersubjective perspective, we might consider the degree to which the observer did not know exactly what their attitude should be in the observation situation, with their feelings of inner chaos encountering the anxieties of the company. The answers given by the observer make them seem as if they are floundering: "My approach is a bit different, I don't go about things in such a structured way". The boundaries begin to dissolve and the interlocutor is prompted to observe "so chaotic!?". The observer does not have a language to define their own role, something which might have enabled their interlocutor to deal with the situation. The meaning of it all remains unclear to Mr. W. and Mr. B. They do not regard themselves as suitable conversation partners because they do not understand what the observer wants.

The observer then attempted to arrange an observation with the police and the military, two institutions which epitomize approaches based on strict structure. The extent to which the observer produced a space of shared uncertainty in the meeting with Mr. W. and Mr. B. can only be answered in quite speculative terms. In this three-person scene, fear is managed via the desire for a structure to contain one's own fears, a structure which each expects the other to provide.

7 Infant Observation in Research

At the University of Vienna, great importance is given to the method of psychoanalytically-oriented observation, based on Bick's method. A research project, "Quality of Life in Nursing Homes", was carried out at the university, under the leadership of Anton Amann, Elisabeth Seidl, and Wilfried Datler (Trunkenpolz et al., 2009, p. 330f.; Trunkenpolz, 2008).

The project revisited the tradition of psychoanalytic observation, here modified according to the requirements of specific observation situations. The technique of infant observation is suitable for observations outside the therapeutic setting and thus works very well as a research method (Poscheschnik, 2005). In 1995, a London-based group led by Margret and Michael Rustin formed a research unit, and in 1997 set up the scientific journal *Infant Observation: The International Journal of Infant Observation and its Applications* (Trunkenpolz et al., 2009, p. 334f.). Similarly, another group under Wilfried Datler began developing research methods at the Institute for Educational Sciences at the University of Vienna, ultimately dividing these into three parts (Datler, 2009).

The first part of the research aimed at specifying the research proposition. Here, the focus was placed on first, the interplay of conscious and unconscious factors for the individual during interaction; second, on their own experiences of relationships and interactions; and finally on how influence affected their interior world. Observation was meant to take place in a naturalistic setting, over a substantial, defined period of time. What previous experience do observers need in order to carry out the research?

The second part of the research project was structured according to the classic Tavistock model: observation, then initial reflection within a small group, using Bick's familiar structure of initial training and further development. However, since this was a research project, observers were not regarded as learners, but were expected to bring characteristics like "mental structuration" to the project (Trunkenpolz et al., 2009, p. 337). Observers should be capable of mentalization, of thinking about themselves in a reflexive way and understanding themselves to be the instrument of research. They should be able to grasp complex situations, and to mentally retain and transcribe them. These observation records are then analysed and given meaningful interpretations within the small group. Reactions within the group represent a central component in the process of understanding (Skogstadt, 2004). But at this point a new step is introduced into the observers' work process: they now additionally review the reports and notes from the group sessions and establish a thematic focus in line with the overall research question.

In the third stage, a newly formed group subjects the material to further analysis: the group here attempts to establish answers to the main research question (Trunkenpolz et al., 2009, p. 336f.)

The research project was designed to be interdisciplinary, featuring cooperation between sociologists and specialists in nursing and in education. Their job was to create an overall plan to research quality of life in people with dementia in care homes. The idea was to develop and evaluate meta-level methods which could understand people's everyday lives while taking "subjective perspectives" into account. Specifically, the project asked how residents experience everyday life in a care home, as well as inquiring into the significance of relationships with relatives and nursing staff, and the influence of organizational structures and nursing staff. Individual and organizational observations were carried out at the entrance, in the lounge area, and at the nurses' station of two separate care homes. In addition, guided interviews were conducted with nursing staff (ibid., 2009, p. 339).

The authors reporting the "Quality of Life in Nursing Homes" research project emphasize the discrepancy between a care-home resident's sexual desire and their dementia, with denial on the part of the institution. Here, the reports are presented by an observer named Ms. Bog. Again, the emphasis here is on achieving an understanding of the scene through the observer's own feelings.

Report excerpt (2):

> Mr Hartz approaches me. He stands very close to me and looks at my cleavage. ... He stands for some time in front of me, without moving, looking at me. I feel that the distance between us is too small and I take a step backward.

A further excerpt (3):

> He opens the door and leaves it open for me too. Mr. Hartz goes to his bed and strokes the fresh linen. I stand in the anteroom area, watching him. ... He stops just in front of me, stroking my chin with his right hand. He runs over it a few times and has his sweet smile on his lips. I do not feel comfortable with this, but I let it take place nonetheless. The whole time I keep thinking about why he is doing this.

The research group gave these excerpts the title "Sexuality in the Encounter with the Observer". When Ms. Bog sees Mr. Hartz looking at her cleavage, she describes the feeling of his being too close. She probably has an idea of his desire for her breasts, which she finds unpleasant in the situation. When he touches her face, she appears to take refuge in the thought "why is he doing this?" and she has an idea of how to endure the situation. She seems to have stood there frozen, allowing it to happen.

A further excerpt follows (4a):

> She [the nurse] puts her hands on his shoulders and he puts his hands on her hips. She removes her hands from his shoulders and places them on his hips. Then Nurse Elfriede asks Mr. Hartz if she could have a little kiss, and he gives her a kiss on the cheek. Two nurses standing beside them laugh and clap.

The research group's interpretation focuses on the humiliation caused by the nurses' laughter, citing the following passage as evidence:

Observation report excerpt (4b):

> Suddenly Mr. Hartz throws up his arms and shouts very loudly: 'Listen, leave me alone! Are you stupid? Damn you [*Sakre du*]!' The nurses laugh and go to the nurses' station.

From an intersubjective perspective, this is a sentence the observer should have said. A jointly constructed reality event has taken place. It is now the observer who defends themselves against the wishes of the patient. There is tension in the observation reports where the observer describes how she allows herself to be caressed or lets the patient look at her cleavage, enduring it all stoically. The observation as an encounter between the two people contains much tenderness and ultimately creates desire. The scene with the nurses, which does not take place in an intimate atmosphere, does not carry the same degree of erotic tension as the two scenes with the observer. Desire and seduction are constructed together. The observer ascribes a "kind smile" to the patient, thus removing any sexual connotation from the encounter, as if her breast were not subjected to sexual desire but solely existed to provide milk.

In conclusion, the researchers at the University of Vienna note the importance of "entering the field of the dynamic encounter" (Trunkenpolz et al., 2009, p. 347). Encounter also means an ability to think about oneself as a participant in the encounter. In terms of the example above, it includes thinking about one's own desires in terms of sexuality, and the fears associated with this. In the spirit of Gadamer's hermeneutics, it is also important to examine this process within the research group. For example, what does it mean for an older researcher when an old man in an observation report expresses sexual or intimate desires for a young woman? This situation can also trigger something in the researcher, and this in turn shapes the interpretation of the material within the group (Scharff & Scharff, 2000; Scharff, 2014). The writer of the text must also consider their own perspective, attitude, and sexuality, in order to open up a space of understanding.

8 Infant Observation in Neonatology

Agathe Israel has described the use of infant observation with preterm babies in a neonatal intensive care unit. In this context, she regards the observer as a person who creates an inner space within themselves, a space where the psychological experiences of these children have a place, in this way lending these premature babies a kind of self (Israel & Reissmann, 2008, p. 9). She emphasizes that since one in ten children is born preterm, we need more detailed research into psychological development in this "psychosomatic borderland on the edge of life" (Israel & Reissmann, 2008, p. 10). In this way, Israel and the photographer Björn Reissmann have opened up a new field for the understanding human psychological development. Israel's principal question is how we can approach the experiential world of preterm children: their chosen method is that of *participant infant observation* (Israel & Reissman, 2008, p. 17). What participation here consists of is not specified and the term contradicts the injunction of non-interference. In articulating her understanding, Israel is guided by the ideas of the Kleinian school, which was also Esther Bick's background. In addition, Bion's idea of containment is central to her explanation of the self's development. She regards preterm babies as existing in a disintegrated condition, dominated by raw states of being, and posits that these states are projected and introjected, taking place within containment via mechanisms of projective identification (Israel & Reissman, 2008, p. 16).

Once a week, an observer comes to a neonatal station and pays attention to one particular scene, without interfering in any way. A record of what was perceived in the scene is written out from memory, then discussed in a group.

To understand how theory guides Israel's conception of these neonatal situations, we can consider one of the observation records cited in her book:

> **Rejection and birth defects**: A mother, wearing a baseball cap and a loud tracksuit top, is sitting in an armchair, holding her newborn son in her arms, at a slight distance from her body. Silently, with a serious expression, she looks at the child and the child looks at her. His eyes are really searching the mother's face; he is astonishingly awake, although he was only born yesterday. His little head has some scratches, bruises, and scuff marks, it looks like it has been beaten. The little guy seems totally pitiful, and the relationship between them, which is so obviously distant on the mother's side, also seems pitiful. I stand with them for a while and I introduce myself. The mother smiles briefly, but doesn't say a word. She seems sealed off. I later discovered that the baby was born at term, but very underweight, just 1,800 grams. His mother already has

> three grown children: he is probably an unwanted latecomer. The mother smoked at least 20 cigarettes a day during her pregnancy, which very likely resulted in placental insufficiency (a dysfunction), leaving the child half-starved in the womb. Even after the child was born, the mother's attention appears to be inadequate. After the mother leaves, the nurse picks up the baby to bottle-feed him. She holds the child in her arms and we both look at him with concern. How will this continue? Will the mother be able to adjust to the baby, maybe with the help of her adult children?
>
> Then the baby is taken for a sonograph. His little head has to be examined for possible internal damage.
>
> (Israel & Reissman, 2008, p. 85f)

The observation, as described here, has created emotion in the observer herself: there is anger at the mother, the belief that one is a better mother. The child and the mother look *pitiful*. The nurse and the observer show concern for the child. Does this reflect concern for the child or more an idea of insufficient care on the part of those looking at him? Aggression towards the mother is experienced as concern for the child. In Winnicott's sense, there is no baby without a mother: in this, *detachment* plays a major role. The observation report seeks to think of the baby without its mother, with the nurse seen as the "better" mother. This distance is emphasized by the mention of cigarette smoking in connection with placental insufficiency. The report constructs an image of physical distance between mother and baby. The baby has to figure things out for himself; the observer is probably influenced by her sense of "pitifulness" and a lack of care. Male figures are not included in this version of the situation, or solely in the form of "the little guy seems totally pitiful".

A further step in the observation process is for the observer to consider the scene via a reflection on their own feelings and to think of themselves as a co-creator or co-constructor of the encounter.

Another of the astonishing case histories in Israel's book can help clarify this idea:

> **Giving a name.**
>
> My attention is drawn by an unusual sign attached to the bed. It gives the family name, the date of birth (14 days previously), the baby's weight, and finally the baby's given name in scribbled handwriting.
>
> 'Aha, it has a name now,' marvels the nurse as she approaches the bed, 'that must be very recent!'
>
> The photographer tells me he was at this bed yesterday, and there was no first name on the sign. Previous to this, he had met and spoken with the parents, and received permission to photograph the child. Maybe, he speculates, the interest taken by a third party in the child was what prompted the parents to finally give him a name.
>
> (Israel & Reissmann, 2008, p. 86).

Here the report conveys that the photographer has devised a meaning, which he then turns into a hypothesis. He suspects that the wish to have the child photographed also provided meaning for the parents, who were now able to give a name to the child. By virtue of the recognition shown to the child, the parents also came to perceive this meaning. He asked the parents because he regarded the child as part of them.

A further case opens up a different world of participation for us. This scene is entitled "Shock".

> ... with mechanical-seeming movements, she pulls the electric pump to her, places it on her breast and pumps out the milk. ... She speaks to me in a similarly mechanical way. She doesn't dare touch the child, she is not yet capable of that ... Then we talk about how important the relationship with each other is and how difficult it is to overcome the shock of separation. ... I emphasize that it is very important that she also feels well looked after, so a good connection can develop. ... When it becomes clear to us that he [the child] is insistently asking us to stay with him, I feel the mother's rigidity loosen slightly, some growing sense of compassion. It is impossible not to see that the mother needs support, so she can endure the reality of sudden separation, and doesn't run away from the child's distress.

The "mechanical" theme is a thread which runs right through this report. Technology dominates the scene; the sentences are like something from a psychology textbook, featuring interchangeable people who have no identity. The mother stays because she is supposed to; the observer also depicts her in this way. Actions are only done *mechanically*. Feelings on the subject of *running away* are not to be discussed, nor should any disappointment about a "defective" [*defizitäres*] child, who can only survive with the help of mechanical devices. The observer constructs the scene. The women remain in a linguistic-mechanistic world, where human drama remains outside. Dissociation is another dominant influence in the scene. The mother as an autonomous person has no place in the encounter. Distress is associated with the child, while support is considered for the mother. All of these ideas feel technically correct, but they lack any individuality.

Theory is crucial in order to achieve empathic understanding, namely a grasp of the particular idea of the baby or mother which is anchored in our thoughts. However, empathy should not regarded as an individual capacity, but as a jointly constructed event (Aragno, 2008; Buchholz, 2017a). In this shared construction of reality, the empathetic is to be found at the point of dissociation of dramatic feelings, feelings which would otherwise overwhelm the mother. Here, the *mechanical* represents the shared construction of empathy within the report: this imposes a prohibition on thinking about the mother's fears and needs, as well as any expression of the observer's own needs.

There seems very little room for fear on this ward, where the boundaries between life and death are so fluid and fragile. Fears are directly addressed in the following observation reports:

> He breathes regularly in and out, which draws his ribcage deeply towards his upper abdomen, as he struggled to overcome resistance while gasping for air. I am shaken: he seems closer to death than to life. Fear wells up in me and I realize that what I thought was vitality was actually agitation.
>
> (Israel & Reissmann, 2008, p. 100)

By naming the fear, it seems to be possible to recognize the baby's agitation as a struggle with death.

Reading the observation reports put together by Agathe Israel's team can trigger many different feelings: the texts convey fear, trauma, and profound emotion. It is easy to see in the texts how the hospital staff, as well as separating off their own feelings so as to overcome crises in the ICU as quickly as possible, try to be present for and empathetic towards the premature babies. Both of these attitudes can be justified in terms of clinical necessity, but to not explicitly name them creates a breeding ground for ambiguity and conflict.

> Gitte, red in the face, screams without tears. But this is not a scream which expresses vitality. Now she spits out her feed, it arcs high into the air. When I get the nurse, she mutters angrily: 'She always does that when she's bored.' She asks me to stand for a moment by the open neonatal cot so she can get a cloth. Gitte is screaming again, and again I feel the urge to tape-record her.

One week later:

> ... as the nurse speaks, Gitte lays her head on her chest without taking her eyes off her and smiles, which the nurse happily accepts. 'Sometimes you could even laugh.' Colleagues rushing past warn her to put Gitte back in her cot, so she doesn't get spoiled.
>
> (Israel & Reissmann, 2008, p. 100)

Intimacy and tenderness are forbidden here. Everyone i collectively on guard against the taboo of wishing something from the children. The personal feelings of the individual – which may instinctively be seen as maternal feelings – must be suppressed with the help of the group. Can I wish for something from the children? Can I be pampered by them? Here, needs are something which can only be ascribed to the children. It would be morally reprehensible to project wishes about one's own motherhood or one's own deficiency – as well as any associated healing fantasies – towards children who are struggling for their lives. But in order to attribute a self to another person, do I not need to associate wishes with them, wishes I can direct towards them? If I cannot develop wishes for another person, I cannot enter into a relation of dependency with them, and my possibility of empathy is blocked. Wanting something from another person means exposing myself to the risk of connection, but it also means giving meaning to them, by making a connection between my emotional regulation and theirs, between my sensibility and theirs. To do this is to lend meaning to the child, which the child can now feel on an emotional level. I am happy and I am sad about what I experience through other people.

9 Critical Reflections on Bick's Method

In recent years, there has been increasing criticism of infant observation (Ludwig-Körner, 2015; Blessing, 2012; Hollman, 2010; Cardenal, 1998). The basic methodological design for observing infants and young children is based on the principle of "evenly suspended attention", considered a cornerstone of psychoanalytic treatment. Many people conducting this form of observation repeatedly feel conflicted: they are torn, on the one hand, between the wish to give into their own impulses and intervene in the situation, and, on the other, the need to adhere to the psychotherapeutic "rule of abstinence" (Aulbert et al., 2015; Hollmann, 2010; Prat, 2013; Blessing, 2012). According to Ludwig-Körner, some authors have distanced themselves from a position claiming *pure* observation is possible (Ludwig-Körner, 2015, p. 1163). This prompts the question whether pure observation is possible in the sense of exerting no influence on what is observed. This viewpoint adheres to the research maxim of the last century, which assumes that observers can avoid having influence on the experiment. Infant observation by Bick's method is still very much caught up in the traditions of Cartesian thought, pointing towards one-person psychology. But some infant observation reports are much less about the task of neutral observation than they are about describing the observer's own inner struggle to allow space for their instinctive reactions.

> At the end of the observation Stefan, twelve months and two weeks old, had not managed to roll over, crawl, stand or walk: he could only sit. Perhaps this is the Stefan the parents saw and that I was powerfully required to see too: my question is, was there another Stefan around, who, with more attunement, could have been encouraged and helped to find his own pleasure and strength in moving?
>
> (Somaini, 2013, p. 158)

Here Paola Somaini asks whether a different perspective is possible and to what extent a different attitude might have helped Stefan's development to move in a different direction. What attitude did the observer bring to the situation, thereby influencing Stefan's ability to express himself? The group reflected on the scene:

> We speculated as to whether her internal world was dominated by persecution and danger. Perhaps she was scared of her own hostility towards Stefan and was grateful to have me around to contain? Though it is true that she was able to put her ambivalence into words, I had a sense that something was often on the edge of bursting out and that perhaps her cutting off and keeping Stefan at a distance was a defensive manoeuvre to keep her and baby safe.
>
> (Somaini, 2013, p. 160).

Another way of thinking through this would be to look again at the group's unconscious, to address the observer's fear of her own hostility towards Stefan: the feeling that she too had ascribed a birth defect to Stefan, with her own guilty feelings expressed through her reflections on containment. If the observer were to allow space for her feelings, something within her could break open, and she would no longer need to maintain herself at a distance, in keeping with the notion of "abstinence". Ambivalence offers a basis to grant the possibility of difference to the other person or to the scene as a whole. In this way, the situation can be mentalized, thus allowing Stefan's psychological inner world to emerge. Only we only understand others via ourselves, and empathy reaches a limit within us, since our own feelings guide us, via interpretation as a kind of understanding. To watch an interaction, suppressing one's own impulses, without intervening to help or to fix things: this is a very difficult thing to endure. Freud asked the analyst to assume the attitude of a surgeon at the operating table:

> I cannot advise my colleagues too urgently to model themselves during psycho-analytic treatment on the surgeon, who puts aside all his feelings, even his human sympathy, and concentrates his mental forces on the single aim of performing the operation as skilfully as possible. Under present-day conditions the feeling that is most dangerous to a psychoanalyst is the therapeutic ambition to achieve by this novel and much disputed method something that will produce a convincing effect upon other people.
>
> (S. Freud, 1912e, p. 380f)

To what extent does this attitude influence the scene under observation? The observer's own repressed affects are projected onto the mother, while feelings of guilt are managed through the concept of containment, specifically with the help of a group where a shared interpretation can be developed. It is difficult indeed to distinguish between projection and empathy; both phenomena go hand in hand. The most palpable form of containment comes from the group, which is very clear about its speculation about the mother's interior world, but does not refer back to their own feelings, which would allow them to open up a world of understanding about themselves. The psychological interpretation remains more of a technical and general kind: "Her internal world was dominated by persecution and danger". One way of reflecting on this would be to include the observer's fears in our understanding of why the mother is so restrained and undemonstrative. The mother's "lack of interest" can only be recognized via the observer's own feeling of interest in Stefan. We may suspect that more energy goes into restraining one's own emotions during observation than into understanding the encounters. The author focuses on the mother's incapacity to see, as well as the associated impossibility of adequately mirroring Stefan. The observer sees all of this and thus likely experiences massive inner conflict around the question of non-intervention. But she does not take her own seeing into account, nor the mirroring associated with it. The question here is how can I give meaning to someone if I do not attribute meaning to myself within the process of observation?

On September 9, 1924, Hermine Hug-Hellmuth, the first child analyst, was robbed and murdered by her 18-year-old nephew Rolf Hug. After his release from prison, Hug demanded compensation from the Vienna Psychoanalytic Association on the grounds that his aunt had seen him only as an object of observation and analysis. Hug-Hellmuth's writings on child development were in fact based on observations of her nephew. As Helene Deutsch put it, children do not want to be watched, they want to be loved.

3 Introduction to Mentalization

1 Why Mentalization-Based Pedagogy?

When working with children and adults, educators will come to different conclusions as to whether and how much early intervention directed towards an individual will influence their later life. More than a century ago, psychology recognized that the earliest years of life are the most sensitive, formative phases of an individual's development. As a practising psychotherapist, the author has daily witnessed the effects of educators' actions. Likewise, his work with educators has frequently exposed him to the limits of pedagogical action.

For two semesters, the author attended a kindergarten in order observe a child interacting with the world around him, as well as working for a short time as an active teacher in a different kindergarten. Surprisingly, it was clear from his own reactions and from observing other colleagues interacting with the children that we all fall back on profound reactions to the experiences we have stored up from childhood This is in spite of high levels of training in self-awareness, specific pedagogical training, psychotherapeutic intervention techniques, etc. Facial expressions and gestures are controlled automatically, not consciously, and not according to learned pedagogical or therapeutic ideas. The question arises: to what extent can changes in a teacher's behaviour be brought about by changes in their inner attitude? Concepts are flexible and interchangeable. Moreover, they reflect our thinking over time. Concepts form explanatory models for our actions which only become meaningful for us when we have thoughts about them. However, if we think about something during a given situation, we place ourselves outside the encounter. Spontaneity and creativity are lived out within *present moments*, as conceived by Daniel Stern (2004). Since the best learning outcomes are tied to affectivity, i.e. feelings, it is not possible to think during the encounter situation itself. It is possible to integrate experiences into future encounters in the form of instructions for action, but these require forethought to be used explicitly. The prerequisite for this is stable attachment. Attachment in the sense used by Bowlby means an emotional-affective relationship with a specific person which endures in space and over time.

DOI: 10.4324/9781003483441-3

The key to understanding the development of mentalization lies in attachment theory. Attachment is a crucial factor for the child (Spitz, 1957), one fundamentally based on parents' understandings of their child's inner world. Attachment is the prerequisite for learning affect regulation and is thus linked to mentalization and attention control. With a good attachment bond (one with congruent and marked mirroring), the child can develop a sense of self-authorship. To understand this development, it must be shown that this complex intrapsychic process can be damaged. Accordingly, the location of children's deficits should also be recognized: this is where they will require greater support. This is also the best place to begin to counteract or mitigate the risk of personality disorder. Large-scale studies have demonstrated that parents' attachment patterns are transferred to their children (Fonagy et al., 1991). The kinds of understanding which young parents received from their own parents is of great importance in whether they can now respond to their children in an understanding way.

Based on this research, it seems that a society's most important task in preventing personality disorders must be to focus on elementary education (i.e. on daycare and kindergarten).

Fonagy and his team posit that the crucial factors are a successful attachment process and a child's capacity to understand interpersonal behaviour in terms of mental states. Mentalizing (reflexive function) is the name they give to this ability. We need this ability in order to organize our internal structures and thus to develop as people and to regulate our emotions.

2 Mentalization-Based Pedagogy: Theoretical Background

2.1 Mentalization

Mentalization can be understood as a *concept* of mentalizing (Fonagy, 1991): it is formed from a combination of attachment theory, developmental psychology, psychodynamic, cognitive-behavioural, trauma-related and neurobiological findings, and theory of mind (Fonagy et al., 2002; Bateman & Fonagy, 2006; Allen, 2009; Allen et al., 2011).

To get a sense of this, we can imagine how the richness of the inner and outer world begins to be revealed when we attain a state of understanding, feeling empathy towards ourselves and others. One of human beings' basic capacities is the ability to experience, recognize, and understand themselves and the world around them. Peter Fonagy speaks of "holding mind in mind", i.e. being capable of thinking of feelings and thoughts. To the extent we can conceive of ourselves and others, attributing minds or opinions to them, we become aware of them as people. This is one of the most important bases of empathy, which in turn represents a crucial element in avoiding violence and preventing burnout.

For Fonagy and Bateman, mentalizing has a meaningful impact on our self-image and thus on our stable sense of self. There can be no constructive social interactions without mentalization, no relation between people, no common ground, no sense of inner security (Bateman & Fonagy, 2019a). In their book *Affect Regulation, Mentalization and the Development of the Self*, Fonagy, Gergely, Jurist, and Target added an element of developmental psychology to the theory, making a connection between mentalization and the idea of attachment. Processes of mentalization are of fundamental importance in child development. In particular, Gergely and Watson, by introducing elements from their research into infant observation, added crucial insights to mentalization as a developmental concept (Fonagy et al., 2002; Gergely & Watson, 1996; Klöpper, 2014; Kirsch et al., 2016). They have also postulated a connection between poor development of social cognition (mentalization) and later psychopathology in adulthood. In doing so, they have attached great importance to human development and the capacity to mentalize. This produced treatment concepts (MBT – mentalization-based therapy) for a wide variety of psychopathologies, including borderline disorders, depression, antisocial personality disorder, eating disorders, trauma, drug addiction, anxiety disorders, and somatoform disorders (Fonagy, 2009; Fonagy et al., 2004; Bateman & Fonagy, 2006, 2019a; Robinson & Skårderud, 2019; Arefjord et al., 2019; Luyten & Fonagy, 2019; Schultz-Venrath, 2013; Staun, 2017; Bolm, 2009; Fonagy & Bateman, 2017). Moreover, a further specialization emerged around issues of "setting", leading to a deeper conception of mentalization, in sites including individual therapy, group therapy, child psychotherapy, short-term psychotherapy, family therapy, and psychodrama therapy, as well as day-care, outpatient, and psychodynamic settings (Schultz-Venrath & Felsberger, 2016; Bateman, Kongersley & Hansen, 2019; Asen & Midgley, 2019; Midgely et al., 2019; Luyten & Fonagy, 2019; Bales, 2019; Kjolbe & Bateman, 2015; Vermote et al., 2014; Bateman & Fonagy, 2006).

For Fonagy and Bateman, these treatment concepts (MBT) differ from other integrative psychotherapy methods by virtue of their complex, interwoven frame of reference, which includes a model of developmental psychology, as well as a hypothesis-generated model of mechanisms of psychotherapeutic action. Moreover, treatment concepts associated with mentalization include a well-developed theory of psychopathology, specifically with regard to borderline personality disorder. The biggest difference between mentalization-based treatments and other psychotherapeutic procedures is MBT's focus on techniques specifically intended to promote mentalization. The underlying idea of psychopathology posits an attitude of non-mentalization on the part of the patient, suggesting that this in turn causes psychopathological phenomena. In a mentalization-based context, the focus is not placed on cognitive restructuring, nor on interpretation and its associated insights, nor on direct behavioural change. The significance of MBT lies in how it captures mental processes: phenomena like restructuring, insight, and behavioural change are all generated as a by-product of mentalizing encounters. Mentalization is a very broadly-based concept, used in almost all psychotherapeutic methods, since the focus of mentalization is on paying consistent attention to the patient's thoughts and feelings.

Along with the development of a psychotherapeutic treatment framework, the second achievement of mentalization-based approaches has been as a concept within developmental psychology. If mentalizing is a human characteristic and can be well developed or badly developed, the question arises whether pedagogy and relationship structures can have influence on this developmental mechanism. Mother-child interactions and the significance of the family are central to these considerations and of great importance for the concept of mentalization presented in this book.

The third fundamental aspect of mentalization, as emphasized by Fonagy and Bateman, is as a psychological process, with an influence on all psychological disorders. They make a distinction between, on the one hand, a disorder of mentalization, which amounts to a developmental disorder, and, on the other, conditions in which mentalization disorders can occur, such as depression (Luyten et al., 2019).

2.2 Definition: Mentalizing

Here are three definitions of mentalizing, first as defined by Bateman and Fonagy, followed by two alternative formulations:

> Mentalizing describes a particular facet of the human imagination: an individual's awareness of mental states in himself or herself and in other people, particularly in explaining their actions. It involves perceiving and interpreting the feelings, thoughts, beliefs, and wishes that explain what people do. This entails an awareness of someone else's circumstances, his or her prior patterns of behaviour, and the experiences to which the individual has been exposed.
>
> (Bateman & Fonagy, 2019a, p 3).

> To mentalize means to experience and understand externally perceptible behaviour in connection with internal, 'mental' states and processes, and vice versa. This inner reality includes, for example, feelings, thoughts, needs, wishes, reasoning, meanings and very personal life experiences.
>
> (Bolm, 2009, p. 29).

> For Fonagy and his colleagues, mentalization means the ability to perceive, understand and anticipate one's own and others' behaviours, seeing them as beings with mental and emotional abilities, or with a psyche. They describe mentalization as a process in which a human being realizes that his or her perception of the world and the perception of others are mediated by the mind, in other words, that they are mentalized. The development of the ability to mentalize depends on attachment and relationship experiences while at the same time having an effect on those experiences in turn.
>
> (Lackinger, 2008, p. 318).

In a nutshell, mentalizing is social cognition. This cognition is composed of imaginative mental activity; it enables ourselves and others to perceive and to interpret. Through it, we can attribute needs, desires, feelings, beliefs, goals, purposes, and motivations to ourselves and others (Bateman & Fonagy, 2019a).

Fonagy's first article dealing with understanding "others' feelings, others' intentions, rules and conventions and that others have mind", which also created a form of clinical treatment methodology, appeared at the end of the 1980s (Fonagy, 1989). The emergence of the concept was also rooted in the impact of austerity on the British social system and the pressure exerted on longer-term therapies. The need for evidence-based therapy, as well as the need to generate funds for treatment, led to the development of manuals providing a specific basis for outcomes research (Bolm, 2015; Schultz-Venrath, 2013; Taubner, 2015). This led to associated research and reflection, undertaken using scientific methods, and also produced new test procedures to subject mentalization to measurement (Fischer-Kern & Fonagy, 2012; Luyten et al., 2019).

These points represent a framework for thinking about mentalization and represent a constant thread running through the works of Bateman, Fonagy, Allen, and Target:

1. Understanding the behaviour of others in terms of their likely thoughts, feelings, wishes, and desires is not entirely a constitutional given but to some degree a developmental achievement.
2. The acquisition of this capacity depends on the quality of attachment relationships – particularly, but not exclusively, early attachments, as these reflect the extent to which our subjective experience was adequately mirrored by a trusted other.
3. The quality of affect mirroring affects the development of affect regulative processes and self-control (including attention mechanisms and effortful control) and the capacity for mentalization.
4. Disruptions of early attachment and later trauma have the potential to disrupt the capacity for mentalizing and, linked to this, the development of a coherent self-structure.
5. The capacity to mentalize has both 'trait' and 'state' aspects that vary in quality in relation to emotional arousal and interpersonal context.
6. Mentalizing and the associated capacities for affect representation, affect regulation, and attentional control normally obscure forms of subjectivity that developmentally antedate mentalization.
7. The failure of mentalizing, in combination with profound disorganization of self-structure, may provide a comprehensive account for core features of borderline personality functioning. In particular, we have argued in the past that borderline personality functioning can be understood as the consequence of the following:

a. The loss of mentalizing in emotionally intense relationship contexts.
b. The re-emergence at these times of modes of thinking about subjective experiences that antedate full mentalization.
c. The constant pressure for externalization of internal states (projective identification), which we consider the re-externalization of disorganized, intolerably painful self-states (the self-destructive alien self).

(Bateman & Fonagy, 2019a)

Don't all educators want to bring children, and people in general, towards this kind of inner psychological stability? But what are the basic requirements for me to be able to act like this? What kind of frameworks and inner attitude am I going to have to achieve? As a teacher, how should I change my own inner frame of reference to be more secure when mentalizing?

Mentalizing is an basic element of ourselves, of our own sense of our identity. We mentalize in every part of our lives: if we move back and forth with wisdom between our inner and outer worlds, it will be possible to gain greater and more complete access to our own feelings.

These subjects are closely linked to the overall tasks of pedagogy:

- to equip the child to empathize with themselves and with others
- to equip the child to reflect on their own behavioural patterns and the cognitive-emotional events they go through
- to equip the child to take responsibility for their own actions

Take for example, the everyday life of a kindergarten teacher:

The teacher mentalizes when they:

- enable the child to feel safe in the kindergarten
- understand the effect of situations on a child, for example separations
- can mirror the child's feelings back them, and give them names
- have the capacity to understand and name a child's distress when they have been distressed by their own experiences or behaviours
- can explain and show to a child the kind of things they can do with a toy
- can reflect joy felt by a child at play, reflecting it back to the child, thus making clear to them that it is possible to change their feelings

3 History of MBT: a Mentalization-Based Treatment Approach

Mentalization-based therapy (MBT) resulted from accumulated needs within local cultural contexts, while also determined by financial circumstances.

Psychiatric care facilities were increasingly being used by so-called borderline patients. Kernberg provided a sound theoretical background for the clinical outline of this condition, building on Stern's description (Steinberger, 2016). But success in treating remained low, with the prognosis for psychotherapeutic treatment quite poor. In German-speaking countries, a treatment approach was developed which specialized in structural disorders or "early disorders", but this received little international attention. PIM, a psychoanalytic-interactional method, was developed in the 1970s under the leadership of Franz Heigl and Anneliese Heigl-Evers; this would became known as the "Göttingen Model". Many recommended treatments which originated in the Göttingen Model can now be found as part of the MBT treatment approach (Bolm, 2015).

The 1990s saw the international establishment of the treatment approach developed by Marsha Linehan, of dialectical behavioural therapy (DBT) and of transference-focused therapy (TFP), as developed in the working group under Otto Kernberg (Steinberger, 2016). Early in the development of MBT, Kernberg was highly regarded, seen as a leader of this mode of thought, but he would later become an opponent of the approach, authoring several articles which point out the weaknesses of its concepts. As the field has developed, Fonagy and his colleagues have made less and less reference to Kernberg's work (Kernberg, 2014).

In the early 1990s, Anthony Bateman took over the management of the Halliwick psychiatric day unit at St. Anne's Hospital in London. The treatment frameworks he found there were primarily aimed at people suffering from psychoses, based on lengthy treatment duration. There were few treatment options for severe personality disorders: if these patients received any treatment it was solely inadequate hospital stays, with no treatment framework (Bateman & Fonagy, 2006; Bolm, 2015).

Around the same time, a working group around Fonagy at University College London and the Anna Freud Institute in London developed a theoretical framework for understanding severe personality disorders. Mentalization was the name they gave this conceptual framework (Fonagy, 1991; Fonagy & Target, 1995).

Bateman's practical implementation of the mentalization framework at the Halliwick day unit in the mid-1990s led to the first research-based and manualized treatment framework based on theories of mentalization. This conceptual framework was further reinforced by the first randomized controlled study of the MBT approach. The success of the study led to further applications of the mentalization concept and the publication of the first MBT manual for borderline patients in 2006 (Bateman & Fonagy, 2006). In the wake of massive austerity measures in the British health system, the treatment procedure also promised to be coherent and empirically-validated, and thus cost-effective. In 2009, the treatment procedure was included in the NICE clinical guidelines, used in the treatment of personality disorders in the public health service in England and Wales (Bolm, 2015).

The MBT model spread very quickly, including to internationally renowned university hospitals. In the German-speaking world, Thomas Bolm introduced the MBT approach to the Christophsbad Clinic in Göppingen. The approach was also introduced at another German hospital, the Evangelical Hospital in Bergisch Gladbach, under the direction of Ulrich Schultz-

Venrath. Both of the institutions would become major pioneers of the approach in the German-speaking countries, each bringing out its own treatment manual (Bolm, 2009, 2015; Bolm et al., 2007; Schultz-Venrath, 2013). In the area of psychotherapeutic pedagogy, Heiner Hirblinger was the first to deal with considerations of mentalization, individualization, and the development of the self, especially in relation to adolescents (Hirblinger, 2011).

4 Psychoanalysis and Mentalizing

As early as the late 1960s, the French analyst Pierre Marty had addressed the concept of mental organization in the sense of mentalization: "Progressive disorganization selectively impairs people whose neurosis, if it exists, assumes the form of a character neurosis, of a poorly structured mental organization" (Marty, 1968, p. 246; Fonagy, 2009; Sieberth & Steinberger, 2013). Marty is here describing the capacity to create psychological representations, and to allow fantasies to arise within oneself. He presents mentalization along three axes, respectively representing qualities of depth, mobility, and stability. For Marty, depth refers to the possible layers of a representation, mobility in representations is a criterion of quality, while stability is an expression of a representation's accessibility (Marty, 1980; Aisenstein, 2008). For Marty, mentalizing means: "Psychic representations constitute the basis of mental life in every one of us [*les reprèsentations psychiques constituent la base de la vie mentale de chacun de nous*]". (Marty, 1990, p. 8). If psychological representation via mentalization does not take place, there occurs instead a physical or psychosomatic expression: what is missing here is "mental" life, with patients unable to represent or organize their affects into higher forms of representation. This way of thinking includes a concrete way of understanding the modes of thinking developed by patients, who are described as having symptoms of alexithymia. For the first time, this way of thinking about of mentalizing brought together mental representations with psychoanalytic mechanisms. Thus Marty introduced the term "mentalization" into meta-levels of psychoanalytic theory (Marty, 1990; Taubner, 2015).

Writing on mentalization, the American psychologist and philosopher Elliot Jurist follows the French approach to understanding alexithymia, which involves the therapist translating feelings into language for patients: "I would characterize my approach to helping patients identify emotions in terms of mentalization ... Identifying emotions entails a process in which the therapist joins the patient in naming, understanding, and tolerating his or her feelings" (Jurist, 2020, p. 22). Jurist justifies his views and their application by presenting case histories drawn from his own psychoanalytic practice. He regards his approach to mentalizing affectivity as profoundly anchored in psychoanalytic theory: "Mentalized affectivity is an outgrowth of mentalization theory, itself a product of psychoanalytic theory. Our experience of emotions necessarily reflects our past history and identity; thus, emotion regulation cannot exist as an abstract category denuded of these factors" (Jurist, 2020, p. 169).

5 Theory of Mind and Mentalizing

For over 30 years, developmental psychology has addressed the question of how we generate ideas about ourselves as thinking beings. What internal system do we have which allows us to access mental states? This question has prompted a field of research known as Theory of Mind (ToM). A number of cognitive abilities are collectively known as ToM or thought-reading: these capacities allow us to predict, interpret, and interact in cooperative and competitive situations by inferring desires, intentions, and beliefs from the behaviour of others (Gergely & Unoka, 2011; Wellman, 1992, 2014; Taubner, 2015).

It is possible to recognize a "naive psychology" in children from the age of about three years. Their evolving ideas at this age are initial models for understanding human behaviour. Concepts enable us to have ideas of things, which in turn allow us to have insights and to ascribe meaning. Experiences are based on the capacity to generate concepts and thus set things in a particular order. From birth on, children are probably developing precursor forms of concepts.

"Naive psychology" is grouped around three psychological constructs: desires, beliefs, and actions. The three constructs are our primary explanations for understanding behaviour. To give an example: I would like to eat something (*desire*). To do this, I go to the refrigerator (*action*) and take something out (*belief that the refrigerator is full*). Desire and belief are not visible: they are what open up a psychological space of understanding for us. What is visible is the action, from which we may draw conclusions about desire and belief.

Recent findings in animal research suggest that humans and chimpanzees are not the only species to rely on the capacity to recognize mental states: "Thought-reading". Other species to have implicit knowledges of this kind include goats, as well as bird species such as crows, ravens, and scrub jays (Kabadayi & Osvath, 2017; Gergely & Unoka, 2011; Bugnyar & Heinrich, 2005; Emery & Clayton, 2004; Hare et al., 2001; Kaminski et al., 2011). These studies demonstrate that animals which interact in social groups in a specific competitive niche are capable of attributing mental states to members of their own species, and to store this information over a long period of time. This knowledge allows them to hide food, monitor hidden food, and mislead other animals.

The transition from naive psychology to a theory of mind occurs between the ages of two and five. This period sees the development of fundamental insights into thinking. Children develop ideas about how the mind and thinking work, and how feelings and ideas influence our actions. Harry Wellman developed a theory of how Theory of Mind develops at this age (Wellman, 1992; Wellman & Gelman, 1992), describing basic interrelated categories which go to form the structure of a Theory of Mind in preschool children.

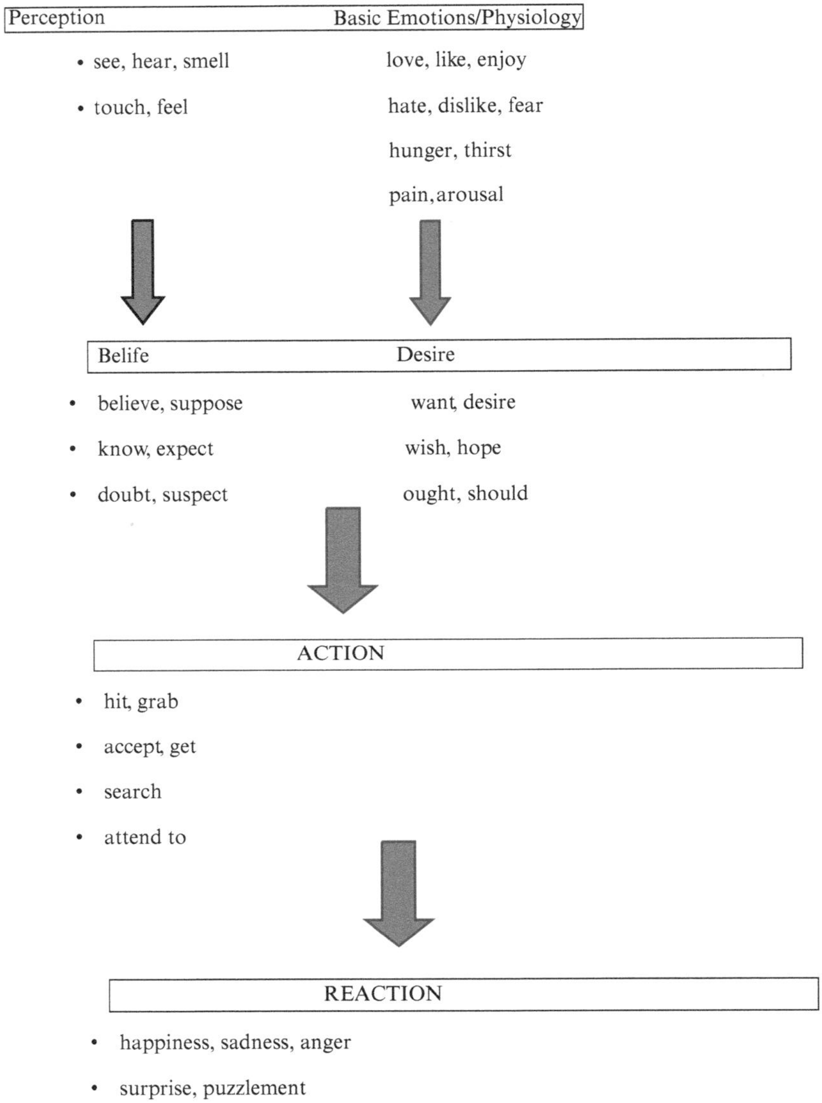

Wellman, Henry M.: Making minds: how theory of mind develops, Oxford University Press 2014

Figure 3.1 An idea for developing the mind according to Wellman (2014, p. 34) und in Siegler, DeLoache, Eisenberg (2003, S. 261).

Wellman's model assumes that beliefs mostly come from perceptions. We already have some knowledge of how basic emotions (Ekman, 2011) can consist of physiological states, and these in turn can generate desires. Preschool children can also already recognize that wishes and beliefs lead to actions, and that these actions can in turn influence or alter wishes and beliefs.

One important building block in developing a Theory of Mind is the ability to contextualize other people's wishes and actions. Henry M. Wellman discovered that the ability is already present in most two-year-olds.

When children as young as two are asked if the person in the story being narrated would rather play with cars than with dolls, they are capable of making a distinction which goes against their own desires. The child might want to play with a doll, but the child in the story prefers to play with cars. In other words, the child is able attribute the desire for cars to the child in the story. They thus create a difference between their own desire and the child's desire as told in the story (Wellman & Woolley, 1990; Siegler et al., 2005). In this way, the child makes a distinction between his own needs and the desires of the child in the story. However, most two-year-olds still have difficulty with the idea of beliefs and their influence on our ideas. If you tell a two-year-old child a story in which a child suspects that a small dog is on a terrace, when the real child knows that the dog is in a garage, the child will think the child in the story is looking for the dog in the garage, not on the terrace. By contrast, most three-year-olds are already capable of believing the child in the story is looking for the dog on the terrace. Three-year-olds also attribute intentions to characters in a story, for example here they can see the loss of the dog as the motivation for action on the part of the child in the story. One possible explanation attributable to the child looking for the dog is that he misses the dog and wants him to be with him (Wellman, 1992, 2014; Bartsch & Wellman, 1995).

Three-year-old children already have a clear sense of the distinction between tangible objects and intangible phenomena like sounds, shadows, light, etc. Most three-year-olds also know how desires and assumptions come about (Wellman, 2014; Pillow, 2012). Attributing needs to oneself and to others, or generating a difference between them, also requires the creation of an I and a you.

> Adam: Want some? (to adult).
> Adult: No. I don't want some.
> Adam: OK. But I want some.
> In this conversation the child, Adam, contrasts two different desires about the same physical reality – you want some, but I don't.
>
> (Wellman, 2014, p. 35)

Adam makes the adult the offer so as to attribute a wish to himself. His own need becomes an attribution of the desire to the adult. The adult turns down the offer, and it now seems to take some effort for Adam to acknowledge his own wish. The word "OK" leads us to believe Adam is turning away from adults, finding a way of standing alone in the world. The use of the word "but" seems to suggest a prohibition has been laid down by the adult. In a wide variety of cultures, encounters are based on the fact that if I offer a guest a meal and he refuses it, another offer is made: the host holds firm, and the guest then reaches for the food. The politeness ritual is actually about shaming. The guest must not be left alone in his desire for food, because this would mean exposing his desire for food.

> Desire:
> Adult: We'll turn it on later.
> Child (2 years, 10 months): You turn it on later?
> Adult: Yep.
> Child: No. I don't want it on later... I want it on now. You said you will turn the cowboys on!
> Adult: I said I'll turn them on later.
>
> (Bartsch & Wellman, 1995, p. 83)

Here a wish can be clearly defined, but it is rejected by the adult. The scene seems to manoeuvre itself into a form of power and powerlessness. This is a very physical world, where everything centres on who has the power to turn on the television. We cannot establish a reason why the television is not to be turned on now. The child suggests the meaning of television by using the word *cowboy*. The meaning of the dialogue only becomes clear if we regard it as a power struggle. In this brief scene, the adult shows no interest in the significance of the cowboys who appear to be on television. Control over the child's wishes is now determined by the adult. The child is likely to be left angry and enraged: the child's needs are under the control of the adult and he has no idea why the television will not be turned on. Moreover, the adult's "yep" suggests a pleasure in exercising power. The adult does not explain their motives but instead enjoys the non-fulfilment of the child's wish.

> Adult: Don't.
> Child (2 years, 10 months): I want... don't want ... I don't want it on [a Band-Aid].
> Adult: Well, you gotta have it on. Leave it on.
> Child: No.
>
> (Bartsch & Wellman, 1995, p. 83)

Here, there is an inner differentiation in the wish: "I want... don't want". The issue also does not seem primarily to be about the Band-Aid. The movement of the event is towards the creation of difference between two individuals. The child shifts the divergence outwards by distributing the wanting and not-wanting between himself and the adult.

Child (2y, 9m): I wanna watch TV, I wanna watch TV.
Adult: You can in a little while.
Child: I wanna watch something now.
Adult: Nothing good is on until 11 o'clock. Why don't we practice for a while?
Child: I don't want to tumble.

(Bartsch & Wellman, 1995, p. 87)

In this scene, the child transforms his wish into physical danger. If there is ban on television, there is a risk of falling ("tumble"). The fulfilment of his wish is here formulated as the prevention of a fall and the possible injury which would result. Because the child's wishes are refused, the adult is now responsible for a possible injury caused by a fall. The child shifts the adult's No onto a physical level.

Belief:
Adam (3y, 3m): Does you think have sugar... some sugar here?
Adult: I don't have any sugar.
Adam: I think you have sugar.

(Bartsch & Wellman, 1995, p. 124)

Adam equates his own need for sugar with that of the adult. The idea of the same desire or need for sugar is stronger than the language-mediated reality of not having sugar. In medical-diagnostic terms, we would call this delusion, if we did not acknowledge that the child feels lied to by the adult and is not telling the truth or is lying to the adult. Here, the adult must apply a theory of mind to give meaning to the child's words that is beyond the realm of delusion.

Child (3y, 10m): Leslie make me angry.
Adult: Why?
Child: If she thinks something is silly. I don't think it's silly at all.
Adult: Oh, you had a disagreement.
Child: Uh huh. She thought her necklace was silly.
Adult: She thought it was silly?
Child: Yeah. But I didn't think it was.

(Bartsch & Wellman, 1995, p. 122)

This scene constructs a triangle: feelings are negotiated here via "Leslie", who is not present. "Something" pushes the meaning of the necklace into the background. The child expresses the feeling "angry" in order to prompt the adult to investigate the background context. The child's feelings run contrary to Leslie's and the child ascribes the thought "silly" to Leslie. The adult formulates the scene and the significance of the child's emotion as a conflict, a "disagreement" with Leslie. With "I don't think it's silly at all", the child introduces this as a thought and not a fact, holding open the possibility of difference, while seeing how the adult emotionally positions themselves toward "silly". In this scene, the child probably wants to influence the adult with their own emotions by behaving in a way that he or she suspects the adult would appreciate.

> (Abe and his father are watching a TV programme about snakes, which has a female narrator.)
> Abe (3y, 8m): Is that a poisonous snake, dad?
> Adult: No.
> Abe: I think, if she tells about it... I think if she says it's a poisonous snake...you're gonna be wrong.
> Adult: You're right. I would be wrong. But it's not a poisonous snake, she just said it wasn't.
> Abe: It looks like a poisonous snake.
> Adult: Yah. But it's not.
>
> (Bartsch & Wellman, 1995, p. 123)

Abe challenges the female speaker's narrative of a possible dangerous reality. If the speaker speaks about it, the image can present a danger, a poisonous snake, even if this is in denial of the television narration. Because the snake is described as non-poisonous, the possibility of danger seems to become apparent. Might the father be staying silent about dangers, or lying about them? Abe goes for a compromise, deciding that the snake looks as if it could pose a danger.

> Child (3y, 9m): Can you eat snails?
> Mother: Some people eat snails, yes.
> Child: Why?
> Mother: Because they like them.
> Child: Mommy, do you want to eat snails?
> Mother: No, I don't think I'd like to eat snails?
> Child: I don't like to eat snails... People eat snails.
>
> (Bartsch & Wellman, 1995, p. 85)

Here the child turns to the mother to obtain a reference point about eating snails. With the help of its identification with the mother, the child can now make a distinction between itself and other people. The child can position themselves in a way contrary to other people. If the mother had said she ate snails, a conflict would have arisen for the child, one which would be difficult to resolve. But the mother's first answer differentiates herself from people who eat snails. The child begins to share the mother's beliefs and adopt them as his own. In their last answer, the child formulates the mother's clear position: "...don't like to eat snails".

6 False Belief Test

At the same time, research into what is known as the "False Belief Test" has highlighted the limits of the three-year-old imagination. This test involves distinguishing between other people's beliefs, as well as children's own beliefs. For Fonagy et al., the False Belief Test is the litmus test for mentalization. One version of the False Belief Test is the so-called Sally-Anne Test. In this test, Sally puts the ball in the basket and goes out of the room. While she is outside, Anne moves the ball into the box. Sally returns to get the ball. The test question is where Sally thinks the ball is. Only children older than three will give the answer that Sally will look first in the basket, where she has previously placed the ball.

Another false-belief experiment is the Smarties Test. The child is shown a box which says "Smarties" and asked what they think the box contains. The child answers: Smarties. They now look into the Smarties box and see that it contains pencils. Now they are asked what another person would think is in the box. Children under three often say that another person would think the box contained pencils. Five-year-olds usually laugh at the mistaken "pencil" belief and say that everyone would think there were Smarties in the box. For their part, when three-year-olds discover their mistake, they state that they already know there are pencils in the box.

The children's emotional reactions in this case are very interesting. Most children probably experience some inner tension when their imagination does not match reality. Five-year-olds relieve this tension with laughter, putting themselves on the same level as those who will commit the same error. Younger children avoid this tension by reinterpreting reality, saying they knew it beforehand.

These results hold true independent of culture: the same results have also been found when testing children in African contexts. For the authors, the test shows that three-year-olds have difficulty in separating their own knowledge from other people's assumptions and in allowing other people to have different perspectives on experience (Siegler et al., 2005).

What usually goes unmentioned in reflections on the False Belief Test is the emotional significance produced by the experiment: so far, the literature has paid little attention to intersubjective elements in the encounter between the child and the experimenter. In the Smarties test, younger children can complete the task if the experimenter introduces the idea of playing a trick on another child. This change makes it easier for younger children to grasp that other children don't know there are pencils in the Smarties box. In this case, the researchers suspected that creating the distinct role of the "cheater" – the figure who put pencils in the Smarties box – made it easier for children to imagine how other children could be taken in (Sullivan & Winner, 1993). Here the difference between child and adult is eliminated. The child does what the adult tells him to; they not alone in their knowledge of the world. Five-year-olds immediately fantasize about other children who would also succumb to the mistake if asked about the Smarties box.

Thus looked at differently, it rapidly becomes clear that an intersubjective event is taking place: the subtlety of the scene can only be understood in terms of the encounter between child and experimenter.

It is not yet clear how this ability arises, whether it represents a specific ability in human development, or if it in fact results from the maturation of general cognitive abilities. Nor is it clear how all of these aspects interact (Taubner, 2015).

Data provided by Simon Baron-Cohen, Patrik Bolton, and Alan Leslie suggests that children suffering from autism have limited or no ToM ability. These children are deprived of the ability to empathize and participate in their environment (Baron-Cohen & Bolton, 2006).

Michael Merzenich's research into brain plasticity at the University of California has suggested that autistic children do not lack a module for empathy, but rather suffer from an imbalance of stimulatory and inhibitory neurons, which do not mutually regulate in their brain, meaning their impulsive excitement cannot be inhibited. To put it another way: incorrect processing of stimuli may lead to the misinterpretation of emotional situations (Merzenich, 2013; Mottron, 2016).

7 Explanations for the Development of Theory of Mind

Autism research data raises a number of questions, but cannot answer why people with autism find it difficult to learn to read other people's mental states. So far it has not been possible to precisely identify what might cause improvement in thought reading. These questions have sparked several discussions in the field (Siegler et al., 2005).

One strand of research investigates the possibility of a separate theory of mind module, i.e. a specific brain mechanism. In normal child development, this mechanism develops during the first five years of life, allowing for a differentiated understanding of other people's inner psychological worlds (Dennett, 1987; Fodor, 1992; Leslie, 2000; Wellman, 2014). Problems with the ability to empathize in autistic children are explained by the biological impairment of or subsequent damage to the Theory of Mind module. Some researchers regard the mechanism for ToM and mentalization mechanism as being one and the same. Gergely and Unoka also cite research to prove that systems of attachment and of mentalization are in fact unrelated: by making this argument, they also oppose the idea of intersubjectivity as primary in the development of mentalization (Gergely & Unoka, 2011).

Another school of thought emphasizes interaction with others as a crucial driver in the development of Theory of Mind (Perner, 1993; Astington & Reiss, 2000; Astington & Baird, 2005). These studies use findings from sibling research, showing that children with older siblings perform better on the False Belief Test than children who experience less interaction.

A third strand of research focuses on information processing as a crucial skill for understanding other people's minds. Since information processing is a very complex operation, three-year-old children and autistic people lack the knowledge to read the minds of others. This explanatory model suggests that information processing ability depends on a capacity for cognition which works with contradictions. This achievement in thought is limited to older children (Zelazo et al., 2003).

All three of these explanatory models probably play a role in the development of thought reading and mentalization. According to the most recent neurobiological evidence, brain maturation, interaction with other people, and increased information processing appear to have both general and specific significance for ToM development (Taubner, 2015; Siegler et al., 2005).

Harry Wellman summarized his own twenty-five years of research on ToM as follows:

> Theory of mind (a) is rapidly acquired in the normal case, (b) is acquired in an extended series of developmental accomplishments, (c) encompasses several basic insights, that are acquired worldwide on a similar trajectory (but not timetable), (d) requires considerable learning and development based on an infant set of specialized abilities to attend to and represent person, and is severely delayed in both autism and in deaf children of hearing parents.
>
> Not all researchers would agree with all these points, but nonetheless this list represents an important consensus regarding theory of mind based on considerable empirical knowledge garnered from twenty-five years of research effort by developmental scientists across a range of disciplines and countries.
>
> (Wellman, 2014, p. 31).

8 Attachment and Mentalization

A key building block for the idea of mentalization has been its connection to concepts of attachment and to research associated with it. By incorporating findings on attachment, Fonagy's working group has resolved the long-standing conflict between psychoanalytic approaches and ideas of attachment. Findings from attachment research are becoming more and more relevant in clinical application.

The attachment model is based on an idea that an instinctual *attachment system* is already genetically present within us (Bowlby, 1973; Gergely & Unoka, 2011). The system of attachment is anchored genetically: it enables us to function adaptively in stressful situations, including threats and separation. In young children, negative affects like fear, exhaustion, etc. lead to reactivation of attachment and they seek protection from their carer. For Bowlby, attachment instinct is important because it protects non-autonomous offspring from danger, thus allowing them to survive. Many mammals have such a mechanism, whereby offspring instinctively seek proximity to the mother in case of a possible threat scenario.

At one time, attachment theory was strongly rejected by psychoanalysts, who considered it to be too close to psychology. Today, the theory is partly acknowledged by Bowlby to be a psychoanalytic theory in and of itself. Theories of attachment offer a connection to general psychology and its approaches to understanding human beings, and they are becoming increasingly important for psychodynamic therapies. With infant research rapidly developing the scope of its knowledge, more and more connections have been made between psychological data and clinical applications in schools of depth psychology.

Bowlby's initial focus in the 1940s was on the relationship between infant and mother. He recognized the link between the quality of the mother-infant bond and the child's psychological condition as an adolescent or adult. As early as 1944, he treated young people found guilty of theft, and later children in care. Here he managed to establish a connection between the behaviour of what were then called "juvenile delinquents" and the lack of maternal attention given to children in care.

Bowlby stressed the importance of attachment and was one of the first researchers to note that infants are born with an active predisposition to interaction. This idea took him close to biological thinking, and his investigation increasingly turned to "attachment behaviour" among children. He also observed that "caregivers" are a safe starting point for children's exploration of the world, with a connection between "exploration" and "attachment". His guiding principle for healthy child development was the child's secure attachment to the mother. If children do not establish secure attachment, they will later experience partial or total deprivation. He later made a connection between symptoms and the separation reactions seen in children, describing the reaction to separation in terms of a sequence of "protest – desperation – detachment" (Bowlby, 1973). He described the maintenance of attachment as a form of behaviour, a claim which triggered controversial reactions within psychoanalysis. As described by Bowlby, attachment behaviour can no longer be explained by a drive model.

The distinction between attachment theory and object relations theorists centred on the idea that the child does not seek the mother as an object, but instead is stimulated by an internal system in its search to be close to the mother. The aim is to regulate a physical state, which is brought about through closeness. This initial goal of physical proximity is only later replaced by a psychological goal, namely a feeling of closeness with the mother.

Attachment theory is important for developmental psychology in understanding the connections between attachment and exploration. When there is secure attachment, i.e. when the caregiver is nearby, the child can become curious about the world (Ainsworth, 1978). If the caregiving figure of attachment is absent, the child is inhibited in their exploration, their going-into-the-world. This suggests that secure attachment contributes greatly to the development of cognitive and social skills. When the child is afraid, it withdraws back to the mother, thus reducing external stimuli. Separations produce two stressful situations for the child: first, separation produces unprotected exposure and second, it takes away the source of protection. The child's fear system is activated by the absence of the caregiver. Behavioural systems of fear, attachment, and exploration regulate the child's being-in-the-world (Ainsworth et al., 1978; Fonagy & Target, 2011, 2003).

In the second volume of his trilogy, Bowlby explained that the presence of the caregiver allows the child to develop ideas about safety and its reliability. Here he links attachment to cognitive development, in particular the capacity for trust (Bowlby, 1973): Bowlby calls these behavioural systems "internal working models". In this way, his work underscored the genuine importance of relationships in human development.

A major step in the further development of attachment theory was made by Mary D. Salter Ainsworth, whose pioneering work introduced what is known as the "strange situation test", an instrument for observing the internal working models used by small children.

In this experiment, the children and their caregiver, usually the mother, are led into a room containing toys, where the experimenter familiarizes the child with the environment. The child is then confronted with seven separate situations, experienced as individual episodes. In two of these scenes, the child is first separated from and then reunited with the mother. Between these two comes another scene, featuring an interaction with a stranger. This person first stays with the child when it is alone, and then also in the presence of a parent. Each episode lasts approximately three minutes. During all of this, the child's behaviour is assessed by observers. From what they note, it is possible to identify distinct behavioural patterns, allowing conclusions to be drawn about the quality or security of attachment. Attachment researchers later introduced a fourth category (Siegler et al., 2005).

According to this research, the first category in attachment theory is that of securely-attached children. These children manage, after a time, to look at the toys lying in the room, occasionally looking to their parents, sometimes showing them the toy they have found. When the parents leave the room, the children are usually – but not always – disturbed and show joy when their parents return, and crawl towards them. The presence of their parents quickly calms them down and they begin to explore the room again.

Ainsworth described two other attachment categories: children she described as *insecurely* attached, dividing these in turn into subcategories of insecure-ambivalent and insecure-avoidant attachment styles. Ainsworth described children as exhibiting insecure and ambivalent attachment behaviour when they stayed very close to their parents or clung to them at the beginning of the strange situation test. These children, when their parents returned, refused to be consoled by their parents. In the insecure-avoidant category, Ainsworth included children who showed defensive reactions to their parents when they returned to the room. They did not greet their parents, instead turning away from them. Researchers also observed children whose reactions were unclear and difficult to understand: for example, they reacted to the situation by smiling anxiously and looking away, or they appeared calm and content, only to then spontaneously erupt in anger (Siegler et al., 2005).

Ainsworth's set of attachment categories can be summarized as follows:

Secure:

- children communicate their distress openly in the separation situation
- can be quickly comforted and soon return to their play
- exhibit a good balance between attachment and exploration behaviours

Insecure-avoidant:

- children show few feelings of distress at separation, but put particular focus on their play
- when the attachment figure returns, they avoid any active proximity
- their attention is largely focused on exploratory behaviour, at the expense of attachment behaviour

Insecure-ambivalent:

- children cry when separated and are difficult to console
- exhibit ambivalent behaviours: a desire for closeness, but also resistance to contact, expressed in the form of annoyance, rage or passive despair
- their attention is largely focused on attachment behaviour, at the expense of exploratory behaviour

Disorganized-disoriented:

- children have no coping strategy during separation and show incompatible behaviour on reunification: stereotypical movements, phases of rigidity (freezing) after seeking intimacy, expression of fear towards the parent
- disorganized behaviour can be found in abused and neglected children, as well as children whose parents have not yet processed their own grief

Secure attachment is a prerequisite for the development of mentalization: only on this basis can children attribute a psychological inner life or mental states to their parents. The attachment system's enabling of exploration extends to children being able to explore their caregivers' inner lives. Securely-attached children are able to build trust in the world and in others, and move on to explore with curiosity. Interactions are increasingly internalized as lived experiences in the child and are thus now becoming increasingly available to the mind. The child's intersubjective experiences become more and more clearly anchored mentally, leading to a generalization of experiences and thus to an expectation of repetition [*wiederholungshaltung*] on the child's part. These repetitions and the associated capacity of abstraction allow for generalization to occur, which in turn guides the organization of intrapsychic structures. These structures are reflected in the strategies we have developed to satisfy our attachment needs. The concept of mentalization can be seen as a structural model, and thus represents a new concept for the development of the self. The capacity to mentalize reflects the self's developmental experiences and its underlying structure, it thus also reflects the self's potential for further development (Steinberger, 2019; Taubner, 2015; Fonagy et al., 2002; Taubner et al., 2010; Grossmann et al., 2015). Fonagy et al. acknowledge that with a dysfunctional attachment environment there is a risk of "depriving the individual of some key building blocks for the development of this structure" (Fonagy et al., 2002, p. 186). The building blocks are attachment experiences; these experiences go on to form a structure, which in turn becomes the foundation of the self. Through the possibility of agency [*urheberschaft*], the child becomes aware of the self.

9 Mentalization and the Structural Model of Self

Traditional intellectual approaches to disorders of character and personality have been based on a clearly described hermeneutics, which focuses on the idea that every individual has an inner psychological structure. In the literature, the concept of structure is presented as a complex phenomenon, used across a variety of disciplines. Derived from the Latin word *structura*, the word's meaning encompasses, first, assembly and construction, and second, build-type and structure (Stowasser et al., 1998, p. 484).

Freud attempted to form the psychological chaos around him into a cohesive structure, so as to "see" it better. To do this, he developed the concept of the psychological apparatus, which in turn supports a topographical model, which regards place or topos as the key to understanding and using structures. Freud tried to form a coherent structure from patterns within psychological experience, including everyday repetitions, and perceptions which constantly surround us. This would remove material from the realm of chaos, and allow for repetition. Freud writes:

> We assume that mental life is the function of an apparatus to which we ascribe the characteristics of being extended in space and of being made up of several portions – which we imagine, that is, as resembling a telescope or microscope or something of the kind.
>
> (S. Freud, 1940a).

With the metaphor of the telescope, Freud places his understanding in a larger context, as described in his metaphorical work *Totem and Taboo*. Our understanding moves on a small axis, meaning we can examine large structures as well as small ones. In their article "A General Model for the Origin of Allometric Scaling Laws in Biology", West, Brown, and Enquist designed a generalized model to understand why larger organisms exhibit an equivalent decrease in metabolism to smaller organisms. The answer lies in genetic fractal building blocks, which are self-repeating, so that only *a single* architectural plan for recurring patterns is needed for complex fractal design (West et al., 1997, p. 122f.). If we assume an equivalent kind of self-similar development in psychological events, as Freud suggested, then the basic pattern of love experiences or parental-bonding experiences would be reflected across all of our relationships. With small shifts and innovations we arrive at a relationship pattern of self-similarity. Using this self-similarity, this fractal quality, we design structured patterns which can be superimposed on our own patterns of interaction.

We tend to impose a hypothetical structure on anything not directly visible, a structure we use to try to depict or describe psychological experience. This structure can only be inferred indirectly (Orange, 2000, p. 543; Doering & Hörz, 2012, p. 2). So these mental models also carry the mark of their own time, including its cultural concepts, be that attachment and apparatus, or microscope and telescope.

When it comes to concepts of structure, psychoanalysis has seen three main strands of development, one quantitative and two qualitative. A quantitative concept of structure tries to establish the extent of pathology, while the two other strands present an elaboration of character pathology and of neurotic structure (Doering & Hörz, 2012, p. 2).

For Kernberg, a structure is something which remains stable, always exhibiting the same patterns of transference and countertransference, subject to recurring defence mechanisms (Kernberg, 2014, p. 130). Kernberg bases his own structural model on a primary motivation system which mediates between biological, symbolic, and intrapsychic structures. Affects lead to the internalization of object relationships, which he sees as the equivalent of Bowlby's internal working models. The affects are anchored in procedural memory, which is not capable of consciousness, they thus accordingly form a representation of the self and the object. As an object relations theorist, Kernberg sets up the object in opposition to the subject, which forms a kind of stored experience (Kernberg, 2014, p. 137).

The self is formed in these encounters with others, creating mental models which internalize, abstract, anchor, and structure these experiences. The understanding of one's own self develops through the ability to mentalize, an activity which gives access to the internally formed schemas (Taubner et al., 2010). An empathetic and secure attachment builds a foundation for high mentalization functioning, in turn enabling the development of an integrated self, as reflected in the awareness of the self's agency (*selbsturheberschaft*).

10 Developmental Stages of Mentalization

Starting from affect regulation, building on attachment theory and the theory of social biofeedback, Fonagy and his colleagues have worked out a theory of development, a permanent work-in-progress, which has their idea of mentalization at its core. The following analysis draws on concepts from the work of

Fonagy et al. (2013) and Taubner (2015, 2010). The capacity to mentalize develops in a continuum, but with different steps. This capacity is the prerequisite for any ability to think about oneself and hence to become aware of oneself.

The various authors here assume that children have a predisposition to recognizing and exploring contingent structures. This capacity enables interaction between mother and child, since they are able to take up alternating roles of listening and vocalizing (Gergely & Unoka, 2011). These contingencies are building blocks for the development of experience, enabling the notion of a self. The awareness of the self occurs along a line of development that leads to ideas of oneself and others as having authorship (*agency*). The capacity to experience oneself as a psychological being occurs as part of a developmental and intersubjective process. This process is based on attachment experiences and can thus also exhibit deficient development, leading to psychological undesirable developments. For Fonagy and his colleagues, attachment has the function of regulating affects. From co-regulation by the caregiver, there is now a transition to self-regulation, and with it the development of a perceived sense of self (Taubner, 2015).

Fonagy and colleagues divide their concept into four developmental stages, placing them on a sequential timeline (Fonagy et al., 2013, p. 53):

- teleological actor (6–12 months)
- self and others are understood as teleological actors:
- understands causality between action, actor and environment
- understands agency exclusively in terms of physical actions and constraints
- intentional actor (12–24 months)
- self and others are understood as intentional actors:
- understands that actions are caused by prior mental states (e.g. desires) and that actions can lead to changes in mind and body
- develops language for mental states and the ability to non-egocentrically infer feelings and desires in others
- cannot yet represent mental states independently of physical reality
- at certain times, experiences inner reality as far more compelling than external reality, at other times as irrelevant (mode of "psychological equivalence" and "as if")
- representational actor (3–4 years)
- understands self and others as representational actors:
- understands that other people's actions are caused by their beliefs
- is increasingly able to solve false belief tasks
- knows that people don't always feel what they seem to feel and are influenced by previous emotional experiences
- temporally extended self-representation (around 6 years)
- ability to relate memories of intentional activities and experiences into a coherent, causal and temporal organization
- formation of a temporally extended self

10.1 Teleological Actor: The Interpretation of Reality

The word "teleology" comes from ancient Greek and means purpose, goal, end, and theory. Teleology is the theory that actions are subject to a goal or purpose. The term also refers to the rationality of our actions. Fonagy and colleagues use it to identify a particular stage of development: the second half of the first year of life. At this stage of development the child begins to experience themself as the author and agent (*urheber*) of their own actions. The baby experiences itself as an actor and is now able to perceive the causality of its environment. At nine months, during what is called the "Nine-Month Revolution", children view actions as expressing an underlying intention of an agent. They can now also see themselves as the cause of actions and take actions to pursue a goal. From adults, children expect logical behaviour on a physical level. When they want something, their gaze moves to the adult, then they watch how the adult reacts to their pointing hand. They internalize these scenes and repeat them over and over again. They now are experiencing themselves as actors (Fonagy et al., 2013; Fonagy et al., 2002; Bolm, 2009, 2015).

10.2 Intentional Actor: Intentional Interpretation of Reality

The concept of intentionality refers to the ability of consciousness to relate to something. The term was introduced into psychology by Brentano, whose thinking also influenced his student Sigmund Freud.

During the second year of life, the child becomes aware of his intentionality: they can now relate themselves and others to their mental states. The child now understands that actions they undertake can be the cause of mental and physical changes. The child now points to objects, for example reacting in frustration if they don't get them. The child now shows clear tendencies in his affect regulation, in this way reflecting its experience of relations with others. The child begins to develop a language to speak about their feelings and can talk about the wishes of others without making a direct relation to themselves. The child can now also complete goal-oriented actions in cooperation with others. But they are not yet capable of separating out mental states from the physical world. Inside and outside remain interwoven and cannot yet be clearly distinguished from one another. This stage of development also sees the transition between equivalence mode and pretend ("as if") mode (Fonagy et al., 2013; Fonagy et al., 2002; Bolm, 2009, 2015).

10.3 Representational Actor: Recognizing the Self and the Other

Between three and four, children begin to develop an understanding that people are driven to action by inner opinions and beliefs. From around this age, children become capable of dealing with the false belief test. The child now begins to clearly establish that people, for example, can feel something different in a situation than what they themselves feel. It can now understand itself and others as distinct actors. This last achievement is regarded as a major achievement in developmental psychology. The child is now capable of empathetic behaviour towards others. Prompted by the idea that people regulate their behaviour via thoughts and feelings, a self-conception emerges in the child, i.e. they develop an idea of their own self. The child can now make jokes and play little tricks, thus expanding their social interaction, they can more consciously use other people to regulate their sense of self. Here we can see the beginning of a process which will last a lifetime, that which makes us interactive beings. We are able to surround ourselves with people who share our interests, attitudes, and sense of humour (Fonagy et al., 2013; Fonagy et al., 2002; Bolm, 2009, 2015).

10.4 Temporally Extended Self-Representation and the Relation Between Implicit and Explicit Knowledge

Over the course of the child's sixth year of life, they begin to store memories of intentional activities as experiences, in order to place them in causal connection at a later moment. As a result, the child is now capable of developing preconceptions and associated expectations. The child now also develops an ability for second-order thought, so they can, for example, recognize lies or use lies or social deceptions themselves, as well as understanding the ambivalent feelings associated with them. Moreover, the child now understands how expectations and prejudices can have an influence on events. These skills also allow the child to deal with their impulses differently: the child can now express impulses through linguistic utterances, discharging them in this way. This leads to a decrease in physical violence and the physical expression of emotions. Aggressive feelings now appear more often as an element in a relational context, expressed in some combination of language, non-language, and turning away (Fonagy, 2008; Fonagy et al., 2013; Fonagy et al., 2002; Bolm, 2009, 2015; Juen & Fizke, 2010).

10.5 Summary

A small child will assume that their knowledge is also known by others and the knowledge of others is also available to them. Only later do they develop concepts of personal uniqueness. Separating out the inner from the outer world occurs over the course of the child's development: it is a process-like event. Small children prone to outbursts of anger or who suffer from frustration are expressing their sense of helplessness and powerlessness, which they go through because of their inability to separate inner from outer worlds. This means they do not understand why the other person fails to react precisely as they do in their inner world. They start from an assumption that other people know exactly what they want. If their self is still sufficiently underdeveloped, they will accept the other's reality as their own reality and therefore as their own need. An alien self emerges within them.

In 2010, there was a further reclassification of developmental lines, outlined in the work of Svenja Taubner, Tobias Nolte, Patrick Luyten, and Peter Fonagy. Contemporary developmental psychology now speaks of interlocking developmental lines which complement and influence each other. There are three strands of development – the social-emotional, the physical, and the cognitive strands – which entangle with one another, like the roots of a tree. These roots form the basic elements of the child's developing capacity to mentalize, and the knowledge of a self which accompanies this.

These revised developmental lines also include the first nine months of life (Taubner et al., 2010, pp. 243–258; Taubner, 2015):

- 0 to 9 months: the self as a physical and social actor
- 9 months to 2 years: the self as a teleological actor
- years 3 and 4: the self as an intentional actor
- age 5 and up: the self as a representational or mentalizing actor

10.6 Birth to Month 9: The Self as Physical and Social Actor

Based on experimental observations, Daniel Stern identified the ability to perceive oneself as a physical actor as being present in the first three months of life. He posits that the infant, through its corporeal existence, influences its environment and perceives connections within it (D.N. Stern, 2003). The infant's complex capacities take in these stimulus events as contingent experiences (Gergely & Watson, 1996).

The development of the social-emotional actor begins before birth, through interactions with the expectant mother. During pregnancy, the mother develops an emotional relationship with her child and the child in return also influences her emotionally. She begins to imagine the child within herself and develop an idea of them and of the relation between them both. Affect regulation occurs via the regulation of physical stimuli, including physical contact, stroking, warmth, and emotional care from the caregiver. This joint regulation of affects – their coordination between mother and child – now leads to structures of mental representation, which in turn influence maternal interactions and modify or replace the mother's original emotion-regulating behaviour. Affect mirroring plays a central role in mentalization theory, with negative affects being reduced by mirroring, which leads to psychological stability in the sense of the contingency maximization hypothesis. Contingency leads to an increase in pleasure in the infant, which also regulates negative affects. The infant experiences its self as the active author of its own affect control. The self-attribution of affects and their influence occurs through the social bio-feedback, as described by Gergely and Watson (Gergely & Watson, 1996; Taubner, 2015; Taubner et al., 2010).

10.7 9 Months to 2 Years: The Self as Teleological Actor

The nine-month revolution is characterized by babies' new ability at this age to distinguish clearly between animate and inanimate objects, and to interpret pointing gestures. At this stage, babies exhibit affective-social understanding. Semantic memory can now also be seen (Tomasello, 2011). Fonagy and colleagues characterize the self during this developmental phase as *the self as a teleological actor* (Fonagy et al., 2002), with the infant now credited with the ability to form "naive theories". In terms of causal relationships, the baby can now influence its own actions and establish a rational relationship between the action taken and the accomplishment or not of their goal. The first mentalistic acknowledgement of a specific figure of external reference appears when the baby uses pointing gestures to achieve goals. The baby's field of action is thus expanded by way of this external reference figure. The child next develops a capacity for meta-representation. This new ability allows them to play games of pretend and make-believe. Equipped with this pretend mode – we could think of it as an as-if "decoupler" – the infant can now work out the complex functions they will need for make-believe play and indeed for play in general (Leslie, 1987). And because play is a reflection of reality, and not reality *in realitas*, we now see the emergence of symbolic representations of actions and objects. Play must explicitly differ from reality and hence must be marked off. Winnicott described the phenomenon of illusion in infants, viewing autoerotic phenomena like thumb sucking and later playing with soft toys in terms of transitional objects to the real mother's breast. He attributes this particular ability over the course of infant development to sensitivity on the part of the mother, which "allows the infant the illusion ... that what he creates actually exists" (Winnicott, 1989; Winnicott, 1997). Here Winnicott describes the fragility of as-if actions and thus also the fragile relations between play and reality. This space of fragility can be seen as a precursor to mentalization and thus represents the transition to mentalization. Negative affects are dissipated or regulated through the possibility of externalization, i.e. being projected onto the outside world through a projection process, which now represents a stage for pretend (as-if) actions and make-believe (Fonagy & Luyten, 2011; Fonagy & Target, 1995; Taubner, 2015).

10.8 Years 3 and 4: The Self as Intentional Actor

From the age of two on, the toddler can be defined as an intentional actor. It now has the ability to attribute feelings to itself which can be influenced by the outside world.

> Adult: Would you like to have a cookie?
> Eve (2, 3): I want some cookies. Cookies, that make me happy.
> (Bartsch & Wellmann, 1995, p. 114).

The child can attribute feelings of happiness to themselves, i.e. look into the future and incorporate the influence of the physical world. This marks a transition from a teleological to a mentalistic worldview, through which the child can attribute feelings of happiness to him- or herself. But for the moment, the child remains within a dual psychological experience. The child's needs may remain within a framework of psychological equivalence, with thoughts still experienced as something very close to the real world, while at the same time the as-if mode also has an influence on the child's psychological experience. Their own thoughts are experienced as real, and the other person experiences the same thoughts and is therefore in the same reality. Eve would make the assumption that the cookies would make the adult as happy as she was. Without the possibility of mentalizing, she would believe him to have the same motives and ideas as she did. In this sense, the world can often appear to be threatening to children when they have negative feelings and fantasies, a world in which everyone knows their thoughts, a belief which can be accompanied by great feelings of guilt. In children's play, this dual mode finds integration, and emotional experience and childish thinking can develop and stabilize. In play, the child learns the meaning of the reality of the game and the reality of the external world (Fonagy et al., 2002; Taubner, 2015).

For Fonagy and Target, the "mirror relationship" has significance in this stage of development. In contrast to traditional psychoanalytic theories, here meaning is located in the parent's response to the child's inner experiences (Fonagy & Target, 1995). As a result, the child acquires a symbolic language for inner-psychic events and develops second-order representations. These experiences of play support the child's development in adopting and stabilizing a mentalist attitude.

10.9 Age 5 and Up: The Self as a Representational or Mentalizing Actor

This phase of development sees the stable integration of the pretend (as-if) and the psychological equivalence mode. By this stage of development, Fonagy and colleagues regard the child as a representative actor in its own right. It can now recognize its own beliefs, and those of others; in this way, it can interpret opinions as being false because they are based on false beliefs. The child can see other opinions and ideas as being different from his or her own idea of the world. Running parallel to this development, memory is now organized as autobiographical memory. Fonagy and colleagues see this kind of continuity of self-experience as being a higher-order mentalization function. The child can now make a differentiated adjustment to psychological experience, capable of looking at situations from various perspectives. Children's play allows for the secure development of a stable mentalization function, characterized by a flexible form of self-experience. Children can now attribute an inner psychological state to other people and understand that this is the basis on which they make decisions.

This new capacity gives the child independence from the immediate emotional reaction of the person with whom they are interacting; in emotional terms, they can now take a different position for himself and create their own idea of the world. In other words, the child can position their own reality in relation to the reality of others and in this way subject it to scrutiny. Inside and outside are no longer experienced as identical, but neither are they now experienced as strictly separate, as in pretend, as-if mode. The child can more easily control their affects, impulses, and feelings: their own idea of themselves becomes increasingly clear, as does the meaningfulness of their own life, combined with the possibility of generating confidence in their own self (Taubner, 2015; Fonagy et al., 2002; Taubner et al., 2010).

10.10 Gergely and Watson's Theory of Social Biofeedback

Gergely and Watson first developed their theory of social biofeedback through maternal affect reflection in 1996. This notion forms the basis of ideas of how the ability to mentalize is developed; these ideas postulate a genetically-anchored process of social biofeedback, one which helps infants become sensitive to their own emotional states. The development takes the form of an automatic process of affect-regulating interactions, based on the "marking" of affective states, which is accomplished by the mother's reflection of these states for the baby. This outline draws on a concept from classic biofeedback theory, whereby the body's own conditions – such as breathing patterns, blood pressure, pulse, blood oxygen content, skin resistance, etc. – are assumed to function in a primarily hidden state, beyond one's own control. Biofeedback, as a form of external feedback, is thought to make these internal regulatory processes visible and therefore controllable. Gergely and Watson then transferred this idea of a sensitization process to the infant's affective states. Analogous to the idea of biofeedback, they describe a mechanism of contingency discovery and maximization; this then leads to the infant's becoming sensitized to affective processes.

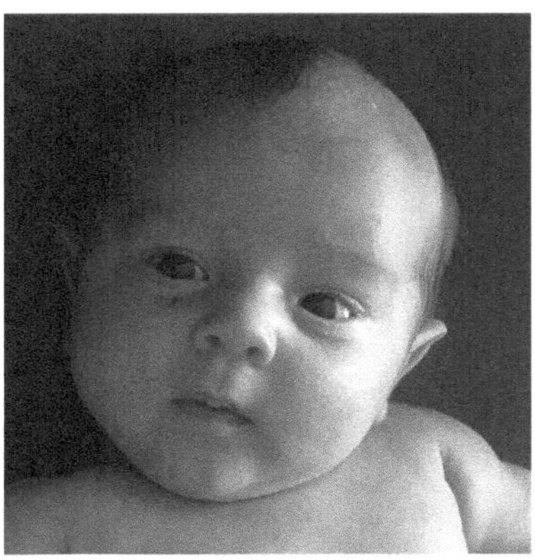

Figure 3.2 Infant (Photography, Claudia Guttenberger 2019).

The caregiver marks and mirrors the infant's current condition; in this way the infant is mentalized in the caregiver, in other words, the infant's state of mind is absorbed and reflected back to the infant as something not belonging to their self. Apart from promoting awareness of the infant's own affective states, social biofeedback fulfils a further task: that of regulating the infant's state, specifically in terms of negative affects. Moreover, as explained above, this marking and mirroring leads to the construction of a secondary representation, which connects to the baby's primary procedural affective states, thus contributing to the possibility of imaginative or cognitive access to affects and thus ultimately to the formation of a self. Furthermore, social biofeedback leads to a generalization of a communication style like *baby talk*: this "marks" affect reflection, through decoupling, i.e. by forming linguistic and facial representations of the affect which the infant has experienced. By making representations like this, baby talk means the infant can have the experience while not undergoing consequences in reality.

Incorrect development of this mechanism can lead to the formation of a false self and thus various additional incorrect developments in the constitution of the self. Bateman and Fonagy have described this abnormal development in terms of borderline personality disorder (BPD); in doing so, they came up with a new etiological approach to understanding this particular pathology (Fonagy et al., 2017).

10.11 Maldevelopment in Mentalization due to Failed Mirroring

Neglect, violence, serious illnesses, and other stressful life circumstances can substantially impair interaction with the infant, negatively impacting

Figure 3.3 An example of a mother reacting to a crying child, showing a facial expression which can be seen as marked and congruent with the infant's affective expression (El Shaddai Photography, Renate Steinberger, 2019).

the caregiver's affect coordination. This leads to attachment disorder and failed affect containment. On the basis of a process of failed attachment, the infant develops defence mechanisms, which Fonagy et al. (2002) regard as an identification with the caregiver's defence mechanisms (Bolm, 2015; Taubner et al., 2010). The whole development of mentalization capacity suffers if this connection fails to be made. Based on the idea of social bio-feedback, marked and congruent mirroring, three possible undesirable developments can be identified:

1 There is no marking of the congruently mirrored affect
2 The marking is mirrored with an incongruent affect
3 There is no reflection of any kind and thus of course no marking

Maldevelopment 1: Lack of marking

If there is no marking, the caregiver does not "succeed" in identifying or marking a distinction between their own feelings and those of the child. Faced with this unmarked affect reflection, the infant cannot anchor its own affect and is thus incapable of building up a secondary representation. This leads to deficits in the child's self-perception of its own affective state, as well as that of the caregiver. Thus, for example, the child cannot decide whether fear is their own fear or that of the mother. Unable to attribute the negative affect, he or she can experience a flood of fears, suffering exposure to a cumulative mini-trauma. The mother provides no containment (Fonagy et al., 2002; Taubner et al., 2010). The lack of marking by the mother – or its insufficiency – leads to the development of a fragile self, which in turn leads to a confusion between *as-if mode* and reality.

The absence of marking when interacting with infants is often found in caregivers with the attachment classification "enmeshed-ambivalent" and is thus more common in mothers with borderline personality disorder (Taubner et al., 2010; Fonagy & Luyten, 2011).

Maldevelopment 2: Lack of congruence

A lack of congruence is due to a marked mirroring of affect, but the emotional expression mirrored is a misinterpretation of the affect in fact displayed by the infant. For example, the caregiver reacts to the expression of affect by becoming annoyed and is thus liable to employ defence mechanisms of their own, such as projection. This incongruent affect is then anchored by the infant as an actual expression of his or her own affect as a secondary representation (Fonagy et al., 2002; Taubner et al., 2010). In making a secondary representation, the infant forms a false impression of their own affect, which results in a distorted self-representation, in the sense of a "false self," an idea formulated by Winnicott in 1960 (Winnicott, 2017).

Figure 3.4 Here, the marking of the child's affect is missing. It cannot be determined from the reflective affective expression whether it represents the child's expression or reflects an emotional state within the mother (El Shaddai Photography, Renate Steinberger, 2019).

Figure 3.5 Here the child is shown an expression of affect which is different to the one it actually displayed to the caregiver (El Shaddai Photography, Renate Steinberger 2019).

Maldevelopment 3: Lack of reflection

In this case, there is an absence of reflection, and thus the infant is not able to internalize secondary representations of their emotions and for this reason cannot develop emotional concepts. For the child, access to their inner understanding remains closed off; they cannot develop a distinction between their thoughts and the reality around them. In terms of psychological development, the child remains stuck in a mode of psychological equivalence. Externally, these children often appear very calm, but internally we see a massive release of stress hormones. Caregivers are unable to form a bond with these children, and usually react to their needs with a hostile and helpless attitude. Children cope with this kind of aloneness by remaining in teleological mode, failing to switch over to a mode of functioning based on mentalization. They cope with their aloneness with dissociative reactions. The child's inner world remains a threatening mental conception, from which the child must repeatedly dissociated themselves (Fonagy et al., 2002; Bateman & Fonagy, 2006; Taubner et al., 2010).

10.12 Subdimension of Mentalisation

Luyten et al. (2019) make an important point relating to the distinction between focusing on one's self and turning or relating to others.

According to the most recent neuroimaging studies, it appears that neural networks for recognizing the self and for recognizing others are identical (Liebermann, 2007; Uddin et al., 2007; Taubner et al., 2010). Here we might cite Martin Buber: "Wir werden am Du zum Ich" ("Man becomes an I through a You"). We are only capable of seeing another person through our selves.

The latest research by Fonagy and his colleagues highlights the importance of a "general psychopathology factor", otherwise known as the "p factor" (Caspi et al., 2014). This factor underlies all psychopathology, describing an impairment attributable to three separate factors. Impairment is to be found in a possible

Figure 3.6 Here reflection is missing. There is no interaction to be seen, either with a child or with other people. The child is left alone with unresponsiveness on the part of the caregiver (El Shaddai Photography, Renate Steinberger 2019).

positive view of a situation, in an associated inability to reassess the situation, and in an inhibition of retraumatizing triggers (Fonagy et al., 2017).

10.13 Critique of Mentalization Theory

Fonagy and colleagues adopt the theory of maternal affect reflection from Gergely and Watson and, bringing together many different research findings, including studies of attachment, have constructed a developmental concept which describes possible undesirable developments, which then lead to known psychological disorders. Basing their analysis on borderline personality disorder, they construct their own view of psychopathology and its treatment.

First, the authors assume that human beings have an innate, internal system which means they deal with contingencies using, among other things, the basic emotions available to them: joy, anger, fear, grief, disgust, and surprise (Ekman, 2010). The second factor is the reflective availability of caregivers. Despite high ambitions for a Cartesian turn in thinking, the authors ultimately retain a causally defined system in which a biological foundation represents the starting point for development. Ultimately, they do not resolve the causal mechanisms in their main work *Affect Regulation, Mentalization and the Development of the Self* (Fonagy et al., 2002). They attribute to infants, as a biological foundation, the *rudimentary* possibility of regulating their emotions via *thumb-sucking* (Fonagy et al., 2002, p. 160). Thumb sucking is usually seen as a transitional object which is transferred to various objects over the course of development, such as teddy bears (Disler, 2017, p. 179).

With social biofeedback, the authors assume that the infant contains a reflexive mode within itself and can notice precisely when the mother marks an affect in a congruent manner. The authors in this way presuppose the mechanism which is supposed to be developed via the process. With biofeedback, the test subjects do not discover their own blood pressure, but rather the connection between mental and physical phenomena, and this "instrument" then shows them the correlation to their blood pressure. It is a training in sensitivity which allows recognition of the indirect connections between physical and mental well-being, on the one hand, and blood pressure on the other. Fonagy and his colleagues assume the opposite path of biofeedback, whereby the mother represents a resonance factor for the child's emotions. The child now has the opportunity to gain an idea of their own feelings, through the mother marking them congruently. In this way, the infant learns to recognize its emotional state and later to use language to give a name to this emotional condition. Through the exaggeration in the mirrored affect, the infant comes to recognize that it is their own emotion, through its mechanism of contingency detection. To recognize contingency, the child needs an idea of his caregiver's authentic emotional expressions in order to have a reference point for the contingent event. To be able to develop a representation, there must be a possibility of a difference from the mother's own emotions, which not only mark pain, but are also affected by her child's feelings and thus now also contain pain about the child's possible misfortune. What is the difference here, in terms of mirror neurons, when we observe that a child is injured, for example, and we reflect that pain without its being *our* pain, when the mirror neurons are signalling something quite different to us (Rizzolatti et al., 2008)? This complex distinction seems to become present only in a very reflexive manner; moreover, as I indirectly infer, this depends on the affective mood of the person conceiving it. The authors in question identify a "contingency discovery algorithm" in the infant which performs all of these complex differentiations, or else guides this process towards conscious awareness. Another factor in this process is pleasure – which they refer to as positive arousal – in the awareness of control, for which they use the example of the "mobile" (Watson, 1972). They thus presuppose a predisposed need for control, which fuels the "contingency maximization strategy". Another difference which these authors presuppose is the notion of time – an idea about the perception of effects – on the basis of which conclusions are drawn, as seen in the example of the mobile. Between three and five months, infants begin to prefer non-perfect contingencies. These findings from infant research confirm that the infant is now capable of distinguishing between itself and an inanimate object. The infant seeks to have the greatest possible influence on their caregivers through the "contingency maximization strategy" (Fonagy et al., 2002, p. 123). Should the infant fail to develop this desire for control, the authors ascribe a developmental deficit to the child, which they attempt to substantiate using findings from autism research. They describe this mechanism as a one-way street; and the infant must absorb all of these reflections, also in the sense of an "alien" self, in other words, if the most important caregiver does not reflect the feelings to them in a marked or congruent way.

Fonagy and colleagues assume an emotional self-knowledge, but it is one in which the knowing subject is absent. They take the metaphor of the contingency system to be a physical phenomenon and describe it as a phenomenon which they consider to be an aberration, namely a system within the infant which generates these representations in order to imagine its own self, rather than the self developing them in the process of becoming aware of itself. As an alien self that generates my self when I become conscious of it, this remains a mechanism, conceived as a metaphor, which creates me psychologically with the help of my mother.

Here there appears to be a gap in the theory of Fonagy and colleagues, despite the fact that it rests on findings from a large number of infant observations. Another weakness in the theory lies in its claim to be absolute. This claim contradicts the concept they are trying to describe, namely mentalization as the interpretation of different opinions and selves. They adopt the idea held by intersubjectivists, then make a further claim to absoluteness by seeking to explain intersubjectivity in its development, in order ultimately to refute it. Fonagy and his co-authors face a hurdle they cannot overcome, between the dichotomy of transferring the cognitive sciences to the explicit level of mind as a human science, and thus remain stuck in the Cartesian world view, proposing a physical explanation of the development of the self (another metaphor from the humanities). Furthermore, there is little discussion of the tradition of Jewish interpretation, thus also missing the core of development as an issue, although questioning as such is the central mode of making-concrete and of giving instructions in developed forms of mentalization-based therapy (Bateman & Fonagy, 2006; Aron, 2016).

The authors were thus unable to carry out two major projects which they initially announced: the Cartesian turn and the explanation of the development of reflective function in human beings.

11 Biographical Information on Peter Fonagy

The paradigm shift from Cartesian dualism, with its dichotomization of body and soul, to a perspective derived from intersubjective and relational theory, suggests the theory of mentalization must be embedded in the personal development of the concept's inventors. Touching on this, I will here sketch out some thoughts regarding Peter Fonagy's own biography. In their 1979 book *Faces in a Cloud*, Atwood and Stolorow put forward a theory that the thought structure of any theory is profoundly connected to the thinker's own life story. As they put it: "We believe that their most powerful source can be found in the subjective experiential worlds of the personality theorists themselves" (Atwood & Stolorow, 1979, p. 5). The theory they developed was intended to form a basis for all *theories of the art of living* (Buchholz, 2014a, p. 355), including a metapsychological view intended to represent a new form of understanding. Something consistently ascribed to Fonagy and his colleagues is that they did not develop a new theory, but rather created a new common ground of thought for all theories (Taubner, 2015; Bolm, 2009, 2015; Schultz-Venrath, 2013). Fonagy et al. claim to have identified an overarching commonality between the relevant psychotherapeutic schools, incorporating the intersubjective schools into their own concept and in this way reversing the direction of thought (Fonagy, 2009). The shared mental construct is not intersubjectivity in the sense of psycho-biographical data; instead, mentalization is the all-encompassing framework of thought (Pap, 2017; Atwood, 2017; Atwood & Stolorow, 2014).

What follows is thus a short digression into the relatively little information available on Peter Fonagy himself. A crucial influence on Fonagy's intellectual career was his father Ivan, who was born on April 8, 1920 and died on April 11, 2005. In 1949, Ivan Fonagy completed a dissertation at the Péter Pázmány University in Budapest, writing on "Secondary changes in the Neo-Latin languages" (Másodlagos hangsúlyváltozások a neolatin nyelvekben), going on to become an internationally recognized linguist, appointed to the Hungarian Academy of Sciences in 1950, with a visiting professorship at the Sorbonne between 1967 to 1970. In 1971, he moved permanently to Paris to become research director at the CNRS. In 1990, he was elected as an external member of the Hungarian Academy of Sciences (Kiefer, 2005).

Fonagy himself was born in Budapest on August 14, 1952: although the war had ended seven years earlier, its effects continued to exert a great influence on the country. Four years later, in 1956, continuing tension resulted in the Hungarian uprising against the Stalinist regime, with widespread protests across the country, and a violent military crackdown. This time of political turbulence undoubtedly influenced Fonagy's upbringing.

Unfortunately, no more specific information than this is available about his childhood or other significant influences. In conversation, he is known to have expressed criticism of the conservative structures of Viennese psychoanalytic training. On February 19, 2007, he was awarded the city of Vienna's annual International Sigmund Freud Award for Psychotherapy, presented at the Sigmund Freud University.

Fonagy studied clinical psychology at University College London, graduating in 1980: he is now head of the department of Psychology and Linguistics at the same institution. His interest in language was likely sparked by his father's specialism: Fonagy senior's work focused on preverbal communication and its relation to linguistic evolution, addressing the meaning of feelings in language and describing the double coding which exists within the affective and cognitive spheres. His work paved the way for a move from an idealized laboratory situation to "natural" language situations. In this way, his work re-foregrounded the meaning of what was said and its motivations, focusing on the possible intentions in conversation. In this way, his work came very close to the idea of the therapeutic conversation, a clear indication of the importance of Fonagy's father's work for the development of mentalization. The work of both the father and the son also addressed "misleading" in language (*pretend action*), establishing the roots of mentalization theory in distinguishing between the expressed linguistic statement and underlying opinions and intentions (Fonagy & Fonagy, 1995; Buchholz, 2014a).

The most striking thing about the theory of mentalization is the absence of culture as an intentional factor. It remains the meta-level of attachment theory, which has general validity, just as Fonagy's father had shown in his linguistic work. Language and mentalizing have another generality, beyond personal influence, which can be found in the culture of family stories. In German-language literature, there is repeated reference to British "understatement"; statements that mentalizing is not new in psychoanalysis are associated with this. Within Austro-Hungarian cultural intentions, as a shared space of linguistic meaning, this statement's intention is very clearly defined in a conception of the importance of the mentalization idea and a sense of its power. Language regulations in the Dual Monarchy meant that the opposite of the intended meaning must always be uttered, to avoid censorship, or to maintain a possible line of retreat, by arguing that one had in fact, intended the literal meaning. This particular linguistic-cultural area, stretching from Vienna to Budapest and Prague, is associated with examples including the literature of Nestroy in Vienna, and the literature of Jaroslav Hašek (*The Good Soldier Schwejk*, 1923) in Prague. Both of these authors create scenarios in which a stupid person wins out over their social superior because his intentions are never clearly formulated or are formulated exactly in terms of their opposite. Today, we refer to this as sarcasm, irony, ambiguity, a sardonic attitude, etc. In this way, British "understatement" acquires different meanings from different understandings of linguistic culture (Buchholz, 2014a; Riecken, 2006).

Against a background of presumed family disunity, changing locations, and thus a different form of search for roots and belonging – something which psychoanalysis in particular can offer – the theory of mentalization represents another kind of a shared superstructure. Despite its claims to the contrary, as a theory, mentalization presents a counter-movement to pluralism, by focusing on the shared core.

In the sense of the Greek *aletheia* (unconcealment, truth), the self which shows itself, which presents itself, is already present in the encounter with the pronunciation of one's name, as in the differing Hungarian and English pronunciations of Fonagy. The self already takes on very different meanings, in the sense that we have many selves within us, and these selves are in turn determined by our interlocutor, in the best sense of mentalization. The pronunciation of my name constructs my self and along with it all underlying affective and cognitive attributions. Seeking to reunite the Cartesian worldview of division, to bring back together all that was mutually exclusive in psychoanalytic history, between drive theory and attachment theory: this reflects a striving for wholeness, which in turn points towards a search for a unique place. The more that a place has been physically subject to fragmentation, the more it requires realization as an unbroken place within the self. One's own sense of being torn enables one to work with the conflict seen in people with a borderline diagnosis and in former prisoners: two fields of work in which Peter Fonagy has been active (Atwood, 2017).

12 Examples of Mentalization Ability in Everyday Life and Education

Below are some examples from various areas of application, which may serve to make mentalization more understandable.

Mentalization in everyday life:

- we mentalize when we try to understand someone else's needs and motivations
- we mentalize when we settle a dispute and present different points of view
- we mentalize when we think about ourselves, when we try to understand our motivations

Mentalizing as a teacher:

- we mentalize when we can offer a child a safe environment
- we mentalize when we understand what a child is experiencing and feeling
- we mentalize when we give a child words for their feelings

The development of mentalization in a child:

- the child can approach their environment openly and with curiosity
- the child engages in role-playing games or plays with hand puppets, the child enjoys taking on different roles
- the child learns to describe their feelings, both about themselves and about others

The research of Jon G. Allen and his colleagues suggests that the process of caregivers giving marked contingent reactions to children can be regarded as a learning process. They regard the development of mentalization occurring in this process to be the most important characteristic of an empathic and humane pedagogical disposition, which is the basis for conveying and for acquiring cultural meanings. Pedagogical learning, like language, develops in a mutual relation with the process of mentalization (Allen et al., 2011).

In the spirit of Fonagy and his colleagues, one can say that mentalization is not a new direction in pedagogy. Instead, it should be understood as a basic requirement for all pedagogical tendencies. The concept of mentalization cannot offer any new instruments for the field of pedagogy, a field already too large for any individual to master. Reflections on this subject tends to focus around a fundamental ability that makes us human (Allen, 2009). To mentalize is to offer the child a framework in which they can develop a healthy self and to gain security, because even in difficult situations, they retain the loved child's sense of themselves. In this way adults can come to have a capacity to tolerate ambiguity and to cope with unstructured affective situations.

4 The Development of the Relational Tradition in Psychoanalysis

> It entails a tolerance of the fragility of those hopes, woven together from realities and fantasies, and an appreciation of ways in which, in the rich density of contemporary life, realities often become fantasy and fantasies often become reality.
>
> Stephen A. Mitchell (2003a, p. 201)

The relational tradition is influenced by many currents; within these, each new thinker has their own thoughts which tend to move off in different directions. The burden of formulating relational ideas and implementing them in the psychoanalytic field has lain with American thinkers.

The main current of a school of thought, including its emergence, is embedded in a particular form of social upheaval. In these moments, new concepts of life are more clearly defined: thus increased debate around feminism and the queer movement opened up new perspectives of thought. Within this new mode of questioning older orders and value systems, a new questioning arose, focused on the treatment perspectives dominant in American psychoanalysis.

Within the tradition of object relationship theories, the relationship increasingly became the focus of psychoanalytic thinking. Hartmann created a particular American school of thought by placing a greater emphasis on the "I". Ego psychology was further fostered by continental European Jewish psychoanalysts who had emigrated to the United States. The traumas experienced by this generation find a reflection in ego psychology; they took the emotions and the involvement out of psychoanalysis (Orange, 2018). Self-psychology, as put forward by Heinz Kohut, deals with the significance of the psychoanalyst within the treatment process by addressing the question of empathy on the part of the therapist. Under its leading thinkers – Atwood, Stolorow, and Brandchaft – self-psychology developed towards constructions of intersubjectivity, within the same atmosphere of American liberalism. Later additions to this tendency were made by Donna Orange and Chris Jaenicke, who has a psychoanalytic practice in Berlin. Freud already addressed the phenomenon of reciprocity and its meaning within communities:

DOI: 10.4324/9781003483441-4

> I once discussed this phenomenon, the fact that it is precisely those communities that occupy contiguous territories and are otherwise closely related to each other ... that indulge in feuding and mutual mockery. I called this phenomenon 'the narcissism of small differences' – not that the name does much to explain it. It can be seen as a convenient and relatively innocuous way of satisfying the tendency to aggression and facilitating solidarity within the community.
>
> (S. Freud, 2004, p. 48).

Historical differences which appeared irreconcilable when they arose now seem like subtle distinctions, small in differentiation. The significance of various factors influencing development is accepted or rejected by authors, or else not taken into consideration, and yet nonetheless interpreted and evaluated differently (Harris, 2017).

Differences can be identified based on the interpretation of terminology. As the focus moved in the direction of *object relations*, terms associated with this also came newly to the fore. Countertransference as an emotion in the therapist was discussed by Freud as early as 1910:

> We have begun to consider the 'counter-transference', which arises in the physician as a result of the patient's influence on his unconscious feelings and have nearly come to the point of requiring the physician to recognize and overcome this counter-transference in himself. Now that a larger number of people have come to practise psycho-analysis and mutually exchange their experiences, we have noticed that every analyst's achievement is limited by what his own complexes and resistances permit, and consequently require that he should begin his practice with a self-analysis and should extend and deepen this constantly while making his observations on his patients. Anyone who cannot succeed in this self-analysis may without more ado regard himself as unable to treat neurotics by analysis.
>
> (S. Freud, 1933, p. 289).

This basic credo rests on the importance of the feelings of the "doctor" and the self-analysis associated with it, which are viewed as great, unchangeable pillars. The shared experience of patient and analyst was increasingly described through concepts of staging or enactment. The meta-psychological term deriving from this is *intersubjectivity*. If we here once again take a macro perspective, it will lead us to concepts of co-construction and *thirdness*.

All these concepts focus on the persons of patient and analyst; they place the relationship between two people at the centre of interest. The elaboration of these terms has influenced how meta-psychological terms are viewed, and these in turn change interest in how different therapeutic phenomena are perceived. It is not small differences which primarily create meaning and change. Rather, resulting attitudes have an influence on the therapeutic process and the metaphors created in that process, in this way making the psychological visible to us.

Both Emily A. Kuriloff and George Makari regard the emergence of relational thinking as indicating a replacement of ego psychology in the United States, where it had previously been dominant. They trace the emergence of ego psychology to the trauma experienced by immigrant European analysts in the 1930s: as a result, these analysts then retreated into cognitive scientific analysis, dissociating their own emotions of trauma. This form of ego-psychological analysis then formed the reference point for a countermovement, wherein analysts were not split off from their own feelings and their significance of these feelings in their lived existence. Thus a path to relational thinking as a countermovement begins to emerge (Kuriloff, 2014; Makari, 2010).

Harris and Mitchell consider relational theory to be the quintessentially American contribution to psychoanalysis. "Indeed, relational psychoanalysis may be regarded as a distinctive contemporary American school of psychoanalysis" (Aron, 2013, p. 19). They asked students and colleagues the question: "What's American about American psychoanalysis?" and traced its roots to the work of William James (1876–1907) and Charles Sanders Peirce (1839–1914), the co-founders of philosophical pragmatism, who had great influence on the specifically American development of psychoanalysis, as Mitchell and Harris have noted:

> There are a number of aspects of William James's (1890, 1910, 1978) far-reaching thought, that we might highlight in the light of the evolution of American psychoanalysis. James distrusted but did not repudiate abstraction. He was determined to ground any understanding in subjective experience, the immediacy and ongoing stream of conscious life. James sought to widen the scope of psychology from problems of knowing to include problems of believing or ethics. Passions are as crucial for ways of knowing as is mind. There are some familiar themes here: an instinctive pull for indeterminacy, for multiple ways of knowing. In James, this democratic, or perhaps more accurately egalitarian, impulse is grounded in philosophy, not ideology. James (1978), writing on pragmatism, on the experience of the self, on his theory of radical empiricism, produced an important and influential network of ideas that feels quite familiar to relational analysts. His focus was on experience. His interest always lay in the particular instance, not the general concept. His focus on experience – not simply of things, but of things and relationships – and his attention to a kind of hermeneutic circular relationship between belief, desire, and action must strike an American (and particularly, an interpersonal psychoanalytic) reader as deeply familiar. This approach in philosophy and critical theory was, quite simply yet grandly, to understand the multiple intersections (James's term) between the individual's knowing of objects, the public shared nature of that knowing, and the problem of how one mind knows another. These ideas

are strong anchors for contemporary American psychoanalysis where the intrapsychic and the interpersonal co-construct, where mind is simultaneously social, individual, public and private. Certainly, one can read James in the light of Sullivan and interpersonal psychoanalysis, finding themes and preoccupations that cannot simply default to behaviourism. Because psychoanalysis, across its spectrum, insists on the centrality of meaning making, CS Peirce's (1955) theory of meaning could be seen as a background influence on perspectivism and the contemporary preoccupations with intersubjectivity. Peirce built a complex triadic structure distinguishing the word, its meaning for the speaker, and its distinct but overlapping quasi-shared meaning for the listener. This complex model of meaning as intersubjective has had powerful influences in the academy.

(Mitchell & Harris, 2004, p. 169f.)

1 Beginnings: Mitchell and Ghent

Stephen A. Mitchell (1946–2000) is seen as the personification of relational psychoanalysis as a movement and is regarded in the literature as its founder (Mertens, 2011; Orange, 2018).

Mitchell was born in Manhattan shortly after the war, at a time when the United States had become a world power, a society particularly marked by the idea that technology could accomplish anything. It was the early days of space travel, while biological advances in fields like genetics were opening up new pathways for thought. The era was dominated by a belief in social advancement: the idea of the American dream had never been closer to reality. The post-war opening up of university access in the United States enabled a major educational offensive. In 1968, in this open-minded educational atmosphere, the 24-year-old Mitchell graduated summa cum laude in philosophy at Yale University. Four years later, he received his doctorate in clinical psychology from New York University. This led him to study psychoanalysis, in which he completed training in 1977. Thereafter he worked as a lecturer at the renowned William Alanson White Institute, offering supervision from 1985 on. Since 1989, he has worked at the same institution as a training analyst, while also working at NYU as a clinical supervisor, as well as teaching as part psychotherapy and psychoanalysis. In the 1990s he and others developed a curriculum for relational psychoanalysis. In 1991 he founded *Psychoanalytic Dialogues*, one of the most open and creative journals in the field, which published texts from a wide variety of fields of knowledge, addressing encounters and relationships.

Mitchell's thinking was profoundly shaped by the diverse cultural changes taking place at this time: protests against the Vietnam War, important debates on gender, and the civil rights movement, led by Martin Luther King. The work of Harry Stack Sullivan at the William Alanson White Institute created a central hotbed for open and collaborative thinking, creating substantial leeway for interpersonality (Buchholz, 2004a; Kernberg, 2011a;

Fonagy, 2009). One of Mitchell's teachers, Emmanuel Ghent, had particular influence on ideas of two-person psychology.

A group of thinkers formed around Mitchell, creating a breeding ground for creativity and fostering constructive exchange. Its members included influential figures, among them Jessica Benjamin, Lewis Aron, Adrianne Harris, Anthony Bass, Jody Davis, Philip Bromberg, Muriel Dimen, Donnel B. Stern, and Irwin Z. Hoffmann. Students, who often posed critical questions, were another important factor in sharpening Mitchell's ideas. He co-authored two books, both intended as textbooks. This genre of writing represents an important basis for the clear formulation of theory and the development of thought; in their presentation of different theories, textbooks contain reference points which can be used in the creation of new ideas. Mitchell's earliest articles, dealing with homosexuality, were characterized by a dissatisfaction with the moralizing, pathologizing approach taken by psychoanalysis to the subject (Mitchell, 1981a, b).

Prompted by their students, Greenberg and Mitchell offered an overview of different psychoanalytic schools of thought:

> The idea for this book grew out of our experiences in teaching aspects of the historical development of psychoanalytic ideas. Both of us had taught courses organized along conventional lines – Freud, the American 'ego psychologists', Sullivan, the 'British school' of object relations, and so on. Although this way of dividing the material has merit – particularly in maintaining boundaries between systems that operate on the basis of incompatible and potentially confusing fundamental assumptions—it also has limitations. We had struggled to help students grasp something of the larger context from which various traditions of psychoanalytic theorizing have emerged and understand the common conceptual problems for which adherents of each tradition have fashioned unique solutions.
>
> ... We needed an organizing principle through which the dialectic tension between competing theories could be understood, and we found it in the currently popular concept of ›object relations‹, the general term encompassing people's relationships with others. These relationships are and always have been central to the clinical practice of psychoanalysis, but assigning them a theoretical role remains controversial.
>
> (Greenberg & Mitchell, 1983, p. viii).

Their jointly-authored book *Object Relations in Psychoanalytic Theory*, published in 1983, addressed a variety of object relations theories, comparing the work of Klein, Fairbairn, Winnicott, Guntrip, Hartmann, Kohut, Jacobson, Mahler, and Kernberg. It drew a contrast between Freud's drive and structural models and the focus on relationships found in the work of object relations theorists. In this context, Greenberg and Mitchell's main focus was on object relations theorists, given the primacy of object relations for their work. They regard object relations as a departure from one-person psychology, based on theories of drive. They question these theories based on their clinical significance, which they then use as a means of deconstructing individual theories. As part of this approach, they focused very closely on terms like internal object, object representation, self-object, and object cathexis, attempting to use these as a basis for clinical significance. Ultimately, they argue that the clinical significance of a theory is a yardstick of its quality (Greenberg & Mitchell, 1983; Buchholz, 2004a).

All of Mitchell's works remain true to this basic idea, clearly expressed in this book: the importance of relationships and how they are viewed in an analytical setting. But Mitchell's concept of relational thinking always remained in the psychoanalytic tradition; he did not set his own thought in competition with other models. Rather, he saw it as shifting focus to relationships and their clinical significance in the here and now. That was also why he did not regard himself as being in competition with classical concepts of psychoanalysis.

The preface to *Freud and Beyond – a History of Modern Psychoanalytic Thought* describes his experience around the rejection of more recent ideas and developments in psychoanalysis:

> The story is sometimes told that in the last years of his life one of the most important innovators in post-Freudian psychoanalysis had taken to bringing a gun with him when he presented his work at more traditional institutes. He would place it on the lectern without comment and proceed to read his paper. Invariably someone would ask about the gun, and he would say, in a pleasant voice, that the gun was for use on the first person who, rather than addressing the ideas he was presenting, asked instead whether they were 'really psychoanalysis'.
>
> (Mitchell & Black, 2016, p. xxiii).

Mitchell wrote *Freud and Beyond* with his wife, Margaret Black. In a similar way to *Object Relations in Psychoanalytic Theory*, the book took a comparative approach to psychoanalytic schools in terms of historical understanding and cultural embeddedness. The ideas developed in the book are very close to relational ideas, especially in terms of the impossibility of possessing truth through statements and of the omnipotence which would come with it. The outline given of a variety of theories already collapses any idea of truth, thus implicitly paving the way for relational analysts: these thinkers and their actions here become the focus of consideration. The book compares numerous great thinkers – for example Freud, Sullivan, Klein, Fairbairn, Winnicott, Erikson, Kohut, Kernberg, Schäfer, Lacan, and Loewald; here, the comparative perspective and the emphasis of viewpoint are already generating a third position. What unites all of these thinkers is the relation in which they find themselves and, when subjected to comparison, their particular relation to each other. Whether they are seen as being in competition, or placed in hierarchy, is a decision which is left to authors and readers, in the third position. If these authors and readers in turn reflect on their own position, with all its affects, feelings, ideas, and cultural integration, they are already in the process of creating a fourth position. This led to paradigm shift, attributable to relational psychoanalysis. As Black puts it:

> He [Mitchell] encouraged the development of a paradigm shift in psychoanalytic thinking, reflecting what he felt was already implicit but not directly formulated in the writing of most of the authors included in this book: humans are not best understood as isolated beings motivated by and struggling with the prefigured innate forces of sex and aggression; rather, human beings are fundamentally social, developing within, internalizing, and shaped by their relationships with important others in their lives. These experiences find expression in the development of internal structure and imagination. They affect relationships in an ongoing way. Culture, gender, race, and sexual orientation all figure into this development as well. Sex and aggression remain fundamental aspects of our experience but are not unmoored energies on the loose, arising in a vacuum. Sensuality and frustration are intertwined with relationships, arising in response to and deriving meaning within experience with others. This alternative vision is referred to as 'relational psychoanalysis' ..."
>
> (Mitchell & Black, 2016, p. xviii).

Here, too, Mitchell and Black remain very close to psychoanalysis, increasingly taking up its historical aspect as a frame of reference. They do so by integrating the comparison of theories more closely into a developmental framework, in this way also lending importance to the cultural circumstances in which any given theory emerged. Mitchell's guiding principles are shaped by a defence of psychoanalysis; this serves as a common thread in his work, providing a constant frame of reference. He puts forward myths to challenge: for example that psychoanalysis was the work of one man, that treatment did not change over time and this was why it fell out of fashion, that psychoanalysis demanded an esoteric cult of submission and required many years of study. The attitude adopted by Mitchell and Black is already predetermined: they want precisely to question these myths, and come to different conclusions. The book was reprinted in 2016 and has already been translated into many languages; it has become an important work in the psychoanalytic community.

Mitchell's second book – his first as a solo author – *Relational Concepts in Psychoanalysis* (Mitchell, 1988) continued to pursue the ideas he had developed with Greenberg, while moving away from his erstwhile writing partner in terms of his thought on relations. Mitchell asks whether the various currents and schools of psychoanalysis have a common core. Do the various currents still fit together: if so, in what form, and if not, why not?

Mitchell believes that all schools are "right" in their lines of argument. They only cover a small segment of the complex events in a psychoanalytic treatment. His approach to comparative research into the various theories and schools is based on this insight. This prompts a selective integration, which in turn leads to a common postulate of the relationship as the basis for treatment and encounters. As Mitchell writes:

> Amid the apparent conceptual disarray in contemporary psychoanalysis are two broad, competing perspectives, Freud's drive theory and a cluster of theories (including British object-relations theory, interpersonal psychoanalysis, and self-psychology) which derive from a set of premises that Jay Greenberg and I have termed the relational model.
>
> (Mitchell, 1988, p. viii)

Introducing the book's basic idea – the existence of a single relational concept within psychoanalysis – Mitchell states: "This book aims at such a unification, by considering the major domains of psychoanalytic inquiry – sexuality, early development, fantasy and illusion, continuity and change – from an integrated relational perspective" (Mitchell, 1988, p. viii f.). By comparing the different orientations of schools and approaches, Mitchell's line of argument is always focused on the relationship and on meaning in all its developmental functions, with a subtle focus on clinical history in treatment rooms. Included is its orientation entirely due to the first book: "The most creative and influential contributions derive from what Greenberg and I (1983) have termed the relational model, an alternative perspective which considers relationships with others, not drives, as the basic stuff of mental life" (Mitchell, 1988, p. 2) Object relations theorists thus provide the basis for Mitchell's own creative thought. At this point, he began to distil from these theories, developing clearer formulations and as a result abandoning linguistic concepts based on Freudian terminology, which he felt had strongly marked the work of Winnicott and Loewald. Towards the end of his short life, Mitchell turned increasingly to Loewald's writings, seeking an understanding in which descriptions of individual elements taking place in treatment rooms could be considered together. As he put it:

> We are portrayed not as a conglomeration of physically based urges, but as being shaped by and inevitably embedded within a matrix of relationships with other people, struggling both to maintain our ties to others and to differentiate ourselves from them;
>
> (Mitchell, 1988, p. 3)

To integrate this shared field of very different tendencies, he borrowed a term from Loewald: that of the *matrix*. Here he is again, in his own, clear expression:

> I use the term 'relational matrix' in an effort to transcend the unfortunate tendency to dichotomize concepts like interpersonal relations and 'object' relations, or the interpersonal and the intrapsychic, as if a focus on either side necessarily implies a denial or deemphasis of the other. I do not believe that interpersonal interactions are merely an 'enactment' of a more psychologically fundamental world of internal object relations or 'representations'; nor do I believe that subjective experience is merely a recording of actual interpersonal transactions. The most useful way to view psychological reality is as operating within a relational matrix which encompasses both intrapsychic and interpersonal realms. The mind operates with motivations concerning self-regulation as well as regulation of the relational field. Like Escher's Drawing Hands, the interpersonal and the intrapsychic realms create, interpenetrate, and transform each other in a subtle and complex manner.
>
> (Mitchell, 1988, p. 9).

In *Hope and Dread* (Mitchell, 1993), Mitchell formulated his ideas with even greater precision, not attempting to create a new "psychoanalysis" but rather to establish a common description of phenomena which occur in therapy. He did not develop specific new words or descriptions for the phenomena he sought to illustrate. His preface is emphatic on this point:

> One of the miscellaneous bits left over in my memory from as 'jargonized common sense'. I have always tried to make the sense I could offer (common or otherwise) as de-jargonized as possible. Because I am, in places, tracing intellectual trends and trying to integrate divergent lines of theorizing, the discussion is at times specialized and detailed. However, in an effort to make the book more accessible to the general reader, I have separated some of the more technical discussions from the text into endnotes.
>
> (Mitchell, 1993, p. xi)

The central questions the book asks are: "What does the patient need?" and "What does the analyst know?" The two questions take Mitchell away from the meta level, bringing his thought directly to the relation between the two protagonists within any analytical setting. The questions can only be answered very individually, outside of any meta-psychological understanding. They call for the relativization of knowledge and truth. The second part of the book questions the concepts of self, and thus also ideas of knowledge and truth which go along with this concept. The final part of the book explicitly returns to the relation, filling the concept with ideas of desires and needs. It concludes with an idea of the mutual construction of hope in the analytical encounter:

> The fundamental assumption in this line of thought is that the patient's experience – the basic data of psychoanalysis, which is to be understood

> or 'analysed' – is fundamentally ambiguous. This is an easily misunderstood concept. It does not mean that the patient's experience is necessarily opaque or mysterious (although at times it might be). It does mean that understanding human experience, including one's own, is never simply a process of seeing it, grasping it, or reading it (depending on whether one likes one's metaphors ocular, physical, or linguistic). The elements of human experience are understood only through a process that organizes those elements, puts them together, assigns them meaning, and prioritizes them. The organization that seems most compelling may seem quite accessible and unmysterious; it is still constructed, through an active organizing process, in the person who is doing the understanding.
>
> (Mitchell, 1993, p. 56f.)

Empathy and experience rely on our capacity to understand our own inner organization by attributing meaning to its individual elements. This is also the means by which we understand our patients: "At the heart of the resolution of each analysis is an individually crafted or, considering the role of the analyst, a jointly coauthored movement beyond either/or solutions to the problem of justification." (Mitchell, 1993, p. 170). For Mitchell, analysis goes beyond any form of problem solving. At the centre of being is shared rhythmic movement.

Mitchell's next book, *Influence and Autonomy in Psychoanalysis*, came out in 1997. His argument remains consistent here, with Mitchell turning to the idea of interaction as it appears in various traditions of psychoanalytic thought. The sixth chapter deals specifically with analysts' intentions in interaction, with the argument increasingly making them active protagonists within the analytical session.

His close reading of theories reveals a number of contradictions. For Mitchell, Kernberg in particular is caught in a trap of contradiction: he abandons anonymity towards patients as a concept but maintains the idea of neutrality. This, he argues, means Kernberg puts forward a fallacy: that this attitude has no significant influence on the therapeutic process and the person of the analyst has no effect on the patient. Mitchell argues that the concept of countertransference should be reassessed and the concept of neutrality abandoned, since the idea means that analysts are constantly being dragged down from the "perch of their authority" into a whirlpool of countertransference, meaning they must then laboriously climb back up to a position of authority (Mitchell, 1997, p. 234). This attitude always produces a duel with the patient and thus, from its conception, bears aggressive – hence also instinctual – ideas within it. "In this alternative view, countertransference is less like a storm from which one emerges periodically to regain one's perch and more like the weather itself" (Mitchell, 1997, p. 234). Our ideas and our metaphors organize our world of understanding and in this way generate our attitude towards patients.

Mitchell also addresses how analysts make decisions when interacting with patients. And it is essential to think about the decision to be made in this situation:

> In actuality, these choices go by too fast to allow prior conscious reflection on all of them. But when I try, retrospectively, to articulate the implicit, preconscious nature of these choices, they go something like this: does the reverie I find myself in now seem related to the patient's material in some fashion, or does it seem to be taking me further away? Does focusing hard and closely on the details or confusion in what the patient is saying open up impacted areas of the patient's experience, or does it feel as if it is diverting me into an obsessional muddle and away from a fuller emotional response?
>
> (Mitchell, 1997, p. 196).

Here Mitchell sketches out various ways in which psychotherapists can approach reflective questions; the therapist comes to realize that they will find no "correct" answers. The answers depend on their standpoint, which in turn is guided by their affects and feelings. For example, if the therapist feels tired, the answer will be different than if they are experiencing a feeling of elation. Nor is there a "truth" about oneself, but only a holding-on to the moment of generating experience. If some new experience flows on into something new within my thoughts, I would call it a *present moment* in the sense used by Daniel N. Stern.

Mitchell again raises the question of constructivism in his examination of whether the psyche is revealed or constructed. This question in turn influences the analyst's approach to the encounter with the patient, hence also the analyst's claim to truth, and the associated autonomy of the patient. Does the psyche [*Seele*] reveal itself in the sense that it is co-constructed – in a shared process in dialogic understanding – or does it emerge through analyst's influence on the patient? This is the central question of *Influence and Autonomy in Psychoanalysis* (Mitchell, 1997).

Relationality – From Attachment to Intersubjectivity, Mitchell's penultimate book, published shortly before his death (Mitchell, 2000), focussed on two major topics. The book's first part returns to Hans Loewald, a thinker Mitchell regarded as under-appreciated, while the second section applies his usual approach in order to explore structural levels of the psyche from the perspective of Bowlby and Fairbairn. His analysis here filters out the shared intersubjective in order, in the final chapter, to confront intersubjectivity in the treatment room, in all its emotional power.

Mitchell takes an idea of a common origin from his reading of Loewald: a primordial density in which human events unfold. In this context, reference is made to expansion of the cosmos after the Big Bang. For both Mitchell and Loewald, a basic matrix exists in which all things are related. This represents a counter-model to the idea that libido and instinctual drive are the factors which determine human beings. Loewald had been a student of Heidegger and was influenced both by his philosophy and his philosophizing; however, he retained an ambivalence towards his former teacher, given Heidegger's involvement in National Socialism (Grunenberg, 2016; Orange, 2020). Heidegger had declared that language was "the house of Being": according to *Being and Time*, understanding requires both of these, with Being only arising within time, while time only becomes conceptual through Being (Mitchell, 2000, p. 47). Heidegger had a reputation of bringing ancient thinkers to life, not simply talking about philosophers, but teaching how to philosophize. During his three years with Heidegger, Loewald also experienced the encounter *in realitas*, taking from this an idea of language as simply a way of conveying meaning, creating reality through relatedness. The second part of *Relationality* then develops an interaction hierarchy, consisting of four levels, which he discusses through a reading of Bowlby, Winnicott, Loewald, and Fairbairn.

Mitchell's final book, published posthumously, *Can Love Last?* (2003a), turns to the phenomena of love, sexuality, eroticism, and desire. He takes as a starting point the biological idea suggesting that drives dominate what happens to us. The argument takes up ideas of how love is to be described, concluding that our ideas about love and sexuality manifest themselves in our behaviour and thus perpetuate it, against our perspectives on love and sexuality. The world of our imagination creates romantic love, which is to say love is perpetuated by drives.

> The traditional derivation of the inherent delicacy and instability of romance from the primitiveness of sexuality has been, for decades, aesthetically and morally satisfying. It has helped us partially disown what we often don't like about ourselves by locating it in an unwanted legacy, forced upon us by our animal ancestors. We have personified nature to enable us to locate within it those aspects of our own experience that we have difficulty bearing.
>
> (Mitchell, 2003a, p. 112).

Mitchell does not systematically work out the meaning of love and its various backgrounds; instead, he takes us on a journey of thought, exploring why we develop our ideas about the meaning of love and sexuality. He categorizes the concept of love as part of the serviceability of emotions: in the sense that love can transform what is "difficult to bear" into something bearable. To this end, he creates a different concept of understanding love: "Human sexuality emerges within relational and linguistic contexts" (Mitchell, 2003a, p. 66).

Sexuality can develop from relationships and linguistic contexts; this thought takes away from the drive the guiding function in understanding our sexual behaviours, desires, and loves. For Mitchell, desire is not a phenomenon guided by the energy of a drive in search of an object, but rather unfolds in a jointly constructed, subjective world: "Longing does not simply bubble up from bodily tissues but emerges in the context of a subjective world [we have] constructed" (Mitchell, 2003a, p. 127).

Relatedness within an indivisible and jointly constructed world is what allows desire to unfold. Eroticism enables us to live our sexuality; for Mitchell, this is based on the discovery of the other in creating differentiation within ourselves:

> In the dialectics of eroticism that constitute the strange loop of our sexuality, our journey into the otherness of the other often surprises us with unknown features of ourselves, and our exploration of our interiority, the ineffable privacy of the self, often surprises us with the presence of others.
>
> (Mitchell, 2003a, p. 146)

Mitchell offers no concrete answers to the questions he raises at the beginning of the book. The gain in knowledge which he offers to readers consists of an exploration of one's own various feelings, in making them visible by embedding them in images and metaphors, allowing us the freedom to think. Once I am able to imagine something, I can construct or deconstruct my own standpoint towards it. And the frame of reference enables a perspective on the world which allows me to have freedom of choice. Whichever form of relationship, love, desire I want to live out, my standpoint determines my actions.

Stephen A. Mitchell's work goes on a journey which ends with his attempt to design a metapsychology, which he attempted by using existing ideas to develop a three-dimensional heuristic concept. At first, he called this "relational conflict theory" (Mitchell, 1988), developing a three-dimensional framework in the form of a matrix or plan of action:

1 pole of the self
2 object pole
3 pole of interaction

Mitchell suggests that a relational approach can be developed from all of these poles. The three dimensions form a *relational matrix*: his thinking at this point sought to integrate all of these psychoanalytic concepts.

The second direction taken by his thought lay in the further development of a relational theory by integrating and balancing the three concepts:

1 the *self-dimension* with its questions of self-preservation, self-regulation, personal identity, self-esteem, authenticity, and coherence within the self
2 the *object dimension* with its questions of the other, the inner object, the real other, identification, and reciprocal regulation
3 the *interaction dimension* with its questions of enactment and staging, interpersonal behaviour, of who has done what to whom

Mitchell also dealt with the experience of our own *agency*: our ability to maintain relationship patterns and permanently shape (perpetuate) them, as well as with the creative re-creation of our own inner world. These topics perhaps belong to the self-pole or may possibly be assigned to a separate pole. Mitchell did not manage to formulate the points with clarity (Aron & Harris, 2010, p. 113f.).

The meaning of Mitchell's work unfolds over the course of a journey through his world of thought. As far as he was concerned, it marked a substantial achievement to use as few technical terms as possible in writing; he did not seek to generate new terms. Instead, he sought to use the language available to him to create a three-dimensional image and in this way represent a manner of seeing and understanding phenomena in which we are relationally embedded, but which also constitutes us. If one attempts to distil something concrete from this, one loses the significance of "that which is unclear". Mitchell wanted to make us see – via displacement, interchangeability, metaphors – something that exists outside of our usual idea-world of drives and dichotomies. He never presented his thoughts in the form of an overall concept, which would have ended up with a thought that "I must decide for or against". He believed it was a matter of a different way of thinking, about phenomena which only crystallize into shape through their very unclarity. For Mitchell, images change standpoints, and standpoints generate new images. Our thinking also takes place in the dimension of a relationship (*agency*), since we always require a counterpart who constructs us or who sets a limit to visibility.

Emmanuel Ghent (1925–2003) was an important precursor for Mitchell's thought, as well as his companion and teacher. Ghent grew up in Montreal before moving to New York to complete psychiatric training; he later became a professor of psychology at New York University. His great passions included music and computer technology, and he became highly involved in electronic music, while also developing computer-controlled theatre lighting, which combined music, dance, and lighting effects. The world of sound also inspired his ideas about resonant spaces in analytical encounters, and the importance of such spaces in terms of uncovering hidden feelings (Lewis, 2003). He formed part of a community with Nobel Prize winners – supported by the Guggenheim Foundation – in which music was created together. Moreover, his experiences of meditation and Buddhism was also integrated into his diverse strands of thought, as reflected in his article "Credo: The Dialectics of One-Person and Two-Person Psychologies" (Ghent, 1989). In this essay, he uses the question of faith to address what he regards as the inevitable consequences of two-person psychology: for Ghent, faith is a conceptual structure which has received too little attention in psychoanalysis. He regarded theories to be beliefs which hide behind cognitive recognition. In the article, Ghent formulates the importance of a belief system for listening within a therapeutic setting:

> And the paradigm – ultimately a belief system that the analyst lives and works by (and there is no assurance that the analyst has full conscious access to the system under which he or she is really operating) – makes a very significant difference as to how one hears, what one hears, how one assembles what is heard, and how one conducts oneself in the analytic setting.
>
> (Ghent, 1989, p. 170)

Here Ghent is already highlighting the importance of attitude and its influence on the interventions made by analysts. Two-person psychology begins in discourse with one's own belief system. As he puts it in the same work:

> But even more important: our patients are there to help us if only we have ears to listen. If we can remain attuned we will discover that all is not resistance, in fact a fair share is counter-resistance, our own difficulties with having to re-evaluate our theories and expectations in the light of experience that we uneasily sense is not fitting well with those theories and expectations.
>
> (Ghent, 1989, p. 170)

Here Ghent very specifically draws on Ferenczi's ideas of mutual analysis, while also formulating the significance of defence, which he understands as an intertwining of transference and countertransference (Ferenczi, 2013). Ghent's analysand was Clara Thompson, who was also analysed by Ferenczi, and is mentioned in his clinical diaries as patient Dm (Demos & Harris, 2017).

Ghent pursued this idea still further in a subsequent article on masochism and submission. In reflecting on the counterparts to feelings, which therapists bring in with them, he had already moved deep into the thought of relational psychoanalysis.

Within the clinical world, Ghent's most cited article is "Masochism, Submission, Surrender – Masochism as a Perversion of Surrender" (Ghent, 1990), in which he elaborates on the distinction between *surrender* and *submission*, placing them in the context of the term *masochism*. He suggests that surrender is the search for or the finding of a true, authentic self, as opposed to submission to an alien self, which he now regards as a form of resistance or adaptation. Surrender is the longing for the object or for the search for the object. Submission serves to ward off fears, guilt, and feelings of shame and can be seen in all its forms of defence, as described by psychoanalysis. Ghent here takes Eastern Buddhist teachings as a reference point, in which *surrender* does not mean *defeat,* but rather *transcendence* and thus *liberation*:

> The guru [analyst] is an illusion – an illusion which permits the disciple to yield, surrender false self, and therein have a chance at finding

> himself. The process may be thought of as allowing the disciple to re-enter the exhilarating world of transitional experiencing – wherein the guru is the transitional object. The 'ego', false self, 'mind' wants to argue; the guru won't argue. He knows that all commitment at this level reinforces the strength of the 'ego' (false self). Surrender in this sense does not need a guru. The indirect object of the surrender could as well be a tree, the sun, God ... anything or anyone, that will not impinge with its own 'ego'. The process is what is important.
>
> (Ghent, 1990, p. 110)

For Ghent, surrender does not need an object at the end of its path. Rather, it is a surrender to one's own authentic self, which in turn is brought to appear through surrender. Here he very much develops his thought around Eastern ideas about the purpose and goal of meditation. In a Western context, he identifies similar understandings of *surrender* in some theories of art. Ultimately, he sees surrender as a universal or innate need which, when its development is deformed, can lead to a false self. As he puts it:

> The main hypothesis of this paper is that it is this passionate longing to surrender that comes into play in at least some instances of masochism. Submission, losing oneself in the power of the other, becoming enslaved in one or other way to the master, is the ever available lookalike to surrender. It holds out the promise, seduces, excites, enslaves, and in the end, cheats the seeker-turned-victim out of his cherished goal, offering in its place only the security of bondage and an ever amplified sense of futility. By substituting the appearance and trappings of surrender for the authentic experience, an agonizing, although at times temporarily exciting, masquerade of surrender occurs: a self-negating submissive experience in which the person is enthralled by the other. The intensity of the masochism is a living testimonial of the urgency with which some buried part of the personality is screaming to be exhumed. This is not to be minimized as an expression of the longing to be healed, although so often we bear witness to its recurring miscarriage.
>
> (Ghent, 1990, p. 112).

As an antithetical point, Ghent developed the idea of sadism as a concept. Drawing on the ideas of Winnicott, he suggests that sadism is necessary for the development of one's self, to destroy the mother in order to experience her survival. In the analytic concept, it means that the patient makes use of the analyst, treating them sadistically in order to develop their own self, through the therapist's survival. For Ghent, the essential form of development is not towards the object as a rigid self, but rather in how the object is used. Destructiveness is the reality principle which creates the quality of externality. To develop object use, an object is needed which can establish a relationship with *surrender*. This kind of transitional experience now forms the basis for a creative experience of the world. In Ghent's own words:

> As used in this paper, surrender implies not defeat but a quality of liberation and 'letting-go'. I have explored the thesis that at least in some instances masochism is the result of a distortion or perversion of a deep longing for surrender, a yearning to be known, recognized, ›penetrated‹, and often represents the miscarriage of a desire to dismantle false self. Similarly, some instances of sadism are traceable to the obverse of this phenomenon: A failure in the consumption of a more active ›penetrative‹ type of surrender as in object usage. Successful transition from object relating to object usage involves an act of surrender and risk-taking on the part of the infant (or later, patient), as well as a degree of surrender on the part of the facilitating caretaker, or later, analyst. To round out the conception of surrender I have touched on related issues such as creativity and the apperception of disorganizing meaning.
>
> (Ghent, 1990, p. 134)

The ideas which Ghent raises here – about the desire to be seen, the complementarity of love and hate, and the longing for surrender as a form of meaning within relationships – have been further developed by Jessica Benjamin, who was Ghent's analysand, becoming the basic pillars of her work.

In the context of the William Alanson White Institute, Ghent offered a highly significant basis for creativity for many future thinkers. Moreover, even more than in his writing, he lived out his own mode of thinking within his network of relationships with his students and colleagues (Demos & Harris, 2018; Bass, 2018).

2 Next Generation: Benjamin, Aron, Harris, Bass, and Davies

Jessica Benjamin (born 1946), a student and analysand of Ghent, has played an important role in the establishment of relational thinking around the world. Her parents were Jewish emigrants to the United States, who later supported their daughter in her study of social sciences with Theodor Adorno at Frankfurt University. She completed her studies in New York in 1978 and proceeded to undergo psychoanalytic training. Thereafter, she belonged to the inner circle around Mitchell (approximately seven people), and in this way developed into one of the most important representatives of relational psychoanalysis.

As a result of her study of philosophy in Germany, Benjamin was substantially influenced by Hegel and Habermas, as she was later to be by the work of Winnicott. Her essay "Beyond Doer and Done to: An Intersubjective View of Thirdness" (2004a, 2018) remains the most widely read article in the field of relational psychoanalysis.

Taking Ghent's reflections on masochism and sadism as a starting point, Benjamin developed a concept which goes beyond ideas of victim and perpetrator: instead, she attributes agency to both positions, in this way assigning responsibility to both partners in constructing a moral third party. Here it is of course a question of active and passive, although she also ascribes to passivity a quality of readiness to act. She links this, first, to the idea of authorship and, second, to being a subject who is in possession of one's self. Change is only possible, she suggests, through this shared recognition, which both actors unconsciously bear within them. Expanding on the concept, she states:

> [H]ow an individual is empowered to initiate agency and authorship, to take responsibility for their own feelings and actions, to be a subject in possession of their own self. A subject who does not regard themselves as a victim and does not constantly have the feeling that something is being done to them.
>
> (Benjamin, 2004b)

For Benjamin, this means to deny identification from both sides, to no longer be in possession of one's own feelings and actions, and to lose one's subjectivity. Based on the ideas of complementarity put forward by Ghent, Benjamin then attempted to create an intersubjective model of how this complementarity takes place and thus becomes visible, and how change can be brought in this way. She presents a new descriptive idea of the third position, which she conceives of differently to Lacan, Green, and Ogden (Coelho, 2016). She speaks of the "moral third position" which emerges when patient and analyst acknowledge they are both responsible for the situation and that both contribute to it. If therapists do not acknowledge their involvement, "there arises a fusing of the third and an insoluble ideal, which leads many analytic treatments into a quagmire of despair" (Benjamin, 2004b). She goes on to argue that this third position amounts to a pattern or principle of a dynamic interaction, in which one's own influence is recognized and acknowledged. She regards it as a moral development if each of the two partners in the interaction experiences themselves as an ethical person.

> The Third refers to a position constituted through holding the tension of recognition between difference and sameness, taking the other to be a separate but equivalent centre of initiative and consciousness with whom calm feelings and intentions can be shared. Sharing begins in the earliest pre-verbal interactions: the creation of alignment in intentions or resonance of feeling, a degree of symmetry or sense of sameness even among unequal partners.
>
> (Benjamin, 2018, p. 4)

This moral third is created by therapists when they also regard themselves as a person who is doing something to patients and in doing so also recognize how they are reflected by their patients. If this recognition does not take place, "thirdness" collapses. Benjamin also says: "Parts of good and bad: we have both. This leads to the emergence of the third in therapy". In her own words:

> All patients, in individual ways, place their hopes for the therapeutic process in us, and for each one, we must use our own subjectivity in a different way to struggle through to a specific solution. But this specificity and the authenticity on which it is based cannot be created in free fall. Analytic work conducted according to the intersubjective view of two participating subjectivities requires a discipline based on orientation to the structural conditions of thirdness. It is my hope that this clinical and developmental perspective on co-created, intersubjective thirdness can help orient us toward responsibility and more rigorous thinking, even as our practice of psychoanalysis becomes more emotionally authentic, more spontaneous and inventive, more compassionate and liberating to both our patients and ourselves.
>
> (Benjamin, 2018, p. 48).

Recognition is a very important concept in Benjamin's work, a notion which also comes from the feminist movement, which Benjamin has been addressing since the 1970s: "The challenge to a psychologically oriented recognition theory was articulated by Judith Butler in 1997" (Benjamin, 2018, p. 17). Butler is of course one of the most significant thinkers in debates around gender.

The baby makes use of the mother: this is also a recognition of the mother, in the sense used by Winnicott.

> I believe that in formal terms the same process of recognition is crucial in social and clinical dimensions of interaction. The process evolves through early experience with accommodation, attunement, understanding into later more complex forms.
>
> (Benjamin, 2018, p. 7)

For Benjamin, recognition in the therapeutic sense has the task of restoring a space of thirdness and thus enabling both partners to feel and to think independently of one another. The creation and destruction of thirdness is the dynamic side of the psychotherapeutic process, an oscillation between deconstruction, dissociation and repair. "The essential point on which recognition theory focuses is the reciprocal response to each other's minds, regardless of its specific form – the awareness of the other as subject rather than object" (Benjamin, 2018, p. 10).

Benjamin's idea of recognition combines two separate paths: from psychoanalysis, relational thinking in the clinical field and, from thinking on society and gender, relationality as it functions between women and men and in terms of developmental psychology. She views recognition – and the failure to achieve recognition – as an important developmental path in terms of the regulation of affects (Benjamin & Atlas, 2015). Based on her book *The Bonds of Love: Psychoanalysis, Feminism and the Problem of Domination* (Benjamin, 1988), she combines Ghent's ideas – complementarity of masochism and sadism – with aspects of recognition as developed within the feminist movement. In her book *Imagination and Gender* (Benjamin, 1998) she further elaborates her ideas regarding the construction of our gender reality; her 1998 book, *Shadow of the Other: Intersubjectivity and Gender in Psychoanalysis* (Benjamin, 1998) further connects her three main themes, focusing on intersubjectivity. "As problematic as the original meeting of psychoanalysis and feminism was, it is becoming increasingly clear that their paths overlap" (Benjamin, 1995b, p. 17).

Jessica Benjamin is now considered the "public face" of relational psychoanalysis and psychotherapy, its most prominent representative, whose work receives widespread international attention.

Lewis Aron (1952–2019) was another member of the William Alanson White Institute, also forming part of the inner circle around Stephen A. Mitchell, and was responsible for the repopularization of Ferenczi's work in the United States (Aron & Harris, 1993). Aron became the director of New York University's postdoctoral program in psychotherapy and psychoanalysis, the only program in an American university which taught psychoanalysis.

Aron was also the first president of the International Association for Relational Psychoanalysis and Psychotherapy (IARPP), as well as co-founder of the aforementioned journal *Psychoanalytic Dialogues: The International Journal of Relational Perspectives* (1991). Along with Adrienne Harris he edited the book series "Relational Perspective". His own two major works are *A Meeting of Minds: Mutuality in Psychoanalysis* (Aron, 2013) and *A Psychotherapy for the People: Toward a Progressive Psychoanalysis*, co-written with Karen E. Starr (Aron & Starr, 2013).

In *A Meeting of Minds*, Aron addresses various aspects of *mutuality*, putting this idea in a clinical context in order to more precisely formulate the way in which it is subject to asymmetry within a therapeutic setting. For Aron, mutuality consists of the mutual sharing of any feelings, which leads to a shared emotional experience: he regards difference as meaning a lack of mutuality, which forms the basis for separateness. In his thought-constellation, psychoanalysis and psychotherapy offer a dialectic between these two phenomena. Autonomy also requires separateness in order to be able to restore mutuality. In contrast to Benjamin's concept of complementarity, Aron's idea of mutuality and its influence highlights the inequality of meaningful influence:

> The definition of mutuality does not include symmetry or equality. Two people may be said to have formed a mutual admiration society, when

> they hold each other in high esteem or share reciprocal mirroring and idealization. There need be no assumption, however, of quantitative equality or functional symmetry for the term mutual to be applied.
>
> (Aron, 2013, p. xi)

In this work, Aron develops the various meanings of mutuality in the clinical process in a highly differentiated manner, discussing them using common concepts from psychoanalysis.

Aron also applied a dialogic approach to the development of concepts: "Just as meaning is mutually constructed within the analytic situation, so, too, psychoanalytic theories are co-constructed dialogically within the community of psychoanalysts" (Aron, 2013, p. xii). Working out a theory within a community or in dialogue with oneself – in other words, the generation of knowledge – is a relational event.

Aron developed this approach based on Atwood and Stolorow's argument on the significance of writers' subjectivity, drawn from their own narratives of experience (Atwood & Stolorow, 1979). His own socialization through the William Alanson White Institute, including its history, had a considerable influence on his theoretical concepts, which were also refined by currents of postmodernism and feminism prevailing at that time. The second chapter of *A Meeting of Minds* elaborates on the distinctions between relational thought and other approaches to psychoanalysis, while subsequent chapters devote more attention to clinical practice, its dominant concepts, and the ways in which they differ from relational psychoanalysis (Aron, 2013).

Here is Aron's own description of his relationship with Mitchell at the time:

> Stephen A. Mitchell has been my teacher, supervisor, mentor, colleague and friend. While he has helped me with my writing from my first analytic paper, I am delighted that he is now officially my editor. I always learn from Stephen and with his great generosity he manages to make me feel that I am also teaching him. No one in the field could be a better model for the practice of mutuality while maintaining respect for the other's autonomy.
>
> (Aron, 2013, p. xviii).

For Aron and the core group around Mitchell, his sudden death was a traumatic experience that brought them closer together but also caused them to lose creativity during their period of mourning (Orange, 2018).

Adrienne Harris was another member of Mitchell's inner circle. Her most cited article, "Gender as a Soft Assembly: Tomboys' Stories", deals with the phenomenon of "tomboys", girls with a masculine demeanour or appearance, using this as a reference point to deconstruct common patterns of femininity and masculinity. She explains her deconstruction using ideas drawn from chaos theory, in particular on self-developing and self-organizing systems. She contrasts these ideas from chaos theory with notion of character, including its expression, fluctuations, and instability factors, pointing out that both conceptual frameworks, although drawing on different perspectives, rely on a structure in which everything is fluid and in motion. She develops this further to arrive at a particular idea of development:

> The developmental theory I am proposing is less a rejection of existing work than a reframing or revisioning. ... In considering a complex phenomenon like gender to be a softly assembled system, we take up gender's meanings within any individual and familial system, along with its function and form within specific tasks in specific environments. Certainly gender could encompass behaviours that have conscious, unconscious, and social interactional properties. Gender and desire would come into their unique and particular forms only in context, context being very widely constructed. Gender and sex would be inseparable from the interpersonal fields in which they are embedded. And gender and desire would not necessarily be linked in preprogrammed or obvious ways.
>
> (Harris, 2000, p. 232)

Harris's approach here decouples the idea of gender from notions of biological drives and associated ideas, instead connecting the development of desire – including in the sense of gender – to specific family systems. In her analysis, gender and sexuality are inextricably linked by their origins in interpersonal fields. She sums up sexuality as having the following task:

> ... express[ion] and contains multiple functions: self-regulation; interpersonal regulation; distancing or bridging; conditioning safety or potential destabilization; courting excitement or danger or sealing it off. Forms and functions of desire would not have an obvious or unremarkable relationship to gender. The assemblage of gendered experiences in sexual life is contingent and emergent, not pre-programmed. Desire and gender may be set up antagonistically or feel seamlessly enmeshed and obvious. The patterns organizing and consolidating in particular forms of desire or identification could all potentially function at conscious and unconscious levels.
>
> This way of thinking would make the tomboy one among many characters about whom we make developmental stories. She could live in her variability but be less estranged from human functioning. One of the ideological distortions in conventional developmental and psychoanalytic accounts is not merely that many forms of life are declared nonnormative, but that any form of ›otherness‹ from the central story is unfathomably different. If developmental theory is written with such broad generality and is so attuned to multiplicity and variation, forms of life we like to keep thickly bounded (gay – straight, boy – girl; sissy – tomboy; identification – desire, etc.) are more alike in their process of formation while retaining the variability of outcome.
>
> (Harris, 2000, p. 232f.)

Harris's essay does not call into question the phenomena of gender specificity it observes; instead, it advocates for a different form of observation and description. She also discusses the importance of historical development and its connection to the body as one meaning of gender construction: "The almost exclusive focus on the vagina as the designated site of femininity almost inevitably makes the female body a body primed for heterosexuality" (Harris, 2000, p. 235). How I look at something has an impact on my experience of reality and thus also on how I experience and live my sexuality. It is not *cogito ergo sum* which gives meaning, but rather the way in which the body is conceived and how it is awakened into lived experience (*Er-leben*) through its interaction with all its social components. With regard to the development of sexuality, Harris also advocates a non-linear approach, suggesting chaos theory as a different model of observation. This leads her to a guiding principle: "Same-sex and different-sex identifications and interactions assume a single and simply categorized identity. A number of critics have argued that these accounts of gender development remain within an understanding of normative heterosexuality" (Harris, 2000, p. 238). The perspective of heterosexuality as a reference point for development should not be viewed as a fixed entity: heterosexuality should instead be understood, in the sense of chaos theory, as a fluid phenomenon which must continually construct itself. Another point that Harris addresses at this point in her work, one which she will also later pursue, is the unconscious transmission of trauma experiences to the next generation and the influence they have on gender structures: "This phenomenon, the haunting of an individual by ghosts, demons, and losses transmitted in some way well below the radar screens of conscious reflection, may find in the structures of gender a particularly vivid and well-elaborated host" (Harris, 2000, p. 240).

The last section of "Gender as a Soft Assembly" takes up the importance of language and the associated construction of reality in relation to gender experience:

> It might be useful to explore not the role of language in gender experience, but the role of speech, specifically the practice of naming or not naming one's experience. I think we need a more careful and complex understanding of what a category is, how it is built, and how complex, contradictory and multiply configured the categories used to describe gender will turn out to be.
>
> (Harris, 2000, p. 243f.)

Here she once again points out how urgent it is to recognize that we only achieve an understanding of ourselves by deconstructing our language categories regarding gender. The categorization of girls and boys comes about through representation by metaphor, metaphors which are created out of embodied experience and develop, as a total process, within a social matrix. Harris's argument thus moves our construction of ideas of gender, and the sexuality associated with it, further towards relational thinking and further towards cultural determination. It no longer assumes these things to be a biological given.

Anthony Bass, another figure within the core group around Mitchell, teaches at Columbia University's Center for Psychoanalytic Training and, along with Harris, is editor-in-chief of *Psychoanalytic Dialogues*. He was also a founding member of IARPP. Like Aron, he is very familiar with Ferenczi's work, and has developed the idea of mutuality in therapy, an idea which Ferenczi was the first to posit. The starting point is the conviction that all psychotherapy is mutual. His best-known article "When the Frame Doesn't Fit the Picture" (Bass, 1999, 2007), which addresses the interplay between an image and its frame, initially takes up a particular clinical case, which he uses to address the fundamental issue of payment for therapy and what it signifies. In the case, it took a long process – over the course of two years of therapy – before the usual payment arrangement between patient and therapist was agreed, with an invoice sent from the therapist to the patient at the end of the month.

The meaning and effects of actions or interventions like "self-disclosure" always depend on the context of the established framework. It cannot be said per se whether "self-disclosure" as a technique is good or bad; only by reference to the framework can we decide whether this form should be used or not. Bass also argues that the frame does not represent a technology which endures over time, but rather a phenomenon which must adapt to conditions within a particular culture at a particular time.

> From another perspective, the movement from omnipotence to an appropriate form of self-regard, for analyst and patient alike, in which both triumphs and disappointments were not only possible but also necessary, was not yet theorized. Social, cultural, and intellectual trends during the past century have contributed to the creation of new norms and therefore different analytic goals and expectations. We would expect that the rules and frames of analysis would shift to reflect such changing mores.
>
> (Bass, 1999, p. 250)

Each era has different ideas about rules of behaviour in therapy, with ideas cycling between greater and lesser degrees of abstinence (Gysling, 2009). The analytic framework is renegotiated for each individual patient; it changes and is re-formed over the course of the therapeutic process. Since, for Bass, the frame represents something profoundly individual, to conceive of the frame in technical terms can only put a strain on the therapeutic process. For Bass, negotiation is also an indispensable element within analysis, since it allows for enactments to take place, and thus for a therapeutic setting to be created. These unformulated aspects of inner life and of shared experience are what enable new paths to be taken. For Bass, the frame means this: "I believe that within the surface negotiation of the frame, deep consolidation of a wide variety of intrapsychic and intersubjective elements are being created, worked through, and recreated, to the ultimate benefit of both participants" (Bass, 1999, p. 264).

Bass's 2014 article "Three Pleas for a Measure of Uncertainty, Reverie and Private Contemplation in the Chaotic, Interactive, Nonlinear Dynamic Field of Interpersonal/Intersubjective Relational Psychoanalysis" looks at what connects the various relational therapists, looking in particular at the work of Seligman, Corbett, and Cooper. All three authors conceive of and examine the function of a "private" space arising in therapy. In examining this topic, Bass is attempting to trace the common threads within deeply individual understandings of therapy and of the non-interchangeability of those involved.

He gives a precise definition of what "relational" means in the context of psychoanalysis:

> In my view what is 'relational' about the analyst's form of participation at any given juncture in a therapeutic process is not whether the analyst is engaging the patient actively about something that is occurring between them, or listening contemplatively in deep concentrated attention, but rather the analyst's careful attention, whether contained or voiced at any given moment, to his or her own experience and how that is shaping and being shaped by the patient's way of being and relating. Recognizing one's own role in at least partially shaping the patient's experience in therapy is crucial, and differs markedly from the traditional view that the central factor in the patient's experience of the analyst and the analytic situation is the transference of early experience into the present by the patient in ways that eclipse to a great extent the current reality of therapist/patient relationships.
>
> (Bass, 2014b, p. 671).

Bass also takes up an idea from Corbett, arguing that the element of time must also be allowed to create space for contemplative things to unfold, which in turn can allow for spontaneity. He also regards enactment as an important aspect of therapy, always present, but which can be imagined and thus understood, through awareness and decoding. As a countermovement to enactment, he recommends the creation of a contemplative space of reflection within the encounter so as to provide for moments of silence too. In Bass's understanding of relational thinking, there is no single correct path: this kind of thinking is instead defined as the converse of preconceived opinions and rituals, which otherwise can spread through the analyst, leading to the colonization of the patient and the shared space. He believes there to be many forms of silence, as well as many forms of individualized, personal listening on the part of the particular analyst. Listening within the context of analysis is paradoxical: it is both highly focused and surrounded by uncertainty. He also goes against the notion of "free-floating" forms of listening:

> Listening is not a function that can be separated from the mind of the listener, and so the analyst's way of listening is never altogether 'free floating', 'value free', or 'neutral'. It is never free from the therapist's own unconscious contribution to the process, and so we can never be certain how we are shaping the patient's experience of us in our ways of listening and participating. We can never be sure of the degree to which what we are hearing when we listen to our patient is an echo of ourselves.
>
> (Bass, 2014b, p. 674).

The criticism of the term "free-floating" may well be justified if it is regarded as a technical term involving a clear instruction, rather than being understood as an attitude to be striven for, in a back-and-forth process which is always in flux.

For Bass, listening in a relational sense thus means that the analyst hears the effect of their own participation in what is happening, "whether that be his contemplative, unintrusive quiet; his withdrawn persecutory silence; his engaged responsiveness; or his intrusive, unresponsive activity" (Bass, 2014b, p. 674).

This form of listening allows relational analysts to pay attention to different levels of experience and perceive the connections between them. It is a form of attention which involves immersion in the inner world of the patient and the analyst, as well as the recognition of how both depend on a shared development in therapy.

Taking up an idea from Cooper (2010), Bass develops an explanatory model for heterogeneity within relational psychoanalysis. This model, he suggests, represents a different order of theory, one which can be conceived as an overarching clinical model, a kind of metatheory, functioning on a different level than discourses such as self- or ego-psychology. Metapsychology as a concept can be understood in terms of the diversity of thinkers within the relational field: hence it does not generate a single, unified theory, something which has in turn been criticized by classical analysts.

Jody Messier Davies, another of the inner circle of New York relationalists, is a sharp, precise thinker in the clinical field, who has written what is one of the most-discussed papers in American psychoanalysis: "Love in the Afternoon: A Relational Reconsideration of Desire and Dread in the Countertransference" (Davies, 1994). This essay shifts the meaning of sexuality away from Oedipal significance and towards its real meaning, whereby it appears within relationality, generating specific fantasies: "[W]e have in large measure cast aside the reality that sexuality is still an outgrowth of shifting physical sensation as it occurs in relation to specific fantasies and interpersonal relationships" (Davies, 1994, p. 159). She goes on to write that it is impossible to reflect on these important issues of sexuality and all of the feelings that accompany them unless we experience and verbalize them. "If we are to enter the clinical realm of erotic desire, confusion and inhibition, it would seem imperative that we gain access to this essential subtext of interpersonal relatedness as it affects both patient and therapist" (Davies, 1994, p. 160). If therapists are afraid of their own erotic feelings, patients' erotic experiences will be prematurely closed off and a large aspect of self-organization will be lost for patients, who will be unable to think about their capacity for erotic desire. Viewing the patient's sexual desire as a joint undertaking is still something which is very difficult for many analysts to conceive and can lead to a retreat into one-person psychology. If the sexual aspect is shared in its emerging significance within the therapeutic space, the patient will not have to feel guilty for their own feelings and hence will not remain an over-excited young child. As Davies puts it: "I would suggest that ultimately, although with careful timing, the patient must come to know the analyst as subject of her own erotic sensation and desire" (Davies, 1994, p. 162).

Using a scene from a case study, Davies goes on to discuss the meaning of the therapist's own sexual feelings, while describing very eloquently the importance of working explicitly with these feelings in a therapeutic context. She also points to the cultural force of ethical institutions, by which she felt mentally confronted at the moment she recounts. The significance, she suggests, did not lie in an acting out of these feelings, but rather in viewing them as co-constructed and in this way coming to new and unexpected insights by allowing shared involvement.

3 The Emergence of New Thinkers and the Influence of Infant Research

Ken Corbett is one of the younger thinkers within relational psychoanalysis, a teacher at NYU's program in psychoanalysis and psychotherapy, whose work focuses on queer theory and developmental concepts of masculinity. His best-known article "Boyhood Femininity, Gender Identity Disorder, Masculine Presuppositions and the Anxiety of Regulation" (Corbett, 2009a) deals with the problem of feminine boys and the associated use of the Gender Identity Disorder (GID) label, a topic also addressed by his first book, *Boyhoods: Rethinking Masculinities* (Corbett, 2009b). Drawing on a large swathe of the literature on the diagnosis and description of gender identity disorders, he argues that masculinity's prerequisites and definitions are simply never questioned:

> The claims of the binary are so powerfully culturally compelled that they are unthought as natural and essential. Gender is routinely conflated with anatomy, and gender is routinely conflated with that which produces our desires and personality traits. Male traits are linked with the desire for female traits, in keeping with the model of heterosexual complementarity, and so it goes. Social order, it is claimed, rests on the reproduction of this masculine-feminine gender complementarity. Boys become boys through the reproduction of fathering, which is presumed to follow on heterosexual desire.
>
> (Corbett, 2009a, p. 355f.)

Corbett no longer regards gender identity – the inner conviction about one's own gender – as a person's fixed identity, but rather as a chaotic complexity, allowing greater freedom for gender variations. Making use of a case history, he argues for a place for feminine masculinity within masculinity and for feminine boys in development, pointing out that the entire discourse about feminine boys does not question masculinity as a reference point. Variance is permitted within postmodernism, within a perspective of "tolerance", but this remains clouded with a sense of the "subclinical". The discourse does not see variance as an advantage but is always experienced as standing on the margins. Our clinical everyday life, he writes, is guided by a particular kind of diagnostic rhetoric:

> ...that corrals feminine boys, and propagates and perpetuates the anxious assessment of a boy's identificatory bonds with his parents. Is the boy properly aligned? Has he identified with his father? Is that identification robust and competitive? Has he separated from his mother? Is that separation secured through the proper degree of disidentification from that which is maternal and feminine?
>
> (Corbett, 2009a, p. 358).

Clinical attitudes influence our treatment processes and contribute significantly to the standardization of our patients. In terms of the feminine man, the reference point in clinical literature is a pathologizing mother, portrayed primarily as boundary-crossing, over-protective, etc., and femininity is interpreted as a regressive lack of separation.

> There is no consideration given to relational transfers that are not the result of dominating or traumatic intromissions. There is no consideration given to the possibility that a boy could identify with his mother, and through processes of internalization and gender mobility constitute his own feminine subjectivity. There is no consideration given to relational exchange or intersubjective transfers that are founded in mutual recognition.
>
> (Corbett, 2009a, p. 359).

In this way, Corbett presents a possible opening up of relational ways of thinking for certain phenomena, in this way generating a different level of understanding. If this fails to happen, he argues:

> The ethical insufficiency that issues from this lack is that it leaves the therapist inadequately prepared to address countertransference, and to recognize if counter-resistance or counter-anxiety is being repeated through normative presumption and reactive pathologization.
>
> (Corbett, 2009a, p. 361).

Anyone who fails to include the normativity of attitudes in their thinking can reactivate the pathologization of the patient. As an example, Corbett cites attachment theory, in which gender and its development are ascribed no relevance for the strength of the bond, although bonding with the mother is considered of great importance when discussing "feminized" boys. Attachment theories always move along normative lines, and in this sense gender is determined by role adaptation. "The psychological discourse on feminine boys is a staging ground for the regimented regulation of masculine expressivity" (Corbett, 2009a, p. 366).

Corbett raises a fascinating question here: why many explanations for the emergence of effeminate and feminine boys go back to the bond with the mother – in all of its variants, from disregarding boundaries to insufficient bonding – but there is no discussion of the significance of this attachment's impact on gender development. In a related way, Corbett also questions our normative view of all of these approaches to understanding; based on his own clinical experience, he suggests there is no connection with the attachment or detachment factors which should supposedly lead boys' pathologization. He argues:

> In contrast to the various prognostications regarding a feminine boy's difficulty in separating from the family, my clinical experience with feminine boys, especially those who have been able to form a transforming nexus with their parents, suggests that, far more often than not, separation does take place, and with the same degree of success and failure that one notes for most everyone.
>
> (Corbett, 2009a, p. 368).

The work of Beatrice Beebe and Frank Lachmann represents an important connection between psychoanalysis, infant research, intersubjective thinking, and the relational understanding of the world. One of their most important articles, written with their colleague Joseph Jaffe and published in *Psychoanalytic Dialogues*, uses a large body of research to address the basis of the emergence of self and object representations. "Mother-Infant Interaction Structures and Presymbolic Self and Object Representations" (Beebe et al., 1997) is used by many relational psychoanalytic thinkers to illustrate the importance of the encounter in humans' development of their being. The essay introduced the concept of "dyadic systems views" into psychoanalytic understandings of the development of the self. Lachmann also made a connection between research results and the treatment of adults, in this way generating new therapeutic perspectives (Beebe & Lachmann, 2010; Lachmann, 2004; Lichtenberg et al., 2017). The dyadic systems view is based on the idea that in interaction – in particular as seen between mother and infant – information is sent and received by both partners simultaneously. Via these reflections, Beebe and Lachmann posit a bidirectional field in which two interactants each regulate and destabilize the other. They regard this research into bidirectionality as the central question over the last 20 years of infant research. "Mother-Infant Interaction Structures and Presymbolic Self and Object Representations" (Beebe et al., 1997) examined every piece of infant research based on a dyadic systems view, using these to construct a model of communications which is not based on linear development. They regard predictions of development to be based neither on the child nor the environment, but rather in how the two interact as a bidirectional system, similarly to the idea of the bi-personal field (Ferro, 2003). They assume a transformational model of development, in which development is in a permanent state of "continuous transformations and restructurings" (Beebe et al., 1997, p. 136). Their article addresses the questions of how a pattern of interaction is represented and the basis for pre-symbolic representation. They postulate a motivational factor which is present as primary in the infant, either endogenously or intrinsically, and which represents the basis for the creation of a matrix in interaction. The child requires this ability in order to explore, and for curiosity, as well as a capacity to reduce hunger, pain, or fatigue. The authors regard this as the child's biological readiness to react to its environment: to actively encounter it. They discuss a wide range of finding, showing how an infant can recognize "discriminations" and contingencies from birth on. The findings of research into memory and affect suggest a connection between the child's emotional state and his or her ability to remember: "Events occurring under conditions of increased negative affect may be stored but not easily retrieved" (Beebe et al., 1997, p. 141). Solid conclusions can be drawn from this on questions relating to amnesia, dissociation, and trauma.

One important step in the infant's developing social interaction is the basic capacity to perceive time, space, affect and stimulus. Through the interplay of these factors, at around three months, infants develop the ability of *feature detection*, as well as the capacity to create schema formations. Schema formation is complete when small children no longer react to stimuli, having become accustomed to them. "The ability to form a schema is an index of a primitive capacity to categorize and create representations, and it predicts developmental outcomes" (Beebe et al., 1997, p. 144f.).

The child now forms a large variety of pre-symbolic categorizations, inferring regularity by perceiving similarities and differences at the same time: "The capacity to abstract what is common among perceptually discriminable entities, and to generalize on the basis of that abstraction, also makes possible a rudimentary form of representation" (Beebe et al., 1997, p. 145). The ability to categorize forms the basis for the concept of RIG (*representation of an interaction generalized*), which Daniel Stern uses to represent the capacity to generalize interaction (D.N. Stern, 2000). By virtue of this generalization, expectations can now be set for interactions and these interactions can in turn organize and generalize principles such as "ongoing regulation, disruption and repair" and "heightened affective moments". Towards the end of the first year of life, generalized prototypes are formed by means of these expected-interaction structures. These in turn form the basis for symbolic forms of self- and object-representation in infants older than one year. The authors conclude: "These early interaction structures at the pre-symbolic level will later constitute largely unconscious organizing structures or memory structures in the child or adult" (Beebe et al., 1997, p. 147).

Based on this wide variety of evidence from infant research, Beebe and Lachmann conclude that psychological structure or organization is formed via interaction in the first year of life. They define this structure as "relatively persistent organized patterns or classifications of information, or a model used in organizing information". These patterns are in turn formed through an active process of "constructing or reconstructing incoming information" (Beebe et al., 1997, p. 150).

One key point presented by this work is the capacity of mutual regulation and associated self-regulation, regarded as having importance for the organization of structures of interaction. For Beebe and Lachmann, this also marks the intersection of one- and two-person psychology, and the site for the associated discussion. They argue that both regulatory systems are integrated through the development of self- and object representations. Sander was the first person to consider a dyadic system as an emergent property of intrapsychic organization (Sander, 2009). In an experiment, Beatrice Beebe showed how a baby can be moved into a complex combination of calming and arousal, putting the child in a state in which neither falls asleep nor remains in a constantly stimulated condition; rather, the infant oscillates rhythmically back and forth between different stimuli. The integration of mutual regulation with the ability to self-regulate is what leads to psychological structure. Beebe ends her considerations with these words: "We are arguing for an integration of one-person and two-person psychologies" (Beebe et al., 1997, p. 155).

Another point addressed by these authors is mutual influence, which they described as bidirectional. During interaction, both partners influence the other through the establishment of a common rhythm. To investigate this phenomenon, time series analysis methodologies were used to predict future developments, in studies which provide a separate assessment of the influence of the mother on the child, and vice versa. There is a complex interplay of facial reflection between mother and child: a mutual representation of affects is taking place, along with associated modes of influence. Using a complex measurement system, Beebe and Lachmann were able to prove that these phenomena of influence and reflection take place in less than one second, more precisely in less than one-twelfth of a second.

They reach the conclusion: "The infant's behaviour is predicted by the mother's and vice versa" (Beebe et al., 1997, p. 158). The reactions of child and mother are almost simultaneous and cannot thus be explained in terms of stimulus-response mechanism. This almost simultaneous process can only take place if the interaction partners are already participating in the actions to come, and are thus in a position to predict them. Co-regulated communication takes place. These events are not phenomena new to the child; rather, they are predictable patterns to which the child can react appropriately. Stern (D.N. Stern, 1991) defines this ability to predict as an attitude of expectation within a temporal-spatial schema.

Beebe and colleagues have more to say on the importance of mirroring:

> Facial mirroring is one of the interaction structures that contribute to the pre-symbolic organization of self and object representations. To the degree that facial mirroring interactions are positively correlated, so that the partners are changing in the same affective direction, the baby represents the expectation of matching and being matched.
>
> (Beebe et al., 1997, p. 160).

Child and mother are playing a shared game of change and influence, which has as its outcome the perception of the self in the other. Another key starting point for this line of research is that the baby cannot escape the emotions which it perceives in the mother's face, as shown by EEG scans. Beebe and her collaborators point to research revealing mother and child only use mirroring on the other for around 30 percent of the time: for the remainder of the time this is a straightforward process of resonant empathy. If mother and infant find themselves in a mismatched state, they can return to a matched state within two seconds. The movement back and forth occurs relatively quickly and is called *interactive repair*. The better this repair function works, the more reliably a good bond between them can be predicted. This repair function is a regulatory mechanism based on mutuality. To sum up, our psychological structure is created through mirroring and ongoing regulation through predictability, on the one hand, and through principles of interruption and repair, on the other. All communication is based on timing and rhythm as organizational principles. In conclusion, Beebe and her colleagues state: "Healthy development may be characterized by an optimum degree of stability, balancing predictability and transformation." (Beebe et al., 1997, p. 174).

This research also forms a connection with self-psychologists and intersubjectivists, a group to which Lachmann has stated he feels he belongs. Their work has been widely cited and offers a wide variety of explanatory models in order to understand developmental processes (Orange, 2018).

Mauriel Dimen is another prominent representative of relational thinking. Her 2011 article "Lapsus Linguae or One-Person and Two-Person Psychologies" deals with boundary violations she experienced in her interaction with her first analyst. In doing so, Dimen sheds light on a topic which has seen little discussion in the analytical literature. Her detailed description takes the reader into her own emotional world of language and speechlessness, as well as her sense – as the female patient of a "powerful" analyst – of relatedness but also of being at the analyst's mercy. She later undertook a second analysis in which she dealt with the events of the first. In explaining why she remained so long in the first analysis, she writes: "Indeed, one prod for staying in treatment as long as I did may have been a dissociated hope for a repeat performance" (Dimen, 2011, p. 38). There was a longing to repair what had happened, as well as her feelings of dependence, which had been triggered by her relation with authority in a therapeutic context. She notes:

> Dr. O's lapse in this strange treatment, which can be considered both a success and a failure. His transgression issued from the mix of what he, as I perceived him, and I, as I perceive myself, brought to it; conceptual lacunae and technique poorly used, and dangers inherent to psychoanalysis.
>
> (Dimen, 2011, p. 39).

She perceives the problem as having been the following: "[M]y muteness wed Dr. O's silence, fashioning an analysis laced with an incestuous streak" (Dimen, 2011, p. 39). She regards silence as a breeding ground for abuse and the germinating soil of incest, as it unfolds within an analysis (see Steinberger, 2016). She describes being trapped in analysis, perhaps made possible by her love for the analyst. The second part of the book discusses her connection to a desire for incest, Oedipal desire breaking through. She uses her later analysis, noting that:

> It may be that all those years with him laid the groundwork for my second analyst's success in helping me to put words to my silence. Or it may be that my second analyst eventually addressed directly that which held my stubborn muteness in place, the helpless shame I wore …
>
> (Dimen, 2011, p. 48).

For Dimen, shame is the leitmotif of her own muteness, having no language for the scene of the "lapsus". She also addresses the meaning of longing and its importance for our desiring, as well as the difficulty she had with this in her treatment with Dr. O.:

> Desire entails several paradoxes, and it seems useful to lay them out here because they manifested so oddly and silently in my treatment with Dr. O. Chief among these is desire's ambiguous location both between and within those who feel it.
>
> (Dimen, 2011, p. 51).

Longing is subject to a paradox which, for Dimen, is only resolved in its encounter with a dualistic solution: "The relational version might be that desire emerges in relationship, but belonging to the child alone" (Dimen, 2011, p. 51). As she describes him, Dr. O. does not experience longing, but rather the narcissistic desire to triumph over young women. The shame in the therapy session is not a relational product: it is not that he was unable to break through his shame and thus become able to overlay the scene with linguistic significance so as to make his desire comprehensible. The analyst left the patient alone with her shame, in this way withholding all agency from her (Davies, 1994). In phenomenological terms, Dimen attributes less intersubjectivity to the analysis; rather, she draws on postclassical models to discuss the question of intersubjective Oedipus, ascribing intersubjectivity both to desire and to renunciation within the Oedipal triangle. "Postclassical models ... redraft the Oedipal story by constructing both desire and its renunciation as intersubjective. Together, Oedipal adult and child forswear their mutual sexual desire, with the former facilitating the latter's renunciation" (Dimen, 2011, p. 56). There has still been little research into parental desire and its significance for the child's sexual development. In order to shed some light on this process, she suggests heuristically separating the Oedipus complex from the incest taboo.

On the subject, she adds: "I cannot quite forgive him the damage he did" (Dimen, 2011, p. 65). She describes her feelings as still being profoundly entangled with her first analysis, despite the second analysis. She feels obliged to note that "the confrontation would likely have been salutary. Still, whenever I think of having missed it, I usually feel more relief than regret" (Dimen, 2011, p. 65). When she leaves her sense of obligation behind, the significance lies in acknowledging what she missed, which she describes in a new version of Oedipus. The acknowledgment of longing and regrets leads to relief. Moreover, once her shame had dissolved, she no longer felt a desire for revenge. Shame was maintained through the idea of a professional code of inviolability for analysts. She describes the conflict she felt as an analyst and as a patient, in which she felt trapped by the rules of the analytical community.

She offers an explanation: "Analysts suffering the dissociated, unforgettable rejection of having been patients may indeed find themselves inducing that very feeling in their own patients, in order to cleanse themselves and, thus cleansed, to become pure and strong" (Dimen, 2011, p. 73). It is important for her as an analyst always to be able to perceive herself in both roles in the encounter with the patient, able to see herself as a patient and remain aware of how her own longing was shamed. She also advocates a further decoding of erotic countertransference, to avoid the trap of prohibition in the sense of a dictum from the superego. Freud regards the rule as the ultimate way out of countertransference (S. Freud, 1962b; Slavin & Rahmani, 2016). One can only agree with Dimen's final recommendation:

> But better than exhortation would be, in my view, a redefinition of abstinence as the pleasure one takes in another's desire, which would afford a way to appreciate the conflicts analysts inevitably undergo relative to patients' – and their own – desire.
>
> (Dimen, 2011, p. 75).

Dimen's essay presents a journey through the self's own entanglement in analysis as well as its profound embeddedness in subjectivity and the longing for a solution.

To understand relational thinking, we should now attempt a shift of perspective, sketching out a landscape which reflects a number of developments. One important node of thought is the turn to *two-person psychology*, created in the wake of Winnicott's dyadic view and explicitly taken up by Emmanuel Ghent. Winnicott developed the idea of transition, in this way assuming a beginning and end point to a journey. Both ends of transition can have an influence on each other. Ghent described this dualism in terms of an interplay between sadism and masochism (Winnicott, 1997; Ghent, 1990).

The analysts who turned to infant research recognized the importance of the encounter between parent and child and its effect on shaping interactions later in life. Researchers including Beebe and Lachmann, Sander, Stern, and the Boston Change Process Study Group have opened up unexpected perspectives on human development as an interactive process.

Together with the Boston Change Process Study Group, Daniel Stern investigated the [experience of the] present moment and the presence of non- and pre-verbal forms of representation, and the encounter between these forms (D.N. Stern, 2014; Boston Change Process Study Group, 1998). It was Beebe and Lachmann who recognized the significance of regulation, disruption, and repair in the process of development, while Sander highlighted the relevance of rhythmicity (Beebe & Lachmann, 2010; Sander, 2009).

Irwin Z. Hoffman and Merton Gill conducted research into what they termed the "analysis of transference", the subject of their book *Analysis of Transference* (Gill & Hoffman, 1982), in order to observe the development of the self towards a two-person psychology. Hoffmann's most important article within the relational community was "Therapeutic Passion in the Countertransference" (Hoffman, 2009), which further develops his ideas in the direction of two-person psychology. The concepts deployed by Hoffman represent a form of radical constructivism, and he draws on Gadamer's hermeneutic circle for his explanatory models (Gill & Hoffman, 1982; Hoffman, 2009).

For her part, Benjamin developed a concept of *complementarity* which begins from the idea of a relationship, fitting seamlessly together with two-person psychology. In this way, she explained how recognition factor can create a new connection, by means of a pendulum-like movement between attachment and the separation associated with it. For Benjamin, this negotiation of recognition takes place in a kind of thirdness: with this thought, she expands two-person psychology into a three-person psychology.

Another important representative of relational psychoanalysis is Donnel B. Stern, whose work focuses on formulating hermeneutic aspects and on the meaning of enactment. His work hones in above all on the micro-language of unformulated experiences awaiting discovery. From a starting point in what he terms unformulated experience (D.B. Stern, 2015b), he went on to develop his ideas by looking at the significance of non-verbal experience in the analytical process: we must manage inner acceptance of this experience, so as to arrive at an overall sense of meaningfulness (D.B. Stern, 2010, 2014, 2015b, 2019).

Another important influence came from social constructivism and the idea of the social regulation of a given society. In Europe, antipsychiatry developed a social viewpoint and connections were made between psychoanalysis and the ideas of Wilhelm Reich, with communist thought having an influence, as cultivated in student and left-wing circles (Burian, 1972). The ideas of the analyst and sociologist Erich Fromm had a great influence on relational thinking in American psychoanalysis (Fromm, 2005, 1996). Influences on deconstruction in society came from Louis Althusser's famous essay "Ideology and the ideological state apparatus", but also from Slavoj Žižek, who addressed the deconstruction of the subject (Althusser, 2010; Žižek, 2010). An important linking figure between relationalists and intersubjectivists is Emmanuel Lévinas, who abandoned the self-importance of the ego and developed a philosophy of ethics (Lévinas, 2012). Muriel Dimen's work subsequently attempted to merge psychological with political and social aspects. As an anthropologist, she was trained to acknowledge the cultural and social contexts of thought: her psychoanalytic reflection incorporated feminist thought constructs on the gender issue, addressing questions of disgust, sexuality, privacy, and publicity. Her Catholic background was of great importance for the conceptual construction of power, regulation, and the emergence of sexuality (Dimen, 2005, 2011, 2014; Dimen-Schein, 1977). In his work, Ken Corbett combines relational traditions in psychoanalysis with a form of gender deconstruction drawn from queer theory (Corbett, 2009a, b). In the climate of 1980s postmodernism, the pathologization of gender and sexual difference came under increasing criticism, helping to ground new modes of emergent thinking based on relationality, queerness, and antipsychiatry. Corbett draws on the ideas of Judith Butler, who sees queerness as a site of shared contestation which can never be fully owned (Butler, 1993). Queer psychoanalysis deconstructs gender, race, and norms and relates them to one another. How do we construct relationships and associated ideas of gender, race, and power in relational thinking? (Fanon, 1981). Psychoanalysis offers different groups of liberation movements a complex togetherness or rejection of the reactionary thinking of a white elite (Harris, 2012).

The emerging women's movement also had influence in this context, giving rise to feminist psychoanalysis, which led to the further investigation of role construction and its social effects. Relationality is significant in that it constructs roles which only unfold in the encounter (Rieken et al., 2011; Chodorow, 1979, 1992). The further development of feminist psychoanalysis goes beyond Freudian and object-based approaches to interrogate political perspectives on how roles and gender more broadly are constructed in society. There was also a link between the social construction of femininity and the pathologization of homosexuality, which served as a frame of reference for questioning social norms (Mitchell, 1981b; Dimen, 2014; Corbett, 2009b).

In the 1980s, queer theory emerged from these confluences, leading to a transdisciplinary entanglement with psychoanalysis (Hutfless & Zach, 2017; Butler, 1993; Hansbury, 2017). This way of thinking enabled a new approach to gender and race, allowing for an examination of their social locations and their mutual influence. Broader connections must be grasped in the form of relational thought. It took a long time for psychoanalysis to arrive at the deconstruction of heterosexual masculinity, whereas the deconstruction of femininity was in focus from the very beginning. Heterosexual normative masculinity can now also be seen in its restrictive and normative traumatizing function (Harris, 2017; Reis & Grossmark, 2009). This work also makes visible the effects of early separation on boys. By deconstructing masculinity, femininity can also be constructed differently in a relational sense; when shared formative influences can be recognized, new paths of knowledge can be taken. The rigidity of normative heterosexual masculinity is currently being dissolved, with its developmental significance viewed in a more dynamic way (Harris, 2004; Corbett, 2009b).

Social constructs are of a fundamental significance for relational psychoanalysts, because the family is present in all interactions at a macro level: this determines meanings in terms of representing the social categories which define our roles, and the political categories associated with them. There is a great overlap here with systemic thinking and thinking about the system from the intersubjective perspective.

These converging lines of development represent a great developmental enrichment for relational thinking. Many leading relationalists work in the fields of gender development and sexuality, examining how these are embedded in society. What influence does the family have in these issues of development, on a personal and social level? Which social forces affect individual and collective life? What influence has the last century had on all these developments, from the American culture of mourning which fed into the First World War, to the great waves of European emigration, to the paranoid era of McCarthyism, and, finally, the destruction of September 11, which further accumulated trauma? Psychoanalysis has not gone uninfluenced by these events; its theories must always be interpreted and understood from its social-cultural context (Harris, 2017).

These forms of re- and deconstructive thinking naturally lead to a questioning of the concept of self. In the book *Hope and Dread in Psychoanalysis*, Mitchell explored the concept of self by asking whether we have a multiple self or a solitary, singular self, and indeed the extent to which we have a false self (Mitchell, 1993). He writes:

> [W]e can get away from a search for pre-social or extra-social roots of the core or true self and focus on what it means at any particular moment to be experiencing and using oneself more or less authentically.
> (Mitchell, 1993, p. 150).

In relational thinking, authenticity as a question of identity means dealing with changing self-states and therefore, in a meta-psychological trajectory, leads to the idea of multiple self-states and the possible connections between dissociative processes. In this sense, identity and identification become visible as a dynamic, flowing process of varying intensity and meaning. Dissociative phenomena lead to a vertical split in relational thinking and thus to the presence of dissociative processes in the dyad. In some situations, splitting is not a horizontal process, but a vertical, dissociative one, in which shame-inducing states within the self must be kept at bay (Bromberg, 2003). Jody Messler Davies and Mary Gail Frawley addressed the effects of sexual abuse, in this way making fundamental contribution to the topic of dissociation, its influence on mental processes and the associated psychological structures.

> Dissociation is the process of severing connections between categories of mental events – between events that seem irreconcilably different, between the actual events and their affective and emotional significance, between actual events and the awareness of their cognitive significance, and finally, as in the case of severe trauma, between the actual occurrence of real events and their permanent, symbolic, verbal mental representation.
>
> (Davies & Frawley, 1994, p. 62).

At the end of his life, Mitchell returned to the work of Hans Loewald to explore the question of how the self emerges in the context of others. Mitchell's sudden early death meant he could not ultimately, as he wished, make greater use of Loewald's ideas to formulate metatheoretical ideas.

For Ghent, the emergence of the self begins in the transitional space where all of life's creativity is located (Ghent, 1990). Mitchell draws on Loewald's relational matrix, which he sees as the place of primal density and, as a former student of Heidegger, connects in this way to his teacher's ideas on being and time (Mitchell, 2003a). For Loewald, object states and their associated subjectivity emerge from a primal density: words take on life in the encounter, in the presence of others. They are the Thing of human subjectivity and object states: they *appear* in Heidegger's sense, by virtue of time, "everything has its time" (Heidegger, 2018, p. 359). Loewald tried to create a bridge between Heidegger and psychoanalysis. Both thinkers, Heidegger and Freud, take Jewish and Christian concepts of the world and soul as a frame of reference. Despite his involvement in National Socialist doctrines of power, Heidegger remained, via his students, very close to interpretation and to Husserl, his mentor in phenomenology. Freud encountered Christian, dichotomizing modes of thought in Freiberg in Moravia (Vitz, 1988). Loewald sees the key to our dyadic life as the balance of power between affective states and their linguistic representations (Harris, 2017). This space in which dyadic forces balanced out through a pendulum movement comes very close to Winnicott and Ghent's idea of transitional space.

Laplanche adopted the relational idea in searching for a general theory of sexual development based on seduction theory. The idea that we are seduced into human sexual development is already based on an idea of commonality. For Laplanche, seduction begins in our original situation, which he defines as follows: "The primal situation [*situation originaire*] is one in which a new born child, an infant in the etymological sense of the word (in-fans: speechless), is confronted with the adult world" (Laplanche, 1991, p. 89–90). For Laplanche, this confrontation is the encounter which generates the force by which identity is formed and sexuality is constituted. "The central figures in this evolution of relational thinking are all people who bridge disciplines" (Harris, 2017, p. 52).

Interdisciplinarity as such already includes the idea of relation, which is used to open up new forms of understanding. Another important advance in the relational perspective on development came from infant research, particularly the work of Sander, Beebe, Lachmann, Stern, and the Boston Change Process Study Group (Seligman, 2003; Burian, 1998). The findings of this research and clinical experience provide a new picture of development processes, with researchers into infanthood emphasizing the importance of shared learning for human development.

Another important influence on our conception of development and connectedness comes from neuroscience, which is also exploring the space of intersubjectivity in which our sense of self and of we-ness are manifested (Gallese, 2009; Iacoboni, 2009).

The development of relational psychoanalysis has been marked by the importance given to knowledge drawn from the clinical process, which has fed directly into debates on relational technique. Clinical observation has also led to very consequential debates with classical psychoanalysis. Mitchell and Greenberg point out that at the end of the day, it is clinical utility which gives meaning to any theory (Greenberg & Mitchell, 1983). Spezzano's contribution to this debate is the pointed article: "Listening and interpreting – how relational analysts kill time between disclosures and enactments" (Spezzano, 1998).

Antonino Ferro's idea of the bi-personal field represents a radical development of field theory: Ferro's account of child analysis uses this theory to construct his own relational ideas (Ferro, 2003). Important contributions to clinical practice made by Mitchell's inner circle have also come from Bromberg, Hoffman, Aron, Davies, Pizer, Bass, Spezzano, Slochower, and, more recently, Knoblauch, Ringström, Hansbury, and Pula (Harris, 2017; Hutfless & Zach, 2017).

Clinical research puts analysts and their subjectivity at the centre of considerations. Where is the interface which allows analysts' subjective ideas to flow into the treatment process, and where do the analysts' narcissistic desires begin, which can become abusive of patients? These questions have accompanied relational analysts from the beginning; they are now increasingly being put by students, which represents a shift in the power imbalance within the clinical environment. Ideas and theories about analysts' influence on events – through their presence within the setting – can generate new ideas about treatment. The concept of projective identification gave a great boost to the idea of reciprocal or mutual influence within communication (Steinberger, 2016). In the wake of the clinical question of shared influence, questions have arisen as to the "equality" of mutual influence. Is there an asymmetry in influence or are both partners equal within it, and what creates the difference between patient and analyst? Questions posed by relational thinkers have deconstructed the frameworks of classical analysis, leading these thinkers to question what psychoanalysis is all about: it is an anarchy, a democracy, or a set of rules? Aron advocates a flexible handling of reciprocity and the recognition of asymmetry in the treatment relationship (Aron, 2013). Hoffman describes this dichotomy as that which maintains both rules and spontaneity, an atmosphere of freedom, a playful approach to authenticity, and a way of bearing responsibility (Hoffman, 1998).

An exciting development in the clinical arena is the use of negotiation paradoxes as a way of thinking about effectiveness in therapy (Pizer, 1992; Bass, 2007; Slochower, 2011). "All these writers are crafting a model of clinical process in which dynamism is its permanent condition and impasse is a collapse in negotiation and the capacity for reflection and creativity" (Harris, 2017, p. 56).

One key aspect of clinical work is the therapist's own self-reflection. Through a relational perspective, the therapists are subject to closer examination and with it their actions in terms of boundary violations or masochistic behaviour in therapy. Therapists can only have a conscious and thus asymmetrical influence on the therapy situation through making changes themselves, but also by recognizing where they do not change (Harris, 2009; Harris & Sinsheimer, 2008; Slavin, 1997, 2010; Slavin & Rahmani, 2016; Corbett, 2014).

Recently, phenomena such as race, racism, and social classes have been brought into the focus of relational thinking. Neil Altman works on these issues in the South Bronx, where he focuses on patients at the margins of society (Altman, 2010). Melanie Suchet approaches the phenomenon of race through her own childhood story in the context of South African apartheid (Suchet, 2007; Dimen & Goldner, 2010). Using clinical examples drawn from her own patients, Lynne Layton deconstructs how social injustices, racial, and ethnic identities can lead to narcissistic wounds. She proposes a new way of defining identity through thought (Layton, 2006). Sue Grand examines the genocide of American indigenous peoples and the meaning of shame and guilt in relation to whiteness and race (Grand, 2018). Philip Cushman asks the extent to which relational psychoanalysis can offer political resistance (Cushman, 2015).

Lewis Aron and Karen Starr address the question of how psychoanalysis came to be defined differently to psychotherapy, and the significance of racism, homophobia, misogyny, and anti-Semitism in the creation of psychoanalysis and psychotherapy. The two authors regard the development of American psychoanalysis since the 1950s onwards as a dead end which ended in an approach based on the power, status, and prestige of white male doctors. They argue for a return to Freud's original humanistic view of therapy for the masses. They also perceive the separation and splitting-off of psychoanalysis from psychotherapy as a reflection of elitist male thinking, in which "nurturing" female attributes were attributed to psychotherapy, whereas "unveiling", for example, formed part of psychoanalysis (Aron & Starr, 2013).

More recent approaches deal with the generative transmission of trauma and its impact on interpersonal relationships between adults (Boulanger, 2002, 2014). Couple relationships have now also become more the focus of relational forms of treatment. Virginia Goldner addresses both elements in her couple analysis, examining both healing and painful-traumatizing processes within couples (Goldner, 2014). Philip A. Ringstrom has presented a concrete model for implementing relational thinking within couples therapy. The model advocates actualizing self-experience within intimate relationships and training one's capacity for recognition of the other, and emphasizes the uniqueness of every relationship (Ringstrom, 2014). In the context of war trauma and the uniqueness of transference experience in therapy, a link can be made to the descriptions of schizophrenia by early pioneers of psychoanalysis. Here the analyst's task is to face up the long-term challenge of the symbolic destruction of order and of time; in this way, the analyst can access and explore the area of death itself (Davoine & Gaudillière, 2016).

The significance of the body is brought into focus when the question of transgender people is addressed (Hansbury, 2005, 2011, 2017; Goldner, 2011; Corbett, 2009a; Critchfield & Pula, 2015). A link to the deconstruction of moral questions can be made via the influence on patients of a therapist coming out, as well the way our ideas of the body determine our attitudes to race, trauma, and class.

4 Critique

In this context, a point regularly raised by critics like Jon Mills is the inaccurate use of philosophical concepts by relational psychoanalysis. Mitchell put *relatedness* at the centre of his reflections, presenting it as an alternative to the widely-accepted drive model of classical psychoanalysis. Philosophy has been concerned with intersubjectivity for over two centuries and its formulations draw on richer knowledge than psychoanalytic thinkers of intersubjectivity. Developmental considerations point towards a dyadic systems theory that functions within intersubjectivity (Beebe & Lachmann, 2010). This moves away from the importance of the unconscious, hitherto the central scientific concept within psychoanalysis. "To privilege consciousness over unconsciousness to me appears to subordinate the value of psychoanalysis as an original contribution to understanding human experience" (Mills, 2018b, p. 324). This statement suggests that the intersubjective system must itself be organized as a separate entity, contingent on an autonomous process without individuality of thought, affect, or behaviour. For intersubjectivists, individuality is a fluid which evaporates at the moment of encounter, in other words the individual is subordinated to the intersubjective system.

The relational turn largely relies on a constructivist epistemology, which has been specifically elaborated by Irwin Hoffman (Hoffman, 1994). In this way, the ideas of social constructivism – present in many movements, from feminism to mathematics – have passed into the treatment rooms of relational psychoanalysts. The wide spectrum of movements making use of these ideas has meant there has as yet been no precise formulation of constructivism in a psychoanalytic context, let alone a formulation of a unified, comprehensible, and consistent body of psychoanalytic thought (Mills, 2018a, 2018b). It remains an open question as to whether a better-defined framework is needed for dialectical work in the field of intersubjectivity or whether the framework itself must always be viewed in dialectic terms, inevitably leading to a wide variety of interpretations and indeed misinterpretations. Is everything subjective and constructed, or do we need a framework in which this mode of thought can develop, giving it a frame of reference in which it can develop in a more incisive way?

> What appears is a pluralistic mosaic – perhaps even a cacophony – of different amalgamated postmodern hermeneutic traditions, derived from constructivism, critical theory, post-structuralism, feminist philosophy, sociology, linguistics, narrative literary criticism, deconstructionism, and – believe it or not – analytic philosophy that have shared visions and collective identifications, but with misaligned projects and competing agendas. For these reasons alone, I doubt we will ever see one coherent comparative-integrative contemporary psychoanalytic paradigm. … There is too much diversity, complexity, difference, particularity and plurality to warrant such an onerous undertaking.
>
> (Mills, 2018b, p. 326f.)

For Mills, no paradigm shift has occurred, since the difference within these modes of thought means no paradigm can be distilled and therefore no transformation can occur.

In addition to criticism on philosophical grounds, it is also possible to formulate a clinical counter-position to relational psychoanalysis. The rejection of drive theory – which contains the ideas of aggression and the death drive, including libido theory – leads to major clinical problems when it is replaced by motivation theory, which focuses on conflicts arising within the self as a result of largely unavoidable traumatic experiences with important caregivers in childhood (Kernberg, 2011b). With attachment theory and Margret Mahler's theory of dependency, desire, and self-assertion, the intrapsychic conflict situation fades into the background and is no longer regarded as an autonomous system within the child. Instead, understandings of conflict shift towards traumatic encounters with others. In an intersubjective world, the child relation is to an adult or to its own emotions, including anger, annoyance, envy, disgust, and openness to stimulus. Kernberg states that relational psychoanalysis has not managed to make connections with neuroscience or, in particular, with research into affects, and does not regard recent research into affects and its clinical evidentiary basis as amounting to a critique of Freud's drive theory. He completely denies the claim that Freud's psychoanalysis amounted to a one-person psychology, claiming that this is simply unfounded. Instead, he regards it as a three-person psychology, encompassing the interplay of transference, countertransference, and a reflective external observer (Kernberg, 2011b).

The analysis offered by relational thinkers has at times confused the "neutral" and "anonymous" positions. An analyst using a technique of neutrality is not without emotions, feelings, memories, or fantasies, but her intervention is made at a point where she has reconciled her feelings with her observations. In the constructivist view, transference is constructed jointly between patient and analyst. Kernberg would say the exploration of the patient's unconscious childhood history has gone missing here, since the primary focus has been put on interpersonal and interactional manifestations of the relationship between patient and therapist. He suggests that one danger which may result is that unconscious experiences will fade into the background and enactment within the situation will be rationalized. This would mean that elementary manifestations of sadomasochistic sexuality and aggression can no longer be examined; analysts would not be in a position to fully explore patients' pathological personality patterns and thus cannot grasp the patient's history in terms of a chronic and recurring character pathology.

Finally, Kernberg points out that relational psychoanalysis works with relatively healthy patients, suggesting it cannot treat patients with serious unconscious conflicts like severe borderline pathology or malignant narcissism (Kernberg, 2011b).

5 Conclusion

The importance of relational psychoanalysis and psychotherapy lies in pointing out the significance of attitude; the difficulty arises when ideas about technique come to be seen as a form of thought. This kind of questioning brings us back to natural science, with its ideas of correct and incorrect, although in Heisenberg's sense the attitude taken towards something changes when one observes, since observation – generating, in a technical sense – creates a different kind of attitude. Conflicts and contradictions will always arise here at the interface, which makes it highly significant for those involved; its influence requires prior clarification. Interpretative thought always draws boundaries, and thus always excludes something; this can only be relationally re-embedded if both discussants take the attitude that their thoughts are generated together, with both of them creators of what does and does not make up their reality. This kind of paradox is very difficult to grasp in scientific language. Recent writings by the generation of thinkers after Mitchell, in attempting to further develop relational psychoanalysis, have moved away from the importance of attitude and now attempt more explicit theorization.

Relational psychoanalysis developed within a liberal atmosphere, permeated by a "spirit of quite contradictory optimism towards the old structures" (Benjamin, 2004b). Jessica Benjamin raised the question of whether a democratic society needs democratic psychoanalysis (Benjamin, 2004b). Is the recognition of the fallibility of psychoanalysts also linked to a "new" kind of patient who also accepts and appreciates this, without the need to call analysts' competence into question? Freud addresses the healing power enjoyed by doctors, which is based on authority. Does a society in which authoritarian forms are cultivated in institutions and education systems require a different kind of therapist, which would avoid their devaluation? What kinds of therapists are needed by different social forms?

5 Empathy – Affect – Understanding

1 Constructing and Deconstructing Empathy

Empathy is increasingly the focus of scientific research and can also be regarded as the basis of our success. What is foregrounded today as a formula for evolutionary success is not so much Darwin's "struggle for existence" as cooperation, recognized as a basic evolutionary achievement (Nowak & Highfield, 2013). Fonagy and colleagues regard empathy in the overall context of their concept of mentalization: empathy means empathizing with others in order to find out something about them while experiencing an affective reaction towards them, for example pity or sympathy. They see empathizing with others as half the battle of mentalizing, affective reactions are what permit the concept of empathy, as adopted from Baron-Cohen, to go beyond the merely conceptual. They regard empathy as something external to the person, only having to do with the state of the other person. For Fonagy and his colleagues, psychotherapy in the sense meant by Rogers is inconceivable without empathy (Allen et al., 2011; Rogers, 1996; Baron-Cohen, 2011). This version of empathy remains embedded within Cartesian dualistic thinking. A person who claims authority can empathize with the other person, and in doing so knows more about the other person than the other person does themselves. From this perspective, empathy is a one-way street: it only requires a particular performance from the subject, the caregiver, the therapist, etc. (Mitchell, 2005). The ideas of Paul Ekman, who made the assumption that reading feelings was a learnable cognitive skill, also belong to this category. A popular book on seduction also invokes this form of empathy (Ekman, 2010, 2011; Savoy, 2009): it reads like a manual for psychopaths or the FBI and CIA, agencies which Ekman helped with advice and training. Empathy is also seen as an intuitive process, consisting of two components: emotion and cognition (Staemmler, 2009). The neuroscientific approach is a major current in the study of empathy: this approach begins from mirror neurons and ends by investigating how neuronal synchronization operates between people. The field's more recent findings clearly posit a connection and a rhythmic synchronization, a physical connection ("embodied-attuned") between two individuals (Brisch, 2011;

DOI: 10.4324/9781003483441-5

Rizzolatti et al., 2008; Gallese et al., 2007). As scientific studies into psychotherapy have shown, synchronization is based on non-verbal coordination between patient and therapist (Streeck, 2009; Ramseyer, 2008).

Empathy becomes empathy in the sense discussed here when it is raised from an implicit to an explicit level. Empathy must be articulated; this usually happens via language, whether external or internal dialogue, through the ability to express feelings, including the expressive use of metaphors.

A metaphor is not only used as a simple comparative concept that seems insightful to us; we also use our own physical experiences to make them understandable and visible as a physical experience to others. A metaphor that uses a physical expression explicitly calls for identification and thus for empathy. we use metaphors to share our physical experiences (Slavin & Rahmani, 2016).

Metaphors appear to be anchored in the body and in our brain and mind. After a quarter century of research in linguistics and cognitive science, Lakoff and Johnson (2003) concluded:

> Metaphor is a neural phenomenon. What we have referred to as metaphorical mappings appear to be realized physically as neural maps. They constitute the neural mechanisms that naturally, and inevitably, recruits sensorimotor inference for use in abstract thought. ... Because metaphorical maps are part of our brains, we will think and speak metaphorically whether we want to or not. Since the mechanism of metaphor is largely unconscious, we will think and speak metaphorically whether we know it or not. Further, since our brains are embodied, our metaphors will reflect our commonplace [bodily] experiences in the world.
>
> (Lakoff & Johnson, 2003, pp. 256–257)

Our physical experiences are the basis for enabling another person's empathy with us, i.e. to make them "capable of empathy".

Patient and therapist together construct an "empathic-therapeutic" speaking, which includes "music", i.e. the rhythmic interweaving of two subjects (Buchholz, 2014b; Steinberger, 2016). This coming together is supported by "local" projects. "Projects" are implicit answers to the always looming question: what are we doing here? What's going on here? Projects are not goals, and they must be negotiated between both partners. They serve the goals that are set together (Goffman, 1978; Alder et al., 2016).

The language we use for things that are invisible, like empathy, is always tied to metaphors, since there are only indirect conclusions outside our concrete world. Metaphors are based on an idea about something, and this in turn is embedded in theories on a meta-level. "Our observations and our attempts to understand depend on these theories, so that very different perspectives on what happens in the analytical situation can emerge from them" (Plenker, 2015, p. 41).

Theories fill our visible world with interpretive understanding. Why is a child crying? What is it going to do now? What does it want? Empathy arises in the consensus of the encounter; I allow myself to be touched by my counterpart, then I raise my state of being moved to an explicit level, clothing it in language, which in turn depends on the metaphors and ideas available to me for cognitive performance.

Empathy can be understood along the lines of narrative analysis, as a phenomenon which can be represented as a cyclical model. Its first step is resonance, followed by "expressed empathy", which finally becomes what is called "received" empathy, within the other person (Barrett-Lennard, 1981; Alder et al., 2016).

2 Empathy as a Controllable Phenomenon

From a causal-linear perspective, empathy means a capacity to understand and interpret the intentions of others (Weiste & Peräkylä, 2014, p. 3). However, this is too narrow a perspective to understand the phenomenon of empathy in its entirety. The process of empathy is not anchored in two individuals: instead, it unfolds as a joint creation between two or more people. In conversational analysis, a method devised by Harvey Sacks, this is referred to as "doing empathy" (Buchholz, 2014b, p. 14). On closer inspection, empathy emerges as a phenomenon that we can permit to happen, or switch off: "Empathy is not a 'thing' but a way of interacting, of putting oneself in another's emotional experience, a mode of apprehending another person's feelings" (Aragno, 2008, p. 714). What does this mode look like, which we carry within ourselves to be able to perceive another person's feelings? To understand empathy, we need to see what empathy does in interaction between two people, writes Aragno (2008). He suggests that the opposite of aggression is not love, but empathy (Aragno, 2014, p. 16).

For Buchholz (2014b, p. 8), empathy has negative as well as positive connotations: empathy is also a prerequisite for "evil". If we see empathy as a more complex phenomenon than aggression, then aggression can be included within the complex of empathy. Only once the capacity for empathy has been developed is it possible for it to be blocked off, to allow aggression or another's destruction, something quite different to the pathological form, a total lack of empathetic behaviour. This also provides an explanation for the violence of "ordinary men" in wartime situations (Browning, 1992). Switching off empathy is not a difficult thing to do, as Hannah Arendt already suggested in coining the term "banality of evil". However, we should differentiate between phenomena that can be considered empathy disorders and those which are subsumed under various models of perversion and severe personality disorders.

Barrett-Lennard breaks down the process of empathy into three phases: "Resonance, expressed empathy and received empathy" (Barrett-Lennard, 1981, pp. 91–100). This conception of resonance is comparable with what

Aragno describes in terms of the other's mode of perception. Resonance is the basic prerequisite for the interpersonal process in which empathy can arise. How do we find this sounding board within? And how does it change over the course of our development? Human beings are fundamentally blind creatures, who spend their entire lives in an exploratory attitude, trying to counteract their blindness. Empathy does not primarily mean understanding the other person in an interactive situation. Instead, it refers to the process of self-understanding, the expression of this to the other, which will in turn permit them to understand. This process involves a constant weighing up of one's inner reality, marking difference from the other person. This means I can only perceive another person through myself. Do the feelings I experience solely represent my inner reality as drawn from the past, shaped by my life story, or do my feelings "in the present moment" (D.N. Stern, 2014, p. 46f.) help me to understand and interpret the here and now? The question always hangs in the balance.

From a neuronal perspective, this is a question of limbic resonance between two interacting systems, as can be demonstrated using physiological parameters, for example, in terms of the mother-infant relationship (Ham & Tronick, 2009, pp. 619–632; O'Brien et al., 2013, pp. 183–197). The mirror neurons seem here to be of great importance, and are reported to have the ability to trigger empathic feelings: they form the neurological basis for internal resonance and are localized in the region of the insular cortex and in the limbic system (Rizzolatti et al., 2008, p. 174f.). A further brain region has been identified with regard to mother-child investigation; Iacoboni and his team localized this region of pre- and supplementary motor areas in their investigation of mothers with children (Iacoboni, 2009, p. 139).

3 First Case Discussion

What is this "inner sounding board" from a psychological perspective, and in what sense are we blind? Or is it precisely our inability to see which brings us to understand a particular situation? A report of a scene made by a student after patient observation will serve as a discussion example. The report was produced as part of a two-semester project to train and use a mentalizing attitude, by means of patient observation (Allen et al., 2011, p. 49f.). The aim of the project was and is to promote empathy, metacognition, inner mindfulness, and emotional intelligence as fundamental prerequisites for developing a reflective capacity for action (*reflexive Handlungskompetenz*) (Steinberger et al., 2013; Sieberth & Steinberger, 2013; Steinberger, 2019; Zeman, 2019; Hajek, 2019; Zöchling, 2019; Stiefmaier, 2019a). One of the main student exercises is the preparation of an observation report after a session. The reports are later discussed in a facilitated group session:

> When we were ushered into the room, at first only the analyst [JS: significantly, although the EEG is carried out by a medical technician,

> the student refers to them as an 'analyst' throughout the case discussion] spoke to him. She speaks firmly, but very quietly and calmly. Mr Ö. doesn't seem to respond at all. I then speak to Mr. Ö. and explain to him what happens now. That electrodes are attached to his head, that he has to stay sitting down, etc. The analyst tries to put a kind of helmet on him, which he expressly resists. Always wants to get up and doesn't understand when you explain that it's an important examination. ... When the analyst explained to me that he would have had to lie still for another twenty minutes, I could only stare dumbfounded.
>
> (Report 2011/OWS)

The scenes overlap. Is the student describing a situation with the patient? Or is there also a sense of the encounter with the therapist coming to the surface in the debriefing? Now who's losing their head? Where does the inner scene begin, and where does it become the outer scene? Or does the outer scene become the inner?

If we continue with the report, we come across the note: "This is when it would have dawned on anyone who knew Mr. Ö. longer than about a day that this would be an impossibility. ... None of the caregivers seem surprised, they all say it was clear it wouldn't work anyway'. This reflects the students' own group situation, who all agree that nothing will come of this "looking inside their own heads". The patient becomes very frightened, as the student observes, but there is also her own fear of dealing with psychological phenomena in a group session. The students had presumed the format would involve them being presented with knowledge, then asked questions about it.

The report ends with the sentences: "Mr Ö. is given medication by a doctor, PP [nurse] and me. This time intramuscular. The patient seems to cooperate with the method", the student observes. Here the student is clearly describing something she herself is familiar with. When writing the report, the scenes observed appear in your mind, along with the idea that the report will be presented to the group, including the moderator. Like the student preparing the report, the other students are also afraid that someone might look into their minds. The report refers to a sense of connection with the group and the moderator. Buchholz (2014b, p. 11) saw this shared resonance as a human need, just as strong as the satisfaction of an instinctual drive. Buchholz also reports the findings of Ham and Tronick, who suggest that when, during an enjoyable game, mothers suddenly refuse to react facially, gesturally, and verbally to the child's utterances, there is in fact increased internal synchronization of breathing rhythm, heart rate, and galvanic skin resistance (Ham & Tronick, 2009, pp. 619–632).

If one applies these findings to our group situation, we may assume that the physiological values for students and the moderator increase when students are confronted with unfamiliar tasks, such as reporting their observations and feelings. The moderator may now intervene to regulate the situation or deploy a more passive attitude, creating a disturbing situation for the students, to which their inner limbic system reacts. The group in this way can partake of a shared resonance, a paranoid attitude as an externally-directed solution, and unity in the face of resonance-denying attitudes from moderator, or the mother.

But why does this scene superimposition occur in the student's report? How does this come about? "None of the carers seem surprised, they all say it was clear it wouldn't work anyway". In therapeutic sessions we decide if we hold back in abstention or we move into rhythmic synchronization with the patient. Patients feel that they are well "handled" by "active" therapists. If we use the biopsychic insights of Edward Tronick, the therapist's response would not be regarded as resonance, but rather as down-regulation of possible emerging resonance, as indicated by similar readings in both individuals, for skin resistance, heart rate, respiratory sinus arrhythmia, and other biomarkers. When a mother and infant play together their biophysical values react autonomously, causing weak synchronization. If one or other of them interrupts or abandons the play, their physiological values react in correlated fashion. Here we can also understand why psychoanalysis speaks of "identification with the aggressor" (A. Freud, 1980, p. 293f.). If these symptoms, and the underlying fear, are not down-regulated, it can lead to rigidity, which in turn can only be solved by identifying the aggressor. "Mr Ö. is given medication by a doctor, PP [nurse] and me. This time intramuscular". Here the student is reporting her own identification with the aggressor, who is now penetrating the patient. She further reports: "The patient seems to be cooperative with this method". The patient seems to want penetration with a chemical substance, in this sense the penetration of a physical boundary. Here we also get a sense of how perpetrator and victim can be interwoven in a shared interactive process.

It is now easy to understand why borderline patients, for example, tend to create stressful situations for therapists in their sessions. The shared stressful situation brings about synchronization, in a process initiated by the patient. This is how the child senses the mother, whose caring attendance on the child cannot create autonomy in the child. The mother's feelings overwhelm the child and do not allow them to develop their own self. An alien self develops in the child (Bateman & Fonagy, 2006, p. 160f.).

The student continues: "Mr Ö doesn't seem to react at all. I then speak to Mr. Ö. and explain to him what happens now. That electrodes are attached to his head, that he has to stay sitting down, etc.". Here the internal synchronization of biophysical markers between student and patient begins. Both of them undergo a wave of stress; for the student, the situation is probably reconstructed psychologically around the encounter with the analyst, who shows no resonance in the group and only wants to look into brains with "lifeless electrodes". The student sees the patient's refusal as aggressive: "Always wants to get up and doesn't understand when you explain that it's an important examination". By accessing her fear of the analyst, the student has closed off the access she might have had to the patient's fear. Very hypothetically, we might speculate that, as a child, their fear was reflected with insufficient congruence, to use the term coined by Gergely and Watson (Fonagy et al., 2002, p. 188f.; Gergely & Watson, 1996, p. 159f.). This means that when we encounter a situation in which we are confronted with another person's emotion which resonates for us internally, we cannot develop a capacity for distancing, and thus the possibility of mentalization remains closed to us. In this way, the student can create an identification with the patient but have no opportunity to reflect on it, since she is only able to "melt into" her own feelings.

Compassion can be turned on or off and, as is expected in many professions, people can be trained in its use. But can it be switched off easily? Or does the current have to be split and differentiated? Can our resonance body be unplugged just like that, can we escape the crashing wave of stimuli?

4 Second Case Discussion

Let us examine at another student report, this time about a mother saying goodbye to her newborn child.

> Ms. X is very quiet, which I had noticed the first time we met, she was very distant and only gave me monosyllabic answers. I attributed this to Ms. X not knowing me yet and having more trust built up with the other carers. So I had mixed feelings when I was told to accompany her, but I thought it would be an opportunity to get to know her… Before this, her mother had come to visit, bringing a friend with her. Since her family had put pressure on her regarding foster parents, even during the pregnancy, so family visits are always stressful for Ms. X. On the way over we chat about things in general, Mrs. X seems very sad and close to tears. When we arrive at the ward, the mother and the friend are already there, although the original plan was for Ms. X to spend time alone with her daughter. So after a while I ask Ms. X if she wants to spend time alone with the child, she says yes and I ask the two women to step out. Then Ms. X takes the baby in her arms, it is sleeping, connected to a monitoring device The nurse says it's because she is restless and 'misses cuddles'. That makes sense, but the statement seems unnecessary, since the baby continues to sleep peacefully in her mother's arms, Mrs. X says it too, a couple of times. She caresses her daughter and is very affectionate. She begins to cry when we say goodbye. I try to comfort her, reassuring her that she has now made a decision which is a solution for her and the baby, and that it is a difficult situation, but help is there. On the way back, Ms. X asks me if I have children and when I say no, asks me if I am sad about it. On the ward, I bring Ms. X back to her room and ask if she still wants to talk. But she wants to be alone now, she knows she can come to the nurses' station if she wants to talk.

A student from the department is chosen to accompany patient X as she says goodbye to her child. This sentence shows how heavily the story can weigh, how it comes back to seeking a "guilty party". This scene is only manageable if there is a separation of emotion; or more precisely, a refusal of resonance mechanisms. Compassion is not obtained from resonance with the inner sounding board. Rather, it is something that is constructed cognitively: "I attributed this to Ms. X not knowing me yet and having more trust built up with the other carers".

The student sends the patient's mother and friend away, as if she wanted to equal things out. The student seems to need this, although she presents it as the patient's need: "After a while I ask Ms. X if she wants to spend time alone with the child, she says yes and I ask the two women to step out". The student and a nurse remain in the room, going against the intention of leaving the patient alone with the child. The student here experiences herself as absent from the scene she is observing. She cannot think for herself and is absent from her own thoughts, just as she makes the patient's mother and friend absent themselves from the scene.

The paediatric nurse states the obvious: "The nurse says it's because she is restless and 'misses cuddles'. That makes sense, but the statement seems unnecessary." This obvious thing is perceived by the student as a breach of a taboo. The fragile relationship between thought and action is made clearly visible by a taboo. When the taboo is spoken, it becomes subject to a reality which would not otherwise be brought to bear. A popular phrase suggests you can "jinx something" by talking about it. Language makes something reality, namely that the infant is missing its mother and the mother is missing her child. Since this also runs counter to morality, a rational explanation for the action must be found: "I try to comfort her, reassuring her that she has now made a decision which is a solution for her and the baby, and that it is a difficult situation, but help is there". The emphasis on a solution having been found indicates that once again there is a cognitive explanation, and no holding of the scene or the feelings associated with it. Help is brought in from outside, as something abstract.

There is another explanatory sequence at the beginning of the report: "I accompany Ms. X to the children's ward. ... She gave birth by caesarean section on Monday and decided the baby should go to foster parents because she already has a daughter, is mentally ill herself and the family environment is also problematic".

Here we find the medical reason why Ms. X cannot keep her child. To "save" the child, it has to be removed from its mother. By beginning in this way, the observation report makes its moral safeguarding clear: it serves as a justification for supporting the decision made. One aspect is of course the orders given to the student from further up the hierarchy. Another factor shown by the scene is the elimination of resonance towards Ms. X and her feelings when saying goodbye to her little daughter. The student is annoyed by the paediatric nurse who mentions cuddling between the infant and the mother. This shifts responsibility to Ms. X's mother and friend, who are also punished by being sent out of the room with the clear implication that Ms. X was pleased with their expulsion. This contradiction remains unquestioned.

The student copes with this situation by switching off her capacities for resonance and offering care at an abstract cognitive level. Her actions are embedded in a medical form of moral understanding. Another aspect concerns the moral requirement to do everything right, the way she has learned it. It is portrayed as necessary to act this way because it is best for Mrs. X and the baby. Ms. X is sick and lives in a "problematic family environment". Morality is not abolished here: rather the content is changed, which makes it possible to avoid inner conflict and avoid being frozen in inaction.

5 Third Case Discussion

The third report comes from a 40-year-old student who already had academic training, with experience in both psychotherapeutic and Buddhist settings (Report, 2017/OWS).

Patient Observation – Report 3:

> Mr L. has been admitted to the ward for several days. He is a thin, grey-haired, grey-skinned man. His eyes are set deep in their sockets and cast deep purple shadows.

She observes the patient very closely, pay attention to him and describes him in detail:

> All in all, he reminds me of 'The Grey Gentlemen' in Momo, but without the nicotine and the constant efforts to save time.

She develops a metaphor to describe the man's emotional state as it is expressed to her. Via the book or the film *Momo*, she has fastened down the feelings she experienced. But now her inner resonance generates an image of a memory, one touched by the patient: "Most of the time leans back on his chair with his arms crossed. At first he is very reserved and has little contact with the other patients. He seems withdrawn and distant. Over time he has made contact and opened up a little".

One can use the student's description to get a good mental image of the patient; she also describes a possible change in the man, as he "opens up". The four sentences begin with concrete observation, placing the scene in the cultural context of the ward. The particular culture here is the shared linguistic exchanges between patients, in which Mr. L. hardly participates; contact with others is a reference point to gauge just how little he actually has. Solitary behaviour and aloofness can only be observed in the presence of others. The third sentence uses the term "to open up" as a metaphor for observed change. The student must have an idea of loneliness in order to generate this observation, a sense of what it is like to be outside a group.

"Maybe he doesn't open up, but just retreats a few meters from his inner abyss and somehow penetrates through to the outside world, so we can hear him and communicate with him". With these lines the student introduces her own subjectivity into her thoughts, offering an alternative imagining of the possible psychological inner life of the patient. She attributes a complex experience of painful feelings to the patient, also describing loneliness, with its inner abysses and its world on the outside. She interprets this as an effort on his part, an action he makes to establish communication. These lines are full of inner resonance and emotion.

"I've been in the psychiatric ward at least long enough to realize that this man is plagued by depression". This sentence represents an internal counter-movement on the part of the student, moving things towards stability. It helps her to position herself in relation to her own resonance.

"Somehow he has this effect on me like a black hole, it pulls everything in, if you cross the event horizon there is no escape". The thought leads her back towards her own inner resonance. She uses very strong metaphorical images to describe the patient's condition.

"I've often noticed that I find it far more difficult to deal with black holes and depressives than with people in manic phases". The student's thinking is again formulated from an inner counter-movement and is clothed in medical nosology; she positions herself as someone better able to deal with manic phases in others people.

"I always think it's down to my latent depressive streak, that I have an eternal fear of ending up in that kind of state, one that seems never-ending". Here, the student's own resonant capacity is dressed up in language and in this way placed reflectively on a meta level. She is also able to relate it to her understanding of the patient, and the danger she perceives of being too much like this herself.

> Mr L. tells me he often came here with his friends as a child and there were many apartments in S. Plus there would be a train going around and how beautiful it all was. Mr. L. has a daughter who visits him sometimes but is very busy at work herself and a partner who apparently only keeps in touch via text message and email at the moment.

The internal positioning is now transposed externally, to real people. The student now begins to position herself as the listener in the real encounter, as opposed to the women who are not present. The patient's daughter has little time and his partner is not physically present at all. At that moment, the student forms part of the scene she describes afterwards. In her mind, relatedness takes place as a process.

> After a few days, that breaks off as well, and I notice that his eye sockets are getting even deeper and dark grey, in all its shades, is spreading across this person. Most of the time he gives answers to my hesitant

> questions, and I try to build him up somehow, encourage him, give him time, etc., but then sometimes I prefer to stay silent and just smile at him or sit with him.

The student is very close to the patient in her description. Their silence could be understood as "containment" in Bion's sense or as a recognition of the third party through surrender. Benjamin draws on Ghent's concept of surrender to make it clear that thirdness does not come about from holding onto things. Instead, it is determined or affected by the space around surrender (Benjamin, 2018; Ghent, 1990; Bion, 1992).

> [T]he Third is that to which we surrender, and thirdness is the intersubjective mental space that facilitates or results from surrender. ... the term surrender refers to a certain letting go of the self, and thus also implies the ability to take in the other's point of view or reality.
>
> (Benjamin, 2018, p. 23f.).

For Benjamin, surrender means the ability to take the other person's perspective, to begin from their reality. Anyone who can surrender and thereby recognize the reality of the other while not losing sight of their own independence is capable of connection. Benjamin also makes a very clear distinction between *surrender* and *submission*. Idealizing someone or giving in to avoid conflict is a way of submitting to the other person.

> He just says that unfortunately the carousel of thoughts almost never stops. After his day out, he comes back very tired and stressed, the outside world has overwhelmed him; he's afraid to return home: to leave the ward. Here at last he could finally sleep again, and he basically feels very comfortable in S., it's nice and quiet here.

When we bring the situation of the text's author into our thoughts and surrender to our thoughts, surrender starts to look like a surrender to the imagination. The tenderness inherent to the student's text begins with the ability to recall images within oneself. How does relatedness arise along with an ability to surrender?

"After a few weeks I happen to walk past the ward and see him still sitting on the terrace. I think to myself for a moment how bad it is, because when I was still there they actually wanted to release him". Here we might reflect on who has the need to be released, the patient or the student. For Benjamin, enduring or becoming aware of different needs forms the basis for the "moral third". The idea can be found in Loewald's idea of being able to design a future for the child or the other person in the parental role (Benjamin, 2018; Loewald, 1986).

Below is another student's observation report. These lines trigger completely different feelings in readers.

I observed a client in his apartment. The client is in a wheelchair, he is 56 years old. I was told beforehand that he is very sarcastic.

Observation: I arrived at the client's apartment and first of all greeted him; he had a special wheelchair. The client's medical history describes him as suffering from paranoid schizophrenia and ankylosing spondylitis. The client initially meets me in a quite friendly way. I tried to begin a conversation, but no matter what I ask, he always has a sarcastic answer. I asked him how he was feeling and he said: 'How am I supposed to feel, I can't even walk, ha'. Client had a very fixed look and kept rolling back and forth in the apartment, constantly[,] he seemed very driven to me. My colleagues and I were busy tidying up his apartment and I asked him if I could use a particular cloth to clean, and he said, 'I don't know if you can'. I ignored it because my colleague advised me not to react to his sarcasm, since he could turn aggressive. When I came to the kitchen, I was able to examine his refrigerator. It was a large metal refrigerator which had countless knife stab marks on it, and there was a sharp knife lying next to it. I had a feeling that I would rather put it to be washed up with the dishes. A little later my colleague asked the client if we should turn on the washing machine. From one second to the next, he became aggressive, started kicking doors and threatening us verbally, he said he would hit us with the washing machine if we asked that again. Then he was in the kitchen and I was quite happy that I had put the knife in the sink. Afterwards we said goodbye and the client calmed down a bit.

Conclusion: Mr. W. has great difficulty coming to terms with his illness; he is easily irritated and quickly comes to feel despair.

Here readers are affected by the violence described. None of the people described are given an identity or motivations for their actions. The student writes little about the fear and massive threat taking place in the scene. Both caregivers are stuck in endurance mode, pushing away the fear.

6 Summary

Empathy is presented to us here as a form of resonance with that which is moved within me, it is then put in context, placed along with personal memories, but also simultaneously separated from the person under observation, to whom a personal self is again attributed, but only as a hermeneutic hypothesis.

The Third, which arises in this situation, is one's own psychological self. My thoughts about my self now arise because I can imagine myself between, on the one hand, feeling moved by the resonance of mirror neurons, and on the other, one's own thoughts and fantasies, which can be ascribed to the other person. I become more and more clear, increasingly differentiated towards myself, depending on how strongly the third emerges within me. The creation of the third is a process; it reflects the relationship back to me.

For Benjamin, the third is the phenomenon of human relatedness (Benjamin, 2004a, 2018). She sees it as something similar to what Winnicott described as "transitional space" (Winnicott, 1989).

To be *touchable* (*Berührtheit*) means my thoughts about myself and my thoughts about the person or scene that I observe, which I can attribute to another as an I for that person. With every thought about the other person, more of my own self emerges; a cycle develops, in the sense of a hermeneutic circle, as described by Gadamer.

Can touchability be imagined as a resonance phenomenon? Some authors view resonance as a directed phenomenon: a passive, spatial state directed towards an active person. The next step would be to synchronize with this other person, producing shared resonance (Breyer & Pfänder, 2017). Ed Tronick refers to this as a "dyadic state of consciousness", divided into several parts, which underlies a structure, or forms one. As an infant researcher, he views the mother-infant dyad as creating a shared system of information relating to one another, which continually organizes itself into a more complex, coherent system (Tronick, 2007). Empathy does not develop through observation, as mirror neuron theory might seem to suggest, if we view it as a rigid dualistic system. Rather, empathy is a shared existential encounter which brings epistemological advantages. For children and for patients, what matters is less whether the caregiver or therapist does everything right, but rather how they do it and whether they enjoy the encounter. The observers are not a mirror reflecting something; it is of crucial importance for everyone involved to have been "correctly understood" (Schlicht, 2013). Understanding is only generated in a shared field of encounter in which knowledge and meaning develop. Verbality and non-verbality develop in relation to another, in having an idea of oneself and of the other: "It is more than just a question of epistemological understanding, and it is the social dimension of shared being" (Buchholz et al., 2017, p. 97). Empathy, as conceived by Gergely, is a phenomenon in which I am touched, but I always know: this is not me and yet it is me, and the other person is only an approximation of what I understand in terms of the feelings triggered by me.

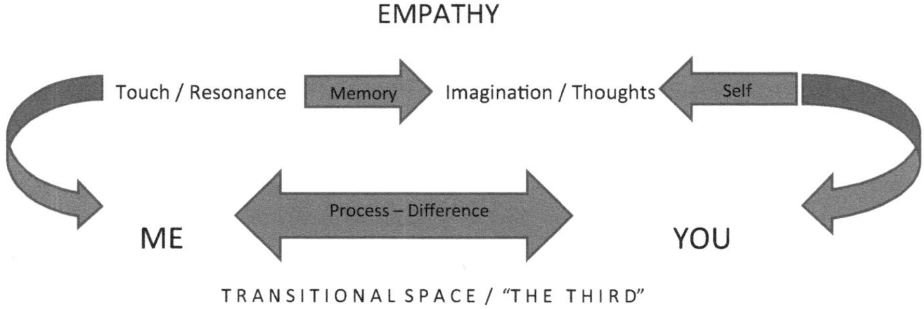

Figure 5.1 Transitional space – the third (own representation).

Benjamin calls these phenomena of remaining aware of oneself as the ability to endure tension, to be different from the other and thus perceive oneself and the other in an attuned manner. She uses the term *"moral third"* or *"the third in the one"*. This "third" is formed through a shared rhythm between mother and child as a principle of affective resonance (Benjamin, 2018). Resonance in the sense of an available resonant body will contribute to empathic understanding if I can grasp its vibrations on an epistemological level, based on all the social micro-encounters I have experienced and which have been anchored in me, through the experience of an empathic person on a resonant path.

Empathy results from encounter; it is a social phenomenon which we must describe and encounter in everyday life. We need this word to make ourselves understood. Academic research seems to have remained long indifferent to it; there is little consensus, it turns out, between the many ideas on how empathy is structured or represented. In operational terms, deconstructing the concept of empathy and dividing the research into different strands might well prove useful.

6 Affect-Reflective Competencies – Developments in Empathy Training – Evaluation

Inescapable romance, inescapable choice
Of dreams, disillusionment as the last illusion,
Reality as a thing seen by the mind,
Not that which is but that which is apprehended.
Wallace Stevens (Stevens & Stevens, 1990 *, p. 333)*

1 Relational, Intersubjective Mentalization Skills in Caregivers

During their training, students will have entered on a path where they are taught to act with implicit competence and confidence in their encounters with patients. In this time, they should develop psychological competence, gaining a sense of self-efficacy and the knowledge that they can use the possibility of attitude to influence situations and reshape scenes.

As part of the ART project, students set out towards professionalization, a course of development which takes them through different theoretical structures and the acquisition of practical "knowledge" about observation and small-group discussion, allowing them to develop greater confidence in their actions. These different levels of experience should help them develop a professional identity in caring for patients, allowing them to make more conscious and explicit use of their specific individual abilities.

Developing competency in professional encounters is connected with a large array of factors, involving various learning and knowledge processes; there will be different paths of knowledge, and these will emerge in both implicit and explicit ways.

Acquiring competence also means the ability to develop specific ideas about a given relationship in a post-reflective phase. Acquiring competence is deeply bound up with a capacity for personal development. Competence is reflected in the confidence with which someone can implicitly decide on a course of action based on their attitude, combining deconstruction and curiosity. The development of competence is closely connected to the educational relationship that students experience with the group moderator, supervisors, teachers, and their peer group.

DOI: 10.4324/9781003483441-6

In recent years, the focus on capacities and their definitions has received much attention across a variety of fields, especially in work-related fields: "Professional competence is a combination of knowledge, skills, experience and behaviour that is used in a specific context; based on this, concrete use can be determined, evaluated, confirmed and further developed" (Franke, 2001, p. 60). Being competent involves having access to a complex network of psychological functions. In interactive processes, a level of expertise develops which allow people to perceive themselves as competent across different fields of work.

We will make use of two conceptual structures here, laid out by Jutta Kahl-Popp and Herbert Will, incorporating definitions of competence for psychoanalysis.

At the centre of Kahl-Popp's considerations for defining competence is a three-part structure:

1 personal competence
2 relationship or relational competence
3 conceptual competence

Personal competence includes the ability to empathize, the capacity to endure the condition of not-knowing or not-understanding, and respecting one's own mistakes without feelings of guilt. For Kahl-Popp, personal competence also includes the ability to trust in the effectiveness of one's own actions and to regulate tensions arising from emotions and conflicts.

Relational competence, in Kahl-Popp's outline, includes the ability to take responsibility for a relationship, as well as high sensitivity towards communicative, intuitive actions and the ability to reflect on the relationship and apply the knowledge gained. This includes ascribing meaning to an encounter and developing a working alliance around it, and offering it as a setting for healing or growth.

For its part, conceptual competence includes developing theory, in the form of plausible explanations for a patient's condition, enabling progress in the encounter in a way that is helpful for the patient. This should also involve having a treatment or care concept that both the caregiver and patient can believe in, as well as the ability to offer reflections which involve different levels, including personality, working alliance, and care concepts, and to respect the mutual influence of these different factors.

From her contextualist point of view, Kahl-Popp thinks of competence as a resource-organizing construct. This organizational competence allows for a development process which provides the resources needed to solve problems (Kahl-Popp, 2007, p. 98f.). Competence is achieved by doing: it is integrated into a process that leads to a skilful application of both implicit and explicit knowledge (Kahl-Popp, 2009, 2011).

Kahl-Popp sees her conceptualization of competence as providing a more general structure for the skills needed in psychotherapy. A differentiated breakdown of competencies for different schools of therapy results from a contextualistic perspective.

Herbert Will's conceptualization draws on a tri-perspectival framework proposed by David Tuckett, involving a first perspective, *the participant-observational frame*, a second perspective, the *conceptual frame*, and a third, the *intervention frame*. Observing and perceiving are important skills which can then be formulated into a conceptual framework, as thoughts, which can be presented in words to the patient (Tuckett, 2017, 2011).

Will's attempt to describing basic skills for analysts grew out of an attempt to find a consensus in his institute on what their work consisted of. For students, this outline of basic skills to be developed should serve as a roadmap for their training.

The analysis presented below draws on the structure described by Tuckett and the ten points which Will developed from it, using them to attempt a definition of competency in the context of the ART project, including relational, intersubjective, and mentalizing competencies.

2 Ten Competencies

Inner attitude, observation, involvement

1 Competence in observation and passive presence based on a mentalizing attitude
2 Competence in working with one's own feelings (explicit/implicit)
3 Competence in interaction/relationality and intersubjectivity
4 Competence in building a helpful relationship (attachment)
5 Competence in dealing with affects (fear, anger, anger, desire) and conflicts
6 Competence in creating a development space and offering an identification model for mentalization

Frame

7 Competence in initiating and designing a mentalization development process
8 Competence in placing one's own and others' actions in a theoretical context (mentalization concept – psychological development: teleological actor, intentional actor, representational actor, self-representation)
9 Competence in self-reflection and in shifting between implicit and explicit attitudes – mentalizing attitude

Nursing

10 Competence in beneficial psychiatric and nursing interventions (congruent mirroring)

Inner Attitude, Observation, Involvement

These competences deal with the relationship with patients and colleagues, and with the scenes in which the caregiver finds themself.

1 Competence in observation and passive presence based on a mentalizing attitude: this covers the ability to observe the surrounding world, to see patients but also perceive what is invisible in them; to radiate a form of existence while observing, to keep one's own energy below the surrounding level, the better to observe one's own enactment; to open a space of understanding for the patient where the caregiver can move back and hold the scene in a containing mode; to hear patients' conscious linguistic expressions, but also to perceive other, non-linguistic forms of expression; to decide on an attitude to have in approaching patients, to exhibit openness, wanting nothing from them, not seeking to get them to do something; to develop questions for patients out of this calm attitude.
2 Competence in working with one's own feelings (explicit/implicit): the ability to understand patients through the perception of one's own emotions; to provide an affective sounding board and to turn the feelings generated in the scene into explicit understanding; to have empathy for patients, the ability to understand them through one's own resonant response; to have external and internal emotional space available and thus explore what is shared in the scene; to be open to one's own feelings so as to establish contact with oneself and patients; to get an idea of an I and a you, to experience each other together but separately at the same time; to endure loneliness so as to be able to acknowledge difference.
3 Competence in interaction/relationality and intersubjectivity: recognition of the shared reality in which relationships unfold; co-creation of the meaning of the encounter, such that reality develops in co-created scenes and can be experienced as such; applying concepts like enactment, role-adoption, staging, projection, projective identification, splitting, the third, etc. on a meta-level, with one's own and the patient's safety in mind; building relationships on a "recognitional" level; grasping interaction as a space of interrelatedness in which the subtleties of an encounter unfold; competence in engaging in role adoption and enactment; ability to express this experience and discuss it with patients.
4 Competence in building a helpful relationship (attachment): the ability to convey security to patients without making them too dependent; being friendly and supportive are the most important factors in building a secure relationship; the quality of a relationship measured by the authenticity of caregiver and patient; by being available, we enable patients to express feelings; we are able to get a sense of what patients need and use us for, and consider how we choose to respond; also relevant here is the ability to endure the process of building relationships

and thus have an idea of helplessness, the ability to offer an atmosphere of openness, warm-heartedness, and support; the ability to experience humour in an encounter.

5 Competence in dealing with affects (fear, anger, anger, desire) and conflicts: the ability to endure ambiguity, fuzziness, tension, and shame; the ground of enactment is what allows these feelings to arise in order to then have a shared idea of the conflict; the caregiver acting out also means enduring feelings of shame that may arise; shared endurance lays the groundwork for the assumption of shared responsibility in the encounter between caregiver and patient; also relevant here is the capacity to recognize and name contradictions and thus to effect confrontational or stressful interventions with patients; to have the courage to face the truth and to ask questions related to intimacy; to be capable of expressing feelings of anger, rage, fear, desire; the ability to confront issues like suicidal feelings, self-harm, the endangerment of others.

6 Competence in creating a development space and offering an identification model for mentalization: being aware of one's abilities and character, being able to respect and articulate the individual relationship spaces within the team. On a sensitive enough level, experiences with the patients are individual and never interchangeable. It is always crucial to return to a curious, unknowing attitude, to have a sense of your own weaknesses and entanglements, and be aware of the limitations of your own actions.

Frame

The frame is a reference for the caregiver, the space in which he or she moves; it thus also forms a frame of reference for perception and interpretation. The conceptual frame of reference is nourished by one's own reflection and by connecting theories about life and experience.

7 Competence in initiating and designing a mentalization development process: to initiate a development process and be able to represent it with hypotheses in care planning; the ability to develop and discuss concepts of nursing diagnostics; capacity to create a lively relationship with patients by expressing mentalizing questions; framework conditions should always be changeable and open to discussion, they should be profoundly linked to individual patient development, with planning processes supported by a positive vision of patient development; care planning should be supported by evaluable theories, which allows them to be viewed on a meta-level without sacrificing individuality; it is vital to ensure a constant connection between what the patient experiences and indications for care.

8 Competence in placing one's own and others' actions in a theoretical context (mentalization concept – psychological development – teleological actor, intentional actor, representational actor, self-

representation): use of theoretical concepts from infant and toddler observation, mentalization, etc.; the ability to develop intersubjectivity and relational psychotherapy through the here and now of encounter, ensuring one does not become ungrounded by the patient encounter, swept away in the flood of excitement; to use alternative concepts as a reference point for differentiated creation of one's own theories and hypotheses; experiences should be organized through thought and recapitulated with the help of concepts; also relevant is the ability to create ideas about a patient's behaviour and their conscious and unconscious intentions; the ability to maintain a common thread through the patient's treatment and care process; the ability to evaluate caregiving techniques used and develop them further in individualized care planning for patients; to gain an idea of one's own effectiveness in caregiving.

9 Competence in self-reflection and in shifting between implicit and explicit attitudes – mentalizing attitude: an openness to showing mistakes and developing an understanding of fallibility, developing this in the team; the ability to meet yourself and other colleagues with a mentalizing, self-reflective attitude; to be open to new situations and theories, the ability to think about other opinions; the ability to offer support to colleagues in emotionally complicated situations; to generate knowledge about patients in a constructive manner, recognizing the individual experience of situations within a common field of understanding; the ability to accept and discuss criticism in order to improve one's ability to give care; to have an idea of one's own weaknesses and strengths; the ability to open up a space for one's own vulnerability and communicate it; the ability to push ideas of right and wrong to one side; the ability to recognize excessive demands and the need for recovery phases, and to make this heard.

Nursing and Caregiving

Nursing, and caregiving, in a broader sense, develops by way of attitudes linked to these competencies. The quality of caregiving activity can only be understood and evaluated in its entirety as described. From reviewers' point of view, interventions occur on an implicit level and can only be presented in an understandable, imaginable form by means of a complex cognitive process.

10 Competence in beneficial psychiatric and nursing interventions (congruent mirroring): the person providing care should have an emotional and cognitive understanding of patients, colleagues, and institution-related phenomena. The key is an ability to clarify misunderstandings, to find possible connections on a psychological level, and to convey this in language the patient can understand; the ability to retain statements and use them to interrupt enactments.

- Caregivers mentalize when we can provide patients with a safe environment.
- Caregivers mentalize when they understand what patients are experiencing and feeling.
- Caregivers mentalize when they give patients words for their feelings.
- Caregivers convey a mentalizing attitude when patients can regain hope in the future.
- Caregivers mentalize when they try to understand patients' motivations.
- Caregivers mentalize when they deal with conflictual scenes with patients.
- Caregivers mentalize when they think about themselves and others in order to understand their actions on a psychological level.

Although Will, in contrast to Kahl-Popp, insists on a specific, psychoanalytic interpretation of the competencies he lists, as explained above, no specificity should be read into this.

Competencies must remain vague in their definitions regarding the development of skills and craft in human encounters, otherwise these lists would read like an instruction manual, and we would have moved from the terrain of art to science, losing all spontaneity and individuality, far from life and lived experience. Individuality and its competent communication are situated within an insecure, uncertain field, and strict competence directives would paralyze the whole thing. Instead, the articulation of competencies provides a framework in which discussions and attitudes can develop. Competency and the lack of competency intertwine in a continuum and form a necessary construct for our understanding of thought which polarizes and discloses.

The goal of ART is to promote and stimulate mentalization and to foster a relational attitude. This is a form of reflection, where a space for focusing on affects can now open up: in other words, the caregiver asks about the patient's feelings or their thoughts on other people's feelings. Personal competence means the caregiver can conduct forms of communication which are embedded in a "soft environment".

3 Developing Empathy Training

What development should students undergo during training? To trace out this path, we use the phase model of Rønnestad and Skovholt. Their research focus is the professional development of those in social professions, as viewed across their entire lifespan. Research into psychotherapy has placed increasing significance on the person of the therapist; their personality is the decisive factor influencing the therapeutic outcome.

> In sum, we define the real relationship as the personal relationship existing between two or more people as reflected in the degree to which each is genuine with the other, and perceives and experiences the other in ways that befit the other.
>
> (Gelso, 2009, p. 254f.)

The focus of the interpretation of encounters is on the authenticity of the relationship, and their capacity to change. Rønnestad and Skovholt drew on survey data developed by David Orlinsky, which included data from 11,000 psychotherapists (Orlinsky et al., 2005). In their model, they describe a transition from non-professional to professional helpers, dividing development stages into five phases, covering the entire working time. Students pass through the first two phases during training:

1 novice student phase
2 advanced student phase
3 novice professional phase
4 experienced professional phase
5 senior professional phase

Students who choose training in nursing and other forms of care work are already embedded in cultural and social environments – their families, their friends – and bring with them ideas about caring and providing assistance. They are deeply anchored in their own cultural understandings of themselves and of the world. The students are already lay helpers and want to undergo training to become skilled workers.

Many students come from different cultures; some have been socialized in large cities, others in villages. They come with different religious ideas, which are very important in terms of their conception of providing help: "There is no psychological experience that is not already constituted by the sociocultural contexts in which we find ourselves. Human beings can never stand outside their contexts" (Frie, 2015, p. 605). This context-based socialization is formed by our cultural environment and by associated historical understandings. We always remain part of our family history (Frie, 2017).

Here we will discuss just a few cultural differences, so as to highlight the importance of these different modes of socialization. In a training context, the western urban world provides ideas about models of illness and psychological functioning. These models of illness very much assume an individual who is in need of help, or who defines themselves as sick. Illness and healing are seen as a problem for the individual, as taking place only within individuals. However, these treatment concepts are only shared by around one third of humanity; in most cultures, illnesses are regarded as a collective phenomenon. Cultures also define phenomena differently: they may locate them in a system of illness or view them as a moral or religious problem (Alsass, 2003).

These cultural differences result in a diversity of suffering, a diversity of definitions of suffering, and even a diversity of what a culture can put into language and thus make explicit. Culture and its definitions are also subject to the particular historical context. Our students bring with them a socialization specific to the time they grew up, an important "culture" that flows into the training situation:

> Each era has a predominant configuration of the self, a particular foundational set of beliefs of what it means to be human. Each particular configuration of the self brings with it characteristic illnesses, local healers and local healing technologies.
>
> (Cushmann, 1995, p. 3)

Every culture produces its own idea of healing. Illness and healing are subject to shared common sense in a given society. This "folk psychology" is so deeply embedded in the individual that our students sometimes react with great surprise if they are told that they should, for example, learn to observe: prior to this, they have taken this for granted as part of their skill repertoire. Listening and speaking come to be seen as a "naturally" existing gift:

> We do not often question the assumptions of many of its theories, such as the underlying ideology of self-contained individualism or the evaluation of 'inner feelings' or the unquestioned assumption that health is produced by experiencing and expressing these feelings.
>
> (Cushmann, 1995, p. 18).

Deconstructing their actions is often a very unusual experience for students; formulating questions which challenge their ideas about the world is scary. At the beginning they hold on very strongly to their own ideas about helping, to their cultural concepts, relying on "gut feeling": the feeling that tells them, as it were, what they should say or what will be helpful in the encounter. They don't need to learn empathy, they think: they all already feel empathetic. They often also question the concept of undergoing training in order to understand other people.

The conceptions of training offered here, which contain ideas of illness, healing, and modes of treatment, are deeply embedded in a socio-cultural idea of individualism. Individualization is an inevitable development process that is necessary in order to be able to use the learning material offered. There is a large cultural interface between the individual and the community, as the learning concepts and the associated skills are associated with concepts of individualization, rather than large or small groups, or forms of family association. In other conceptual worlds, concepts of identity and illness develop from a group understanding. Vamik Volkan, for example, speaks of "tent identity" (Volkan, 1997, 2003).

Do we need a new form of psychological understanding of development, ideas of self, etc., which would give explicit understanding to these various cultural differences? Are our generalizations less universal than we would like them to be? Manfred Stattler highlights some very elementary differences in psychological experience between rural and urban cultures and uses the example of supervision and coaching training to point out deficits in our current training curricula (Stattler, 2017, 2018).

The *zeitgeist* exerts great influence on ideas about healing. Most people-facing professions are subject to the given paradigm of scientific and medical understanding. Predictability and control are currently the dominant action concepts.

One question that should be raised is the relevance of gender roles in the training and professional situation. Relationship professions like nursing are usually connoted, in social terms, as female professions. To what extent do gender constructs influence ideas about careers and how people learn their way into them? What influence do gender and role stereotypes have on our understanding of empathy and how it can be learned?

We will first turn to the first two phases (the *novice student* phase and the *advanced student* phase), which make up the training period and describe possible development steps. These two phases comprise ART's six-semester training program.

3.1 Novice Student Phase

We define the novice phase in nursing training as the moment when students begin their first internship. Beginning the course, taking on a first internship, and working with patients all make for an exciting and demanding phase for students. They have received a lot of learning information in advance and are equipped with knowledge from their first specialist literature. They now have conceptual specialist knowledge to help them find their way around their internship site. In this phase, students tend to stick very closely to skills they have learned, applying them according to rule. Most students feel insecure and anxious during this phase, faced with their first internship. Very often questions arise like: Am I cut out for this kind of work? Have I made the right choice of career? Feelings of professional self-doubt and insecurity are common. This is an important developmental step for most students, which indicates that they are recognizing complex challenges of caring for other people. These doubts are also an important step in maintaining control of divergent feelings when meeting people. In the first internships, the pressure to perform and the need to carry out unfamiliar tasks create fear and uncertainty. At this stage it is very important to have success in meeting people and develop a feeling of effectiveness, which will help keep the tensions of uncertainty at bay. A committed attitude and positive expectations towards the first internship can compensate for a lack of experience and have positive effects on patients. Rapid, overwhelming fatigue can present another real challenge at this stage, when many unfamiliar things must be processed rapidly. Students expend a lot of energy practicing "correct" care and applying the methods they have been taught and shown. Demonstration and imitation are important learning elements in this phase. During the internship, students look for experienced careworkers who can look over their shoulders and also serve as role models. These more senior careworkers try to reduce the complexity of tasks and make greater use of techniques.

Knowledge is generated from a wide variety of sources including formal lessons, books, databases, trainers, internship instructors, colleagues, patients, personal experience, and cultural influence; all of these have an influence on decisions made by beginners in carework. The students experience this time as *overwhelming*, feeling as if they have been plunged into water and are now at the mercy of currents.

Imitation is the preferred learning tool. The students want to be like the teachers and colleagues they admire: they want to emulate them, although this can run the risk of setting unrealistic goals, which can in turn lead to fear. An important development step is the distinction between students imitating care in the sense of role play or if they identify with their teachers and internalize what they have seen. Later, this internalization dissolves as the students can allow themselves a feeling of competition, while professors can allow themselves to feel a loss of competence, using this attitude to convey to students that they will surpass their professors and further develop the nursing profession. In this phase, when it comes to basic knowledge, professors are often very pragmatically oriented; they can inhibit students in the short term, but it provides a good frame of reference for creativity later on, when it will make it possible to deconstruct basic knowledge.

In nursing and other forms of carework there is still little tradition of stepping out from the crowd, establishing independent scientific work, in this way making oneself available as a figure of identification. This makes it difficult for students to find role models outside of ongoing encounters and teaching contacts.

The basis for improving professional competence must be curiosity and an openness to experience, fed by an interest in knowledge and a willingness to learn. The desire for simplification can be an obstacle to development; in this phase, there is a very great desire for rules and instructions promising repeatability. Development is also reflected in the willingness to recognize the complexity of professional work and increasingly bear the tension of not-knowing. But this tension also fuels curiosity and in this way also professional growth. Developing students are more active in handling tasks, more inquisitive and explorative. Students who want to manage their inner chaos and fears seek security via structure and repeatability, exposing themselves to the risk of stagnation.

Internship managers and supervisors play an important role in providing encouragement and criticism. In this phase, students are very open to praise and positive evaluations of their work; indigestible criticism can lead some to entirely reconceive their work and even to change careers. Positive evaluation in this beginner phase is something very elementary, which will be remembered throughout an entire working life. Feedback is particularly helpful in the first year of training, as well as teachers, trainers, and supervisors opening up spaces for reflection. In the second year, patients are viewed as the most important learning resource, with educators now in second place.

The social and cultural environment determines the content of learning. Well-known training centres are committed to contemporary questions, including social challenges, these days dominated by issues of cultural difference, immigration, trauma, consequences of war, linguistic diversity, the future, gender, etc.

Peers are an important regulatory mechanism at this developmental phase. Most people feel very understood by their classmates: they feel on a more equal footing and can share similar experiences. Feedback from peers is usually very supportive, rarely critical. Some peer group members are greatly admired, additionally serving as identification figures. In conversation with colleagues, sensitive topics are discussed which are not shared with anyone else.

The family of origin is still a crucial support element in this phase. The student's newly acquired psychological knowledge flows into the encounter with their own family, allowing new understandings within the family unit. Given the emphasis put by ART 1 on self-experience, the personal development process is strongly internalized and primarily introspective. This novice phase sees an intense process of psychologization, which comes with generation of meaning and psychological experience. A phase of questioning the notions that prompted one's worldview and career choice also begins, and the student usually also asks questions about the future. These questions usually go unanswered; their meaning lies in how they open up a psychological space. Many findings in this training phase are not transferred to work with patients, rather they are important for understanding their own lives. Theoretical concepts are filled up with personal experiences, or else discarded. The students are very busy with themselves and in reshaping their experience.

The search for a professional role as one understands it is in the forefront of students' minds; concepts are criticized and condemned, helplessness in caring for patients dominates the field. It is important to offer emotional support to every single student here. Dropping out from training is most likely to occur in this phase of development. Feeling isolated and lonely in your search for a role often leads to the breaking-off of training.

> By using a few ideas from theory, students can transform the unmanageable complexity of trying to understand the client's life into a comprehensible simplicity of concrete and specific instructions for how to act.
>
> (Rønnestad & Skovholt, 2013, p. 65).

The students gain security through the teachers' acting as personal role models, as well as theories which can reduce complexity. At the same time, there must be tolerance for complexity in caregiving and carework.

Rønnestad and Skovholt use their research data to divide student attitudes to theory into four distinct styles:

> 1. Laissez faire refers to an attitude of not valuing theory or not being invested in any conceptual system. For the few students with this attitude to theory, previously held notions of common sense coexist with a variety of ideas from theory/research, clients, supervisors, peers, and one's personal life. Some of the students in our study claim that experience is the primary knowledge base (practice-based knowledge). Typically, these students seem not to be highly reflective on the epistemological base of their practice, and we may hypothesize that these students may typically not be strong in tasks that require high cognitive complexity to be completed successfully.
> 2. The student with the one-dominant 'open' attitude to theory, which was the one most frequently endorsed, has given priority to learning one conceptual system, but has maintained an openness to other systems.
> 3. The student with the 'true believer' orientation has focused intensively on learning one method and actively rejects other viewpoints. As was hypothesized for the laissez-faire therapists, the 'true believer' may also not be strong in tasks requiring high cognitive complexity.
> 4. The student we described as having the multiple attachment attitude to theory is typically a serious student with many ideas, but one who gives no priority to any one system.
>
> (Rønnestad & Skovholt, 2013, p. 68f.)

Training experiences show that students who take a very loose stance on theories, holding practice to be the only means of conveying knowledge, run the risk of limiting their potential development. Another risk is that of coming to a standstill in development, as seen in the emergence of students who identify as "true believers". Students with an open mind, coupled with a certain scepticism, and students with many ideas and relationship experiences show good development prospects (Rønnestad & Skovholt, 2013).

Meaningfulness in the role as a nurse or careworker is experienced through a perception of one's own effectiveness, with much depending on patient satisfaction and development. Job satisfaction is linked to patient satisfaction. Chronic illnesses or difficult personality disorders, on the other hand, are experienced as very stressful and demotivating. Experiences of violence by patients can often lead to the termination of training during this phase. Feedback, in particular resource-oriented feedback, is very important in this development phase, helping to give students security.

The developmental task in this phase is completed when students have achieved the established criteria for conceptual knowledge, when they have fulfilled procedural skills and found a way to deal with emotional challenges. They can make dynamic decisions between openness and isolation, managing this in a conscious way.

3.2 Advanced Student Phase

We will here use this phase as an explanatory model for the second and third years of training, in which ART II and ART III are delivered, including practical support. Five development steps are defined here, which students must master:

- to understand the theories taught in ART II and have an interest in creating your own image of humanity
- to master procedural competence, i.e. sufficient mastery of skills and being able to demonstrate them
- greater openness to seeing information and theories on a meta-level
- the ability to let go of unrealistic images around care and counselling
- coping with your own confusion and uncertainty with regard to the increasingly complex subject matter in ART II

The first two steps require adequate knowledge and skills to be present, as well as a recognition of what one doesn't know, and a willingness to continue training accordingly. This recognition of necessary knowledge also means recognizing the need for knowledge to be relevant and going about acquiring this specific knowledge. Students show great enthusiasm in their actions but are also often afraid to work independently and like to get reassurance about their actions from superiors, teachers, and internship instructors. Many students not only want to do everything "right", but to do it to a particular level of perfection. Tension within a person increases because the intention to do everything correctly can lead to rigidity, prompting them to act cautiously, with tension, and not very creatively. There are still few "playful" moments and little humour in the encounter with patients; students feel very monitored in this phase. There is a feeling of uncertainty, coupled with a process of letting go, the realization that there is a long way to go. Most people do not feel very competent at this stage of training. Feedback from outside is very important in one's own assessment as to which competencies are necessary to actually attain an authentic role in a professional context.

4 Influences on Student Development

The ART-II project is a major challenge for students in this phase of development. They have only begun to build a fragile, rigid world of experience for themselves, to know and follow rules, and are now having their idea of work roles deconstructed, via tasks of observation. Once again they must now digest and contain the tension of uncertainty within themselves.

In this phase of development, experiences with practitioners, other student's levels of qualification and the experiences of beginners in the field are used to create a frame of reference for action. In this interaction, students gain experience with themselves and others; these are evaluated through feedback and behaviour can be modified accordingly. Through positive feedback, students gain confidence in their actions. Methods and techniques which seem to work are reinforced by positive feedback.

Later, model-based learning takes a back seat and students increasingly come to interrogate theories. They have learned to grasp situations in a more differentiated manner and thus to apply methods more precisely. They no longer have to believe everything they are told by experienced colleagues; rather, they have collected their own experiential reference points and thus can position themselves differently in relation to work suggestions. Students now also trigger fear in experienced colleagues, who no longer show things to them as readily. The desire to observe interactions with patients is no longer satisfied to the same degree; they are increasingly involved in the scene in the sense of working together and are thus now held more responsible for the result. Students can now evaluate colleagues' performance more critically. They have clear ideas about "wrong" and "right", in terms of care and advice, judging other approaches as not being up-to-date. Their self-image is still fragile, based on an idealization of "perfect" skills.

ART II now increasingly puts students' personalities at the centre of dealings with patients. Students experience themselves as the source of learning and significance in developing professional skills and attitudes. The more their own character traits, injuries, and influences come to be at the focus of their actions, the more role models and the desire to imitate can take a back seat. Getting involved in the encounter with patients means deconstructing the training lesson itself. The individuality of caregiver and patient becomes clearer. There is tension between certainty and uncertainty now, between the radical specificity of experience and behaviour in interaction; however, loneliness now also appears; the student is now having to make the ultimate decision in the "moment of now". Some students treat themselves to self-awareness sessions during this phase of training, as the desire to find out more about themselves becomes stronger.

ART III wins great influence over the behaviour of the students; there is a transition from uncertainty – ultimately caused by deconstruction – to a self-motivated certainty of personal development. Students appear more confident in teams and can increasingly bring in their perspective in attempts to understand patients.

Some students cannot follow this developmental step, remaining tied to clear technical instructions. For them, the psychological world does not unfold as a world of understanding and reflection; they remain in a constructivist world and only "believe" what they see. They find it difficult to attribute psychologically differentiated motivations to patients and colleagues. They react with fear in the group in ART II and ART III, and view mentalizing about scenes as an invention and a presumption: everything can be completely different, only the spoken word and its meaning are relevant. They also find it difficult to accept that the group leadership is fallible and subjective in assessing situations. This disappointment with superiors, while simultaneously respecting the competency of experienced practitioners, creates a tension that not all students in the ART project are capable of managing.

The students experience instability in their feelings: they fluctuate between feelings of certainty, thanks to their growing expertise, and feelings of failure and incompetence. They can also drag their educators into these fluctuations, as they oscillate between "positively-toned dependency to disappointment and anger, a shift that can be quite uncomfortable to both parties" (Loganbill et al., 1982, p. 18).

Most students increasingly contribute their feelings to the small group and assess the group leader's reactions towards the authenticity and practicability of the image of humanity they convey. During this phase of training, many feel very open to new things, but also very vulnerable when it comes to criticism. For the group leader, there is a balancing act between students' desire for them to be open, while at the same time feeling vulnerable and sometimes reacting intensely to criticism.

However, they become increasingly independent of patients' statements and can now make different assessments of interpretation. Students' focus is increasingly on ideas of enactment and its significance. Patients' reactions are an important factor in their self-image and their resulting development.

Peers are still very important in this phase of training; working together gives a great feeling of security and of being understood. A lot of "material" which has been experienced or gained is still shared with peers but withheld from superiors. But students are now also beginning to look after beginners, finding this very enriching for their own work.

How students react to scientific literature is determined by problems experienced in internships, and usually there is a desire for quick solutions to problems determined by nosology. The students would like to have rules for schizophrenia, depression, borderline, etc. and in this way put limits to their uncertainty. On the other hand, common sense reactions are also questioned, as is any suggestion that gut feeling can be a basic tool for empathetic reaction. The complexity of professional empathy means students are beginning to recognize the difference between this and sympathetic, friendly reactions to patient needs; ideas of professionalism are becoming more and more influential within the students' decision-making framework. Phrases from care planning, such as having "a relieving" conversation or offering "a shoulder to cry on", are questioned. Students begin to have a clearer picture of their professional role. Their earlier formulations about motivations for beginning training now seem superficial to them; concepts of helping or wanting to help are become more differentiated. They ask themselves questions like: is there more to helping than these concepts, and if so, what might that be? They become more and more curious, but also react with greater unsettledness to the psychological phenomena surrounding them. The psychological dynamics which exert an influence throughout life are becoming increasingly clear to them, in all their complexity; providing help is seen as more difficult than they initially assumed. Conversations which require more than empathetic listening – talking about suicidal fantasies, addiction problems, psychotic experiences, panic attacks, etc. – can quickly give rise to uncertainty. This phase is a very delicate balancing act between "holding" and containing patients, while not being overwhelmed by your own fears.

Students attempt to master complexity and keep their professional role manageable in the face of their increasing specialist knowledge. But they are also deeply involved in the dynamics of the training institution; teachers are working on many development topics. These teachers are admired or rejected by students, although it is less about realistic assessments of their ability than ascribing particular positions to them. Other questions also arise, including where the students would like to work in the future and which fields of work are exciting now. Deconstructing their ideas about their profession, students are often disappointed and unsettled, but they can use this openness to look for new paths and act in more experimental ways.

Patients are now experienced more individually, techniques are no longer seen as absolutes, and are pushed into the background. The search for a solution is more focused on the patient's individuality. Some students adhere to clear clinical diagnostic guidelines in order to reduce anxiety by holding to clearly structured tasks. Students still oscillate between individual solutions for the patients and the structured application of manuals, which allow patients to fade once more into the background. The notion of being able to help everyone is still very strong and chronic illnesses are perceived as very stressful, while helplessness in the face of dying patients is experienced as traumatic.

Assignments are carried out with great seriousness, students are not very playful and their behaviour is not very authentic. Ideas about doing everything right and being perfect are now in the foreground.

Students go through a process of becoming more involved in the encounter with patients, who now gain significance as a person, rather than an object for a particular technique. This experience strengthens students' self-confidence, allowing them to endure the experience of being unable to help. Students no longer outsource their feelings of helplessness to other professional groups to the same degree, no longer referring patients as often to psychotherapists or doctors, for example. Their more developed attitude allows them to contribute more to the overall atmosphere within the work area. They begin to radiate help out to the team, making help available to the whole group in a context of containment.

Students get a clearer sense of what is important and unimportant, allowing them to manage their resources better. They also permit themselves not to remember everything and rely more on implicit knowledge.

By now, the importance of praise from superiors is giving way to a desire for recognition and collegial, equal exchange. Fluctuations between feelings of competency and incompetency are still very large, and there is still much comparison with one's peers, in order to regulate one's state of mind and as a general reference point.

A long process begins – years long – in which students increasingly experience implicit feelings about their importance and effectiveness in encounters with patients and are thus now less dependent on external feedback. Their experience lends them a new sense of freedom, made up of self-efficacy and decision-making capacity. The students now realize that giving up control can help reduce fear, rather than the opposite.

A new phase of development now begins for students, where they identify more closely with their professional role and their working world, breaking their dependence on the training institution and their peers, while also withstanding the disillusionment which comes in the early years of their careers. They begin to follow paths encompassing their own definition of the work role.

Rønnestad and Skovholt describe three characteristics by which they define professional practitioners:

1. That the person has acquired highly differentiated and scientifically-based conceptual frameworks that are necessary in order to understand what causes human suffering and concerns.
2. That the person has an integrated competence in using themselves as instruments, which also includes the application of a wide range of established therapeutic procedures for helping another person.
3. That the person has sufficient background knowledge in the natural, social, and humanistic sciences that is necessary for flexible and ethical assistance to be provided; assistance that is contextualized and adapted to the needs of the individual client.

(Rønnestad & Skovholt, 2013, p. 47f.)

These descriptions of the novice and advanced students describe our experiences with students very well and correspond to development steps we have also taken.

5 Evaluation

5.1 Evaluation of Practice Locations

The evaluation of practice locations is the overall responsibility of training institute management. At most internship sites, an internship instructor will take day-to-day responsibility for training, support, and assessment. When examining students, management at the internship site is usually asked to carry out the assessment. For the most part, ART II and ART III leadership is not in contact with internship locations, although urgent questions will be answered by telephone. Inquiries and concerns raised by the internship site are handled by a person with no group leadership role in the project.

5.2 Evaluation of Teaching

Our evaluation of teaching is based on four building blocks (1) self-evaluation; (2) "convival" survey instruments; (3) dialogue-driven evaluation and constructivist evaluation; and (4) mentalization-promoting intersubjective evaluation.

Quality assurance is reflected in a form of knowledge combining the evaluation itself and the facts gleaned from it, which is used to develop teaching and thus have exert improvement on all parties. We prefer an integrative model of self-evaluation, based on the findings of the Fourth Generation Evaluation, safeguarded by the rules of the Joint Committee on Standards for Educational Evaluation (Guba & Lincoln, 1989; Yarbrough et al., 2011; Riegler, 2012; University of Applied Sciences Northwestern Switzerland, undated).

Dialogue-driven evaluation is based on constructivist epistemology. It assumes that knowledge is based on individual interpretation. Each interpretation is therefore individually and subjectively determined and cannot be understood by using categories of "right" and "wrong". The use of "dialogical evaluation" presupposes a basic mentalizing attitude which assumes the counterpart's subjectivity as a form of knowledge (Beywl et al., 2004; Bateman & Fonagy, 2019a; Fonagy et al., 2002).

5.2 Self-Evaluation

Self-evaluation not only enables the implementation of control, but also timely and flexible reactions to learning-relevant topics and thus rapid implementation. This is not thus an imposed regulation from outside, but rather a development rooted in the process itself. As a result of this interconnectedness, evaluation is not seen as a mode of control or an instrument imposed externally: it forms part teaching, continually feeding back into the development processes of individuals, the group as a whole, and the institution (Hattie, 2009; Stephenson, 2014). Through self-evaluation, teachers and learners undergo a shared cognitive process which only uses dialogue as way of stipulating or fostering insight. For both parties, this can bring about change in the here-and-now encounter, as well as in the future, and in this way promote the quality of teaching and learning (Beywl, 2012).

Professional self-evaluation should produce meaningful data that triggers a new process of development, which in turn is evaluated in a timely manner. This will produce a successful quality assurance instrument. Students and teachers form part of this process, but they are also in control of it and are thus responsible for data quality and for the insights they arrive at from it. Everyone involved can immediately see the benefits of this evaluation method, which is an important motivating factor for implementation. The foundations for this kind of evaluation are laid by the evaluation culture of those in charge of training, which creates the culture that in turn fosters the inner attitudes of all involved (Merkator & Welger, 2013). In Beywl's judgment, self-evaluation is an instrument which holds everyone involved accountable. It should always be viewed and implemented in the context of a teaching or project event. Beywl also refers to the procedures as "convival evaluation" (Beywl et al., 2011): this form of evaluation not only saves costs and resources, but since it takes the form of "work in progress", it includes immediate evaluation and thus has a flexibility not present in any other method. Speakers' internal impulses will prompt them to immediately adapt their thoughts to the community's process, thus creatively moving this process forward. This form of self-evaluation includes all involved parties, leading to an increase in learning (Beywl, 2012; Stephenson, 2014).

5.3 Dialogue-Driven Evaluation – Mentalization-Based Evaluation (MBE)

The significance of mentalization-based evaluation (MBE) as a method lies in the fact that all participants and evaluators serve as "cognition instruments". This requires that everyone involved make some contribution to the process. The basic attitude is a mentalizing developmental attitude: this means that everyone in the process can perceive themselves as individuals with their own thoughts and feelings. This inner attitude should foster a tolerant attitude towards others. The capacity to mentalize develops according to attachment and relationship experiences which unfold in a dialogic relationship (Steinberger et al., 2013). The group should learn the ability to express criticism, including encouragement for those who feel inhibited. By learning from a model of emotional involvement, individuals involved in the dialogic process can perceive the conscious and unconscious reactions of the other person, enabling them to frame their statements in their own emotional context. This immensely important learning aspect enables the students to have the learning experience for themselves, showing them how to open up a space for criticism or reflection for future students. Rather than let off steam in the anonymity of an online "shitstorm", they learn that criticism only leads to satisfactory change if it takes place within a dialogic field. Participants ultimately absorb the specific content of the dialogic-mentalizing evaluation, but they also learn knowledge of their own affect regulation. By reflecting on and evaluating this process, students learn how it will be possible to open up and direct these spaces of affect regulation in future fields of work. This form of evaluation includes a variety of cognitive processes which develop on a range from explicit to implicit knowledge.

Cost is a significant factor here. This form of evaluation is embedded in teaching and learning activities, and is carried out by teachers and students, acting in mutual evaluation. Evaluation also means teaching the group leader: in other words, it includes an agreed change in roles. The dialogic mentalizing evaluation can be used for individual small ART II groups but also in larger, institutional groups.

At the end of the process, explicit content can be written down to serve as a future reference point. Implicit knowledge can be made explicit through linguistic symbolization and thus also anchored as conscious knowledge. However, we consider implicit knowledge, in learning to regulate affects, to be more significant here for the development of students and teachers.

The evaluation process is subject to development. At the beginning of the course, for example, we assume that many group participants will prefer to take a passive role. The moderation function should be carried out by teachers – later by students in higher semesters – who are familiar with this form of dialogic-mentalizing evaluation. A staff member may also take on a confrontational role towards the staff member doing moderation. The aim here is to offer students a model of dialogue and the associated emotional experiences, as well as ways of reacting to the affective experience of dialogue partners and adversaries.

Another aspect of the task is to recognize the interests of group participants in the conversation. The moderator should have the ability to evaluate and mentalize themselves in the moment, thus deciding for example to make implicit group content explicit, recognizing that the group is only "playing" at being an evaluation group, with participants discussing content. This ability to mentalize is expected by the group leadership. This in turn means that the group leader and students must be offered further training in dialogic-mentalizing evaluation.

This form of evaluation is integrated into training as an overall process, and can thus both demand and promote an attitude of mentalizing thought. We currently use this process at the end of ART II and it is continually under development.

5.4 Implementing Dialogic Mentalization-Promotion Evaluation (DME)

This form of self-evaluation will be offered in a variety of formats, including open spaces, discussion groups, workshops, etc., in the foreseeable future. The evaluation processes can be handled in different ways. The crucial factor is framework design and how the process is begun.

Either students or teachers can take the initiative in implementing an evaluation forum. If a relevant issue arises for someone involved in teaching, they can make use of these tools. This is currently happening within various ART groups.

Group leaders will ensure that a dialogic mentalization-promotion evaluation forum is held for any ART activity, at the very least at the end of the training year. For example, the students may contact the group leader and set her the task of organizing a DME session. The group leader is responsible for carrying out moderation themselves or else choosing an alternative person with the help of the group. At the end of the individual group process, a report is produced which can be sent to the person responsible for training programmes.

DME makes it possible to be flexible in setting times for meetings but also in the time covered by the process. Questions from the past can be asked reflectively or evaluatively (summatively). This can be a reflection of a current situation within the group, aiming to produce an interim evaluation (formative), or the question might be aimed at the future, for example in support of planning (prospective) (Merkator & Welger, 2013).

Further establishment of this evaluation method is planned. A DME can react very flexibly to events and can be established as required, including variation in group size and tailoring time and place. A group leader can be selected based on the main thematic focus. How the group will function, including didactic methods used (projector, flipcharts, cards, stimulating lecture, role play, set-up, sculpture, etc.) can be designed independently by the group as a whole, or by those who initiated the process.

The DME process should be documented so as to integrate the evaluation material it produces into the training structure.

The more unfamiliar a group is with the method, the more responsibility lies with the group facilitator. In this case, they will chose a firmer structure and explicitly ask group participants to express their criticism and suggestions. Whether non-verbal elements are used as a didactic method depends on the facilitator and the group. The better a group is in achieving reflective or mentalizing mode, the less internal didactic structure will be required. Here, the focus of leadership is on adhering to time structure and making sure that every group member is involved. If criticism is levelled directly at a teacher, the facilitator must have excellent mentalizing skills, in order to separate substantive topics from implicit ones, and later to reintegrate them. For example, if the group wants to discuss phenomena of violence or disrespectful behaviour by a patient in the latest project, then, apart from the specific content, there will be an actual re-enactment of the incident for the leadership, so as to anchor their emotional reaction as implicit knowledge. At the same time, explicit knowledge which is claimed is checked for functionality: can the person leading the project authentically and experientially represent the knowledge they express in language?

5.5 Synopsis

To evaluate teaching, we use self-evaluation in the form of dialogic mentalization-promotion evaluation (DME) and have recently begun using it in ART III groups. In future, DME should gain greater importance in teaching reviews, and will be continuously integrated into the work of the training institution. Students help us in what is a joint process to further develop the ART project and make it even more effective for future students.

Competence development, personality development, and evaluation are part of a single structure; they develop within a continuous process. This process should also serve to convey to students that change always occurs, in every phase of life and work.

7 ART II – Observation, Didactics, Mentalization

"Man becomes an I through a You."

Martin Buber

1 Leading Training Groups with Affect-Reflection

Many courses of training struggle with the important intersection between teaching psychological phenomena – including empathy and understanding non-visible phenomena – and the means used to teach or impart them. Psychological mechanisms function in permanent encounter; they must be imparted, yet can only be imparted through the mechanisms themselves. Reflection on psychological dynamics must pass through the psychodynamics prevailing at the moment of reflection. By making these visible, I change the dynamic, which is in a permanent dynamic process.

Thus, for example, the classic training idea in teaching psychoanalysis and psychotherapy separates self-awareness, technique, and supervision: this was put in place in the 1920s, in the form of the Eitingon model. This construct does not correspond to the actual circumstances of an encounter, since the separation of these elements only arises from a certain conception of understanding: in fact, these elements always unfold simultaneously in the encounter. The interpretation of language determines the formulation of the situation and perspectives on it. In every situation, we are psychological beings who need language in the form of technique to make something visible and find out something about ourselves and others. This unfolds in the form of self (-experience) and others (supervision).

While the prevailing guiding principle here is the importance of separation, within the encounter itself the idea of technique predominates, placing the focus on scientific views of teaching. If value is shifted towards psychological existence, a referent for the description of psychological phenomena will be lacking; there will be no separation from emotional experience nor any adoption of a meta-position towards this experience. Naming or imagining technique momentarily freezes the phenomena to be imagined, making them visible and conceivable. These experiences of possible modes of thinking are always

DOI: 10.4324/9781003483441-7

embedded in the flow of dynamic, invisible psychological experience, accompanied by feelings and affects.

Training courses always run the risk of supporting students' conformity in the interests of the institution and of manoeuvring them into an infantile position (Kernberg, 1996, 1998, 2014, 2016, 2017; Scharff & Scharff, 2000, 2014, 2017). If the focus is shifted to the point of self-awareness, there can be an atmosphere of regression, but this in turn can be compensated for through a pendulum movement moving back and forth to the cognitive meta-psychological level. The flexibility of this pendulum movement is what characterizes a learning group which works dynamically and succeeds in using both elements of affective learning.

The separation of self-awareness and supervision – in the sense of formalized technique encounters with patients – creates a gap in which a field of learning or self-awareness can open up in every encounter between people. This is where one's own involvement develops. This interpretation blurs the line between who is the teacher and who is the learner, allowing the exchange to be experienced in a common way.

"In short, affects are the engine of self and object organization, in the brain, in the individual mind, in relationships, and in groups" (Scharff & Scharff, 2017, p. 1621). Generating experience through one's own self, as self-experience – or to put it differently, gathering experience with or through one's own self – is the engine for constructing an inner structure. It is we ourselves who provide the tools for the (psychotherapeutic) encounter. Mitchell asks how many selves we may have, deconstructing our idea of a stable self (Mitchell, 1988). Every encounter constructs its own self, which only becomes an idea in the momentum of encounter.

ART II encompasses a multi-channel development system for students, based on a form of "observation" which involves a training of empathy, in the sense of developing an inner attitude which is mentalizing, intersubjective, and relational. This knowledge transfer is cognitive, emotional, interpersonal, relational, and mentalizing, making use of a multi-layered system in which observations are discussed and developed in emotional terms. Cognitive knowledge or theories are needed in order to construct a frame of reference for one's ideas around and about something:

> 'If you don't have a good theory of the interaction process, you are at the mercy of it', says Peter Fonagy. This doesn't mean you need the 'right' theory, but you need to have a firm and a good theory to hold on to. Otherwise the interpersonal encounter with the patient is so powerful that it simply washes you away.
>
> (Boynton, 2002)

Pedagogical instruction takes place via affective group learning experiences, which offer a continuum of experiential learning based on reflection on processes, carried out within the group. The connection between cognition and affect leads to new learning experiences which can be more deeply anchored emotionally and thus open the way to new experiences.

Experiences are constituted by affects, which form a motivational structure and in this way constitute a motor for organizing the self or the ego at the level of the mental apparatus of neurological processes, in relationships and groups. Relational experiences form the basis of our internal structure; they influence the functioning of our psyche, acting as the organizing force in our relationships (Scharff & Scharff, 2014, 2000).

This gathering of experiences through an embedding in relationships, guided by affect, is woven into a shared strand of understanding. Interpretative learning processes generate experiences and can thus also be subject to reflection. How do we learn? And what do we experience while we learn?

Learning develops in an intellectual climate in which affective resonances are linked to cognitive theories. Concepts are lived and understood through one's own experience. For this reason, students must have the opportunity to perceive the described phenomenon for themselves and generalize about it by means of abstract theory.

Through this kind of knowledge transfer, participants' unconscious needs increasingly become the focus of understanding. Learning takes place primarily through a process of identification aimed at the group leader and other participants in the student group. These feelings, which develop on an implicit level, are brought into a field of understanding through spontaneous expression. Through association, students can experience how they participate in the group process and how they can thus influence it.

The group leaders are all psychoanalysts or psychotherapists, with experience of groups and a knowledge of their dynamics. A reflection group for group leaders enables them to discuss their experiences with students. This way, the work of the leaders is removed from secrecy, and they, like their students, learn from these experiences through participation in a group.

Students' competence is demonstrated by their capacity to engage in the affective process in small groups and promote processes of understanding.

2 Group Phenomena

This model enables an adequate study of psychological phenomena and of experience as a form of permanent conversation, as well as the pedagogy of affective learning spaces and many critiques of training (Kernberg, 1996, 1998; Kahl-Popp, 2007).

The group offers a space of public learning and experience, subject to mutual regulation, where affective phenomena can be explored together. As a public space, the group protects participants from feelings of abuse which manifest through concealment (Steinberger, 2016). In the group, different perspectives can be developed and different values demonstrated. In this way, a group conception of value or a moral standpoint can be arrived at in an open manner.

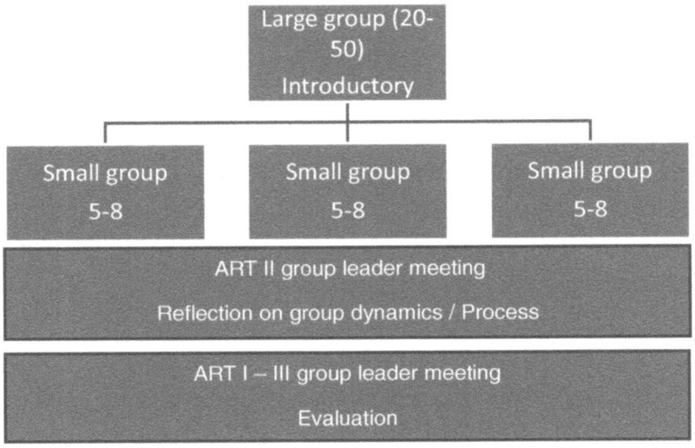

Figure 7.1. ART II – group size of the large group is thirty to fifty people, comprising four to six small groups, each with five to eight participants.

> On the other hand … [a reflexive group] emphasizes the development of intersubjectivity in the participants by participating in a … group which focuses on precisely this. This may even be the actual effective factor … because it is ultimately about developing an ability to mentalize, which can only be acquired intersubjectively within the framework of an attachment relationship. … Only a sufficiently secure attachment relationship – or, if applied to the therapeutic group, an adequate climate of connectedness – allows for moments of encounter which open up the process of self-reflection and the experience of self-efficacy as an ongoing process of co-creation.
> (Felsberger, 2014, p. 5f.).

In the concept of ART, the group is an affective habitat where empathy can be learned or improved. The feelings undergone by group participants form the basis for cognitive understanding of the material presented and the scenes described. The learning content introduced by the group leader and its members become a secondary form of understanding, always based on affective content. In doing so, most group members participate again in the cognitive material, with affectively charged content.

The group is a very important constitutive factor in maintaining institutional cooperation. The group often presents a small scale version of how a large institution structures itself externally. The group reflects the smaller cosmos of a larger institutional process and thus forms the basis for psychodynamic understanding of group phenomena (Stadler & Kern, 2010; Yalom, 2016).

> Only learning from the group experience allows radical institution wide questioning to ensure each individual's personally selective internalization of the object relations way of working and analytic sensibility to group dynamics so essential for building a healthy institution.
> (Scharff & Scharff, 2017, p. 1619).

Self-object relationships shaped by affects represent the basis for psychological structure, which is expressed on an unconscious level by phenomena such as projective identification, thus forming a template for unconscious communication among group participants. This unconscious communication between participants is a reflection of affectively charged topics within subgroups. "Resistance" and enactment are examples of how the group can express fears about learning psychological concepts of understanding via their own unconscious feelings. Group processes bring the patient's issues and concepts to life, making them tangible. Raising the subject of the group to conscious conversation is more effective in bringing concepts to recognition than debating them on a purely intellectual level.

The group offers a safe space for all participants to confront what are often burdensome feelings, making it possible to express them in a spirit of understanding, and to experience them as meaningful. The group is a sounding board for the implicit emotional worlds which develop through the material presented; the group generates its own perspective or explicit influence on the observation presented. As a result, students experience a sense of belonging to a peer group and do not feel alone with their own emotions and perceptions. Concepts used for affects or feelings serve to bring these to life in the group, as each participant transforms knowledge into a deeply personal learning experience. Material cognitively presented or theories discussed are understood in intellectual terms, but they are also anchored on a more emotional and profound level of the self.

A willingness to anchor learning experience in this context depends on the group's ability to contain affects and thus maintain excitement towards their learning, while not allowing themselves to be overwhelmed by affects such as fear, anger, shame, etc. Cognitive learning moves in a space of sustained tension, leading to curiosity while protecting against excessive affects which would drive participants into "escape mode".

The peer group makes it possible to lend one other words so as to formulate and thus perceive one's own feelings. A feeling of freedom arises, of no longer feeling so exposed to one's own emotions, of being able to formulate emotions: to abstract them into words, making it possible to obtain decision-making power over oneself. This also reduces the shame associated with being alone with one's own feelings and helps one experience them as a gift, something which appears at the end of a learning process. This is because with the feelings I now experience, I can understand myself and others and experience them more consciously.

This form of learning experience – one of being held by the group – allows students to develop an ability to experience themselves more authentically in interactions with patients and thus to react more empathetically and understandingly. Students can now feel more secure, no longer experiencing emotions which patients bring to them as anxiety-provoking to the point of being unbearable. At the conclusion of the group learning experience, students have more confidence in their clinical skills, in knowing how to authentically attune to encounters with patients; in short, students develop a sense of self-efficacy. They come to know, through assuming this newly feasible attitude, the ability to influence situations with patients by changing the affects experienced.

In the group, the separation between learning and teaching becomes less important; the two activities are now seen as a shared process of development. Knowledge develops as a process of growth for everyone involved. The group leader's own experience changes, via the ongoing process of exchange with the group. In this form, learning and growth are an attitude of a co-created experiential process, deeply anchored in a continuum. It is up to the group whether this is a process of self-awareness and if individual group participants develop curiosity about their own neurotic behaviour or suffering: it all depends on where the focus is placed, and thus what interpretations and conclusions are applied to the here and now. With the help of the group, the group leader determines the construction of meaning in relation to experience, thus creating a shared reality, deciding whether this represents a group reaction, an individual reaction, the concerns of an individual, or a reaction on the part of a patient. The psychological unfolds in every encounter; we determine meaning together. Freud (1915a), for example, constructed the concept of transferential love to address this dilemma.

These cognitively underpinned structures are guided by psychodynamic ideas, which in turn are fed by concepts of relation, intersubjectivity, and mentalization, as well as current research on infant and toddler observation.

The small group is the cornerstone of experiential learning. Group participants also have the job of observing the group process and reflecting it back into the process itself. They should go through a flexible thought process: between being involved in the group and reflecting within it, and on the other hand looking at these experiences on a meta-level, which will allow them to draw conclusions about the progress of the group.

Each individual in the group has the task of expressing their feelings about the material up for discussion in the small group, in this way allowing others to be touched as well. This in turn helps them to shape the understanding process through expressions, becoming aware of themselves and learning to develop ideas of meaning and self-efficacy within the group.

The learning and experience group is embedded within the larger context of a training institution. Via this close relationship, the experience of imparting material and being affectively involved also flows into group activities. This is strongly influenced by the atmosphere of the institution and, on a lesser level, the attitude of the person in charge of the cohort of training groups, who does not get involved in ART II and III. The attitude of management and the course leader have a great influence on the group and thus determine the extent to which students are prepared to engage with this form of learning. In our training institution, this form of teaching represents a cybernetic process inherent to learning and makes a decisive contribution to the future design of training and development.

At the start of ART II, the entire training course is up for discussion. In a four-hour time frame, a large group of 30 to 40 students engages with concepts of construction and deconstruction, as well as observation situations, relational perspective, intersubjectivity, and mentalizing. These concepts are later deepened in small groups of five to eight students. Participants remain with the small groups until the end of their training: they are intended to offer students a language for formulating psychological phenomena.

When giving a lecture in a large group, my students often react with a lively discussion about approaches to thinking which are new to them: these modes of thought are closer to the humanities than the sciences and thus operate with a modus operandi of interpretation. But this can also move students quite far away from scientifically-influenced medical subjects. The first deconstruction in a large group can trigger uncertainty, but also a sense of freedom, an opening up of new spaces for thought. The larger context can motivate students in the group to participate in the lecture with thoughts, questions, and feelings. In this sequence, they also learn to find the courage to interrupt a speaker and thus create a collaborative process. The process can also be accompanied by increased anxiety, which can find expression in comments motivated by concrete reflections. Students very often experience feelings of shame, especially with regard to ideas of being "seen through" or "analysed". In this open encounter dynamic, frustration towards learning, the institution, etc. can also become apparent. Learning experiences from students' educational past, experienced as traumatizing, can now take hold in an open dynamic. "Allowing the direct expression of negative feelings towards faculty frees the mind at least for learning from and with faculty" (Scharff & Scharff, 2017, p. 98).

In the large group, the students get a sense of how reality is jointly constructed or deconstructed through their interactions with the speaker. By offering different approaches to understanding mental phenomena, the moderator encourages the group to avoid identifying with a "correct" opinion. The presentation of several theories with different heuristic concepts makes it possible for students to develop reference points and thus reveal the advantages and weaknesses of each approach. Via these forms of thinking, students lose the shameful sense of having to use "wrong" and "right" when making statements. They become braver in putting forward thoughts for discussion.

At the end of this large group sequence, students receive written instructions about the framework of reports and a time structure for observations to be completed in their internships. The more detailed work, including questions about the instructions, now moves to a small group context.

3 Observation

The main task of observation is to offer students the opportunity and encouragement to expand their inner world, opening it up to include richer and more diverse experience.

Students' newly-acquired inner worlds open broader understandings of intersubjectivity and relationality, which they can use to further develop cognitive processes. They also learn to deal with the awkward problem of a lack of objective observation of reality and thus a lack of objective truth. Against this background, there is no such thing as a "correct" observation: students should instead be encouraged to deepen their interest in their own observations and thus gain an understanding of others' intentions.

The group leader leads students in a process-like experience of their shared inner perceptual world, and in turn allows them to construct a subjective understanding of reality as a shared co-construction. This co-construction refers to students' inner and outer worlds. The dichotomization of the world is merely a construct that is established in encounter. Empathy for or an understanding of the other does not emerge from a search for a "true" (scientifically-based) reality that satisfies objectivity criteria. Instead, recognition occurs through absorbing and being touched by affective stimuli; we come to understand the mental construction involved (Hoffman, 1998). Because I am initially uncertain about the meaning of a scene triggered in me, the possibility of enduring – and the ability to do so – an observation begins to be present in me. Uncertainty is linked to affects of fear: this allows us to slide into inner enactment, which can now lead to external action (Mitchell, 2005, p. 287). How far can I face a micro scene and hold it, that is, maintain my inner feelings? How much enactment do I need to be able to endure an observation?

Only through my observation's capacity to describe subjectivity can I grant patients their autonomous space and thus a freedom or a free space where development can take place. The group leader uses their own idea of subjectivity to convey that their interpretation of the material and the feelings they express about it do not correspond to repeatability in a scientific sense. Rather, they are based on what Gadamer called "pre-judgments" from our "tradition" which manifest in our thoughts. These represent the reference point of our interpretation: they are always in a state of flux (Gadamer, 2010; Orange et al., 2001).

Students' competency develops based on an inner conviction that their own observation is the equal of that of the group leader and their authority. This inner shift in turn offers a responsive soil in which the patient can develop. The group leader presents a number of models or a theoretical frame of reference for interpreting affects, thus linking them back to a possible understanding of patients' implicitness. Students must also learn different frames of reference for understanding psychological experience; these are metaphors, for example nosology in its medical, psychoanalytic (intersubjective, relational), and systemic forms, etc. For human beings, development begins when we understand the subjective characteristics of our inner perceptual world. The more metaphors I have available for comprehension, the more space of understanding I can open up for myself. Not everything is arbitrary or can be deployed as self-understanding. We subject our cognitive, logic-dominated thought patterns to this examination and, in a multi-layered interaction, recognize whether a theory suits us or whether we reject it. From this point, a common sense can emerge, which in turn is culture-dependent and paradigmatically bound.

Students should learn to use the theories presented to find internal reference points for understanding. Only via structures of inner understanding can we draw the implicit wealth from the depths of our experience. Experienced clinicians can change, dissolve, and reassemble their theories, thus creating something of their own; in this way, they use their subjectivity to understand human implicitness.

The group leader teaches students that their observations influence their material. There is no such thing as not influencing a situation. Observation changes situations; more specifically students' intentions have an impact on the observation. This always involves the group, which observes or influences the material of the observation. Every conversation about a report changes the understanding of the scene under observation. Every act of looking influences the result, as outlined by Heisenberg (Mitchell, 2005; Kunzke, 2011; Pohlmann, 2013).

I allow the scene to penetrate me and create an intimate encounter within me. In terms of empathy, permeability represents the ability to generate one's own images, which in turn reflect the emotional condition of the other person. The gaze directed into me confronts the intersubjective totality of an encounter which has yet to be shaped, or the construction of a shared reality in which we feel ourselves understood (Mitchell, 2005).

ART II is not about teaching students the "correct" observation or interpretation. Rather, it is about conveying how ideas about events in the observation can be developed by expanding one's own inner experience. Competent leadership does not lie in a very complex pedagogy of theories which will allow students to understand patients; instead, it manifests by giving students the chance to use their own understanding to create a space of subjectivity where their own limitations can be interpreted and accepted. The group leader offers "a view of the analyst's knowledge and authority [as that of] an expert in collaborative, self-authorizing self-reflection, in developing useful constructions for understanding the analysand's experience" (Mitchell, 1997, p. 227.).

The training group is led or moderated through multi-dimensional mediation. The group leader repeatedly encourages people to take a reflective or mentalizing position about what is happening in the group: why do I react with these feelings to the material presented? What conclusions about the case study can be drawn from the content of a reflection, which allows us to better understand the situation described? The students specifically learn to work with their emotions to interpret the situation and to reflect on the process. For example, why does the group react with these emotions to the material presented and how can this be related to the situation? In any given moment, this process presents itself as an ongoing flow, where every reflection about individual or group reactions marks a cognitive or affective change. Every reaction prompts a different thought, which in turn can influence affects.

Theory is primarily introduced by the group leader: this can be models of relational psychoanalysis, intersubjectivity, work discussion, mentalization concepts, infant research or field theory. At the same time, the group leader deconstructs the theory and points out that it is based on a particular kind of knowledge, which is itself relative. We need theories to give language to the non-linguistic, enabling our cognitive access; without them, we would have no way to discuss it and would be swept away by the feelings patients trigger in us (Boynton, 2002).

Students should also understand theories as a kind of metaphor. They are models of understanding which can bring the non-visible to visibility; they do not represent truths, but must be viewed as a blur, as Heisenberg showed (2011). Mental dynamics can only be represented through metaphors because they involve movement, and every theory which we see as truth takes us away from a reflective level of understanding, causing both object and our thought to become rigid and inflexible. In short, this means that mental models about psychological events cannot represent the truth because they exclude or destroy what they seek to capture.

Someone who cannot question themselves cannot question anything, and thus cannot formulate a question which shifts concrete thinking into an implicit relational world. As an identificatory figure, the group leader has the job of constantly questioning students and their theories, in this way helping to open a space for creativity to develop, offering a chance to freely play with ideas and express thoughts. It is impossible for students to express thoughts without subjecting them to censorship. Our school culture conveys an attitude which normatively distinguishes "wrong" from "right". To identify with this means subjecting my thought to internal censorship: questioning whether it is "clever", whether it fits in, whether I will be recognized for it, etc. Here experiential learning is of immense importance, beginning by offering students an opportunity to identify with the group leader. Identification is an emotional learning experience: it precedes cognitive insight and is based on mirror neurons (Geißler, 2012, p. 20).

Group leaders are not drawn from the institution's own staff; they are outsiders, paid a fee to do the job of leading the group. This allows them to maintain a certain distance from the training institution, which in turn helps to insulate their position from prevailing institutional rules.

Group leaders themselves undergo processes of change and development. Like the students, they learn through experience. They meet at regular intervals to reflect on group work from their own perspective. This transparency also enables group leaders to become reflexively aware of a situation of competition or pressures to perform.

Opening a space of observation begins with observing the patient or scene. Every form of looking is based on intersubjectivity, the look both creates and influences the observation space at the same time. My observation shapes and changes the scene and thus in objective terms it remains blurry. Mentalizing now means I can see what my mother saw in me or how she saw me. Opening up a space of seeing depends on the ability to look within oneself. An intersubjective field of observation is created from many worlds of experience. These worlds are based on the experience of encountering the relation with other people. My mother sees me, therefore I am. Seen by my mother, I can see her. Autistic vision is functional, yet its sufferers remain blind to the non-visible (Fonagy et al., 2002). Hans-Peter Dürr (2016) tells us that material does not exist, there is only the in-between!

Dürr also says we can only see things by paying attention to them; only in this way can they be classified as real. What we constitute as reality is created by leaving out the unimportant. General statements which we use to construct a shared reality are based on inaccuracy, and for this reason can allow us to create general rules, like in natural science (Görnitz & Görnitz, 2016). The more closely we observe, the more difficult it becomes to summarize reality into scientific laws, and to generate the repeatability of its basic structure.

The accuracy of observation leads us to the individuality of our perception and how disconnection from others' realities can lead to loneliness. Human beings want their perceptions verified by other people. A perception of disconnection can destabilize us: we may react to this realization with excitement or with fear. When we imagine the instability of the organism, we may feel crazy and doubt our senses. Reality consists of construction and influence.

4 Preparing to Adopt an Observational Attitude

The students' task is next discussed in small groups. What attitude do I need and what attitude do I want to develop in order to become someone who "sees"?

In the first small group session, various topics come into play, including: how do I become a good observer? What fears and fantasies might I be confronted with? Many students' fantasies revolve around an idea of ongoing emergency: are they permitted to intervene or do they "have" to simply continue observing? How do I achieve a form of attention that is "holding", containing, evenly suspended? How do I shift my focus away from enactment and towards observing "everything" and perceiving it all as being of "equal value"?

The issue of providing help or refusing to do so strongly points towards students' need to move within the concrete world and receive answers there. On most questions, the group leader cannot give instructions for action, as this shifts the dynamic away from the inner life towards a possibly incomprehensible world of action. Instead, it would be helpful to think about the affects leading to this question, seeking to explore the psychological meaning within it.

One of the most difficult tasks for students in ART II is to adopt an attitude in which their passivity, enactment, and flow of affect remain below the prevailing level of stimulation. Many people do not regard observation as difficult, since they do constantly throughout in their lives. They experience "participatory" observation as an easier task; most people find it very difficult to take a quiet position as an observer in the room. This aspect only becomes visible and comprehensible for students when they actually try out the role. Many regard action as a socially-recognized activity, thinking of observation as non-work. At the beginning of our training project, some hospital wards reacted to the students with anxious fantasies, expressing fears that students might prompt patients to become paranoid. In fact, this has never happened since the project began in 2010. The fears lie with the institution and not the patients. One concern from students is that they are given an internship where there is nothing to observe.

The intersection of the two often lies in "defensiveness" towards the training situation, where many affectively charged topics have accumulated in the previous three semesters, and in fears arising from a possible observation situation.

Another fear is connected with the idea of putting observations on paper, when this is not an "objective" observation and description of symptoms, but a phenomenological observation including all associated feelings. In some groups there is also a lot of talk about the question "how do I write?" in order to motivate students to find their own material.

An observational attitude also includes the universality of every observation and the associated view and understanding of a scene and the interactions I perceive. There is no wrong or right observation.

Developmental progress is reflected in a change in how students respond to observation reports, moving from concrete interpretations to the expression of feelings, thoughts, etc.

The more I weave my affects into description, the more my own boundaries between what is sick and healthy dissolve. People become more individual through observation, but they come closer to me through the feelings the observation triggers in me. Since understanding is about me, understanding only reveals itself through myself and can also lead to fears that my experience of patients I observe may be too similar to theirs.

5 Tasks of the Group Leader

One task of the group leader is to explore the paranoid structure which prevails in groups, especially in hierarchically-run hospitals, and in this way to ensure a collegial relationship between students and the group leader and between students themselves. To ensure authenticity – an essential prerequisite for starting work – collegial interaction between teaching staff and group leaders must be maintained and any feelings of envy, superiority, inferiority, etc. must be dealt with reflexively. By coming together in class, the groups which were formed out of the larger group have an opportunity to express judgments or divisions between the various group leaders. Varying employment and salary conditions can also cause considerable opportunities for friction among group leaders.

Group leaders attempt to create a containing attitude for students, giving them an emotional sense of what this feels like. They offer their group a space where feelings can be discussed without students being overwhelmed with shame. The leader's questions should establish a link between the emotions of the student who is reporting, the group, and the scene described. What can we understand about the patient through the feelings we experience? With this inner attitude of goodwill towards students' thoughts and feelings and the individualization of the feelings they experience, dichotomies of "wrong" and "right" become meaningless. Every feeling presented is deeply individual, while still allowing us to understand the scene and the patients. This inner attitude also allows the students to develop an attitude of letting be (*Gewährung*) towards themselves and others, what Emmanuel Ghent (1990) described as a *surrender*.

Group leaders ask students to express the feelings triggered by the reading of the report, in this way reflecting on what these feelings can tell them about the scene. Reading the report makes it possible to stay much closer to phenomenological aspects of the scene, returning again and again to particular paragraphs. In this way, students have the experience of their thoughts changing and developing every time they go through the material. Group leaders structure the material for the group, encouraging students to remain with it, think about it, and express any associations it prompts. The group leader decides where the group can and should move towards, structuring explicit themes by introducing theories coming specifically from an intersubjective area. The reaction of the group as a whole is brought to consciousness within the group by the leader; this reaction is examined in turn for possible significance in terms of the report read out.

6 Institution and Implication

The groups take place as part of a broad training in mental health nursing and are based in the facilities of a training institution, which in turn is subordinate to an overarching institutional facility. In our case this is a hospital. Each institution has its own structural conditions and its own expectations of students and the training institute. Kernberg speaks of hidden, atypical "rules and regulations" and concealed topics (Kernberg, 2000, p. 119). Since our students conduct observations in different institutions, there were a variety of paranoid reactions from their respective managements. A very common argument as to why the students could not be allowed to carry out observations was the claim: "The situation would make patients paranoid". The paranoid nature of the institution became more pronounced the more closed it was and the more "conspiratorial" the team seemed, particularly if students described the team in terms of division. Where the institutions were very closed, the team constantly moved in an atmosphere of tension, torn between an urge to hide things and the fear of revealing them. In this tense atmosphere, an atmosphere of abuse reigns, which suspends every staff member in authoritarian moral conflict. The problem of the "total institution" (Goffman, 1961, p. 11) becomes more prevalent where no third perspective can be imagined by its interns, students, etc. Here, one hears time and again the argument that the "intimacy of care" may be disrupted. This is indeed true, but this creates a breeding ground for conditions which ultimately produce a treatment institution or situation where staff are no longer protected in taking corrective measures with regard to their own actions.

When the project was introduced to training sites, its initiators were exposed to resistance from some staff, above all passive resistance, which brought students into conflict, so that some students adopted an attitude of rejection towards the project, in a way that went beyond personal motivation.

The more interesting aspect of this lies at the intersection of, on the one hand, convictions regarding the project and its social usefulness, and on the other hand, limiting resistance, so that the project is not "switched off" by internship institutions and students remained motivated to carry out the observation. Some students carry out their observation almost casually, merely standing or sitting nearby, then recording the observed scene later on. The task of carrying out an explicit, declared observation would trigger too many fears on the part of the institution and in this way would direct the prevailing atmosphere of abuse in these institutions towards the students and the project. In this context, students must in effect carry out their task in secret, then report on it to the small group, which of course also encourages a certain cohesion as a "conspiratorial", adolescent group. The group outsources the conflict to the group leader, who must now decide whether the task was completed in accordance with specifications and whether the reports provided are sufficient. Of course, the primary means by which an institution protects its staff is by obtaining an outside perspective, which is what the interns provide. Moreover, the idea that "observation is taking place", i.e. looking at a situation, introduces the idea of reflection and in doing so tears the institution's work away from the common approach, one based solely on action and enactment. Simply introducing this level of thinking into the institution permits it to have a substantial change in perspective. Everything which is brought onto the level of thought brings with it the possibility of deciding between action and inaction, and does not have to be conveyed via a psychosomatic "language". This therefore offers a great opportunity for the institution to increase its resilience.

7 Exploring Students' Feelings Towards the Material

The more open and collegial the group atmosphere, the more students can bring in their own feelings and in this way develop the material in more depth. The group leader carefully asks about students' fantasies, feelings, moods, and perceptions, who repeatedly contribute their thoughts during the group process; by reflecting on events, they get an idea of the process and the development becoming apparent in the material, but which can also be understood in terms of the group and themselves as individuals. The group co-constructs a common reality: the material serves as the basis of the process, with students learning that the material studied changes every time it is addressed by the group or an individual. It must be looked at dynamically; to put it another way, the dynamics of looking permanently changes the process of psychologically understanding the material. This is where the intersection between these dynamics and the location of the material becomes significant.

Of course, this kind of work also touches on the students' deeper conflicts, which in turn requires an extremely tactful approach from the group leader. The longer the group works together, opening up a space for exploration, the more that students will put forward personal narratives. Here the intersection begins between self-experience and the possibility of understanding the material. It is important that the group leader makes a connection between students' emotions and the material they are working on. However, the group should not merely become a pool of personal experience: it can sometimes be subject to a regressive desire for this personal experience, which diverts the focus from the observed material and manoeuvres the group leader into an exalted or motherly/fatherly position, abandoning the collegial aspect of collaboration. At this point, the leader of the group is faced with a narcissistic temptation. At the end of this process, students should understand that they must look within themselves in order to develop the capacity to observe and interpret their observation. Implicit knowledge becomes explicit knowledge. This transformation can only be carried out by the students and the group. The students and group serve as catalysts for understanding at the conscious level.

The group leader's role inevitably exposes them to idealization. Being aware of this protects one from seductive aspects of the situation, and from possible associated guilt feelings. The group's regressive nature will become apparent if students assign themselves a role of ignorance, with the group leader posited as the knowing one: this in turn encourages the leader to adopt a sadomasochistic approach to the group. One part of the group will attack them, another part will reinforce them in their supposed superiority, which can provoke an opposite reaction from the group leader.

The group leader behaves correctly towards students who express criticism; towards adoring students they should behave benevolently while reinforcing collegial behaviour. In this dynamic, the group has already moved into a regressive state, more concerned with itself than with the material presented about patients. A collegial attitude is lost if the students are no longer able to explore the feeling that they, along with the group leader, are responsible for what happens or does not happen in the group. The group leader must always hold open a space for reflexive, mentalizing thought about what is happening in the group.

The group leader should be able to come across as a human being, avoiding mystification and being seen as the holder of oracular knowledge. They more they are elevated to a Delphic pedestal, the more they will encourage the group to regress. This also hinders students in their creative process, forcing them to take up a masochistic standpoint towards their own observations and interpretations. The group leader must redirect the recurring idealization of themselves into a creative, benevolent, and collegial relationship. Here, in keeping with the precepts of mentalization, it is important to bring together interpretations and perceptions put forward by all group participants, framing their contributions as important and meaningful in terms of the material. The group leader should both promote and challenge communication between group members, in order to call their own leadership status into question and avoid the "guru function" which can develop quickly in hierarchical institutions.

8 Exploration of Feelings Developing Towards Material in the Group

It is important for the group leader to have an idea of the dynamic factors which can be at work in a group: they must always be thinking ahead. First, there should be an exploration of the emotions triggered by the material presented; then the group leader should summarize the spectrum of thoughts brought up, helping students to think about how these feelings are related, possible connections between these emotions and understanding the scene, and places where students' own personality structures make an appearance. As a simplifying idea, the example of splitting can be put forward as a mental model. In the group, inherent contradictions can be reflected clearly in students' different identifications and can be traced back to unconscious elements in the description of the observation scene. We can understand or think through this phenomenon using the theoretical idea of concordant or complementary transference with the material. Through this kind of affective group work, students can also ensure that they can hold on to different feelings, by recognizing different participants' perspectives as meaningful. In this way, they develop their capacity to accept ambivalence.

By identifying with the leadership figure, which opens up space for impossibly conflicted feelings which may arise, students learn to be more tolerant towards themselves and thus to better understand patients' enactments. In this way, they are better able to develop their own ways of acting. In changing their inner attitude, students can have more explicit knowledge at their disposal in a variety of situations, allowing them to undertake spontaneous action. The group offers the opportunity to experience the many facets of the situation as described; deconstruction by the group leader makes these aspects visible, available for conscious integration. Finally, the group leader should also not lose sight of the intersection between the group's identification with the material and its own preexisting and emerging dynamics.

9 Responsibilities and Pathologies of Students and Group Leaders

If students have learning or developmental difficulties, it is important that staff look closely at their causes. Since internship positions in ART II are changed twice and we have experience going back to 2010 with most internship sites, their influence on student development allows more precise conclusions to be drawn. Students may express developmental problems through an attitude of rejection, for example citing negative attitudes towards the ART project on the part of the class leader or the management of the hospital unit; this can be explored by the entire group and verified with external information. Another aspect here will be the personality of the group leader, their attitude and manner of thinking, which could in fact form part of the learning problem.

But the question arises whether the student themselves are the cause of the problems in their development, either because of cognitive or personality problems. A language problem can sometimes underlie cognitive difficulties, if German is not the student's primary language. Differentiated language must be used in order to understand psychological phenomena on a differentiated level of perception. Language and phenomena are mutually dependent in student development. In addition, it is often difficult to decide from the material presented whether there is a problem of written expression – because the student is using their second language – or if there is an underlying cognitive problem or an issue with undifferentiated perception.

Another difficulty for students is if someone faced a dominant narcissistic personality issue, with a pervasive borderline structure. This student will often be enthusiastic about new ideas, but enthusiasm soon gives way to disillusion and dismissal. The affected person can no longer learn anything since they already seem to know everything. Ideas expressed by the group leader are often not seen as metaphors used to put the psychological into words, but as direct instructions for action and simple patterns of understanding. Here too, the group leader must establish the extent to which this is a cognitive limitation, or whether it actually is a narcissistic problem, meaning the student is unable to attribute mental activity to another person.

In cases of borderline personality structure, this kind of work quickly causes anxiety in students, who feel they have been "seen through" or "diagnosed", etc. They then very often attack the group leader, criticizing their "pathologization" of patients, or else attempt to position themselves and the material presented by the group in terms of "normality" and "abnormality".

Another problem can arise in groups which are dominated by emotionally immature students. Their own immature identity development – and the fragile self associated with it – can make it extremely difficult for them to let their feelings be observed or to examine them in a reflexive way. The group is often characterized by a very closed posture: students sit with legs and arms crossed, turn away from the action, or keep looking at their phones to communicate externally. These situations always cause frustration in group leaders, since student development is at this point still very important, and this can cause specific tasks and learnings to be deprioritized. Only if my ego boundaries are at a certain level of development, with clarity about my ego, can I recognize the other as an autonomous person, and allow them to enter into a relation with me, in this way making a clear boundary between the I and the Thou.

10 Reports

The students make independent decisions about the situation they observe and later write up the report. The reports are read aloud, and students can use intonation and reading style to shape the report in a particular way. At first, the group focuses on the report as a whole, but later individual sequences are discussed, with conclusions repeatedly drawn from the movement between the two levels.

Formal criteria

In order to pass the subject known as Patient Observation, students must satisfy the following criteria:

- minimum attendance of 80%
- 100% of written observations must be completed (to be discussed, collected, and assessed for each unit)
- One or two student reports are discussed together in each session
- The observation is scheduled to last for one hour and forms part of the time the student devotes to practical training
- It is up to students to inform the unit where they work about the task of observation and its general conditions
- Travel time is not counted as time devoted to practical training

As part of the Patient Observation course, students write observation reports, which should use the following format:

1. length: at least one A4 page
2. written on a computer
3. font: Arial
4. font size: 12
5. line spacing: 1.5
6. side margin: max. 2 cm on all edges
7. Reports should initially contain the following information:
    a author's name
    b date of observation
    c place of observation

Patient Observation Guide (ART Research Study Group, 2016)[1]

To successfully complete the subject, students must carry out one observation for each of the seven group sessions, writing an observation report in each case. One or two observation reports are discussed per group session.

The observation itself is scheduled for one hour (60 minutes) and forms part of the student's hours of practical training at their training location. The observation should include the following:

1. During the observation, no one on the clinical unit should attempt to direct the student to do other activities, except in case of emergency. The unit should ensure that the student can concentrate during the sixty minutes, except in case of emergency, and that they are not engaged in other activities, including "casual activities".
2. The priority for the observation is to see the patient in an environment of your choice. If this is not possible because patients either do not remain long enough at the location or observation has a negative impact on their health process (although this must be discussed with the group leader), what are known as "situational observations" may be substituted. This involves observing a waiting room, a liminal space, entrance area, anterooms, etc.: they should at any rate be functional rooms which are regularly used either by patients, staff, or both.
3. Nothing is to be noted or recorded during the time of the observation itself.
4. During the observation, the observer must adopt a passive attitude. During an observation you can come into contact with the patient, but the student – NB – should not take the initiative. If the patient wants to speak to the student, this is possible, but the student is required to conduct the conversation passively, not intervening in any way. Patients may also ask you about the reason for your presence; they should be answered honestly and frankly, but without delving too deeply into the subject.
5. After each observation, an observation report must be written from memory. It is essential that no writing takes place during the observation; the report must only be written afterwards.
6. The training site must provide the student with a free hour (sixty minutes) to carry out this writing, during which time they are permitted to withdraw from other activities and work in an undisturbed place. The student is responsible for demanding conditions which allow this; it is the training unit's responsibility to make this possible for them.
7. The student's assignment is to carry out seven observations and prepare an observation report for each one.

We look forward to successfully working with you!

(ART Research Study Group, 2012)

11 Observation Skills

While working together in the group, students should be able use observation to develop hypotheses which reflect a vivid and coherent picture. They should also gain an idea of how scenes develop and how they may have come into being, in this way developing their overall integrated thinking.

12 Group Process during the Semester

In the first small-group session, the group discusses ideas and anxieties regarding the observation, as well as the structural conditions of their internships and possible reactions to observations. In some groups, discussion focuses on possible feelings, nascent fears, and the challenge of the task; some groups address the overall conditions of the work, and how to produce a "correct" report, discussing what might happen if they are asked what they are doing there, if a patient leads them to become involved in a scene, etc. Group leaders try to convey what it might mean to act with one's reactions to the environment in the context of a passive situation, in this way gaining a different perspective on enactment. Terms like "reverie" and "evenly suspended attention" are discussed and the small group will already note the group leader's authenticity and capacity to convey this attitude.

Another frequent theme is the fear of putting something on paper and whether it will be "right". Past experiences of fear of failure and fear of school are expressed. At this stage, writing reports which go beyond the visible world already requires psychological understanding and a knowledge of "inner life". I have to recall what I have seen, generating images and putting them on paper. During this phase, we also talk to the students about generating internal images or scenes. They learn to grasp details in their depictions and immerse themselves in them: this includes space, colours, clothes, and even descriptions of facial perceptions. All of this must be combined with the feelings which accompany these images.

The group leader is confronted with a wide variety of feelings in themselves, including destabilizing feelings: is the task too difficult for students, are they overwhelmed? But feelings of curiosity about students also arise when they are looking forward to this new kind of learning, etc. Groups react to these learning experiences with joy or with expressions of protest, for example saying that everything is very difficult and they will never have the conditions to observe in peace. Group participants rationalize their fears and present them in terms of the internship conditions. Other groups react to their task with great curiosity; some students enjoy writing and display great enthusiasm for the project. Each group is individual and reacts in its own way, and each member of the group reacts very personally, with all of their emotions. The group is steered by those who speak up, some hold back and say nothing. The group leader intervenes to structure the discussion, asking each group member to express the feelings they experience. They bring the fantasies expressed into a framework of possible future scenarios, in this way indicating that events within the group will represent a possible point of understanding, since the reality of the observation is still in the future. In this way, the group leader introduces possible forms of meta-level reflection.

In the second group session, we talk about students' experiences completing the observation and the feelings they encountered, how they felt while observing and writing the report. One student is encouraged to read out his or her report. Here, too, we see a wide range of possible reactions: these range from a medical description, where the writer says little about their feelings, to documents where the author's emotions are included, tightly enmeshed with description.

During this phase of the group, students trust psychological constructs and theories from scientific literature more than their collective understanding as a group. Only through an emerging process do they begin to trust themselves and the group's subjectivity; now they can attach importance to their feelings when seeking to understand the other person.

In subsequent sessions, it frequently becomes clear how many of the images the students use are drawn from their own lives and experiences, how they are strongly driven to express their own life stories, their experiences in school and of internships. The task of the group leader is to link these ideas to the report, to find their meaning for the group, and in this way to make use of the group's attitude to set a direction for them. The idea is that the group should not focus on self-experience; instead, they should use elements of it, while also learning that understanding patients is only possible through their own experience. Weaving in a meta-level of theoretical structures can in turn permit students to develop a frame of reference: this will allow things to be made visible from relational, intersubjective, and mentalizing perspectives.

Subsequent group sessions are guided by the group leader breaking down the structure to an increasing degree, allowing space to more and more uncertainty: this enables students to feel safe in moving beyond "right" and "wrong" statements. In this way, they should learn to make individual contributions towards understanding the patient, but also to present original and even unique observations. Here, they must maintain a contradiction: authentically experiencing feelings, and in doing so expose themselves to a unique form of loneliness, while also feeling embedded in the group's emotions, experiencing reality as a shared process. The way to hold contradictions within oneself is to recognize this tense relation between authenticity, loneliness, and the creation of reality with and through other people.

The specific scenes described determine the group's themes; fears, aggression, and helplessness are often discussed. In the kind of hierarchical structures seen in clinics, students are exposed to a considerable amount of trauma, including encounters with dying and death. Because of the emotional scenes described, it is hard for the group leader not to be left speechless. The place of sexuality in the reports (which often deal with transgressive scenes) is always a very important topic in group sessions.

In group sessions, we see an increase in the ability to reflect on one's own experience and the significance of group experience. By now, reports are being written with greater and greater individuality. Descriptions of individuals become more vivid, far easier to imagine for those listening. Scenes and images emerge more and more clearly in the listener and thus inner resonance increasingly begins to pulsate.

The end-of-semester meeting represents another attempt to capture change within individuals, as well as changes in the group and its process in language and in theory. The end of the sequence includes looking forward to the next semester, or to the dissolution and separation of this group, and the prospect of beginning ART III the following semester.

Group members also come to better understand this form of learning, where there is no beginning and no end, but only an impetus to a change one's attitude, a change which can be integrated into one's own life process. The students should also have an idea of how they can put themselves "on the line" and thereby create meaning for themselves and others.

13 Summary

Individual students have the job of preparing their reports for each group meeting; they read their reports aloud between one and four times a semester, making them available for other participants to discuss. Every group member participates in discussion of the report read out. Students bring their own emotions and associations to the material, which tend to be dominated by emotional, intellectual, and personal reactions. Everyone attempts to enter into a shared conversation via the statements they make. Groups also reflect on the meta-process of group activity and how that develops with regard to the materials. The small group has a particular position in training: its intimacy is like that of a peer group or a nuclear family. The size of the group means that all of their emotions, ideas, and cultural associations can be experienced and processed together. The small group enables emotional, shared learning in which clinical observation material can be assessed and experienced emotionally. It also offers a space in which students can get an idea of their own self-efficacy: what influence can an individual have on the group? In the group, connections between "inside" and "outside" can be created, a shared, co-created space can form, and ideas of mutual recognition can be tested and developed. It becomes possible to consider the influence of theories on the group, and vice versa. Concepts are lived by and through the group; in this way, they are anchored on an emotional level as a learning experience. The group experiences theories and events within the group; these can be conceived and discussed through the metaphor of theoretical constructions, which are constantly subject to change. This anchoring of concepts on a deeper and more emotional level will remain available to students later on:

this will be the knowledge which forms their attitude when encountering patients and will thus in turn influence their interventions.

Learning experience in the groups takes place at a number of levels, with the focus on promoting empathy. Theory, reflection, and knowledge develop in a shared and tangible space.

In the meetings of group leaders, the experiences of the group and the concepts presented there are evaluated and checked for relevance. Adjustments to the program are discussed on a more structural level in meetings with those in charge of the institution, and those responsible for the ART program. The ART teaching project is subject to a process of change, through which it also exerts an integrative factor on the training institution.

Note

1 A guide given to students at the start of the third semester (OWS research group).

8 ART III – Supervision in the Group

"umuntu ngumuntu ngabantu [A person is a person through persons]"
Bantu proverb (central and southern Africa)

1 Introduction

The module ART III, taken in semesters 5 and 6, focuses on the ability to make use of supervision without anxiety, while also demonstrating self-reflective behaviour towards patients and staff. Students should by now have the ability to connect declarative knowledge to procedures.

This concept entails a supervisory process which is embedded in an intersubjective field, constituted by the subjectivity of all "three" participants. The significance generated here is always regarded as context-dependent and thus stands in opposition to dichotomization. The intersubjective field is co-constituted during supervision: interpretations always depend on a given context (Jaenicke, 2014, p. 124). Group leaders or supervisors regard the moments of understanding produced as the shared outcome of a creative process which only takes this form of expression in a particular moment. The group leader is aware of the influence they have on the material presented, which is reflected in their attitude; they will also be aware of the Gadamerian circle and of their own thought process (Gadamer, 2010). One major similarity between supervision, on the one hand, and psychoanalysis and psychotherapy, on the other, can be seen in the form of the asymmetrical relationship (Gambaroff, 2012).

2 Intersubjective Field and Co-Construction

Chris Jaenicke, the most important representative of intersubjective psychoanalysis in the German-speaking world, understands supervision to be:

> ...an intersubjective field constituted by the subjectivity of the three participants, and if we understand meaning as context-dependent, then dichotomies collapse. The co-constitution of the intersubjective field and

DOI: 10.4324/9781003483441-8

> the context-dependent interpretation of meaning apply to the supervisory context as well as to the context of treatment.
>
> (Jaenicke, 2014, p. 124).

Here too, we face the question of whether we should "treat or teach" in the context of supervision. For Jaenicke, the difference can be seen by taking into account the different levels of discourse, which in both cases are asymmetrical and bidirectional, as well as the primary distinction between two conversation partners, i.e. therapist and patient. On the asymmetrical level, a supervisor attempts to help the supervisee to understand his or her patients in their subjective world, to develop them and support them in their transformation (Jaenicke, 2014; Sarnat, 1992). The asymmetry between supervisee and supervisor is determined by the definition of the task, and the resulting supervision process. For ART III as a training context, this asymmetry is reinforced by the educational context. Due to asymmetry which goes with the training institution, supervisors enter into a field of tension. The reality of this field is often denied, but it nonetheless exerts a very strong influence the supervision session in its bidirectionality. In ART II, the focus is more on students learning to build intersubjective understanding. In the following module, the focus shifts to coping with the scene described, and how it bears the inherent possibility of transformation; here discussion should always include the dichotomous idea so favoured by students, who seek to distinguish between "wrong" and "right" answers. If the asymmetry is not defined in the training context, students will demand concrete proposals for solutions, which they then later describe as ineffective, conveying the asymmetry to their supervisors, who offer inadequate solutions which do not lead to "success".

The difference between supervision, on the one hand, and treatment or coaching, on the other, becomes clear through the interrelated levels of discourse, which Jaenicke (2014) presents as two points. His reflections focus on the existing "inequality" or role difference within the encounter, which unfolds on a bidirectional level, as part of a shared, dyadic system:

1 Asymmetry of Encounter

The group process develops together in an intersubjective sense, with the clarity of **asymmetry**.

> The ... process develops ... together, but in an asymmetrical way. One participant makes themselves available primarily as a helper, healer, and researcher [the supervisor]. For the other, it is primarily a question of finding relief in terms of their emotional life ... In the process of development ... one of the two participants takes on the task of providing orientation, while the other tries to organize and reorganize their experience in a less painful way than previously.
>
> (Orange et al., 2001, p. 19).

Supervision is a form of professional relationship between two participants, in which the prevailing roles ascribed to supervisee and supervisor are asymmetrical. The authors emphasize the necessity for the process to develop and for everyone in the encounter to be involved, meaning there are no equal positions in the group. They refer to this as asymmetry. "...the asymmetrical role of the supervisor is embedded in his awareness of how three participants mutually influence each other; at the same time, the role emerges from this awareness" (Jaenicke, 2014, p. 127).

Asymmetry is defined here as an attitude based on participants assuming different roles. Asymmetry is also nourished by supervisors' assumption of responsibility, which makes it possible to precisely define the positions of the "three" people involved, integrating the possibility of influence, while not producing overly strong contradictions. The possibility of introducing one's own limitations within a dialogue, in this way opening up a field of intersubjectivity, is based on recognizing the roles of patient, supervisee, and supervisor. If this recognition and its asymmetry were to fail, the working alliances would have to be abandoned.

Supervision aims to provide a space in which inner images from the work can develop, initiating a process of change for supervisees through the scenarios presented and co-created. The process unfolds via a joint creation of images, created by what has already been said by each participant. The closeness of the group is reflected, among other things, in the spontaneity with which participants express ideas about aspects of the material presented. The more group participants can interrupt each other in a tolerant and mindful way, the more spontaneous and thus more creative will be the shared process as it unfolds. However, the more fear there is in the group, the more structured the process becomes, with the group leader forced to increasingly encourage people to express thoughts. The stronger the supervisor's anxiety around not being able to accompany the group in its emotions, the more he or she will structure the group.

Supervisees should become subjects who determine their thoughts, feelings, and actions (Löwer-Hirsch, 2001). The process develops through building relationships, on the part of everyone in the group. Group members operate with feelings and sensations and in this way create an intersubjective field. In other words, this can be defined as a space of transference and countertransference (Jaenicke, 2006, 2010, 2014). For Beebe and Lachmann, intrapsychic and relational processes are of equal importance in generating processes of understanding. They see this process as an interactive interconnection of self-systems, which are constructed by everyone involved (Beebe, 2006; Beebe & Lachmann, 2010; Lachmann, 2003). So-called intrapsychic processes are based on a process of relational events: these produce our thoughts. We can create a relation with something if we are able to mark out a difference or a contour. On an emotional level, the boundary around us is the symbolism of language, which forms a structure of difference, allowing our thoughts to unfold. As an explicit phenomenon, thinking is based on the capacity to create relations within ourselves. Symbolization in the sense of metaphor is what gives us the ability to mentalize.

Ogden regards all that has arisen between those involved as "the third" (or "the analytic third"). The group leader is responsible for giving a voice to this "analytic third":

> In other words, a voice that has lived within the intersubjective analytic third, has been changed by that experience, and is able to speak from it and about it to the analysand (who has also lived the experience of the third).
>
> (Ogden, 2004, pp. 169–170).

The resulting third is the new element which emerges in dialogue and in this way advances the common process, creating a hermeneutic circle. The phenomena of transference and countertransference are embedded within this overall dialogic process. The process of discovery emerges in a shared dialogue in which none of those involved knows what the next step will be. What connects us is our recognition of a shared, constructed subjectivity in which "truth" is created. Postmodern epistemology always views "truth" as contextual (Bohleber, 1999).

Supervision creates a "supervisory third party". The focus in intersubjective supervision is on the professional competence of supervisees in encounters with clients and staff, and how they are embedded within the organization. "The background reference is the world of work, non-familial work in and with organizations and the images which correspond to it, evoked in individuals" (Löwer-Hirsch, 2001, p. 54).

The intersubjective turn in group work goes back to a conceptualization developed by S.H. Foulkes. As early as the 1950s, Foulkes was writing about the "transpersonal" and about "location", developing the idea of a "group matrix" (Potthoff, 2015; Friedman, 2014; Schultz-Venrath & Felsberger, 2016). The group matrix is formed via shared interactions within the group.

> Supervisors who work in a psychoanalytic-constructivist way … are clear that they do not bring "reality" closer to their supervisees, but can only relate their own way of dealing with reality to that of their supervisees, seeking to construct a shared "reality" in an exciting process
>
> (Sies & West-Leuer, 2003, p. 171).

One crucial aspect of supervision is that "reality" takes place in the here and now, its truth unfolding in the present moment, as described by Stern. The way in which supervisors engage with the material presented to the group bears authenticity within it, as well as the empathic feelings of all those who participate in understanding the material. The language of supervisors is embedded within the group matrix and remains on an unconscious or implicit level in terms of facial and gestural expression. Supervisors can use their emotions in a targeted way, in order to crack a case or break a deadlock. In doing so, they prompt a process of negotiation, aimed at understanding the scene and reducing anxiety in the group, which can paralyze supervisees' creativity.

2 Bidirectional Level

On the **bidirectional level**, supervisees come to experience using subjectivity at the interconnection of their individual strengths and the inadequacies of both participants, where both can be worked through. In the 1960s, the Barangers introduced the term *bipersonal* into the language of psychoanalytic understanding, borrowing a meaning from physics to describe the dynamic field in the analytical situation. In the bipersonal field, analysts move from being observers to being participants. In later works, the Barangers replaced *bipersonal* with the term *intersubjective* (Will, 2010). Jaenicke understands bidirectionality to be the recognition of an intersubjective field: the meaning of the bidirectional level lies in the "encounter of differently organized subjective worlds" (Jaenicke, 2014, p. 128). Unfolding on this level is everything related to supervisees and supervisors and subject to mutual influence (Jaenicke, 2014).

The term bidirectional is borrowed from telecommunications and describes signal transmission occurring in both directions, and is also used in biology in the sense of reciprocal action in two directions.

> If the analyst recognizes that reciprocal commonality is actually bidirectional – that is, to put it in terms of intersubjectivity theory, he recognizes the intersubjective fields in which we live and which determine the nature of the analytic exchange – then he must be capable of allowing himself to develop further, and this creates fear of possible consequences.
>
> (Jaenicke, 2006, p. 27).

For Jaenicke, the encounter between supervisee and supervisor represents a bidirectional level whose formulation is reminiscent of the Barangers' field definition. However, he does not clearly work out the extent to which he is concerned with influencing two people, or alternatively, the extent to which, within the common field, two people construct each other or a third (Baranger & Baranger, 2018; Benjamin, 2018; Ferro, 2003). Jaenicke also notes that we should be conscious of "our dual role as an actor as well as a product of an intersubjective field" (Jaenicke, 2014, p. 128).

> The supervisor should … convey to the supervisee that it is not a matter of excluding his or her subjectivity, but rather that both participants' idiosyncratic strengths and shortcomings intermesh on a bi-directional level, and can be worked through at a later point.
>
> (Jaenicke, 2014, p. 127).

The term is very much based on ideas from physical world; it is mainly used there as a description of receiver and transmitter, in order to describe a data interface as bidirectional. This is entirely in the tradition of Freud, who also used the receiver as a metaphor to describe his ideas. As yet, in terms of understanding psychological phenomena, the concept has not yet been defined precisely and productively enough to generate better understanding.

Jaenicke (2014) develops pragmatic guidelines for intersubjective supervision, summarized here because of their importance for the ART III project:

1. atmosphere: ensure a level of safety for students in which they remain true to their feelings and can consciously make use of them in understanding patients
2. individuality: recognize the distinctiveness of students and their experiences
3. recognition of fallibility: supervisors should convey their ignorance as well as their knowledge
4. working tactfully with supervisee's subjectivity: exploring the supervisee's influence on the scene as well as mutual influence between supervisee and supervisor in terms of the material presented
5. clinical attitude ("believe your supervisees") – "hermeneutics of trust": supervisees should be taught a fault-tolerant attitude so that they can reduce their fear of failure
6. empathy and listening: from patients' reactions we can deduce whether they are able to develop their intersubjective world through empathetic listeners. Empathy also finds expression through the accuracy of the phenomenological description of the encounter scene
7. move the focus away from the content and use affects for underlying motives: looking at emotional meaning and in this way creating a contextualization of psychological life
8. transfer from patients to supervisees – organizing activity of the encounter – transfer to group: patients/colleagues transfer their unconscious, affectively controlled perceptions to supervisees. The transference organizes the relationship in a construction of intimacy and distance, with a view to stabilizing the self
9. dream: this aspect can be used in ART III when a student tells of a dream involving the group; via free association, meaning can be attributed to events in the group which are manifest in the dream
10. setting – "treatment" versus "crisis": one important factor is a clear definition of supervisors' attitude-generating response. Are their answers aimed at understanding the scene described, which is characterized by slowness, or does the group discuss instructions for action so as to have a roadmap for recurring crises? The linguistically imprecise definition of "treatment" and "crisis" leads to major conflicts and feelings of incomprehension on the part of students and staff working in institutions.

3 Starting Supervision

Supervision development can be divided into two different strands: as a development from the social field of work, and as a development out of psychoanalytic training:

1 as a development from the social field of work

The term *supervidere* comes from ideas monitoring or looking at, recognizing, inspecting, checking, checking something (Petzold et al., 2003; Edlhaimb-Hrubec, 2004). The term supervision appears in medieval, British, Irish and Latin sources, also describing activities including watching over and exercising control.

Around 1884, the pastor Samuel Barnett and his wife Henrietta founded a university-affiliated institution in a London slum, which they called "Toynbee Hall" after Arnold Toynbee, the historian and political economist. They wanted to bring "educated" and "uneducated" people together so as to make people's needs and social problems comprehensible to the educated classes. As part of this project, students at Toynbee Hall discussed social, economic, and socio-educational issues (Stattler, 2017; Belardi, 2013).

The history of supervision in a social context goes back over a century, with origins in the United States of America. The traditional development of autonomous citizens and the absence of the state, especially in providing care and security, led to the establishment of private aid organizations. To maintain a certain standard of care, assistants were taught and supervised by professional assistants. These "paid agents" were the forerunners of today's supervisors in the United States, ultimately going back to the Charity Organization Society (C.O.S.), founded in New York state in 1878. Towards the end of the nineteenth century, there were 78 relief organizations (C.O.S) in the country, employing 174 full-time or part-time social workers, exercising teaching and control functions over two thousand volunteer members. In 1911, a supervision training course for these "paid agents" was offered for the first time. Psychoanalysts began to emigrate from Europe in 1933: they became increasingly involved in social and welfare work, leading to increasing influence by psychological and psychoanalytic models of understanding. As early as 1920, Otto Rank had analysed a number of social workers in America. Now, aspects of monitoring receded more and more into the background, with the focus of social work increasingly shifting to the importance of the relationship (Stattler, 2017; Petzold et al., 2003; Sauer, 1997).

The emergence of supervision in Austria was strongly linked to emerging findings from the field of depth psychology. Depth-psychological findings could be profitably implemented, especially in the educational field, as well as in care work.

Beginning in 1912, Ilse Arlt offered a training program called "United Specialist Courses for Public Care" (*Vereinigte Fachkurse für Volkspflege*) for those working in caring professions. She developed her "Basics of the Science of Care" to further advance the professionalization of caring professions and as a tool for those working to help people. Governmental support, created by the Social Democratic politicians Ferdinand Hanusch and Julius Tandler in Vienna, underpinned all such emerging efforts towards regulated care work.

The discoveries of Freud and his colleagues revolutionized the understanding of the human psyche, drawing attention to the connection between the development of neurotic suffering and social, cultural, and familial influences.

2 as a development out of psychoanalytic training

Before its institutional development, psychoanalysis saw various personal agreements made between analysts and training candidates, intended to safeguard the monitoring of analyses. In 1925, an official training curriculum was set up to establish standards at the International Psychoanalytic Congress held in Bad Homburg. This included the following elements:

- training analysis
- theoretical and academic-clinical training
- control analyses conducted under the supervision of experienced analysts

This three-part model, which is still used today, was developed at the Berlin Psychoanalytic Polyclinic under the leadership of Max Eitingon (Sauer, 1997; Stadler, 2017).

The 1933 guidelines for teaching in the Vienna Psychoanalytic Association include:

> Point III: Education: c) Practical psychoanalytic work: at least two analyses under the control of designated analysts over the course of two years.
>
> (Huber, 1977, p. 235)

The supervision model established in this way is still used by most psychotherapeutic training courses.

From 1925, Wilhelm Hoffer – a colleague of the psychoanalyst Siegfried Bernfeld, and his deputy at the "Baumgarten Children's Home" (founded 1919) – ran courses for teachers at the Vienna Association's teaching institute. Graduates of these courses also underwent analysis to develop a better understanding of children's needs (Sauer, 1997; Mühlleitner & Reichmayr, 1992).

In 1919, after the end of the First World War, educational advice centres were established under the leadership of Alfred Adler. These were banned between 1934 and 1945, but today still represent a fundamental part of

Vienna's social provision. Alfred Adler recognized very early on that parents, teachers, and educators needed guidance around difficult children and created a new possibility of understanding and help:

> ...the various professional groups involved in the education of children were able to observe Alfred Adler's work, practice it themselves and reflect on it within the group. ... This requires a special type of learning – learning through experience and reflection on this experience, as well as taking emotional involvement into account, alongside an effort to increase awareness of the subjective factors in action and interaction. Today, this differentiated learning process is summarized in the term 'supervision'.
>
> (Fiala, 1986, p. 35).

Supervision took place on different developmental paths: a social work track and, later on, pedagogical and depth psychological tracks. Self-awareness and the role of supervisors were already of great importance in the early days of psychological study, already representing a point of intersection between "treatment and teaching".

4 Leadership Competence in ART III

A review of the literature mainly shows a focus on the skills to be learned by the supervisee: there is little information about the qualifications needed by the supervisor. Since this is a training program, there is also a question of supervisors' responsibilities and the ability of students to evaluate the skills taught. The focus is on a collegial encounter with students, who should always be assessed reflexively through evaluation by supervisors, in order to enable creative exchanges with and within the group. Any authoritarian atmosphere cultivated by the training context should always be reflexively questioned, to prevent feelings of superiority or inferiority destructively dominating the functioning of the group.

Among the most difficult issues for supervisors working in a training context is the problem of supporting students and critically evaluating their statements. Usually the assessment of students – and thus also supervisors' responsibility for student performance – has little place in supervisors' training and teaching. There is still much catching up to do, both in research and literature. Many training associations hide these problems behind terms like "abstinence", the "analytical" attitude, etc. An intersubjective attitude presents an ongoing challenge to supervisors to think with the group about common actions and activities. This kind of conversation will in turn make it clearer to supervisees that the supervisor's interventions develop individually from the case presented, and are thus subject to relativism, and do not represent truth in the sense of an absolute. This will in turn reduce the gap in authority and knowledge between supervisor and students. This reflection on the joint generation of thoughts about the case presented also opens up a possibility for participants to perceive and reflect on process in this kind of scene. In this way, participants recognize their own involvement in the process, as well as the responsibility which goes with it. They can no longer view the process of reflection as involving "divine" knowledge on the part of supervisors; instead, they understand it as a jointly designed process, which should also be anchored in them.

Another question to be worked on is the choice of terms – and associated theories – used to describe scenes and emotions presented. Which theories do the supervisors use to clothe the invisible in tangible images? The various models of psychoanalysis offer a highly differentiated language for psychological events. Here we can find very precise, differentiated descriptions of mental phenomena. The more supervisors consider the phenomenological aspects of description, the less they will need theory as a metaphor and a tool to render the invisible in words. Here too, the principle of mental transposition prevails: theories are necessary to move a thing into linguistic abstraction. Only in this way do we have the possibility of developing ideas, supplementing and repeating them in the sense of free association, and generating describable phenomena. Putting students' intuitive answers into theoretical constructs enables them to find themselves within a socialized world of knowledge, liberating them from imprisonment in their individual "gut feelings". Theoretical ideas allow us to order the world and thus generate repeatability. Scenes can also be transposed, allowing them to be formed flexibly in thought, opening up another possibility of change for students. The mental construct offered by theory is necessary for deconstructing a theory, as a starting point for changing the terms of a case or for deconstructing it. If conversation within the learning group is only produced through intuition, the individuality of expressions is foregrounded and remains so, and each encounter will need its own construct or theoretical structure in order to be understood. In turn, we would in this way construct ourselves as individualized, autonomous monads, since theory, by its act of recognition, presents itself as an intersubjective event. From his students' case descriptions, Kernberg can recognize which person is supervising them. Despite supervisors' intuitive reactions to material brought by a supervisee, an individual view of misinterpretation endures.

For Kernberg, intuition represents an ability to very quickly put a theoretical frame of reference around material consisting of unconscious and preconscious elements (Kernberg, 2016, 2017). These unconscious and preconscious components are fostered by supervisors' attitudes, which they carry within themselves in fluid form, thanks to their experience and specialized reading. Supervisees should also have an idea of their supervisors' theoretical background and an understanding of the frame of reference for their language. This knowledge will enable supervisees to learn to understand and cope with a specific situation, but also how to develop a more general framework from these individual situations. This framework can in turn be deconstructed with regard to specific situations and in this way, thanks to phenomenological understanding, can become profoundly individual, not replaceable by another. Theory also offers the possibility of decoupling supervisors' knowledge from their individual persons, integrating this knowledge rather than viewing it as the all-powerful inspired knowledge possessed by the wise. The supervisee can trace statements back to a more general theory and recognize them, realizing that this theory could also offer different constructs for understanding the scene. Supervisees should now be able to develop their own constructs for understanding material and express alternative ideas for understanding the scene described. This also changes the omnipotent position of the supervisor, putting the focus of meaning more on the describability of the invisible than the validity of theories. This means there is no competition between different theoretical models which attempt to put the non-visible into words and thus into conceptual structures. The common denominator of theories lies primarily in making visible that which is not visible. Alternative mental models already represent a visualization of the previously-presented mental model, in the sense that structure as a phenomenon only becomes apparent in de-marcation, thus becoming visible in the sense of Martin Buber: the I becomes visible in the Thou. This form of supervision counteracts authoritarian forms of theory and technique; supervisees are called on to develop their own models of psychological understanding and subject them to deconstruction.

Supervisors have a responsibility to express themselves explicitly about their own theories and thus always be capable of taking a meta-position towards the material presented, something represented as a Gadamerian circle in the structure of thought. Theories presented are in turn developed based on the case history, in this way illustrating the originality of the case and its individual irreplaceability, as reflected in the creative encounter in the group.

Supervisors also present their own feelings to the group, as a form of reflection on the scene presented. This attitude is characterized by its recognition of individual expressions of feelings which are different from all others and thus do not represent guidelines in the sense of "right" or "wrong".

5 Institution and School: Framework Conditions

In this project, supervision takes place within the framework of a school organization embedded within a structured hospital organization. Hospitals have their own rules, with particular structural characteristics; they have corresponding expectations of students. Institutions on this scale are subject to a closely administered, hierarchical order, governed by formal and informal rules. Supervisors must shift between, on the one hand, the creation of a trusted space in which students can express experiences, observations, problems, and concerns, and, on the other, their acceptance of training obligations, in the sense of defined goals set down by the institution which pays them. The institution, for its part, is under constant pressure from funders with regard to costs, as well as from the expectations of future nursing staff.

The transparency of the connection between supervisors and the institution and their demands for student achievement in training should always be openly addressed in the group, whereby the group can refer to the real situation in which trainees are in. The training process also develops cascading connections, as the group discusses situations involving people who have also undergone this training and who may be known to supervisors. It is not problematic if the group has a prevailing atmosphere of individuality and the material's uniqueness. This means ideas of right and wrong will not arise; they would put supervisors in a decision-making dichotomy in which they would be asked to position themselves alongside one of the people involved.

Student conflict with the unit they are associated with can occur in the group in the form of displaced conflict, especially with supervisors. Supervisees may want to bring it into the meeting as a way of gaining recognition for their experience: they want to have the supervisor "show them" the reaction to their problem (Slavin & Rahmani, 2016). The supervisor's reaction to the students – and thus to the here and now of the relationship – brings with it a strong learning effect, conveying a sense of authenticity. This form of knowledge generation requires open, collegial interaction within the group. Questions arise as to how much criticism is possible in the hierarchical atmosphere of the institution, the extent to which institutional structures can be questioned, and whether supervisors are tolerated or protected by the institution if they open a space for this dimension, thus giving public recognition to criticism.

Various levels of understanding unfold in the encounter with supervisees: first, the level found in the direct student-supervisor relationship; second, the relationship between student and patient or student and colleagues; a third level can be understood in terms of institutional conflicts resulting from feelings between student and supervisor. These levels do not contradict each other as long as an attitude of individuality prevails in the group, opening a space for reflection. The attitude of shared and co-created reality is paramount if we are to be able to think through these phenomena.

6 Empathy in Counter-Transferential Exploration and the Bidirectional Field

In a collegial atmosphere, drawing on aspects of ART II – working with one's feelings – the students and group leader develop a bidirectional, intersubjective field as well as generating specific ideas and hypotheses about the scene presented. There is a cascading progression here: the feelings of the student discussing the case are traced back to the scene in question. Then, using the feelings experienced in the group, this emotion is woven into a hypothetical web of understanding, with the thoughts of every participant carrying an attitude of change, in this way taking Gadamer's (hermeneutic) circle into account (Gadamer, 2010).

One crucial question is the exploration of aspects of the students which contribute to patients' reactions. The question always follows the attitude: what can we understand about patients through students' emotional reactions and involvement in the event? The group and the group leader also form a bidirectional field: they are jointly responsible for the thoughts expressed by students about the case. The difference between self-awareness and supervision lies in the direction and attitude of group participants when asking questions. Supervision is not about the students, nor about the elements of their own experience which they bring with them, nor is it about their conclusions about the past. The focus is always on thinking about reactions to the patient and other people in the material presented.

Given a high degree of trust between group members, there is often a desire to also move into a space of understanding and to present one's own trauma for "third party recognition". Here the group leader must decide to what extent they will accept these offers, which lead the group into a regressive state. In the case of traumatizing experiences with patients – such as suicide, violence, bullying, etc. – group members may ask them to address these events rather than work on a case history. Here there is often a great desire to outline one's own traumatization in the world of work and to experience recognition from the group. The group leader's job is now to surrender to the group's wishes for recognition, while not losing sight of the reality principle of an institution and hierarchical organization with structures of responsibility. If the group wants to experience this at the level of action, the supervisor often finds themself positioned on the side of the institution, as both representative and cause of the traumatization committed by the organization. Some students seize on the regressive ground on which the traumatization is staged, seeing the group leader as refusing to serve group members if they do not give concrete instructions for action and do not immediately intervene personally in hierarchical institutional structures Supervisors can then feel helpless; they are attacked if they do not act. The theme of helplessness is repeated in the shared field, which in turn is experienced very strongly by students. The group or its individual members now create a situation in which the group leader experiences these feelings. These encounters contain one of the most important learning experiences, as they can now experience how supervisors react to them, and which psychological characteristics they now display. How do they respond to their own feelings of helplessness? How do they process this without despairing?

The question is whether the group can recognize the group leader's helplessness and thus respect the fact that they are embedded within hierarchical relationships. Students describe experiencing scenes of powerlessness and dependence. In contract, they perceive the management as very powerful. They often find it very difficult to attribute feelings of powerlessness and dependency to leadership figures. At this point, there is an opportunity in supervision to empathize with supervisors, recognizing their powerlessness and thus no longer feeling so helpless. Perhaps students can also recognize that the helplessness of the supervisors is co-constructed by students, who demand concrete action or instructions from them. Some students remain in their concrete world, unable to open up the psychological world of shared events and enter into a reflective space.

The level of mentalization – in the sense of being able to attribute thoughts, feelings, intentions, etc. to the other person – now descends into concrete demands and actions. Above all, group members are needed who can move within this psychological space in a holding or containing manner. Demanding concrete solutions, thinking in terms of "wrong" and "right", "black" and "white", can gain a strong dynamic in groups, infecting other group members and thus closing off any space for reflection.

Feelings of envy – hence of destruction – may develop in the group, as a way of gaining control over supervisors and thus escaping one's own feelings of longing and associated traumas from one's own past. If this takes place, it can only be put into language through a collegial, supportive atmosphere. If the group leader can acknowledge students' pain or trauma, they can now move from the level of action to thinking about their own feelings, in this way recognizing feelings like envy and the associated desire for control.

A certain idealization of supervisors forms part of group activity, and supervisors can also demand it, within the bidirectional field, so as to express their role as knowledge brokers and receive recognition for their competence in the role.

With a shared attitude, one in which knowledge and insight can only be created jointly – constructing or deconstructing reality – a creative space unfolds in which feelings of ignorance and devaluation fade away into the background. Supervisors should always make their thoughts comprehensible, rather than expressing oracular knowledge from a higher source supposedly intended only for them. Without this clarity, the structures seen in faith communities would establish themselves in the group: this is particularly often the case in psychoanalytic training associations (Kernberg, 2016). Within this regressive atmosphere, many students also tend to "submit" to supervisors and thereby experience feelings of devaluation.

Shared exchange between students – as for example with intervision groups – can open up a space for some students where they are less dominated by feelings of ignorance than they would be with a group leader who behaves like a guru (Kernberg, 2014, 2016, 2017).

7 Dynamics within the Supervisee Group

Phenomena contributing to change are anchored in process-like series of events. A group changes over its time together, reflected in an increase in its knowledge and experience. The group makes it possible to shed light on many aspects of a scene and to understand participants' thoughts as jointly-created material. Within this intersubjective space, very diverse aspects of group-dynamic phenomena can come into play.

Providing a sounding board for participants to express feelings enables a process to develop which can trigger different emotions in different participants. They create individual feelings for the material by means of their own history, which forms part of this sounding board. The statements made now allow conclusions to be drawn about the group's understanding of the scene described. Another task of the group leader is to weave these different strands of emotion into a constructed configuration which demonstrates understanding for the patient while integrating opposed affects into an ambivalent, complex, psychological form of understanding. The more knowledgeable a supervisor appears, the more they will attract dynamics of emotion, including inferiority, anger, etc.; in this way the focus of understanding may shift away from the material presented. Without their own involvement, they will not be able to create an encounter with group participants, in other words, create a learning effect. However, there is always an opportunity to reflect on shared feelings and experiences on a basis of collegiality and to consider the extent to which they contain aspects of oneself, and to what degree they arise from the presentation by colleagues. The significance of emotional or affective narrative colouring for understanding the situation is another question that can be asked.

An important institutional dynamic can stem from the fact that the program is moderated by several group leaders. This can lead to competition, when students talk about different styles or interject what another colleague might say about a situation: this can be experienced as contradicting a statement made by another group leader. Of course, rivalries between group leaders also have considerable influence on groups. Since these feelings are important, they should be conceivable fields for supervisors, so as to make them constantly reflexively available. When an attitude of intersubjectivity has been clearly established within the group, a collegial attitude arises towards all transmittable emotions. In their co-construction of reality, students also experience their responsibility towards supervisors' feelings if they are influenced by competitive thinking. At the end of the learning process, students recognize the common influence on the material, the originality of their own thoughts and feelings, and in this way they also experience self-efficacy in their actions. Feelings of powerlessness, envy, inferiority, devaluation, etc. fade into the background, and students can experience a new way of thinking about situations.

Students should develop their own integrated frame of reference for understanding psychological events, generating a freedom within themselves which allows them to think about their psychological reactions to situations. In this way, they can evaluate actions reflexively. They can be aware of both their limitations and their effectiveness, thus achieving autonomy in their own assessments and value judgments.

8 Developing Student Competence: Scenes and Themes Introduced by Students

Students have the opportunity to freely choose topics and present them to the group in advance. Supervisors pick what they consider to be priority material, paying attention to traumatizing scenes, including the experience of suicide, violence, and frightening situations. Most of the time these scenes are the ones which make the group most emotional and can thus be well supported by them. The more frightening the material, the more the group leader must offer support; they can offer individual supervision in cases where the material is too onerous and has too much influence on students' own life story.

The focus in ART III is on students' oral reports about their experience on hospital units and other internship sites. For Kernberg, this is a source of information which provides excellent access to student attitudes and parallel processes unfolding in the group (Kernberg, 2016, p. 124). For Kernberg, parallel processes represent unconscious reactions which unfold in the process of transference and countertransference.

"Accuracy" in recording dialogue, which can only be guaranteed through audio or video recording, plays a subordinate role in this form. Since every encounter produces its own material and interpretations change every time a video sequence is viewed – in the sense of Gadamer's hermeneutic circle – the idea of "truth" postulated through recorded dialogue is also eliminated (Gadamer, 2010). The focus of ART III is on training one's own attitude and on its associated influence on a situation developing outside of words. The fact that action influences attitude is very much anchored in our Western educational tradition. We thus focus on how the attitude I take in certain situations can influence the action. Skills shown by the group leader should show productive development via students' identification.

Research into the development of competency by therapists, undertaken in recent years at the Personality Disorder Institute of the Department of Psychiatry at the Weill Medical Collage of Cornell University and the Westchester Division of New York Presbyterian Hospital, can be summarized as follows: the capability of supervisors consists in working on the predominant affective themes of the group. To do so, they need clarity in formulations, so as to represent ambiguous phenomena and bring them into common discourse. They also must understand conflicts and put them into language on different levels in order to gain an understanding of attitudes. All of this should unfold in a flexible way so students develop an approach to understanding spontaneous material which often only unfolds in the moment. An intervention which comes too late remains a merely intellectual exercise (Kernberg, 2016, p. 125).

Experts are not characterized by instructions for action, but the ability to react spontaneously and quickly, not to hold a conversation, but rather to let oneself be led by the conversation. The focus should be on letting oneself be guided by hearing or, to put it more precisely, being guided by what you hear, brought forth by the sounding board that generates perceptions (Gadamer, 2010; Buchholz, 2013a, 2017).

An important skill which students should acquire is improved emotional-cognitive regulation, a process through which they will have more freedom of choice in apparently stressful situations. Through the possibility of regulating affective processes, different positions can be imagined as making a difference in stressful situations, which in turn helps regulate the affective process. Here we come across, in a different research discipline, the thing which Gadamer defined as a circle. Gelo and Mergenthaler speak of a Therapeutic Cycles Model (TCM): their study proves that the use of unconventional creative metaphors in psychotherapy has an effect on processes of cognitive and emotional regulation (Buchholz, 2013a; Gelo & Mergenthaler, 2012).

With the ability to offer changes in thought by presenting metaphors for a situation, students have the opportunity to distance themselves from their own burdensome feelings and to begin reflexive processing. The more creative the metaphor chosen, the more the students will experience themselves as individually recognized by supervisors. The more general the transposition or metaphor, the more generally the supervisee will experience the intervention. Generalizations also allow a distancing on the part of the supervisor but require a certain emotional stability in the moment so students can remove themselves from the emotional situation, developing the ability, for example, not to be at the patient's emotional centre. These phenomena are described, among other terms, as projection or splitting. The more general the term chosen, the greater the risk that supervisors will be perceived as particularly knowledgeable or as gurus. The therapists' expertise lies in this use of explanatory models or metaphors. Theories are always metaphors of psychological, invisible phenomena. Supervisors must lead the students out of their dichotomous attitude by offering them an alternative concept, but they should not choose one too far from students' own understanding, otherwise the supervisor will be regarded by students as "standing above" things and their comments will be experienced as "making it easy". Supervisors must present a metaphor, in this way showing that they are "inside" the subject matter, simultaneously showing concern while acknowledging student experience. Students can then experience supervisors' reactions as "authentic"; group leaders have now "shown" them how to handle the situation.

This moment of change represents an interwoven experience between supervisor and student, one in which supervisors allow themselves to be emotionally touched and help co-create a situation in which there is acknowledgment of students' suffering. They offer a shift in language or a metaphor for the situation described, in this way making possible an offer of psychologically integrating the scene for the student. If students do not feel recognized in their emotional experience, they will reject the metaphor and feel they have not been understood. If they cannot experience the metaphor as a psychological shift and a moment of change, they will reject the supervisor's emotional involvement, often saying: "And what do I do with this now?"

Buchholz has designed a model for the supervision process, containing both vertical and horizontal dimensions. The horizontal dimension deals with task orientation between supervisee and supervisor. The encounter between the two roles is defined in terms of a specific task, describable as an overarching task conducted in a certain period of time, or as a task to be negotiated hour by hour.

For Buchholz, two-dimensional representation is about supervisee development, although supervisors also go through development and change. Through supervision, supervisees should attain higher levels of skill in encountering people. The task changes with the process of development. Both elements exert influence on each other. Supervisors are expected to be able to adapt to the development levels of each supervisee and/or to offer it recognition. Supervision is learning in and on the field. Formulations must be worked out with supervisees in mind, in this way enabling their development (Buchholz, 2013a, 2013b, 2017b).

Supervisee development is revealed through more differentiated styles of reflection when thinking about situations they are involved in. They are able to creatively develop an image and attributions, i.e. working out an explanatory model for the intentions and needs of patients or colleagues. The ability to mentalize should be developed and promoted. Supervisees should also be in a position to assess, with increasing clarity, how scenes and people develop, the influence they have on their environment, the influence of their interventions, and the extent to which they themselves change every individual scene. Security in encountering people lies in respecting the uncertainty which exists in every individually-formed scene, having the certainty to grasp something intuitively and respond on this basis. The goal of this training journey is competence. To put it another way: there should be a conception of a path which leads to competence, which must be generated and repeatedly re-found, as a different form of development at every age. Rønnestad and Skovholt conducted various surveys on how therapists develop; Neuweg has addressed competence development in pedagogy. Both findings trace similar lines of skill development. It can be concluded that there are common factors in the development of people working in the social field (Rønnestad & Skovholt, 2013; Neuweg, 1999).

Transitions between developmental stages are addressed via particular paradoxes, leading to a new attitude and in this way to clearer role definition and identification with the chosen profession. Development always involves knowledge about oneself and thus comes very close to the border between "teach or treat" and to a point where it is important to again explicitly discuss the task of supervisors, and thus shift the focus away from treatment. Although this is merely a cognitive construct, it can be very anxiety-relieving for students and serves to prevent regression. The task thus defines attitudes in the encounter, as well as the distribution of roles. Seen from outside, people sit together to listen and talk. Only definition, not action, leads to clear rules in encounters (Buchholz, 2013a, 2013b).

Supervisors should change their approach as the supervisee develops. Buchholz suggests a three-level system in which supervisors should behave or intervene differently towards their supervisees.

At the first level, the supervisee's fear of errors and criticism is at the centre of their development. Supervisors should seek to reduce anxiety, offering plenty of support and guidance. Above all, they should support the supervisees, offering encouragement and taking a less confrontational attitude towards them. Close observation and detailed reproduction build on their experience of ART II. Supervisors put observations into the context of theories about psychology, in this way enabling supervisees to distance themselves from involvement in their material. Students should have a reflective framework in which to reflect on their effectiveness in the situation. This will give them an idea of their "self-efficacy".

When moving to the second level, the supervisors reduce theoretical and practical advice and instruction. Student independence and originality should become more autonomous. The focus of reflection should shift to ideas about process development and psychodynamic understanding.

At level two, students still focus on many topics touching on conflicts of autonomy and dependence. The focus is on the institution and on the training situation within the teaching institution. Ideas of ability and of failure still vary widely. Students develop an increasingly effective empathetic understanding of the situation and of patients. They can more consciously develop a sense of self-efficacy, more consciously regulating mood swings in themselves and others. They also develop more clarity about what is possible and thus also about their own limits as to what is possible. They develop more and more individualized answers for patients and develop their own individual and conceptual ideas about psychological occurrences, increasingly regarding themselves as having an influence on events.

Supervisors' interventions should focus on promoting student autonomy. They are pleased with their students' development and focus more on what happens between student and supervisor as equal colleagues, who do not generate truth about a situation, but rather immerse themselves in reflective understanding. They increasingly ask students to come to terms with situations by making use of their uncertainty, abandoning ideas of certainty by offering different mental models for the same situation. Supervisors also challenge students more, gently provoking them, in this way increasing their sensitivity to attention. They treat group participants with greater and greater individuality, describing students' respective strengths and weaknesses as integrative factors in their personality and as a deeply individual tool of encounter.

The transition from level two to level three will increasingly foster professional identity. Students should further sharpen their understanding of their own psychological functioning in a professional, reflective context. Clear distinctions must be promoted, so that students can include their influence and their own life events in their considerations, and thus experience their influence in a more conscious way. Motivation and curiosity must increasingly be captured in language.

At the third level, students can more and more decide how to react to a situation, whether calmly or with emotion. They become increasingly flexible in encounters, able to recognize developments in themselves and in patients, and think about prognoses about people, teams, and processes. They experience doubt and uncertainty as a resource in their encounters with people. They develop an idea of how they can offer patients space for thought and reflection, thus creating a helpful situation. Students can absorb and integrate a wide variety of information as acquired material, achieving a large degree of autonomy while at the same time achieving a concept of identity and their own psychological understanding of connections with other people (Buchholz, 2013b, 2017b; Scaife, 2013, 2014).

9 Intersubjectivity – Supervision – Relational Thinking

Intersubjectivity and relational thinking encompass both the aspects of "one-person psychology" in which intrapsychic process research predominates, and those of "two-person psychology" where the focus is on interaction: intersubjectivity represents an integration of the two schools of thought. In the encounter, supervisors are never detached from their own psychological realities nor from influences from their own past and present histories. The histories and psychological realities of supervisees and supervisors are woven together into a new psychological reality. Both create a new reality through the transference they bring from their own life stories, which at the same time also forms a sounding board for understanding. The prevailing asymmetry in the encounter is determined by the two roles, and the attitude taken towards them (Berman, 2005, 2004; Buirski & Haglund, 2001).

By this definition, transference is a phenomenon which represents the need for understanding and the ability to empathize. Perception relies on the sounding board of one's own psychological understanding and one's definition of feelings. This ability to understand is developed by naming or through a shift in language, accomplished through metaphor: its purpose is that we are no longer at the mercy of our own impulsivity and the actions associated with it. To be "objective", we must be deeply "subjective" in our understanding. Without the exertion of influence, no understanding can develop, nor can we have influence on the construction of reality.

Supervisees first find themselves touched by patients in various aspects of their own selves; they generate a shared reality through "vulnerability" and the life story they bring with them. Supervisees bring this shared reality, now in part internalized as experience and explicitly available to them, into supervision as linguistically-processed experience. Here in turn a new reality emerges whereby the supervisor, through his or her resonance, and shaped by their own story, shapes the interwoven story of analysand and patient into a new story, in collaboration with the person to be analysed. In order to "understand" patients, we need the subjectivity of our own experience, from which generalizations can be constructed, which we then experience as "objectivity." Each encounter creates an original experience, and any supervisor would develop a different experience and understanding of the individual supervisee's narrative. One's own life story creates reality: it determines our understanding of reality, or else constructs it, as empathic understanding brought about through human resonant capacity.

Transference and countertransference are permanent processes which can be activated and shaped, and which proceed on a cyclical course. Observing these processes with care generates a new emotional climate and represents the reflective space of supervisory work. Within analytical understanding, a transitional space develops where supervisory work can take place.

From an intersubjective perspective, it is not about the supervisor avoiding phenomena like transference and countertransference, but that they explicitly recognize these aspects, as well as the associated construction of understanding the situation in a reflective framework:

> That is, all therapists experience countertransference whether or not they name it as such or devote much consideration to it in their work ... Therapists of all theoretical persuasions, by virtue of their humanity, have unresolved personal conflicts; try though we might, no professional credentials or experience shield us from the human condition.
>
> (Hayes, 2004, p. 24).

Countertransference describes a phenomenon which takes place in the encounter between supervisee and supervisor, beyond all theory and technique. A kind of handhold is needed to face these challenges and to profitably use their crucial potential for understanding. A survey of 127 therapists has suggested they experienced counter-transferential reactions in 80 percent of their sessions (Buchholz, 2013b; Hayes, 2004; Hayes et al., 2011).

Technique forms the framework in which a physical idea of the encounter is embedded. Technique and meta-psychological ideas form a frame of reference for a linguistic shift, i.e. a description of that which is not visible. Repeatability and the reduction of anxiety are based on an ability to abstract, to generalize, and find language in a general sense for what concerns us.

The application of correct technique, which is what many students want, ignores the importance of supervisors. When phenomena such as transference and countertransference enter the discussion as technical terms, they cannot be considered without thinking of the individual. Supervisors should always point out the importance of their feelings as part of the process of understanding. Buchholz summarizes the importance of theory and technique with the sentence: "Theory serves to deal with fear" (Buchholz, 2013b, p. 147). Fear should not be pushed aside, but rather seen as a vehicle for understanding the evolving situation between everyone involved. Technique is linked to the conception of theories, and to resulting behaviours, described in the form of interventions. Theories imply expectations of developmental goals, ideas about what is right and what is wrong. Because of their personal background, supervisors are deeply involved in their own life story, but in addition their meta-psychological ideas are based on it. In this way it participates in the collective shaping of relationships. We should also emphasize again that one's life history influences one's ideas of theory and the resulting technique, which in turn shapes understandings of one's life story, allowing it to be interpreted.

The further that technique recedes into the background as explicit knowledge, the more phenomenological work comes to the fore, in the form of precise observation and a differentiated view of the situation narrated, which unfolds in the context of supervision. In order to work with this interconnectedness, we need to share the feelings which develop during the encounter. In addition, a space for reflection must be created to understand why feelings develop, or transference and countertransference, and what one might as a result understand about patients and one's encounter with them.

Küchenhoff has addressed the importance of theory for everyday clinical practice. He divides theory into four dimensions: first as a worldview held by therapists or supervisors; second as an ideological background influencing life and therapy or supervision; third as a metapsychological conception; and fourth as the preconscious, implicit idea present in every encounter (Küchenhoff, 2004). In doing so, he addresses the constructivist acquisition of knowledge, paving the way for pluralism and the intersubjective field. This approach contradicts models which aim at "truth". Truth-based models imply the exclusion of less "effective" models, moving entirely within a Darwinian tradition of thought in which only the strongest survive and everyone else dies off. Pluralism is not arbitrary: it is based on the need to form a frame of reference within which thoughts can develop. Within the framework, these thoughts reveal psychological understanding, creating space in thought discourse so that thinking about the framework also becomes possible. Frames of reference, like those represented by technique and theory, are subject to mental construction and thus move away from a belief system.

> If theory formation is regarded as a conscious activity that has an undercurrent of unconscious libidinal encounter, theory itself is questioned psychoanalytically. As this again is a theory, it can be applied against itself: the very concept of unconscious motives underlying theories is a theory built on unconscious motives.
>
> (Küchenhoff, 2004, p. 11).

To subject this passage to deconstruction: the tool of deconstruction again requires theory and technique. Theories should not be arbitrary, otherwise they run the risk of being superficial. Many thinkers have engaged with psychoanalysis to develop concepts of understanding within this overall framework of thought. All of these shape our understanding of the psychological. But the development of beliefs goes through a paradigm shift, passing through deconstruction and in turn construction, as part of a cycle of knowledge generation. Psychological development and psychological freedom are seen in one's involvement in life and in the capacity to reflect on one's own thought. Fear seeks truth: it looks for repeatability in the sense of security rather than generalization, and for reference points in the process of making-visible. Lear summarizes it as follows: "The problem is that even if you do need psychoanalytic experience to understand the theory, it is also true that if you don't understand theory you can't really understand the experience you think you are having" (Lear, 2003, pp. 16f.).

Kantrowitz addresses the change undergone by therapists in the process of encounter, where conflicts arising in the therapist, prompted by their own life story, intersect with the patient's conflicts (*similar*). She attempts to use empirical material to establish the extent to which this is important for processes of change in patients. Therapists' own conflicts are reactivated during analysis and they must thus subject themselves to constant self-scrutiny. The ability to mobilize one's conflicts, affects, thoughts, and feelings from the past is the key point in understanding the patient; this is the basis for empathy.

> Studying how analysts perceive changes in themselves over time allows for a longitudinal view of the impact of the analytic process on a group of people who have devoted themselves to this process as their lifework. For most analysts this means that the psychological issues explored in their personal treatment are not re-repressed, as they might be following termination, but rather are kept actively alive in their work with patients. As a result, the analyst has the continuing opportunity to rework these issues on a potentially deeper level. Every analysis an analyst undertakes is in this respect potentially a reanalysis for him- or herself.
>
> (Kantrowitz, 1997, p. 130).

Influence over patients comes from the knowledge which therapists gain about themselves: through this they can develop a different attitude towards patients. She gives an example drawn from an interview with an experienced therapist: "Once the analyst had this realization, without his saying a word, the patient relaxed and said, 'You're with me now'" (Kantrowitz, 1997, p. 134). The therapist's transformed attitude was already influencing the encounter with the patient, without it being explicitly expressed in language.

The question is how analysts process analytic experience in their field of work, which in turn raises the question of supervision and its significance. If we start by assuming that it is significant that patients experience change undergone by therapists, then effective supervision relies on supervisees experiencing this process of shared change in the supervision. Supervisors must be involved to such an extent that supervisees can also anchor their change in the form of implicit learned knowledge.

> Although the asymmetry of the relationship means that the analyst is by definition in a 'safer' position than the patient, the former, once this emotional openness is permitted, engages in an emotional risk. Without this emotional risk, no psychological change can take place. To be truly engaged is to allow oneself to be vulnerable to another.
>
> (Küchenhoff, 2004, p. 36f.).

The recognition of shared involvement and the shared fear of what might be discovered is reduced by ideas of correct theory and technique. Examining two people's interaction and entanglement in the encounter leads us to deconstruct transference, countertransference: precisely our theories and our techniques.

As early as the 1950s, Harold F. Searles confronted us with the claim that patients are their analysts' therapists (Searles, 1974). Searles worked in schizophrenia research, and anyone who has worked with patients of this kind knows how deconstructive and paradigm-shifting the encounters can be. In this context, the concept of psychotropic drugs (Atwood, 2017) comes to be added to therapists' use of theory and technique – quickly deconstructed by patients – as a means of escape and anxiety reduction.

This was echoed in Georg Devereux's warning from 1967, which exhorted us to pay attention to the significance of researchers' fears (Devereux, 1973). But it is not simply a question of fears on the part of the analyst or supervisor. It is about recognizing the co-constructed experience of these emotions, recognizing mutual dependence, without which witnessing, in the sense of a "third party", would simply not work (Benjamin, 2018).

"The psychoanalytic process arises in a mutual interaction between analysand and analyst" (Szecsödy, 2004, p. 54). These words come from a well-known researcher in the field of supervision. He picks three points from the concept of mentalization, clarifying its importance for the development of psychological understanding:

> Mentalization is important:
>
> - first, it enables the individual to see people's action as meaningful through the attribution of thoughts and feelings, so that their actions become predictable, which in turn reduces dependency on others.
> - second, it allows for recognition of the fact that someone is behaving as if things are a particular way does not mean that things are like that.
> - third, without a clear representation of the mental state of the other, communication must be profoundly limited.
>
> Finally, mentalization can help an individual to achieve deeper experiences with others and, ultimately, a life experienced as more meaningful.
>
> (Szecsödy, 2004, p. 58f.).

For Szecsödy, the relations is the centre of change in the therapeutic relationship. He draws on the mentalization concept of Fonagy et al. to lend this change a comprehensible and thinkable concept. Learning under supervision works best when the focus is on deconstructing and reconstructing patient-supervisee interaction, in order to view it as a system functioning within the boundaries of an overall framework (Szecsödy, 2017).

Change in supervision happens within a shared structure: "[I]t is not 'the' supervision ... not 'the' method which achieves something, but rather the particular combination of method and person" (Buchholz, 2013b, p. 155). Buchholz also puts the focus on the opposite case: what it means to cause damage in supervision and how this might be measured. With regard to the shared field, there is also the question of how much damage patients or supervisees can inflict on therapists.

The intersubjective field develops as a joint construction between two people who are present and one person who is absent, or in a group including one person who is present in the form of another person's representation of them.

This person who, or the scene which, is described by students contributes significantly to the formation of this intersubjective field, although they are absent. Every time the scene is told, differently processed by the narrator, it is changed again, in contrast to written ART II reports. The process of listening undergoes continual change as it constantly manifests itself anew. We always hear different elements in a story. It is probably also changed repeatedly when reading it, as readers go through their own process and, if it is re-read, read it differently every time. Attention is not only paid to the content of the scene, but to the process, which is in constant flux. Contemplation on the meta level is always based on an attitude which posits reality as created through jointly-constructed influence, through the efforts of co-creators. This view requires critical self-reflection in order to bring the field into one's thoughts as a reality.

This reflexive metacommunication allows participants in a group to go through a process of personal growth. But if the supervision process becomes increasingly content-driven, this personal growth process is inhibited (Berman, 2004).

Growth also involves reflecting on the feelings of inhibition, shame, ignorance, etc. which always develop between a supervisor and their students. In supervision, these feelings are usually denied and rationalized away. But supervisees' emotions have a massive influence on the shared process. It is important to always open a reflective space for these feelings, without in turn encouraging emotions that are too strong, like envy, fear, competitiveness, etc. Negative reactions on the part of supervisors are based on "prolonged, unrecognized transference-countertransference disjunctions and the chronic misunderstandings that result from them" (Stolorow et al., 2014, p. 42). Misunderstandings which cannot be articulated can lead to a chronically negative reaction on the part of supervisors.

It is also important for students to develop an ability to allow new thoughts and tolerate their own recognition of ignorance. Some students experience envy towards statements made by supervisors, with reactions – e.g. a masochistic attitude – taking hold, devaluing, and destroying what comes from the supervisors. If the process helps the development of the group and every individual in it, these archaic feelings of envy and destruction are minimized because of a shared recognition of knowledge and ignorance, and how the two processes take place together. In dichotomization, feelings of envy, destruction, etc. come into play. Good supervision is shaped by a shared recognition of blind spots; the roles of teacher and learner are interchangeable and fluctuating. In order for a process to take place, everyone involved needs to change. At the end of this process, there should be colleagues in the group who act as a peer group, enriching and influencing each other with their thoughts and statements.

Conflicts arise for supervisors when students demand that their pain be acknowledged in a professional situation, with supervisors also acknowledging the helplessness of the person involved in the scene described. If they then try to give students freedom of action in relation to feelings of dependency and attempt to understand the feelings of one student or another, they will manoeuvre themselves into being rejected by the students. At this point, a dynamic of helplessness is taking hold: supervisors are now very close to students, since they now also feel helpless in their suggestions.

We will quote Sarnat to show a path of development leading out of this dynamic:

> A supervisee's character problems become a focus of supervisory attention. The supervisor's conflicts (i.e. their impatience to see her supervisee change, and her need to assert her own competence through too-active intervention) played into the student's problem (i.e. submissiveness), contributing to the development of supervisory crisis. An intense, emotional transaction occurred in the process of resolving this supervisory crisis. The supervisor responded quasi-therapeutically when the supervisee 'invited her in' via an expression of intense affect to the supervisor.
>
> The supervisor's acknowledgment of her contribution to the crisis seemed to shift the interpersonal context to one in which the supervisee could safely and vividly experience and process her own conflict, even in the absence of complete confidentiality.
>
> Had the supervisor tried to 'help' her with this problem, while pretending to be the uninvolved expert, the supervisee would very likely have felt humiliated and endangered.
>
> (Sarnat, 1992, p. 399)

Sarnat points out the importance of equality between the people involved, to preserve the dignity of supervisees, so they are not obliged to disavow feelings like shame and humiliation. Dignity is an important constant in therapies and supervision, and in pedagogical fields, but it is not usually spoken of with adequate reflection in the intersubjective field (Orlinsky, 2018).

Another major unexplored area in supervision is the subject of eroticism between the people involved. Here is one example from Berman:

> As is usual, I encouraged the supervisor to tell me of any past interactions we had that might influence her feeling in supervision. She brought up an interaction from years back, when we had been acquainted professionally in another setting, in which she had experienced a compliment I gave her as seductive. Our straightforward conversation about that episode turned out to be a valuable springboard for our subsequent work on eroticized transference issues, because the possible resonances between sexual currents in analysis and supervision (e.g. the erotic atmosphere that might evolve in supervision when the analysand's sexual fantasies about the analyst are discussed) became less threatening to both of us as a result of the effective working through of such topics in our own relationship.
>
> (Berman, 2004, p. 204)

The supervisee was now able to address the subject of eroticism during supervision and much more easily able to think about her erotic feelings in the encounter with the patient. For Berman, this sequence was important in her development, opening up a process of understanding erotic themes in her own supervisory relationship. If the topic does not emerge as a surprising moment, it will remain, at most, an element of technique in supervisory discussion (D.N. Stern et al., 2012). If the erotic component between students and supervisors does not find space in the group as a genuine sequence in the encounter, it can only be processed in terms of technique, without the affective participation of those in the group. This is among the most difficult topics in supervision as an intersubjective field. In the above example, too, the appearance of the subject was put outside the usual framework, to avoid embarrassing a supervisor for having previously paid the supervisee a "seductive" compliment. The supervisee was the one to bring the erotic moment into the supervision. In the asymmetric field – as postulated by Jaenicke and as described by the Boston Change Process Study Group – it is possible to discern forward motion and change in the field, from supervisor to supervisee. The supervisor is the one who follows, while the supervisee moves ahead, taking the supervisor with her: the supervisor then goes along with this, using it to expand their working relationship.

The supervision process is not a parallel process to the work as actually experienced or the process of encountering the patient, in which the supervisor, from an abstinent position, would provide "correct" explanations for past and narrated events. Instead, the moment of change takes place in the group encounter, in the present moment (D.N. Stern, 2005; D.N. Stern et al., 2012). "Contemporary supervisors attend not just to the patient being presented, or to the therapeutic dyad, but to the supervisory relationship itself as part of the clinical/supervisory frame of reference" (Bass, 2014a, p. 540).

Our attitude as supervisors is based on recognizing our own limits and the limitedness of subjective understanding, that is, of how we perceive and shape our experience. This attitude also takes into account our influence on students and the fact that they can now also recognize their own influence on patients. This attitude is expressed in the fact that "every reflection offered and every question formulated is done so tentatively, since we are aware of the complexity of our dual role as an actor and as a product of an intersubjective field" (Jaenicke, 2014, p. 128).

Supervisors' answers reflect their own subjectivity by formulating it, presenting themselves in the presence and uncertainty of the spoken word. Supervisees often seem disturbed by this type of answer, but it means they can allow their own patients more independence and also learn to give them tentative answers.

10 Embedding in a Training Institution

Supervision is anchored in cultural understandings of the training institution, and its understanding and attitude have an influence on groups' attitudes towards reflective thought. Intersubjective thinking by implication includes organizational, historical, and cultural influences on the situation of students and group leaders. It is always possible for feelings which develop in a supervision group to be reflected in an institutional context; the atmosphere established in the training institution always rubs off on students and group leaders (Berman, 2004). Of course, the training centre likewise places demands on students and educators, and this in turn reflects demands on the part of the institutions where students work in internships and later pursue their profession. These fields of tension are guided and affected by the influence of political agendas. Many students experience this tension when their internship site or the people working there devalue the knowledge they have acquired, telling them that it is unrealistic or what they are learning does not correspond to the needs of practical work.

Group leaders are paid by the institution and should fulfil its wishes regarding the education of the students, at least on an implicit level. Questions arise as to the moral values established by the institution: what idea of ethics should group leaders attend to? When should they break confidentiality, in the event of problematic situations? What happens if a group leader classifies a student as unsuitable for a caring profession or wants to suggest further training in self-awareness? Does the rule of confidentiality offer protection to all participants and does it relieve supervisors of their responsibility for students vis-à-vis the institution, colleagues, and patients? Internship institutions and instructors, in turn, outsource issues concerning students to the supervision group. This raises the question of who bears what responsibility within the structure.

Many issues raised by students are complaints about their training, reflecting their helplessness and the traditional learning experiences they have had in hierarchical schools. Students very often address personal development and autonomy issues, especially in the age cohort between 20 and 25. Group leaders are often equated with the institution and confrontationally held responsible for experiences during training. These subjects very often slide into unconscious preoccupations with efforts at autonomy vis-à-vis their family of origin. A space in which reflexive attitudes can develop presupposes the appearance of an autonomous ego and its recognition of its individual autonomous development. My personal recognition first requires the possibility of reflexive behaviour and thus also the recognition of difference, of the existence of an I and a you. If the group leader's statements were viewed as enriching, as something they had themselves generated, it could lead to the abandonment or destabilization of one's own identity. Many subjects discussed in the group deal with this desire for recognition and identity. A desire for recognition on the part of the students often overshadows other topics, or emerges via the material presented.

In this field of tension too, the group leader must move between elements of self-awareness and moments of responsibility towards the scene described by students. The pressure is increased when scenes focus on the subject of training. Students taking on personal responsibility means being critical of their own actions and learning to accept discussions about challenges, from their own perspective. Students quickly feel criticized or offended, and struggle with feelings of invalidation.

> Effective learning, I suggest, is most enhanced by a supervisor who is openly critical but also self-critical and who is willing to openly explore the way this criticism is experienced – reducing as much as possible any reporting to external authorities, and discussing any such reporting openly within supervision.
>
> (Berman, 2004, p. 213).

All these influences can put a lot of pressure on participants in a supervision group. It is necessary for the leadership of the group to continually reflect on all of these factors, in a process of intersubjective understanding.

> The best and most creative supervision takes place when the supervisor trusts her organizational structure to support her ability to use her voice uniquely and creatively, and to encourage her supervisees to do the same. ... For the supervisor to continue to grow and to refine her own voice as a clinician, supervisor, and community member, she must be able to rely on her organization to be a facilitating environment that is willing to and capable of holding a tension between conformity and deviation; between old and new; between the experimental and the tried and true.
>
> (Frawley-O'Dea & Sarnat, 2001, p. 243).

To enable this in the group, supervisors need the training institution's containing function. If this atmosphere cannot be maintained by the institution and cannot be restored when breaks occur, students will ultimately suffer, specifically in terms of their ability to manage a supervision situation in their professional field.

But the structure of an organization, a training institution, is also supported by fragile human beings, operating in a fluid of instability.

> There is also a need for limits that protect the overarching goals of the organization. If one joins an organization, institute, or training program, there is some responsibility to hold, to protect, and to facilitate the voice of the organization at the same time that one is held, protected, and facilitated.
>
> (Frawley-O'Dea & Sarnat, 2001, p. 248).

These two authors point out the interconnectedness and shared responsibility of the organization and those who are working there, as well as the responsibility borne by students. For some supervisors at ART III, the external position which they hold – they are paid fees but not employed – offers a certain freedom, which is reflected by introducing theories into the supervision which supervisors are currently dealing with and which they want to teach. These levels of interconnectedness present a delicate structure of varying needs and perceptions, reflected in pendulum-like movements between structure and freedom.

11 Boundaries between Supervision, Therapy and Analysis

Further questions arise: to what extent should a group leader have an understanding of students' psychological structure in order to develop an intersubjective understanding of the situation described? To what extent is it important to convey to students that within an intersubjective field, understanding is always something developed together and that every understanding of scenes or patients always opens up self-understanding for students? In relational understanding, there is no clear line between "teach and treat".

Since students have less practical experience in a work context, they often come up with examples from their family background, to understand the scene under consideration. Supervisors can more easily draw on experiences of meeting people in everyday working life, but can also make links to family experience, including their own children, since they may be in a similar life situation to their students.

"Without direct communication about personal matters, we may remain at times in the dark as to the significance of what we observe in supervision" (Berman, 2004, p. 218). One's own life story can be a gateway to understanding the patient and should have a place in supervision. For students, understanding patients comes from their own life history. Empathy develops through students' experience of feeling moved. The job of the supervisor is to record their feelings and associations and carefully bring them into the context of the case presented, rather than allowing them to be diverted into self-awareness, where these elements are always present. Supervisors take responsibility for directing how work continues with the particular associations presented. If the associations presented by students remain concealed, the intersubjective field will close over: what will remain is a knowledge-generating reflection about patients, with the viewpoint remaining solely that of two "experts". The influence of supervisees on the scene presented remains hidden because the supervisors block their access to an understanding of their own life history.

The distinction between self-analysis and analysis of a described scene lies in the conscious direction undertaken by the supervisor, which repeatedly places associations presented by students into the context of the event described. The feelings which supervisors experience in turn flow into the construct of understanding regarding the patients. These emotions open up a common space in which to reflect on feelings unfolding in the encounter between supervisor and student. Negative or erotic transferential feelings in supervision should be used as moments of understanding for the case history. If students now learn how supervisors can work with these feelings, they will also learn how to attain security regarding these feelings in patients during their encounter.

Many students struggle with a fear that they themselves may be "pathologized" or "seen through". The more abstinent supervisors are in this situation, the more these feelings will come into play in the group. Understanding the patient means looking within yourself and becoming involved with your own feelings. This understanding now generates closeness to the patients but also the fear of becoming very close to and understanding of their "pathology". These anxieties should always be brought into a reflexive process. The involvement of supervisors and the expression of emotions to generate empathy reduces supervisee anxiety (Frawley-O'Dea & Sarnat, 2001; Sarnat, 1992).

Frawley-O'Dea and Sarnat turn to well-known voices in psychoanalysis to make the argument that "a rigidly impenetrable boundary between teaching and 'treating' in supervision is neither desirable nor truly achievable" (Frawley-O'Dea & Sarnat, 2001, p. 159).

This distinction presents a similar construct and indeed the same dilemma that Freud dealt with in distinguishing between transferential love and "real" love. The need for differentiation is not due to the primary separation of the two phenomena, but to control fear on the part of students and supervisors (Slavin & Rahmani, 2016).

Supervision, thought of in a relational sense, requires transference from supervisee to supervisor and supervisor's countertransference in order to understand what is happening with patients.

> The analyst's experience of the patient is central in understanding and guiding the analytic process. Within this context, the 'teach/treat' dichotomy is no longer a meaningful distinction, for 'treating' corresponds with illuminating the analyst's experience, a necessary process for 'teaching'.
>
> (Fosshage, 1997, p. 202).

This dichotomy, as Fosshage aptly mentions, hinders our flow of thought in understanding supervisees. It is a fear-reducing mental relic which has the purpose of maintaining clear structures for external use. There is no teaching without personal involvement.

If we start from the paradigm that both empathy for and understanding of supervisees develop when supervisors can look within themselves and define their own contribution to the encounter, then the idea of *not* including the personality of supervisees in their understanding is an untenable construct.

This is how Frawley-O'Dea defines the boundary between therapy and teaching:

> How, then, does this relational model of supervision differ from analysis or psychotherapy? The answer is – it depends. Primarily, it depends on the unique parameters developed by each supervisory dyad as to the boundaries of relational explorations. Generally, however, the discussion of transference-countertransference paradigms and relational derivatives of parallel processes within supervision is focused differently than in treatment. Specifically, within supervision, the overarching objective is to further the supervisee's competence and comfort as a psychoanalytically-oriented clinician. In other words, the development of the supervisee as a clinician is the paramount task. Although there may be some overlap with the supervisee's work on growth and character analysis taking place within his treatment, this is a secondary point of focus within the supervision. For instance, in the example above, my supervisee and I did not spend much time discussing the possible etiologic antecedents of her compliance, nor did we address the particulars of this style across relationships. Rather, our focus remained on our own relationship and its implications for her work with her patient.
>
> (Frawley-O'Dea, 1997, p. 9).

The more clearly defined the recognition of supervisors as participants in the supervisory relationship, the less problematic the boundary between teaching and treatment appears. Supervisors also undergo change through their encounter with students, and only by defining the asymmetry is it possible to distinguish whether this is a shift in understanding, and thus a gain in knowledge for supervisors. Or are the students teaching the supervisor in the sense of exploring something new and unique? Here too, distinctions between the meaning of learning, teaching, knowledge, self-awareness, etc.

become superficial constructs, which can be deconstructed and will thus lose their function of anxiety-reduction.

12 Intersubjectivity in the Group Setting

Working in and with groups already includes relational and intersubjective thinking, where transference and countertransference develop between participants, representing elementary aspects of the group. The group analyst S.H. Foulkes is also considered a pioneer of the intersubjective paradigm shift, thanks to his formulation of terms including "transpersonal" and "location". As early as 1948, Foulkes described a shared connection between all group participants as a *matrix*, a term which Mitchell later adopted from Loewald, meaning an unconscious primal connection. His metaphor for the connection was X-rays invisibly passing back and forth between participants.

> Group analytic conceptualization of the social unconscious preceded its time by emphasizing such intersubjective concepts as multiplicity, mutuality, and radical openness, long before intersubjective or relational writings were first published. We can conceptualize the intersubjective field as a co-creation of the psyche of the people involved in the interaction, meaning that it is not the simple result of the people's unconscious but is a new co-unconscious belonging to neither participant.
>
> (Weinberg, 2015, p. 195).

Haim Weinberg does not regard the unconscious as an individual phenomenon. Rather, as he puts it, "we are talking about creating the unconscious and acquiring 'knowledge' about it with the help of the other through conversation" (Weinberg, 2015, p. 195; 2007). He refers to this unconscious as the social unconscious, constructed jointly by the members of a group. Every community, every group, every nation creates a shared social unconscious, which has its meaning implied in reflection: on the group, or the learning institution, or in the context of ART III, the internship site.

There are similarities between group analytic concepts and intersubjective, relational thinking, but the two divide on approaches to neutrality, as well as to an associated phenomenon: the participation of the group leader as a separate actor in the group process. In conceptual terms, the group leader remains in an abstinent, non-participating position. The members of a group are always embedded in an equal position. For this reason, the group is, a priori, always already intersubjective in its essence (Hirsch, 2010).

Group analysts see the group as a healing factor, with its members acting as "healers" through the relationships they enter into. Pathology, in Foulkes' conception, can only be understood through relationships: "pathology" and "healing" develop in the group through the relationships formed within it.

> The complicated position of the group leader in the context of intersubjective approaches to clinical work should be discussed and practiced, so that we can better understand what it means to be a 'leader-in-a-group' rather than a therapist who keeps his patients at a distance.
>
> (Friedman, 2015, p. 20).

The group fulfils a holding, containing function for all participants: in a functioning transitional space, this proves to be a manifold phenomenon, one which reshapes relations (Carvalho, 2010). Beate West-Leuer (2011) has defined five key points for intersubjective supervision in a multi-person setting:

1. There is no "objective knowledge"; rather, there is a complex network of relationships between the team, the supervisor and the client being supervised. This process is influenced by formal and informal rules and the culture of the institution where the supervision takes place. The decisive source of knowledge is "intersubjectivity".
2. By means of a specific setting and interventions, the group creates a transitional space where insights can develop. Reality is generated in an intersubjective field of tension, and not in reconstructing the past.
3. Insights are gained in the "in-between" as the group goes beyond manifest content, tests itself intuitively in debate, thereby generating new insights.
4. Supervisors are in an external position and thus automatically outsiders to team members. Reflecting on this outsider position, this alienation, generates knowledge and insights about clients and also about patients' lifeworlds, something equally alien.
5. Understanding can only come through discussion with group members, and there is no way of proving the correctness of insights gained in supervision.

13 Transitional Space – Representational Space as Intersubjective Staging

The group offers a space of possibility in which supervisees can reenact unconscious conflicts they experience in their work. By transposing them to the group, conflicts can be brought to awareness and in this way coped with. The group leader reacts to the material presented or to the supervisee's transference with second-order countertransference. These resonance effects of the group and the group leader, triggered by the scenic function of the ego or by mirror neurons, shape the "transitional space" as involvement in the scene. Unconscious relationships with clients and colleagues are now re-staged or they model the representational space (West-Leuer, 2011).

Group members offer a sounding board and are now identified with the material presented, with supervisors able to take a new metaposition towards the group, in turn helping to shape the process via the affects they have experienced.

> If the patient makes the supervisee into an all-powerful helpful object, the group often undergoes a vicarious feeling: this is either hypomanic, active or full of good advice (symmetrical countertransference) or overwhelmed, paralyzed, critical, making the 'student or supervisor' aware of their failure (concordant countertransference to the reported scene).
>
> (Lohmer, 2017, p. 23)

Supervisors retain the function of "alienated" feeling, in this way raising the affects they experience into language and developing the process further, for example by giving space to excessive demands and the emotions associated with them. For Lohmer, stepping back from an active ego to an observational ego – reflected in the emotions experienced – is the central supervisory skill of the group leader. The supervisor interprets the group's reaction and its dynamics on a meta-level, in the sense of an understanding of the supervision case being described (Lohmer, 2017).

14 Not Knowing: Group Leaders with Low Field Competence

Supervisors are confronted with students' different internship positions and usually have little field expertise in this heterogeneous institutional landscape. Students usually feel alienated in their new internship position and convey this alienation, and associated feelings, to their supervisors. West-Leuer assumes that "alienation" is expressed as a primary feeling in the transitional space. The scenes described feel just as alien as to students, who find themselves in an outsider position during their internship. This also makes it easier for students to identify with supervisors, since both have a "outsider" or meta position in relation to the workplace. Compared to their colleagues at the internship, the students have an outsider position and can thus offer perspectives and questions to the team, put forward, for example, as "blind spots". Not knowing represents a large reservoir of understanding in which repressed, denied aspects of the client can unfold in a hidden team dynamic. The group leader always traces associations expressed back to the material presented at the beginning: this in turn enables associative conclusions to be drawn. A shift in focus to the initial scene of the story to be processed prevents too strong a regression to one's own life history and its associated neediness, as well as one's own traumatizing life story which struggles for recognition (West-Leuer, 2007, 2011).

15 Conclusion

ART III represents a final process point of a three-stage training, which should accompany the students in their professional development, promote growth, and support them in finding their future professional role. Many students hold great expectations about their future career, hoping that training will provide them with "tools" to support their practice and promote autonomy. They go through phases of fear and uncertainty, along with ideas of capability and superiority, based on their newly acquired knowledge. Most people experience a certain disillusionment in internships in terms of expectations of their chosen career and the applicability of the knowledge imparted. This can lead to increased frustration. Training confronts students with a deconstruction of their own ideas and expectations of themselves and the profession, in order to achieve an authentic experience in work situations and thus enjoy greater security (Rønnestad & Skovholt, 1997, 2013; Skovholt & Rønnestad, 1997).

The ART concept holds that professional maturation is tied to making a connection between the professional and the personal. In this way, it thus leads to ease in action through a feeling of authenticity. Students should deal reflexively with complex work situations, position themselves and others in an accepting manner, recognize ambiguity in situations, and be able to recognize different solutions to the same problem, as well as be able to withstand the pressure to act, above all, in order to generate solutions. "This pressure is expressed in the slogan 'Don't just sit there, do something!'" (Rønnestad & Skovholt, 1997, p. 301).

Reflection should transform lived experience (*Erleben*) into known experience (*Erfahrung*). Complexity should be recognized in its entirety and processed in this way. Change which cannot be illuminated through a reflective process is subject to dangers of pseudo-development and stagnation.

The relationship with supervisors and the qualities of that relationship, based on respect, empathy, authenticity, clarity, and openness, are the decisive factors in students' developmental success.

Through their relationship skills, supervisors make a significant contribution to maintaining a constructive group and learning process. They should create an atmosphere that reduces anxiety, while offering some degree of structure so as to develop a space for reflection with all its rules. At the end of the path is a shared development process, a stimulating one, which everyone in the group has enjoyed and experienced as enriching.

9 Methodological Approach

1 Empirical Investigation of the Training Process

The initial situation of students at the beginning of training, as with the cohort described here (beginning of third semester), has received little attention in the literature (Fiegl, 2016). The primary assumption is that personality variables are already present in students entering a social profession. One of the first to address this question was Carl Rogers, who believed that qualities like empathy, warmth, and congruence need to be taught as part of psychotherapeutic training. He later came to the opinion that these characteristics cannot be taught, but must be brought with them by students (Hill & Knox, 2013; Fiegl, 2016; Fiegl & Sindelar, 2014; Rogers, 1957). Truax and Carkhuff represent the position that "helping skills" for counselling and psychotherapy are both teachable and learnable. They discuss this in terms of empathy, warmth, and genuineness, qualities they see as important for people in counselling and therapy professions (Truax & Carkhuff, 1973).

There is no obvious research data on what characteristics students should already have, and what skills they can learn, in training for the counselling and psychotherapeutic professions. There are no basic reference values for different stages of training to answer the question of initial requirements, and the associated question of support (Fiegl, 2016). Pollmann's dissertation addressed admission criteria in psychoanalytic training. Heimann, Reik, Balint, and Greenson all assume that students possess skills as existing predispositions, which cannot later be acquired (Pollmann, 1985; Fiegl, 2016).

But students do not arrive as "blank slates", as Ulvik and Ronnestad so aptly put it. Each person undergoing training brings with them a cultural background which has shaped them (Lorenz, 1935). Individual students bring ideas about illness and models of help (Rønnestad & Skovholt, 2013): "Healing practices are embedded in the culture in which the practices take place. Cultural embeddedness, or contextualization of practices, is a fundamental principle in cultural psychology" (Rønnestad & Skovholt, 2013, p. 38).

Culture has a greater influence than personal characteristics on students in terms of healing professions, and this in turn brings the culture of the educational institution to the fore. Training culture is determined by learning

DOI: 10.4324/9781003483441-9

processes. At the outset, the person undergoing training tends to adopt an imitative role, adopting a professionally-adapted attitude dictated from outside. Individuation takes a back seat at the learning stage (Rønnestad & Skovholt, 2013, 1997).

In terms of supporting students, their relation with trainers and supervisors is the decisive factor in successfully becoming a therapist or counsellor. The relationship is also crucial in the encounter with patients. The most important factor in successful psychotherapy is the relationship (Orlinsky et al., 1994). "I believe the critical element of any successful therapy is the ability of the therapist to safely manage the relationship between patient and therapist" (Strupp, 1996, p. 1022).

Significant relationships with supervisors and teachers are the basis for learning, in terms of the quality of students' relationships with patients. "The quality of a relationship between supervisor and supervisees influences learning at every level of experience" (Rønnestad & Skovholt, 1997, p. 301).

Satisfaction with training and later the treatment of patients is largely determined by the relation with trainers and with institutional culture. The experience of relationships with trainers, embedded in affective learning, in turn shapes relationships with patients.

Undertaking this learning experience requires "high emotional intelligence," which in turn is linked to above-average formal intelligence (Fischer, 2011). Even for Tom Levold, who begins with the individual personality, a "therapist personality" cannot be trained because it emerges from a long process of development, encompassing all personal experiences (Levold, 2004). Deconstructing or overcoming training should take place very quickly, so that one can react to situations in patient encounters: "Even at this early level of training, one can learn how to overcome training, and learn that one has to overcome it, because in a psychotherapeutic situation you must always fall back on yourself" (Buchholz, 1999, p. 347).

Buchholz describes the paradox of successful education. Recognizing difference leads to independent forms and the anchoring of authentic action in the encounter. Attachment research has confirmed that in fact secure attachment, and thus also the exploration of the world, are not tied to an all-comprehending mother. In terms of mentalization: it teaches difference from others, enabling the development of a self, and of a subjective world view (Fonagy et al., 2002).

The question that comes up here is relevant to every training course: what do students bring with them and what do they need to be supported in? Research as it is cannot provide a clear answer as to what should be brought to training in social professions, in particular training as a professional therapist, and what can be learned. In principle, training positions are not allocated based on pre-determined skills; instead a ranking is created based on candidates' skills. Selection criteria will shift according to the number of candidates available. Relational aspects, which are equated with skill in reflection, are the determining factor in being accepted for a social profession.

It is only possible to make distinctions between skills which candidates must already possess and character traits they should possess in a speculative way. What is the significance of their cultural background and their ideas about illness and healing? What kinds of necessary skills – including empathy, authenticity, and sensitivity – can be taught in training, and which should already be present in some form, so as to develop them? These terms are very abstract and subject to many interpretations. It is astonishing how little research material exists on these questions.

2 Theoretical Reflections on Choice of Method and Survey Sequencing

The quantitative methods used here were developed in a collective discussion process in our ART Research Study Group (ART-RSG). Our first attempt assembled a questionnaire using descriptive statistics (Raab-Steiner & Benesch, 2012). By putting together our own research questionnaire, we did without an internationally standardized test, including reference data such as standard values. The following year, we decided instead to use a long-established procedure in the scientific world, which would clearly meet our quality criteria of objectivity, reliability and validity. Another consideration was the idea of a test procedure which included psychoanalytic categories, allowing conclusions could be drawn. We also shifted the emphasis, going from investigating the intrapsychic to an understanding of interaction by students. A colleague with experience of the Giessen test in Berlin prompted us to introduce this test to the ART Research Study Group. Most statements in the Giessen test focus on the test subjects' relations with other human beings.

The initial study results are discussed here; we continue to generate and disseminate data. The data presented here was collected in semesters three and four: it relates specifically to the second training model of three-phase affect resonance training (ART).

3 Selection of Methodology

In deciding to use the Giessen test, we felt it was advantageous to pick a psycho-diagnostic personality test which had not primarily been designed as an individual diagnostic instrument. Our test would ideally also focus on relationship aspects of the students' personalities. Another reason we went for the Giessen test is that it is an objective, individual-psychological instrument with medium bandwidth and precision in relevant depth-psychological categories, but also reflects social attitudes and reactions and for this reason is also an instrument to measure intersubjectivity. The test focuses both on a person's self-attributed characteristics (self-image) and on characteristics ascribed to other people (the image of others) (Böker, 1999).

When interpreting findings, intersubjectivity must always be taken into account. In other words, the Gießen test asks for internal and external assessments of individual characteristics, but it does not capture objective characteristics (Böker, 1999; Beckmann et al., 2012a). As a criticism, Hell (1982, p. 41) points to a lack of clarity between the test's construction and measurement, on the one hand, and the conception and interpretation of its psychodynamic model, on the other. Given that test statements and intersubjective or psychodynamic concepts have not been proven to be congruent, metalinguistic interpretations of the test findings should be avoided (Böker, 1999; Hell, 1982).

The findings discussed here, based on a survey of self-image, have been correlated with other group data. Given its medium-range precision, the test offers a relatively limited range of information. In interpreting it, we should also note that this is a standardized test procedure and thus has a limited measurement range (Böker, 1999; Beckmann et al., 2012b; Ermann, 1987; Eckert & Biermann-Ratjen, 1985).

4 The Giessen Test Self-Image

The first part of the study – the results of which are also discussed here – attempts to capture the self-image of students of psychiatric nursing over the course of eight years. Data collection was intended above all to capture personal and interpersonal aspects of students' idea of relationships. First, we assume that internalized object relations play a significant role in shaping current relationships, and second, we sought to capture the importance of intersubjective influence on self-image. We then put this data into a broader group context. When interpreting the data, the focus is not primarily on basic psychosocial data like gender, age, social class, or duration of relationship, but rather on the quality of encounters between students and of students with trainers. Can conclusions be drawn from group data about the significance of psychodynamic factors in group members and the quality of their relations with trainers? Conclusions about relationship quality in groups and with trainers are made via statements on self-image. These are considered to be a determinant of self-esteem, while also serving to judge the regulation of narcissistic balance within the group. In terms of group development, differentiation from the institution and from trainers is also considered as a quality of relationship.

5 Description of Test Materials

5.1 Origin of Giessen Test II

The Giessen Test has been used in clinical-diagnostic and research contexts for 40 years. The test, invented by Dieter Beckmann, Elmar Brähler, and Horst-Eberhard Richter, is now in its fourth edition and was slightly revised and brought up to date in its most recent edition in 2012, with the main changes focused on user-friendliness. The manual also contains the first standard values of a sample based on a survey of around 5000 people in Germany. In recent years, the area of application of the test has also shifted, moving towards socio-psychological, sociological, and political studies.

5.2 Definition of Giessen Test II

The Giessen Test II is an inference questionnaire with several dimensions. Test subjects can assess their self-image, their image of others, or their ideal image. Its basic composition is based on psychoanalytic and socio-psychological concepts. The test includes six standard scales: a) social resonance (negative socially resonant versus positive socially resonant); b) dominance (dominant versus submissive); c) control (undercontrolled versus compulsive); d) basic mood (hypomanic versus depressed); e) pliancy (permeable versus retentive); f) social potency (socially potent versus socially impotent). These six scales are collected using forty statements. These bipolar statements (3–2 - 1–0 - 1–2 - 3) are assessed according to their importance for test subjects and are checked by them (Beckmann et al., 2012; Brähler, 1989; Beckmann & Richter, 1979; Proske, 2014).

5.3 Areas of Application

The test was primarily designed for adults but later expanded to include teenagers. It can be carried out either as an individual or group test. Its most common use is in clinical practice, specifically as a diagnostic tool and for monitoring the course of psychotherapy. Its use has steadily increased in scientific investigations, including social psychological research (Beckmann et al., 2012a).

5.4 Quality Criteria

The manual accompanying the material provides precise instructions for conducting, evaluating and interpreting the standardized test, in this way ensuring objectivity. With regard to reliability, the retest reliability (with an interval of six weeks) in the standardization sample for the scales is between 0.65 and 0.76. The test is also valid in terms of content; various studies have been carried out on construct validity (Beckmann et al., 2012b).

5.5 Standard Values

The t-values, percentages, means, and standard deviations for statements and scales are maintained as standard values. Differentiated values result from gender and age. The current standardization is based on a population-representative sample from 2006, ranging in age from 14 to 92 years (N=5,036) (Beckmann et al., 2012a).

5.6 Group Diagnostics – Analysis of Mean Profiles for Collectives

The Giessen test can be used for group diagnostics going in opposite directions. First, for interaction diagnostics, the interest lies in relationships between group members. The second case is a group diagnosis in which average characteristics of groups, as well as all typical characteristics of all test subjects, are used for analysis, in comparison with standard values or in comparison with other groups or control groups. The data presented here refer to this second form of group diagnostics (Scheer, 1979; Beckmann et al., 2012a).

6 Test Implementation and Procedure

The ART project has been running since 2010. The Giessen test was put to cohorts from 2011 to 2014 (training duration six semesters). For cohorts which began training in 2011 and ended in September 2014, began in 2012 and ended September 2015, and began in 2013 and ended September 2016, the whole class filled out questionnaires for self-image and ideal image in pencil during class time. The questionnaire for assessing others was carried out in the ongoing small groups. For this, a report was read to the students, which they then used to do the test. Beginning with the March 2014–2017 cohort, the test was digitized, uploaded to the school's learning platform. Procedural instructions for the test on the platform were given as a teaching unit in the large group. If there were further questions, members of the ART-RSG were available to answer them, either in person or via email. The test duration was designed to be 15 minutes. Response rates ranged from 70 to 85 percent. There were large differences in the response rate from class to class. Students failing to complete the test were reminded to submit it, by mass or personal email. The data collected was recorded manually, and later electronically using SPSS 24.

7 Evaluation

Standard values (t-values) for the test's six standard scales and percentile ranks (PR) for attitude scales E and M were used as the basis for evaluation. The raw values for M and E are generated by a simple count; M is made up of the number of undecided marks (0 or 4), while E is made up of extreme marks: those furthest to either right or left (3 or 1 and 7).

Missing values or double marks were replaced by the mean value in the item, as recommended in the test manual (Beckmann et al., 2012b). Here are some examples of the procedure:

- serial number 79; preGTFm, two missing values (items 26 and 40) replaced by means of the remaining item values (=6), this affects scale 5

- serial number 70; preGTS, one missing value (variable 15) replaced by the mean of the remaining item values (=3.8, rounded to 4), this affects scale 6
- serial number 81; preGTI, one missing value (variable 30) replaced by the mean of the remaining item values (=3.6, rounded to 4), this affects scale 6

7.1 Self-Image

An examination of pretest self-image mean was conducted. N=199, covering eight training years (cohort 2011–14 September; cohort 2012–15 September; cohort 2013–16 September; cohort 2014–17 September; year 2014–17 March; year 2015–18 March; year 2015–18, September; year 2016–19 March).

7.2 Summary of Calculations

There are clear differences between individual classes. These differences are significant in classes 1, 2, and 3, with the subsequent classes. The first three years are the classes in which the testing was carried out in large or small groups with a supervisor present. These differences are particularly evident in scales 1, 2, 5, 6, and E.

7.3 Scale 1: Social Resonance

Scale 1 deal with ideas of the subject's own impact on their surroundings.

Here, items 9 (evaluation of work by others); 16 (popularity); 23 (general evaluation by environment); and attractiveness are combined, since correlation is expected. Furthermore, self-assertion and social validation, as well as a desire to look good, correlate with attractiveness and popularity. The main theme in Scale 1 includes interaction with one's surroundings and self-experience within that environment, and the idea of whether one is perceived well or poorly. This is a question of self-presentation and of being noticed. Hysterical modes of experience, with exhibitionistic-voyeuristic elements, are indicated as character traits. Role expectations are placed above underlying character traits. Inauthenticity is assumed at high values on this scale, with conclusions drawn regarding hysteria. The mean for unsorted neurotics is given as t=42. In general, neurotics show a negative assessment of their resonance (Beckmann et al., 1979, 2012). The

Table 1 Social resonance scale (Beckmann et al., 2012a, p. 25).

Left	*Right*
negative socially resonant (NR)	positive socially resonant (PR)
unattractive, unpopular, disrespected, criticized at work, not assertive, uninterested in looking good	attractive, popular, respected, valued at work, assertive, interested in looking good

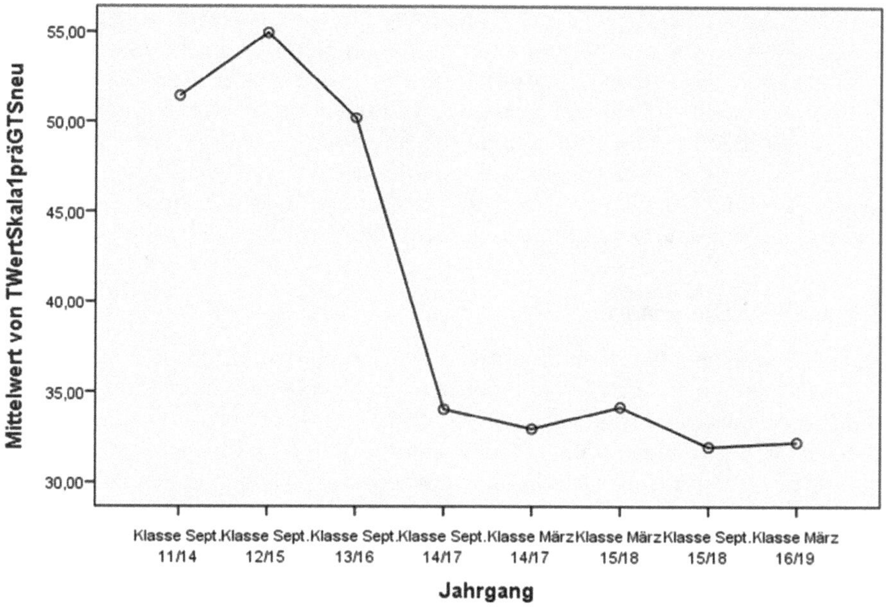

Figure 9.1 Scale 1 (ART Research Study Group, 2016).

assessment of one's self-image in terms of social resonance is t=29.905 for depressives and t=48.190 for alcoholics (N=21, depressives; N=21 alcoholics) (Wolf, 1976). The self-assessment of myasthenia gravis-pseudoparalytica patients[1] (N=34, of which 25 female, 9 male; average age 36 years) is t=46.88 (Paschotta, 1976); the self-image t-values of male homeless people (N=15) are t=49.44; and for female homeless people (N=15) t=53.00 (Kleinschnitger & Meyer, 1977).

7.4 Interpretation of Scale 1 Results

As can be clearly seen from the scale, cohorts 11–14, 12–15, and 13–16 have a t-value of over 50 and are thus in positive range. They experience themselves as valued, assertive, and respected in the community. The other four cohorts have a t-value below 35 and thus also below the average for neurotics, which is 42. These cohorts perceive themselves as less attractive, disrespected, with less ability to assert desires and needs. The significance of the external impact of cohorts from 14–17, 15–18, and 16–19 cannot be interpreted as not as relevant and correlates with groups diagnosed with depression or with myasthenia gravis pseudoparalytica. In terms of positive self-image, the values of cohorts 11–14, 12–15, 13–16, and 16–19 correlate with groups of alcoholics and homeless people. Depressed patients and those suffering from myasthenia gravis pseudoparalytica experience themselves as unattractive, disrespected, and not assertive. Patient groups and the homeless were gathered together into a single group in the Giessen test, whereas with the students, the group already existed as a class community. Group dynamics and student attitudes are influenced by external conditions, which in turn lead to the formation of two subgroups across the six years.

Alcoholics and homeless people experience themselves as being heavily involved in their surroundings and self-determined in their actions. There is a feeling of being able to assert one's own interests in life.

7.5 Scale 2: Dominance

Scale 2 represents complementarity between dominant and compliant.

This scale shows complementarity between aggressive, dominant, possibly sadistic behaviour versus submissive, balancing, calm, possibly masochistic behaviour. Beckmann, Brähler, and Richter describe as character traits sado-masochistic behaviours classifiable between controlling and wanting to be controlled. Furthermore, they believe that patients with psychogenic disorders tend towards dominance while "healthy" patients tend to present as docile and willing to adapt. The mean for patients with psychogenic disorders is t=46. The mean value from the 2012 manual is used here, since the earlier work (1981) gives the mean value as t=42. In terms of dominance, depressives' assessment of their self-image is t=50.952 and for alcoholics it is t=50.952 (N=21, depressives; N=21, alcoholics) (Wolf, 1976); the self-assessment of myasthenia-gravis-pseudoparalytica patients (N=34, 25 female, 9 male; average age 36 years) is t=46.88 (Paschotta, 1976); the self-image t-scores of male homeless people (N=15, ages 18–34) are t=43.22; and for female homeless people (N=15, ages 18–34) t=47.17 (Kleinschnitger & Meyer, 1977).

7.6 Interpretation of Scale 2 Results

As in the results for Scale 1, Scale 2 also has large shifts in values between the first three years and the following four. The first three classes tend to be predominantly located above the t-score of 46. The later four classes are clearly below the mean, with the shift clearly in the direction of docility. In the interpretation of the authors of the Giessen test, classes 4 through 8 would be considered "healthier" than grades 1 to 3 (Beckmann et al., 1979, 2012a).

Table 2 Dominance scale (Beckmann et al., 2012a, p. 26f.).

Left	*Right*
dominant (DO)	compliant (GE)
often involved in arguments, stubborn, likes to dominate, talented at acting, impatient	rarely involved in arguments, docile, likes to be subordinate, untalented at acting, easy to cooperate with, patient

Figure 9.2 Scale 2 (ART Research Study Group, 2016).

The values for cohorts 2011–14, 2012–15, 2013–16, and 2016–19 do not correlate with any of the group values used here. Their values very clearly tend towards docility. As a group, they present as very submissive. These values also go towards an idea of being patient and easy to work with. In contrast to the authors of the test, an interpretation tending to see them as dependent groups in the sense of Warren G. Bennis would also be possible. The values can also be understood as being related to group dynamics and precisely not to be determined from individual values of the participants, which were combined into groups using data from the literature. Years 14–17, 15–18, and 16–19 tend towards counterdependency (Bennis, 2009; Majce-Egger, 1999; Antons-Volmerg et al., 2001).

7.7 Scale 3: Control

Scale 3 deals with the two poles of uncontrolled versus control and their defence mechanisms of the id and superego.

Table 3 Control scale (Beckmann et al., 2012a, p. 27f.).

Left	*Right*
uncontrolled (UK)	compulsive (ZW)
inept at handling money, untidy, comfortable, tends to pseudo-logicality, unsteady, capable of exuberance	gifted with money, over-organized, over-zealous, quite fanatical about truth, steady, incapable of exuberance

Scale 3 shows textbook psychopathology, especially in its leftward shift. There are also no statements asking about dealing with others or the emotional significance of others. Rather, the significance lies in the intrapsychic field as a battle between the id and the superego. The poles range between instinctual character and compulsive structure. Object relationships are only indirectly affected, even though a person's environment can often suffer as a result of their behaviour.

The t-value is 46 in the 2012 manual and 43 in the 1981 book. In patients who have been diagnosed with compulsive structure, the value shifts to the right (t-value 60; Psychosomatic University Clinic). The authors also point out the cultural aspect and age rigidity. Students seeking help at a psychotherapeutic counselling centre deviate to the left on this scale, although the issue of age is also very important. The assessment of self-image for depressives in control is t=50.391 and for alcoholics t=45.381 (N=21, depressives; N=21 alcoholics) (Wolf, 1976); the self-assessment of myasthenia gravis pseudoparalytica patients (N=34, 25 female, 9 male; average age 36 years) is t=48.79 (Paschotta, 1972); the self-image t-scores for male homeless people (N=15, age 18–34) are t=41.78; and among homeless women (N=15, ages 18–34) at t=42.50 (Kleinschnitger & Meyer, 1977).

7.8 Interpretation of Scale 3 Results

Classes 1, 2, 6, and 8 range between 46 and 47 and are therefore very close to the mean t-value of 46. Class 3 has a value of 52 and is thus the only

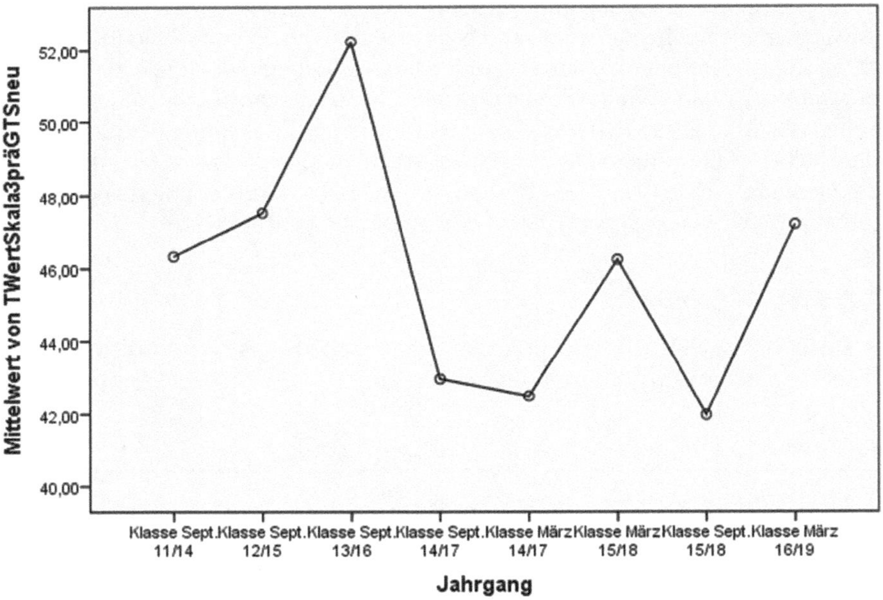

Figure 9.3 Scale 3 (ART Research Study Group, 2016).

group placed towards the right-hand scale. A certain kind of order and structure can be assumed in the group. Groups 4, 5, and 7 have a value of 42 and are hence the groups tending towards non-control. These three values can also be divided into the group dynamic factors coined by Bennis and Shepard: 1. Dependency group; 2. Counterdependency group; and 3. Interdependency group (Bennis & Shepard, 1956; Majce-Egger, 1999; Antons-Volmerg et al., 2001). Groups 4, 5, and 7 are in the same scale range as the group of male and female homeless people. In terms of group dynamics, these values can be attributed to the counterdependency phase. In this phase, for example, the trainers/teachers in a group are questioned. There is much debate about the structure of learning and schools.

All five groups have attributes of being boisterous, untidy, and spending money easily. Group 3 correlates with results of the "depressed patients" group, but in terms of the t-values it is still far from the group of obsessive-compulsive patients.

Groups 1, 2, 6, and 8 are in a scale range of 2, along with alcoholics and myasthenia gravis pseudoparalytica patients.

7.9 Scale 4: Basic Mood

Scale 4 represents the basic mood and its aggression orientation.

Scale 4 shows the tendency of the basic mood, whether it is towards hypomania or depression. Linked to this is aggression, thought of as energy potential that is directed outwards and thus strengthens the drive or is expressed as a self-suppressing form as depression. The right scale is associated with self-insecurity, anxiety and dependence.

Patients at Giessen Psychosomatic Clinic achieve a t-value towards the right of 64. The self-assessment of basic mood for predominant depressives is t=67.714 and for alcoholics t=58.190 (N=21, depressives; N=21 alcoholics) (Wolf, 1976); the self-assessment of myasthenia gravis-pseudoparalytica patients (N=34, 25 female, 9 male; average age 36 years) is t=57.24 (Paschotta, 1972). For homeless women (N=15, ages 18–34) t=49.67 and for female homeless people (N=15, ages 18–34) t=53.33 (Kleinschnitger & Meyer, 1977).

Table 4 Basic mood scale (Beckmann et al., 2012a, p. 29).

Left	*Right*
hypomanic (HM)	depressed (DE)
rarely depressed, less inclined to self-reflection, less anxious, hardly self-critical, anger more likely to be outwardly directed, tends to be independent	often depressed, strongly inclined to self-reflection, very anxious, anger more likely to feed inward, tends to be dependent

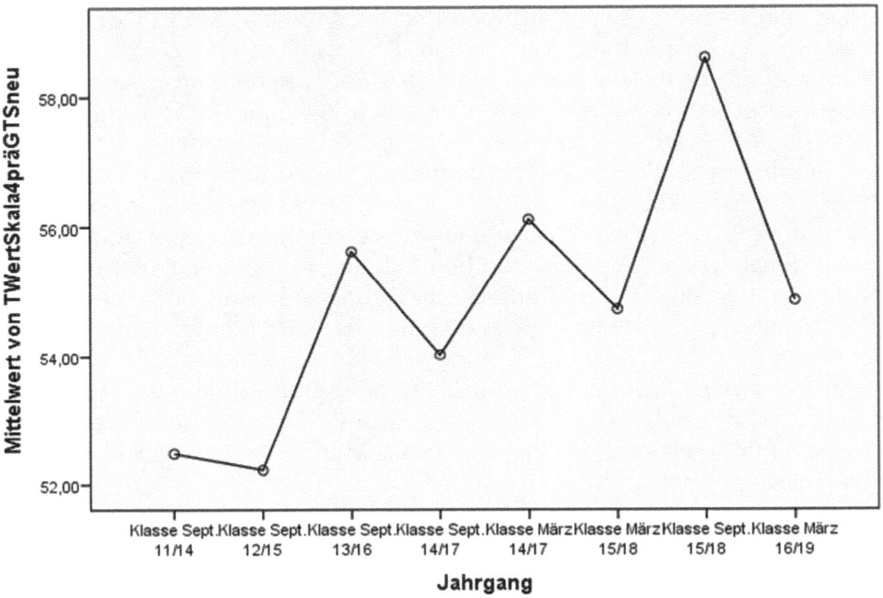

Figure 9.4 Scale 4 (ART Research Study Group, 2016).

7.10 Interpretation of Scale 4 Results

All groups range between the values 52 and 58.5. If we take the patients at the Giessen clinic as a base reference for the groups, we see a clear shift of the t-value towards the left, compared with 64 for the clinic patients. Regarding the values, the two measures for depressive groups (t=67.7 and t=64) are relatively distant from the other groups. The values of the 15–18 cohort are in the same range as the group with alcoholics and the group of patients with myasthenia gravis pseudoparalytica. The cohorts for 11–14 and 12–15 are on a similar scale to the female homeless group. In terms of group dynamics, this could be interpreted as a tendency towards the counterdependency phase.

7.11 Scale 5: Pliancy

Scale 5 returns the focus to psychosocial relationships. The dimensional range includes pliant on the left and retentive on the right.

Table 5 Pliancy scale (Beckmann et al., 2012a, p. 30).

Left	*Right*
pliant (DU)	retentive (RE)
open-minded, close to others, more likely to reveal, expresses need for love openly, tends to be trusting, able to experience love intensely	closed, distant from others, not very revealing, love needs rather reticent, tends to be suspicious, not very capable of experiencing love

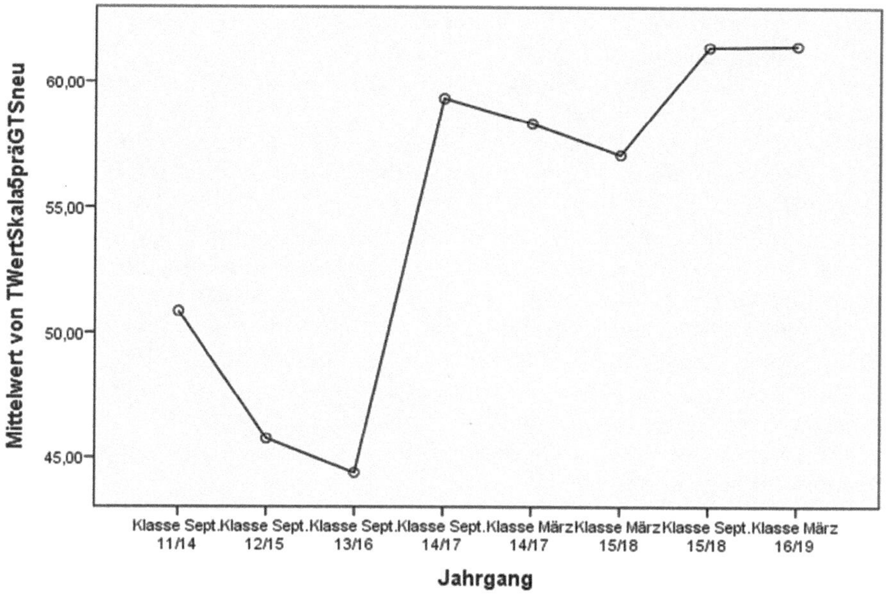

Figure 9.5 Scale 5 (ART Research Study Group, 2016).

This scale deals with the experience of contact with others and with behaviour in contact with others. In a psychoanalytic sense, this addresses categories of very early orality and anality. They are also touch on Erikson's terminology: *basic trust* versus *basic mistrust* and *autonomy* versus *shame and doubt*. The scale definition aims to inquire into the fundamentals of security in relationships, or on the other hand, a schizoid, autistic contact disorder. A sense of being in the world can lead a person to develop openness, sociability, and a positive worldview. A move to the right suggests a paranoid worldview, one characterized by withdrawal. In this case, distrust determines the prevailing mood in contacts with other people (Erikson, 1998).

On average, neurotics at the Psychosomatic University Clinic in Giessen show increased retentive traits (t-value=58). In terms of pliancy, self-image assessment for depressives is t=59.524 and for alcoholics t=55.000 (N=21, depressives; N=21 alcoholics) (Wolf, 1976); self-assessment of myasthenia-gravis pseudoparalytica patients (N=34, 25 female, 9 male; average age 36 years) is t=49.18 (Paschotta, 1976); the self-image t-values for male homeless people (N=15, ages 18–34) are t=44.67; while female homeless people (N=15, ages 18–34) stand at t=53.33 (Kleinschnitger & Meyer, 1977).

7.12 Interpretation of Scale 5 Results

Group 1 with a value 49, group 2 with a value 46, and group 3 with a value 44 cluster in a more or less shared group, contrasting with group 4 (t-value 60);

group 5 (t-value 58); group 6 (t-value 57); and group 7 and group 8 (each with t-value 62), all of which tend to the left of the scale. This result suggests these groups are much more open-minded and sociable than other groups. Groups 4 to 6 come close to the reference values from the clinic, while groups 7 and 8 exceed the values for neurotics. They tend to form a strong, closed, paranoid group, the kind described by Bion as a *fear and flight* group (Bion, 2001). The cohorts 14–17, 15–18a, 15–18b, and 16–19 tend more to the right (retentive). This correlates with groups at the Psychosomatic University Clinic in Giessen and with the group of depressed patients. The years 11–14, 12–15, and 13–16 correlate with myasthenia gravis pseudoparalytica patients and with the homeless group. As a group, they describe themselves as open-minded, close to and trusting others. From a group dynamic perspective, these groups can be seen as being in the interdependency phase. Solidarity and harmony are at the forefront of group relationships (Bennis, 2009; Majce-Egger, 1999; Antons-Volmerg et al., 2001).

7.13 Scale 6: Social Potency

Scale 6, like Scale 5, relates to relationships and the focus of mature development.

The focus in Scale 5 is on early development, characterized by oral and anal components. The focus here is on later development, describing a social, potent person, coming very close to a description of "healthy". In the psychoanalytic sense, this is a strong, phallic person who has positively overcome the Oedipus conflict and is very satisfied with themself and their environment. This contrasts with the inhibited, neurotic person who goes through life with great hesitation, hardly committing to anyone, avoiding confrontation.

The assessment of social potency for predominantly depressives is t=55.000, for alcoholics t=57.619 (N=21, depressives; N=21 alcoholics) (Wolf, 1976); the self-assessment of myasthenia gravis pseudoparalytica patients (N=34, 25 female, 9 male; average age 36 years) is 50.27 (Paschotta, 1976); the self-image t-scores for male homeless people (N=15, age 18–34) are t=44.56; and for female homeless people (N=15, ages 18–34) are t=49.50 (Kleinschnitger & Meyer, 1977).

Table 6 Social potency scale (Beckmann et al., 2012a, p. 32).

Left	*Right*
socially potent (PO)	socially impotent (IP)
sociable, at ease in heterosexual contact, very devoted, clearly competitive, capable of long-term relationships, imaginative	unsociable, restricted in heterosexual contact, not very capable of devotion, barely competitive, barely capable of long-term relationships, poor in imagination

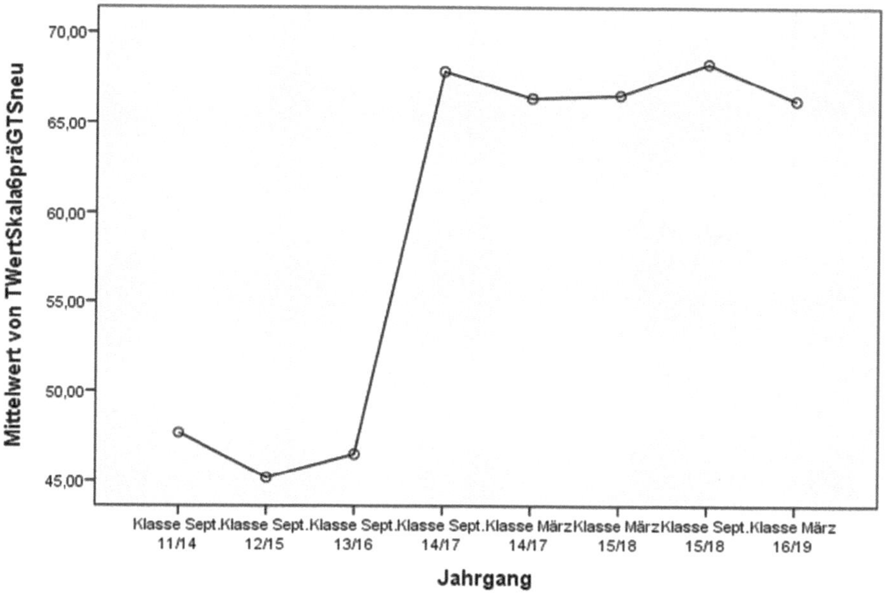

Figure 9.6 Scale 6 (ART Research Study Group, 2016).

7.14 Interpretation of Scale 6 Results

Here, we see a similar picture to scale 5 with a distinction between groups 1 to 3 and groups 4 to 8. Groups 1 to 3 tend to have values towards the left (values 45–46), while groups 4 to 8 lie between 65 and 66. Years 14–17a, 14–17b, 15–18a, 15–18b, and 16–19 perceive themselves as highly socially impotent compared with all groups used here. An argument can be made here towards a dependency phase: a highly defensive attitude towards fear and associated dependency. There is a very considerable lack of imagination in these groups, which represents a problem for student groups.

7.15 Description of Scale E (extreme marks) and Scale M (average marks) Results

Scale E refers to the extremity of the marks made by survey participants. The frequent use of extreme marks indicates active behaviour and little self-control or impulsive behaviour. Beckman et al. cite another result with a tendency towards E values; in depressed patients E is preferred (Beckmann et al., 2012a, p. 33f.).

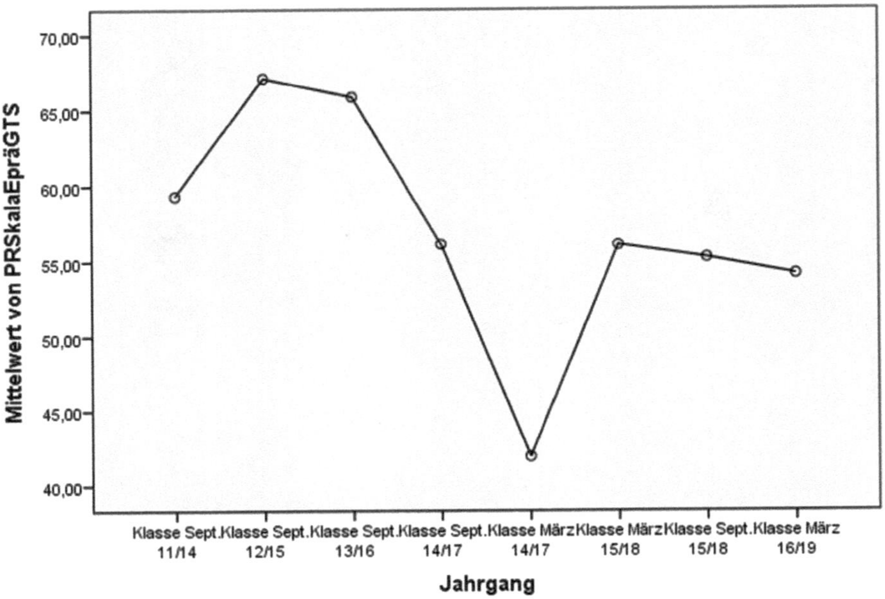

Figure 9.7 Scale E (ART Research Study Group, 2016).

7.16 Interpretation of E-Values

Groups 1, 4, 6, 7, and 8 range in values between 50 and 60. Groups 2 and 3 have a value of 66 and group 5 of 43. Groups 2 and 3 have the highest level of extreme marks made by survey participants.

Self-image E values for male homeless people (N=15, ages 18–34) are t=50.56 and for female homeless people (N=15, ages 18–34) are t=57.83 (Kleinschnitger & Meyer, 1977).

The M scale assesses the level of average marks made by survey participants.

A high level of M marks can indicate an emotional indifference towards the questionnaire. This can be caused by non-reflective, compulsive behaviour or can also result from a hypomanical attitude of denial, whereby the patient sees no sense in doing the test or regards it as meaninglessness.

The self-image M values for male homeless people (N=15, ages 18–34) are t=42.78 and for female homeless people (N=15, ages 18–34) are t=33.83 (Kleinschnitger & Meyer, 1977).

7.17 Interpretation of M Values

Here, results for groups 1, 3, 4, 6, 7, and 8 range from 39 to 47. Group 2 returns a value of 30 and group 5 a value of 54. These values correlate with the scattered M values of male versus female homeless groups.

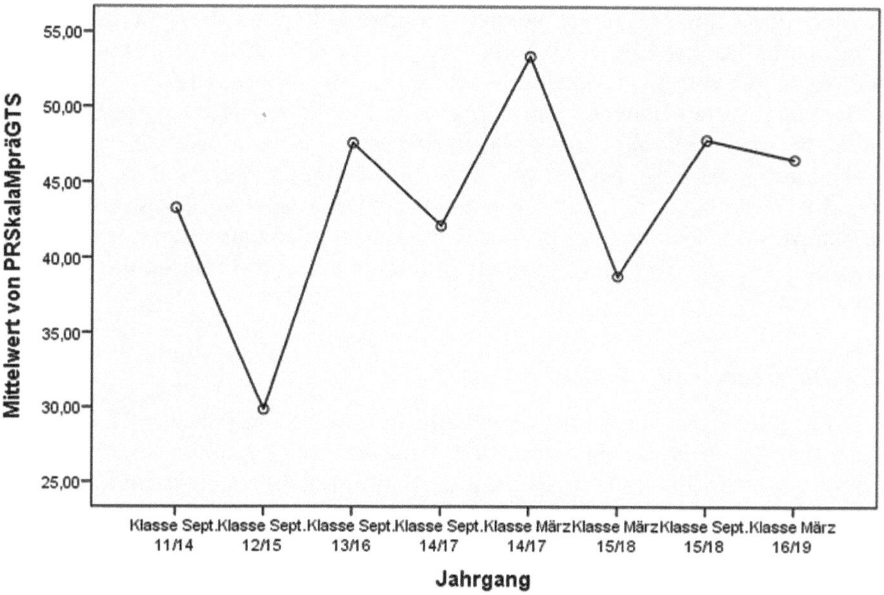

Figure 9.8 Scale M (ART Research Study Group, 2016). P. 190

8 Giessen Test Self-Image Group (GT-S): Summary of Results

8.1 Differences Between Training Groups

In standard scales 1 to 6, there is a significant difference between cohorts 2011–14, 2012–15, and 2013–16 and the cohorts 14–17a, 14–17b, 15–18a, 15–18b, and 16–19 with regard to scale 1 (social resonance); scale 2 (dominance); scale 5 (pliability); and scale 6 (social potency),

The authors of the Giessen test state that a raw value shift of around 5 to 6 is significant in evaluating therapies (Beckmann et al., 2012a, p. 33). For scale 1 (social resonance), the raw scores of the two groups mentioned lie at least 15 values apart. For scale 2 (dominance) the two groups are at least eight values apart; for scale 5 (pliability), the difference is at least seven values; and for scale 6 (social potency), the difference is some 20 values apart. Scale 3 (control) and scale 4 (basic mood) do not correlate with the group findings mentioned above.

The difference between the two groups lies in the fact that they are based in different school buildings and thus have a different weighting of teaching staff. Another important point is the mood of the main training hospital; in recent years there have been increasing signs that the hospital will be closed, which has had a major impact on staff working on its wards.

The data obtained suggest both the importance of teachers and of the fundamental atmosphere and sense of community in an institution. Students or student groups are intersubjectively embedded in the shared ground of a school and the institution extending beyond it; this contributes to their mood and sense of community (Stephenson, 2014, 2017; Pap, 2017).

The largest gap between the two groups mentioned is on scale 6 (social potency). If we interpret this scale in the sense of "competence" and consider the values described in it – thus: unsociable, self-conscious, not very capable of dedication, barely competitive, barely capable of long-term relationships, poor in imagination – then the question remains: what is the burdensome mood enveloping students of one group at their particular training location?

8.2 Difference with "Patient Groups"

Patient values can be found repeatedly in a wide variety of ART cohorts, with depressive group data on scale 4 (basic mood) being a small outlier. There seems to be a clear diagnostic relationship between depression and values. The group with depressed patients has a t-score of 67.7, while the highest value for any cohort is 58.5.

Finally, we can establish that effects of community and teachers' capacity for intersubjectivity are more important than various diagnoses might suggest them to have. Influence on the group's experience and understanding is exerted by its interlocutors, reflected in the "thou" of their teachers or their colleagues on the hospital ward; but the overarching significance of the institution as a living organism also has a determining influence.

The importance of the initial situation, the skills that students bring to training, and the selection criteria for training in social professions fade into the background. After two semesters of training, our findings suggest a major importance for environment, and by contrast, speak against the significance of admission criteria currently in use (Steinberger, 2019).

Note

1 *Myasthenia gravis* is a neuromuscular communication disorder caused by autoantibodies, which block acetylcholine receptors on the motor endplate (endplate disease). Clinically, this leads to muscle debilitation, leading some authors to refer to the disease as a "muscle disease".

10 Evaluation of Observation Reports

"In order to find the patient, we must look for him within ourselves."
Bollas (2018, p. 202)

1 Method

Given the availability of student observation reports, the method used to examine them is objective hermeneutics, which can bring out latent structures of meaning. The technique belongs to the interpretive social research group and is embedded in the traditions of qualitative research.

Qualitative social research is a tendency within broader social research which emerged from various research strands during the 1960s and 1980s (Steinberger, 2016). The sociologist Ulrich Oevermann and his colleagues developed objective hermeneutics as a method in the 1970s, as part of research into socialization theory and family sociology. The approach was developed in conceptual terms by his team and repeatedly modified. Oevermann and his colleagues referred to objective hermeneutics as "art theory", implying that interpretation technique cannot be acquired like a cognitive knowledge. Instead, it should be regarded as something based on experience. Text interpretation is a methodically guided, skills-based competency. Objective hermeneutics is considered a logic of reconstruction and comes with basic theoretical assumptions, principles that can guide research, and thus also methodological procedures (Oevermann et al., 1979; Hug et al., 2010; Kleemann et al., 2013; Hofer, 2014).

The technique focuses on latent structures of meaning, which are very close to the interpretation of implicit knowledge, moving away from deliberate structures. These structures of meaning are largely hidden in the reports made, only later are they subject to reconstruction and analysis. The gain in knowledge achievement by evaluating the report lies in the scene described in its context, as well as its wider embedding in cultural and historical knowledge, and in implicit (reconstructed) structures of meaning, as well as possible generalizations and categorizations.

DOI: 10.4324/9781003483441-10

2 Attitude

Freud writes:

> [I would] spend a long time before them trying to apprehend them in my own way, i.e. to explain to myself what their effect is due to. Wherever I cannot do this, as for instance with music, I am almost incapable of obtaining any pleasure. Some rationalist aspect of my mind, or perhaps analytic, defies being moved without knowing why or by what ... I realize this comprehension cannot merely be intellectual; what must be grasped is the reproduction within us of the emotional condition and mental constellation which impelled the artist to create.
>
> (Freud, 1997, pp. 122–123)

Freud here is concerned with observation, describing a sensual understanding of observation, without which one is "incapable of pleasure," incapable of grasping what is perceived. He also mentions the emotion arising in him as an observer: he wants to understand this, so as to be able to lend an identity to the other: i.e. to the artwork, the creation. He must reach within to find the trace of understanding; he must allow himself to be moved, to grasp the feelings arising within and connect them to the other. For Freud, the rational comprehension of a phenomenon does not involve understanding in the sense of grasping the emotional content of what is observed. This also rules out the possibility of mentalization.

Freud recognizes quite clearly that understanding the other entails a dynamic process. This is based, first, on allowing oneself to be touched emotionally, and then, opposed to this, on a particular mental attitude, which he regards as rational and analytic, which prevents us being overwhelmed by our own emotions. The attitude allows emotions to be clothed in words, enabling the observers to generate meaning beyond the specific, concrete scene.

Freud is a close observer here, attempting to use body metaphors to describe empathy and its significance. As his thoughts continue, they remove us from the emotionality of what is happening, bringing us back to the generality of his drive theories. Here Freud points out that something in us must be touched *again,* in order for the other to emerge as a created being (*Geschöpf*). He is already suggesting that only what is already within us can emerge to consciousness, through language and spoken encounter (*Sprache bzw. Be-sprechung*). He locates language in a rational, analytical *aspect of mind,* and through many theories he has made a major linguistic contribution to understanding and grasping that which cannot be seen.

> ... ultimately a belief system that the analyst lives and works by (and there is no assurance that the analyst has full conscious access to the system under which he or she is really operating) – makes a very

> significant difference as to how one hears, what one hears, how one assembles what is heard, and how one conducts oneself in the analytic setting.
>
> (Ghent, 1989, p. 170)

Ghent's groundbreaking essay "Credo" already argues that our conduct and our attentive listening (*unser Er-hören und unser Ver-halten*) are determined by our internal attitude (*Haltung*). We can only hear and see what we find within ourselves, thus only this can we hold and preserve (*halten bzw. be-halten*). Our attitude determines our reactions to our environment and the thoughts we develop.

We have a resonant sounding board within us, organized according to our experiences; we use this to relate to our environment. "In any individual, this scheme is lakes as the result of unfolding interactions between the growing child and significant people in that child's world. Features of, and relationships with, these early figures come to be internalized in stable ways" (McWilliams, 2018, p. 88). Our experiences determine our view of the present. Or, to be more precise, they determine, first, the relationship structures anchored emotionally within us, second, how we ascribe meaning to the images we generate, and thus how we focus through the dazzle of stimuli which bombard us. Our desire, our capacity to love, are connected to these "schemas"; out of these experiences we choose our partners and re-enact our repetitions, so that things may after all unfold somewhat differently (McWilliams, 2004).

Freud tried to summarize attitude with the formula "evenly suspended attention". Ogden and Bion wrote of an inner attitude of "reverie", adopted so as to listen to and hear patients. Casement calls this attitude towards patients *emotional influence*, by which patients should be able to sense the analyst's involvement (Casement, 1993, p. 1016).

Openness is a prerequisite for all psychodynamic practitioners who perform analysis. They must actively turn towards openness, as a practice of curiosity. Openness prompts a second prerequisite: an attitude of awe and reverence. "It involves feeling very small in the presence of the vast and unknowable" (McWilliams, 2018, p. 91).

Another important factor is recognizing the complexity and ambiguity of the psychological phenomena all around us, how we can hold ambivalent feelings and contradictory needs within us, and thus coming to recognize intrapsychic conflicts as they occur.

This attitude also requires a recognition of subjectivity and an ability to endure a lack of knowledge. And yet this very subjectivity is our only tool to identify with what we see.

The following sequence of reports, drawn from the ART project, present a number of scenes. Via these scenes, we will address how different attitudes can allow us to grasp the different kind of perception at work in these reports, which were all prepared under comparable constraints of time and context.

Report a/17/PA

... When I came into the room he was asleep. He was lying there, the only one in a double bedroom. I sat there and looked at everything in his room. The heating was turned up to 6, with all the windows closed, of course. But the temperature in the room seemed OK, it wasn't all that warm. Maybe that was because of the windows, which were already old and no longer properly sealed (they were windows with sashes). There were a lot of things on his bedside table like glasses, plastic drinking cups, two bottles of Pago juice, wet wipes, a bumbag, and a mobile phone. There were several packages on the window sill, like packets of colostomy bags. There's also a refrigerator in the room.

After about half an hour, the patient opened his eyes, then closed them again shortly afterwards. About ten minutes later he finally woke up and asked what I was doing in his room. I replied that I had an assignment from school about observation or perception. 'Oh, I see,' he said.

He also asked me to get a small rubbish bag because he wanted to empty his colostomy bag. He was very careful when emptying it so as not to break the ostomy plate. The process took approximately seven minutes. He then asked me to dispose of the used materials.

Mr. P. then took the bottle of Pago, poured it into a glass, and drank some. He then asked me again to get a 'Resource' drink (coffee flavour) for him, because he likes to drink it. I went out, grabbed two of the 'Resource' drinks off the shelf, gave them to him and finished my assignment with him.

I think on the whole Mr P. coped pretty well with the hospital situation.

In the description, the student seems little affected by what she sees. Her inner attitude seems determined by anxiety associated with doing everything correctly, just as she learned at school. The patient is given little identity, in the sense of ascribing psychological states to him; he remains almost exclusively in a concrete world. The description makes the student seem absent, functioning by rules she has learned off, according to concrete instructions she has taken in, so that she and her surroundings appear mechanical. There is no inner life revealed, she does not take the chance to look more closely at the scene; she does not use the opportunity to nuance the description. The student's attitude seems to be guided by determination to get on in life, fulfilling all assigned tasks. Her description of the observation has a superficiality which allows for little emotional reaction and develops no curiosity towards understanding. Her observation makes the student seem like a child who has received little attention, was not much seen, and for this reason was unable to develop an observational gaze.

Another excerpt follows, from a different student:

> Report d/18/PA
>
> Ms Z. had been admitted a few days earlier. She was brought in by the police after she more or less had to be 'evicted' from her current place of residence. For more than ten years, Ms. Z. has been living in the forest under a bridge, but this now is in danger of collapse, and the space where she lives is no longer safe. Very soon after, the patient arrived on the ward and quickly made contact with the other patients. When I asked my practice supervisor where her tablets were, I found out that she receives no medication. I am amazed: she seems to be the first person in the geriatric psychiatry unit to have nothing in their drug dispenser. I briefly think about how striking the empty box is, standing out among all the other boxes, which are full of psychotropic drugs, and I wonder what is different or special about this woman. Maybe I'm happy for her that she can get by without that stuff. But on the other hand, how has she even ended up with us? Couldn't she have stayed with friends or family, and not in a psychiatric hospital? At lunch I introduce myself properly and make my first attempts to get to know this lady. She seems friendly and open, interested in having a conversation. Over the next few days, we speak more often. Ms. Z. says she would rather be in the forest, with the animals that she feeds. She says she came along with the police, because she has close contacts with 'top-ranking police' and also with the 'mafia'. She receives a lot of information, she says, but it's very secret and confidential. She broke off contact with her family completely a few years ago and doesn't want to resume contact. Ms. Z. says that they can't take her blood because there are gold rings and jewellery inside her body, and also she also has a villa in Vienna and a lot of money, but her cooperation with top-ranking police means she can't go there yet, a lot of things are still to be arranged. At the start I had some difficulties in carrying on the conversation. Apparently at other times Ms. Z. clearly says she wants to make films, modern adaptations of 'Grimm's Fairy Tales' making reference to society and politics in our own time. She studied philosophy at the University of Vienna, but dropped out before completing her bachelor's thesis. She says directly that all this must sound a bit odd or crazy and people say she is some kind of forest woman who feeds trolls and fairies, though she only feeds animals, because the other ones don't exist. Her body is slim and athletic; she reports no major pain or discomfort. When she was asked what happened to her face, which has many cuts and scars around the eyes, she said she regularly pierces her skin and prescribes herself treatments requiring a lot of sun, so they are mostly only possible in the summer, when there is most light and it lasts longest into the evening.

This report probably has a greater effect on the reader; it has an interweaving that offers paths to connect with their own experience. The student allows herself to be moved by the images and affects readers with the words she writes. To understand the patient, she allows images to resonate internally with her; she formulates her thoughts based on her experience of perception. She constructs her interlocutor through her own self. She conveys a sense of holding her feelings as they take place within her, preferring to position the patient in terms of difference. The student searches within herself for possible ways to like the patient, associating the scene with an idea of uniqueness, since the patient has been strongly rejected by others. She avoids constructing shared loneliness by means of her individualized love, constructed around the idea of togetherness. We are the lovers rejected by the world around them. Loneliness is based on an ability to see the reflection of a psychological inner world. In the first report there was no loneliness: it requires resonant space and some form of language.

The second text explicitly speaks of making "attempts to get to know" in an attempt to cultivate curiosity. A game of recognition and rejection begins to develop. Who can impress whom? The wish to get something from the other creates a sense of manipulation. What do I have to invest to get something? When we love, it expands our opportunities to be loved. Encounter is based on the possibility of developing one's own resonance and of finding a rhythm to synchronize our fields of affective possibility: in a general sense, our capacity for love.

Students repeatedly express a desire for explicit instructions on how to observe, searching for the purpose of the assigned task. They are given a task which they constantly do anyway during their waking hours: observation, defined as perceiving and processing environmental stimuli, becoming aware of and interpreting these impressions. Students are free to decide what to observe and when. For many, this freedom seems too vague as a basis for getting down to observation; they must carry out an activity in order to record it afterwards. The "freedom" to decide what I write and the scene I choose brings some students into major inner conflict. What the reference should be is not suggested in instructions or technical guidance. It remains an open question whether there is a right and wrong way to do observation.

> Lost among this plenitude, however, is the sense that, while each type of intervention is justifiable, they derive from distinct and in some instances incompatible theories of therapeutic action. These stances can direct physicians to different qualities of the patient or the interaction, and can require divergent clinical intents.
>
> (Tublin, 2018, p. 67).

Now we do not examine this plenitude within the observation itself: I must constantly decide what I observe, what I create in myself through being moved, and what can be formulated as a result. The process unfolds again when one thinks back to the scene. As I write down the scene and read through it again, different images will unfold within me. All observations are subject to Gadamer's hermeneutic circle (Orange, 2004; Sassenfeld, 2015).

Tublin writes about being lost in the abundance of thoughts generated within us, which we often find incompatible with what we have learned. Our attitudes lead to different qualities of interaction and thus bear different clinical intentions within; these in turn pose the question of doing observation "right", and having the right clinical attitude to go with it.

Associated with all this is a fear of observation, and the way that fear as an emotion influences my observation and my thinking. Fear can shape an observation, prompting us to remain stuck in the concrete, factual world, only describing what is "visible". This will mean the observed scene will not be filled with life; there will be no attribution of goals, feelings, intentions, or other phenomena of psychological significance.

> Excerpt: Report b/14/PA
>
> Mrs K. had a subarachnoid haemorrhage in February and has been on our ward since April ...
>
> Nursing visit with Ms. K: she is sitting in her wheelchair at a table in the hallway, her best friend is visiting. We ask if we can sit down with her to discuss a few things. What progress has there been so far, how does she see things herself, and what does she think will happen after her release? The ward manager sits to her right, she asks questions the whole time, and there is a nurse sitting opposite the patient, while myself and another student stand to her left. She is asked questions about when it is, where she is, who she is: the questions seem to overwhelm her; she looks at the ward manager, then at her friend, then at us, or else she stares into space. She looks for answers, only questioning and expectant faces look back [at the patient]. That's how it was with almost all the questions.

This part of the report is located in the visible world; the intention of the questions is unclear. The scene is deconstructed and embedded in a concrete worldview. What is the inner attitude behind it?

Attitudes are formed by concepts and theories, ideas we have about what it is to be human. Being able to see and attribute meaning to what is seen is linked to having been seen oneself. If feelings, intentions, wishes, etc. have been attributed to me, I can also use them as metaphors to generate images within me. What does not appear in the visible realm can be clothed in language using metaphors.

In our clinical view, an attitude becomes a professional one when "it is structured around a coherent theory of ... action that defines the ... clinical intent – e.g. ... the articulation of unformulated experience" (Tublin, 2018, p. 70). I can only formulate something if it already exists within me as knowledge and has already been articulated. "Engaging with" observation means an ability to attribute meaning to images seen or imagined, via my own self. The report goes on:

> Or else she laughs, as if we're not taking her seriously by asking her questions like that. 'Well, it's obvious,' and yet she doesn't know the answer. She seems uncomfortable with this. Like an interrogation. I want to cry. Everyone knows the answer and then their faces when it's not the answer they expect, the one they want to hear. It's shameful but scary too. Why can't she think of it? A black hole? How does it feel for her? I feel sorry for putting her in such an uncomfortable situation. Why are we putting her in such a shameful situation? She is the same age as my mother was when she had her accident. There are so many questions! What is worse, to have no control over your mind, or be paralyzed from the neck down? Embarrassing things happening because you're always forgetting numbers, facts, and information. Losing control of your brain.

The student is guided by her images: she has the courage to allow them to rise up inside her. She experiences the situation as shameful: bombarding the patient with questions, literally interrogating her in order to show her that she "obviously" doesn't know. She empathizes very intensely with the patient, starting from the idea of shame, her thoughts turn to her own mother's situation. She weighs up ideas of not knowing or having no control over your brain, creating a difference between the patient and her mother.

The report is determined by different back-and-forth movements, going from emotionless description to emotionally loaded thoughts to memories of her mother's situation. The student then re-introduces the patient by raising the question of paralysis from the neck down, and the mind that can't be controlled. The difference between the patient's situation and her mother's is considered in terms of a trade-off. The path to understanding a situation is by allowing your own ideas about situations to move, along with the associated emotions. As a scientific phenomenon, neutral observation is revealed, on closer inspection, simply to be a mental construct. The idea of neutrality allows us to have an idea of reference. Without a counterpart, i.e. a reference point, no world can be generated and I would have no conception of the existence of my own self.

Finally, we can note that observation generates attitude and attitude shapes observation. This dichotomous relation is a basic prerequisite for creating an idea of ourselves and others. Most of the metaphors we use to describe our world come from physical language, as movement creates our ideas about the world. Before thinking there is movement. Movement generates difference, which in turn is symbolized in words as an other, a counterpart, enabling us to imagine. When we ask something and someone tells us we are asking something, this positional movement creates symbolic meaning within us and is also linked to the feelings we have at the moment of doing so.

Here is more from the same report, about attitude, fear, and seeing things in concrete terms:

> Report f/16/PA
>
> Later that day, as we had been warned, we experienced the first insults. But before this happened, I was able to put my ideas into practice, verbalize my role in the process, and sort of reassure myself. So it was my job to observe and get (*be-sorgen*) missing utensils if there were any. Perfect! Close enough to see and experience something, with little potential for screwing up (*verbocken*) and nobody with any real high expectations of me.

The student conveys his attitude before the patient was brought onto the ward by reflecting back on the start of the case. He assigns himself a role in which he is safe: it gives him security and reduces his anxiety about "screwing up". The German word for this conveys the image of an animal (a goat, *Bock*) which serves to verbalize the fear of being shamed for having acted incorrectly. The metaphor *expectations* suggests the idea of maintaining tension through waiting. Tension that wants to create movement should be endured: here, putting up with not moving while waiting. The tension is not discharged as an affect. The student neutralizes his "worry" (*Sorge*) about getting (*be-sorgen*) things through his use of "Perfect!" Movement is experienced as an expression of worry, in this way, it is located as meaningful and experienced as significant for one's own self. This expression generates an image of a potentially positive aspect of feeling, expressed as meaning.

With this inner attitude, what does our student now see?

> When the lady arrived, I looked closely at her on the ambulance stretcher and felt a little sad. She had just been sitting and talking with her son in the coffee house when suddenly she couldn't say anything anymore and it started. That must have been a terrible feeling for the son.

His vision is a glimpse of *a little sadness*, the image of a coffee house in which she sits at the table with her son and is no longer able to speak when *it started*. What does this speechlessness do to a woman and what is the *terrible feeling* it creates *for the son* at the same time? The scene experienced creates a speechlessness that manifests itself in the lines as the idea of an "it" that suddenly sets in. The lines maintain a hold on what might be frightening for the patient's son.

The counter-movement from speechlessness leads to images of external action:

> The lady was immediately taken to the stroke unit, where a nightdress was put on her, the necessary access points were made for any impending lysis, and she was prepared for CT. ... A TEA [transient epileptic amnesia] was suspected after the CT was normal. However, the impressions (*Eindrücke*) turned out to be quite exciting and instructive for me, and I was in a good position to learn and observe as much as I needed to.

The position is described very well by *me*; there is so much speechlessness in this scene, which crystallizes in not being able to find words or having no words available. Through the generation of meaning, the ego is located again in the scene of the observation task and is described as deformed by the *press* of *impressions*. Observation deforms the ego and can attack it when feelings cannot be contained; seeing depends on generating one's own images and the associated ability to use language as a metaphor.

Seeing is a complex interplay of metaphor, language, experience, and the capacity to hold. Seeing *impresses* us and creates attitude. Attitude, in turn, is an internal reference point used to create a movement which anchors us in the world and creates impressions (Lakoff & Johnson, 2014; Buchholz, 2003).

Anyone who speaks must also accept that they are taking action, and action is connected with significant gaps in self-perception (Greenberg, 1996; Searle, 1974; Tublin, 2018). Language begins with resonant images constructed in a shared reality. Disclosure or "(playing their) cards face up", as Renik postulated for psychoanalysts as early as 1999, "try to articulate and communicate everything that [...] will help the patient understand where the analyst thinks he or she is coming from and plans to go" (Renik, 1995, p. 485). Openness begins with the ability to unfold one's own thoughts via the imagination of images experienced. An observer should play with their cards face up, in this way beginning to radiate authenticity. Personal involvement does not begin with other people, but rather with the recognition of involvement in order to make the invisible visible or to generate significance and meaning. Diversity and creativity come out of an ability to become personally involved, by recognizing or allowing inner images, which are transformed into something which can be formulated, using the resonant sounding board thus made available. What I recognize or do not recognize in myself takes on significance with regard to reality, in the encounter with myself and with others.

To take up another idea from Stephen A. Mitchell, a founder of relational psychoanalysis, we can consider: what should I express, which thought should I take up and try to formulate? Mitchell answered the question: "It depends" (1997, p. x).

> It depends on what has transpired between these two people before and on the meaning to this dyad of particular course of action. It depends on the ... sense of whether an action might provide something new or repeat something old.
>
> (Tublin, 2018, p. 81).

Through images which form within me, prompted by external stimuli, something from my own history can be located or seen as something new. It takes both phenomena to see that it is now up to me to decide which meaning or path of knowledge I want to pursue. The construction of old and new is just a construction, since it is never possible to pass through the same river twice, but it requires the old one to serve as an idea of the river. The images that our seeing makes possible are only filled with meaning at second glance, but seeing occurs via the attitude to which we attach meaning: "It is not what the analyst does – but to an elegantly nuanced habit of mind. … self-reflective emotional involvement" (Tublin, 2018; Mitchell, 1997, p. x). A mental attitude and emotional involvement enable us to see the staging [*Inszenierung*] which forms and unfolds with us and through us. "History provides not the procedures for managing that interaction, but the constructs the analyst employs to understand it" (Tublin, 2018, p. 77).

Donnel Stern was another relational psychoanalytic thinker who addressed dichotomization as a phenomenon. He described what he brought with him as the *cultural*, whereas what he was confronted with was the *immediate* (*cultural and immediate*). With both positions we create connections and thus look for attitudes towards meaning. Stern describes attitude as the philosophical commitment to freedom in the search for meaning, aside from rules and technical structuring (D.B. Stern, 1999, 2003, 2010, 2014, 2015a, 2015b, 2019).

The co-construction, conceptualization, and recognition of the third take place via the meaning of the experience. They are constructed as a hermeneutic circle, which had already been present as a requirement, but now continues to unfold in cascading form, allowing both reality and meaning to emerge.

3 Existence and Listening as Attitude

Attitude controls my listening and forms the basis of encounters. Listening is not only based on the perception and processing of acoustic signals. As a process, listening works through signals in an emotional sense. To make this form of listening understandable, Freud coined the metaphor of "evenly suspended attention". Reik called it "listening with the third ear" and Ogden called it "dreaming", while Singer dubbed it listening with the internal organs. Barsness summed up the ability to listen as "conversation that is at hand" and understands this as a concept including affects, dissonances, and awkwardness, in this way going beyond the content of words. In his study on psychotherapists' relational core competences, he describes this form of listening as such: "I look deep within myself to find my patient"; "I ask myself, what is my body saying?"; "I wonder what is going on with us"; "What are they repeating here with me?" Another active element listed by Barsness is the ability to hear what the patients no longer want to hear, because of their life story and its associated defensive strategies. This unheard element nonetheless finds expression through a wide variety of channels (Barsness, 2018, p. 104). Freud said these phenomena were inaccessible to human beings, calling it the unconscious, which is always present:

> He that has eyes to see and ears to hear may convince himself that no mortal can keep a secret. If his lips are silent, he chatters with his finger-

> tips; betrayal oozes out of him at every pore. And thus the task of making conscious the most hidden recesses of the mind is one which it is quite possible to accomplish.
>
> (S. Freud, 1962, p. 78).

The unconscious does not lie in the depths, notwithstanding Freud's great yearning to be an archaeologist. Instead, the unconscious is reflected through listening, an active momentum which provides a resonant sounding board; to put it another way, one's own unconscious serves to construct the shared meaning of the encounter. Listening is hearing one's own resonances and the associated affects, feelings, stimuli, then transforming these into language to construct a shared world.

> Therefore, the relational analyst seeks to be highly attuned and self-reflective, paying a great deal of attention to what is happening within their own mind and their own affective state, recognizing that what is being stirred within them is in part a transmission of the patient's internal and external world, yet unknown or unspoken.
>
> (Barsness, 2018, p. 104).

Existence, listening, and attitude are prerequisites for participating in the world. From an ontological point of view, it is the basis for grasping our being through what is (*unser Sein im Seienden zu erfassen*). In his Zollikon seminars, Heidegger suggests it is a preliminary exercise in "seeing", "contrasting against": a necessity in order to create the difference we need in order to see (Heidegger, 2018, p. 166). For Heidegger, detachment is necessary in order to separate something, thus making it visible, allowing them to emerge as two things or to create an "against", so as to justify difference. The difference of the *unknown* and *unspoken* mentioned by Barsness can only be sublated by elevating it to a metaphor. And these lines also reflect the basis of our physicality, since we generate language through bodily conditions. At the same time, elevation involves a physical idea of a movement, which leads to difference.

Pizer summarizes the attitude we bring to the encounter: "As analysts or therapists, we possess a capacity for generous involvement simply by virtue of our being human, with our existence embedded in a relational context" – meaning we are able to offer generosity by being embedded in relationships (Pizer, 2018, p. 105).

Our existence can have different meanings or be significant in different ways. If we have had good relationship experiences, we can be generous and giving, ascribing a different meaning to ourselves, in this way radiating a different attitude and thus also listening in a different way. With this, we are on the trail of physical metaphors involving the third ear, dreaming-listening, and the ability to hold (to contain). Pizer sees this "generosity" as a therapeutic tool, regarding it as a caring connection with the patient: as such, it means we should ask why we sometimes lose touch with this attitude and what meanings we can take from that. Its loss or sublation enables us to create meaning through difference by attributing meaning to the physical metaphor of "losing something".

The recognition of the other is one of the great aspects of life, and it requires no words, but my existence generates recognition and gives the other and me, as separate beings, the meaning of existing, of being there (*Da-sein*). While I remain technically abstinent, I recognize the separateness and thus the loneliness of the other person. If I am connected by my action of holding, then I recognize the other person in their affective experience, as a whole person. When I put the unspoken into words, I expand the consciousness of the encounter, enabling my interlocutor to expand their self. The meaning of "I am with you, I see you" is an attitude which creates a deeper sense of sensuality in the encounter but can be named through linguistic formulation. We generate meaning on the physical level through our ability to symbolize, available to us through language. Existence and holding lead to a recognition of the other person and thus to a sensual and meaningful event. Pizer explains this phenomenon:

> Generosity is an innate property, 'elemental' and 'instinctual', yet I also assume that, as with the expression of most genetic potentials, generosity is contextually shaped – certainly by past developmental influence, and likely by conditions of the immediate moment.
>
> (Pizer, 2018, p. 109).

The ability to be generous i.e. capable of conveying meaning to others, lies in our innate attachment behaviour, described in detail by Bowlby and later Answorth. Recognition and non-recognition are anchored within the same world of experience. Seeing is not the same as recognizing:

> Report a/17/PA
>
> [The] patient I am observing today is 66 years old and for 8 years on and off has been receiving treatment for addiction problems, along with severe depression with psychotic content. The aforementioned lady went to the station with police and rescue services [on] the morning because she couldn't stand it at home anymore. She cited arguments with her long-term partner regarding financial problems as well as relationship problems as the reason for her impulsive break-outs, which resulted in alcohol-related incidents. The patient is barely accessible verbally, screams, curses, and spits and threatens to kill herself. The doctor on duty decides to admit her because she is considered a danger to herself and others. While she is being restrained, Mrs. P. threatens to talk to her lawyer: she wants to speak to her husband, feels understood by no one, screams very loudly with the words 'I'll kill you all if you don't leave me alone.' … What a morning, I have never experienced anything like it on the ward. It occurred to me how strenuous the work must be for everyone involved …

There is a lot to see in this scene described, which is dominated by physicality. The fear of everyone involved is at the forefront.

> Report e/16/PA
>
> Mr L. has been admitted to the ward for a few days. He is a thin, grey-haired, grey-skinned man. His eyes are deep in their sockets and they cast deep purple shadows." She observes the patient very closely, turns to him and describes him in detail: "All in all, he reminds me of 'Momo's Grey Men', only without the nicotine and haste." Most of the time leans back on his chair with his arms crossed. At first he is very reserved and has little contact with the other patients. He seems withdrawn and distant. Over time he has made contact and opened up a little. Maybe he doesn't open up, but just retreats a few meters from his inner abyss and somehow penetrates the outside world, so we can hear it and communicate with it. I've been in the psychiatric ward at least long enough to realize that this gentleman is plagued by depression. Somehow he has this effect on me like a black hole, it pulls everything in, if you cross the event horizon there is no escape. As I have often noticed, I find it much more difficult to deal with black holes and depressives than with people in manic phases. I always think it's due to my own latent depressive streak, that I have an eternal fear of ending up in such a seemingly never-ending state. Mr L. tells me that he often came here with his friends as a child and that there were many apartments. Plus there would be a train going around and how beautiful it was there. Mr. L. has a daughter who visits him sometimes but is very busy at work herself and a partner who apparently only keeps in touch via text message and email at the moment. After a few days, that too breaks off, and I notice how his eye sockets are getting even deeper and the dark grey, in all its shades, is spreading across this person.

In both reports, there are people looking on. The first report, through its physically described scenes, moves the reader, but does so differently to the second report. The focus of the first observation is on holding on to your own fear, as well as transferring it to colleagues. This is not a way of recognizing the patient as a psychological being, nor of recognizing the observer in the scene. The two reports convey two different ways of looking at a scene, and thus two possible ways to hold those involved, two ways finding a form of benevolence. Failing to recognize oneself and others leads to forms of observation and of treatment which are fundamentally technical in nature. Action can convey recognition, as shown in one of Ghent's examples, where he hands a blanket to his patient during a session and in this way acknowledging that she was cold and shivering (Ghent et al., 2018). Failing to recognize an expression leads to a demand to deny a feeling or its expression, or to a physical rejection, as described in the first report on the experience of violence. The patient experiences recognition through the strong physical expression created by the joint staging of violence. Recognition can occur through the symbolic power of language, which is metaphorically based on physical experience or is transformed directly into meaning through physicality. A culture-related influence also seems to predominate here, with girls tending to favour the linguistic level, while boys usually receive physical recognition by being asked to do some kind of sporting activity. Cultural and historical comparisons do not confirm biologically-based gender differences. Adolescent girls, for example, increasingly express their emotions physically, which is now beginning to be reflected in forensic statistics. Freud developed his ideas about human beings through the cultural idea of physicality common in his time and through the interconnectedness of bodily difference, divided into male and female. From this, Freud developed many of his psychological concepts, which he decouples from the visible differences of bodies. It does not appear that genetics is ultimate meaning of our being, nonetheless physicality is the basis of our thought, the means through which we develop ideas about ourselves and the world.

As early as 1953, Harry Stack Sullivan developed an interpersonal theory in which he explicitly pointed out the importance of others' reactions to the formation of our self. Our self is constituted by others' recognition of our fundamental need, and the particular needs associated with it. We come to recognize ourselves through our needs; appropriate measures of care are used to alleviate our distress. Sullivan regarded the need for tenderness and the tensions associated with this as deeply rooted in individuals: this idea already comes very close to Bowlby's idea of attachment (Sullivan, 1983). "Tension of tenderness" was the concept Sullivan used for difference and the separation associated with this, which is what makes phenomena visible. The tension between the need for tenderness and the giving of it is what connects mother and infant: it is the basis for mutual recognition. Pizer compares this to his conceptualization, which posits an instinctive movement toward tenderness, which then meets a spirit of generosity, thereby indexing recognition (Pizer, 2018). The infant researcher Trevarthen formulated this innate search for the pre-existing wish to be "relationally" embedded in a community, or to achieve a "we-ness" (Trevarthen, 2009).

For these authors, this desire for community – for recognition – is a striving towards the beginning our emergence and thus represents our fundamental motivation of striving for emergence. The self's development in order to generate ourselves as meaningful beings occurs by means of a circular movement. Our striving for recognition lies in a desire to abolish difference, which in turn only comes about through difference or detachment in the Heideggerian sense. Attitude is thus also an ability to turn towards one's own self and towards others. Distinction, as a process, only takes place later: thus the distinction between drive and object only becomes possible later on, and is not primarily present as a biological phenomenon. The problem is that thinking itself is based on difference and this can only later emerge as a thinkable thing, since our means of comprehension are limited.

4 Empathy as the Interplay of Attitude and Charisma

An attitude which prompts us to hold a scene, causing us to radiate something others experience as warmth and goodwill leads us to an idea of empathy. An essay by Coltart approaches this line of thinking:

> The people whose manners we genuinely admire and enjoy are those who, without it being obvious, skilfully enhance our sense of significance and worth. All contact, whether conversational *or silent,* is accompanied by an atmosphere of warmth and generosity; this promotes trust and openness.
>
> (Coltart, 1992, p. 137; italics in original).

Charisma is not only produced through conversation, but also by silence, triggering a sense of significance and worth in the other. Or we experience an attribution of meaning, about ourselves or about the scene, which leads us to experience significance and worth. If we understand meaning in our experience, we can be trusting and open in our attitude. The idea of empathy is something co-created: it presupposes an attitude towards what I seek to create; the process of creation is already underway within me. It is not the product within me which creates empathy as an attitude. Rather this process should be reflected within me as an attitude towards the other: in this way empathy can manifest in a flow of permanence, in the sense of a hermeneutic circle.

An attitude that manifests as empathy, in the sense of openness and trust, is also a willingness to allow oneself be touched and for this reason, it also radiates a presence of existence.

> By clinical generosity, I do not mean lax attention to the frame or sloppy guidelines of practice, but rather, a serious, and at times, even unsettling re-evaluation and openness to amending any and all aspects of analytic practice in light of the patient's forward edge strivings.
>
> (Corpt, 2011, p. 5).

That patients are moved is something important to Corpt. But what is it that should *move* patients, if it is only us who are here? They can only move within us, and we are the patients, and what is disturbing is this new thing and the evaluation of both people involved in the process. Attitude is often equated with the capacity to provide containment for patients. "By containment, I mean a welcoming of the patient's multiplicity of states and feelings hero in an abiding negotiated relationship" (Pizer, 2018, p. 98).

Pizer sees containing as an unstable process, an offer which must constantly be negotiated with patients. Active negotiation is a process of containment in the sense that patients are offered a living relationship. This can happen through communication and through silence; the dynamic process in which everything that is embedded fluctuates is the containment of change, the process of transformation of what Bion called the beta and alpha elements. For Pizer, acceptance is an attitude of being conscious of patients' feelings and of one's own feelings as evoked by patients. Psychotherapists maintain an internal struggle with patients' feelings, so as to treat their anger, helplessness, fear, and anxiety with respect. In doing so, therapists also show their willingness to put pain, confusion, self-doubt, etc. into a process of shared negotiation and thus entanglement. This willingness, which is brought into the encounter process in the form of an attitude, is a prerequisite for entering into the painful process of working through, since it can convey to patients to give everything they have to the process, sparing nothing of themselves. Psychotherapists indicate their capacity to participate in the shared process which lies ahead. Through this kind of attitude, therapists express that they are able to bring their feelings into the encounter and that they are not overwhelmed by them, so they can give patients recognition and accept them as independent people, recognizing their separateness. Pizer sums this up with the words *containment, acceptance*, and *recognition*. This attitude should then become the implicit expression: "I am with you" (Pizer, 2018, p. 111).

So what now would be a countermovement to achieve a difference, and when is there no return to the place of encounter and a loss of this attitude or of patients? The movement which creates a scene is an embrace of emotion. Showing compassion is an active act which amounts to a movement towards feeling. It involves a complex kind of witnessing, the opposite of being a mere spectator. Imre Kertész, the Hungarian writer and Nobel Prize winner, places witnessing at the centre of his work.

"And he does not flinch, Kertész wants to bear witness, to get close to the truth which always eludes him, even if he knows he will never grasp it" (Bielefeld, 2016). Bearing witness, in the spirit of Kertész, an Auschwitz survivor, embodies an existence to witness, in all its tragedy, to seize what threatens to sink into namelessness. His texts are full of witnessing but they are not about watching. Witnessing is based on an inner struggle with the shaping and blending of external realities, which construct themselves as truths, but which one can only approach, and for this reason can only be movement.

Witnessing, in this sense of compassion, is *a moving towards the feeling*, as Pizer puts it. A movement to bear witness requires the emergence of an event whose witness I can be. If, in striving to witness, I can only see myself, this merely expresses the needs and deficiencies of my striving to witness, my unwitnessed life. It is a back-and-forth movement within me, seeking a witness for another person. If I am overwhelmed by the lack of witness within me, the other will remain hidden from me, and the witness will become an active orchestrator of his own pain. Freud described it to Ferenczi as *furor sanandi*, a search to bear witness which can no longer find a way out of the soul's own wrong tracks. In this context, repetition compulsion can be understood as a quest for a witnessing of my life's drama and trauma. Compassion is not simply forward motion; it is movement both inward and forward, to present witnessing and compassion (Pizer, 2018, p. 111; Ferenczi et al., 2013).

Recognition, as formulated by Jessica Benjamin, also includes the capacity to make use of the other. Since compassion is a witnessing of active movement, we need a reference point: the ability to witness the other. I need you to be able to recognize me, in other words, I need your witnessing. The back-and-forth movement turns viewers into witnesses by recognizing the witnessing carried out by the other person. Technical neutrality, which is only a mental construct, would be an attempt to move from witnessing to spectatorship. But since every movement creates a difference, it is always also a witnessing, including as a witnessing which denies (Benjamin, 2016a, 2018). For Poland, learning to value yourself and others is a single process, the only difference being one of perspective: "The capacity to appreciate the self and the capacity to appreciate the other do not simply go hand in hand: they are the same unitary phenomenon of growth seen from different angles" (Poland, 2016, p. 29f.).

Growth is movement: to focus on it is to divide the phenomenon, so it merely means the same thing as what we consider as the self and other. We become the Thou via the I; we only experience the Thou through the I. On this, Poland writes: "In the analyst's regard (witnessing the face of the Other); looking and caring and separateness (interpretation) are one" (Poland, 2016, p. 32). This is a process in which looking, witnessing, caring, and separateness unfold. The formulation in the sense of interpretation leads to separateness in the sense of symbolization through language, and this enabled the process to be conceived. According to Aron, interpretation is: "The principal process by which analysts position and reposition themselves interpersonally in relation to their patients" (Aron, 1992, p. 504). Interpretation means to relate to something, and this reference leads to a repositioning, which in turn generates new thoughts, thus changing the position and keeping it dynamic.

5 Sensitivity – Resonance – Complementarity

According to Stuart Pizer, *sensitivity* can be described as "deep listening" or as "a capacity for generous involvement simply by virtue of our being human, with our existence embedded in a relational context" (Pizer, 2018, p. 105) – a great philosophical thought, grounded on an idea of inner generosity. Perhaps this generosity means treating myself and others with a free-floating attitude, trying in a moral sense to be aware of my judgments. My cultural background and my ways of seeing influence my understanding of the world and construct my personal perspective. Sensitivity is embedded in the awareness that I am constructing phenomena and in this way creating them. In this sense, I am acting in a profoundly subjective way. This insight leads me towards a path of "generosity", as Pizer tries to convey. If we lose this generous participation in the event, observation becomes a technical event: I have a lack of a caring connection with myself and thus also with the scene taking place in front of me. Sensitivity is also expressed through a capacity to give meaning to myself and thus to the observation. Only by giving meaning to my existence is it possible to bear witness to the scene. If I cannot give meaning to my existence, I remain hidden even though I am being watched. Sensitivity is the "face of the non-negotiable: containment, acceptance and recognition" (Pizer, 2018, p. 107).

Sensitivity is the innate anchoring of the search for attachment. We are in this world to form community and be embedded within it. We are looking to feel connected (Trevarthan, 2009). A further significance of this lies in enduring the tension of uncertainty, in this way holding open the development of an image; it is thus also a possible form of reticence in interpretation. All the images I absorb are subject to a constant negotiation: they must be related to each other, or alternatively the tension of uncertainty must be maintained. Sensitivity is an inner struggle with feelings which are touched, the capacity to hold them within oneself, to bear witness to oneself and what one sees, in this way recognizing the reality formed by stimuli and by feelings like fear, anger, joy, etc. This recognition of a subjective reality is transformed into a vastness of experience through an attitude of generosity towards the feelings experienced.

Observing and being compassionate is a "feeling with; generous involvement entails a moving toward the feelings, being a witness who is not a bystander" (Pizer, 2018, p. 111). Anyone who is merely an observer in a scene will not be able to leave the meanings of the concrete world: they will not enter into a psychological space in which resonances and rhythms unfold.

The philosopher Emmanuel Lévinas ascribes responsibility in his representation to the other whom we see: the *face of the other* is the name Lévinas gives to how the other presents themselves and the difference from my idea of them. This face can be destroyed at any time; it is what allows beings to arrive at expression (Lévinas, 1969). Seeing the other is a rhythmic perception of the other's representation, of my own resonance and of the new which arises from all this. In Lévinas's sense, the other has now emerged as an individual with identity. Donna Orange's response to Lévinas's other: "Me voici – me here" (Orange, 2011, p. 47) – affirms an inner existence, so as to give the other a face or to grant him recognition within myself.

Giving the other a face, being capable of holding them within yourself, is closely connected to a process of growth which ends in bearing witness to the face of the other. To again cite Poland: "Looking and caring and separation are one" (Poland, 2016, p. 32). Resonance is there in interpreting or imagining what is seen; it is thus a second process of vision. By thinking about what I see, I have to repeatedly position myself interpersonally, in the sense of the affective scenes within myself. In this way, I enter into a relational process which allows "new things" to emerge (Aron, 1992, 2018).

Sensitivity and resonance mean being able to surrender to what you see, getting emotionally involved, being able to endure conflicts while being deeply involved in the scene.

Complementarity is a kind of resonance: it refers to how we respond to images. What we see turns us into "prisoners of the coercive projective power of each other's vision," as each person "becomes hopelessly defined by the other" (Davies, 2008, p. 15). What we see influences us and we are defined and shaped by these images. This phenomenon represents the basis for intersubjectivity: mutual influence takes place in a rhythmic cycle. This can be defined as *complementarity* (Benjamin, 2018; Sander, 2009). This complementarity unfolds between, on the one hand, the images I see and my resonant capacity on the other. This resonance has been formed through all of my affective experiences, as well as my reaction to them, which is here "the common third", if we were to define this intersubjectively. Identification is based on the mechanics of rhythm: I am moved to oscillation by the affective touch of my experience. The more strongly that affective experiences are expressed, the more that one feels trapped and hopelessly exposed, the more one's self is plunged into a looping experience of repetition. The sooner that insight is formed – in the sense of the newness inherent to any scene – the sooner these feelings can be clothed in change and insight. Shared recognition of this constructed complementarity allows us to adopt a new position and to accept new affective experience. Benjamin honed in on this constellation when she acknowledged the existence of the "moral third". The recognition releases one from a dualistic viewpoint, in which "only one can live" (Benjamin, 2018, p. 215). Complementarity is sought, only to be destroyed in the next movement. This is not a rigid system, but rather a rhythmic movement in which one can feel trapped. In this context, Benjamin uses the metaphor of a children's seesaw (Benjamin, 1999a). However, complementarity can be resolved through shared recognition, which produces the possibility of creating reciprocity together.

This recognition is a witnessing or a working through of a trauma which prevails within us, a chaotic, violent primal scene. "One aspect of experiencing unconscious resonances of the primal scene is the intense conflict concerning with whom to identify, and we often manage such conflict by rigidly identifying with one actor and disidentifying with the other," writes Aron. He goes on: "This oscillating function is the basis from which a person can participate" (Aron, 2018, p. 125f.).

This oscillation or rhythmicity brings with it an ability to change positions, to rise to a meta-level, to get an overview, and to express all of the bodily metaphors of the triangular position. Indeed, the space opened by the movement is often described as a triangle, dissolving the duality of the seesaw. When our thoughts move up and down on a seesaw, we feel trapped, at the mercy of our fears and aggressions. But if we can dissolve these constricting structures, we make a triangular space: it is here that new forms of thinking and feeling can unfold: "Thinking and feeling within the newly created triangular space allowed ... a shift from the limiting structure of a polarizing flat line to a space with possibility and depth" (Aron, 2018, p. 129).

Complementarity can be viewed as a phenomenon of touch, a matter of reacting to one's inner resonant sounding board. It is the prerequisite for triangulation or thirdness. It is always a processual event.

Resonance can be viewed as a pattern of synchronicity and asynchronicity, a movement hidden within us like a wave. Only displacement (*Verschiebung*) creates visibility, doing so through energy that unfolds (Görnitz & Görnitz, 2016). This phenomenon has been represented using a variety of different conceptions, including nonverbal, sub-symbolic body functions, body memory, procedural memory, physiological awareness of feeling, and implicit memory. Wilma Bucci, in her theory of multiple coding, divides these systems into three levels: a) sub-symbolic system, b) nonverbal symbolic system, and c) verbal symbolic system. The sub-symbolic system is what corresponds to the phenomenon mentioned above, coordinating the motor activities. The system is also able to dedicate itself to thought, but this is not conscious thinking in the sense of cogitated thought. Instead, this is thought which organizes us, in the form of resonant emergence, expressed as enactment (Solano, 2010; Bucci, 2011). Resonance means the provision of an emotional schema, with its organizational core at the level of the sub-symbolic system:

> Emotion schemas are types of memory structures that constitute the organization of the self in the interpersonal world. They are formed on the basis of repeated interactions with caretakers and others from the beginning of life. The sub-symbolic sensory, somatic, and motoric representations and processes constitute the affective core of the emotion schema – the source of the varieties of arousal and pleasure and pain that constitute emotional experience. In each event of life, the processes of the affective core will be activated in relation to the people, places, and activities that figure in that event; Thus we build memories of people and events that give us pleasure or pain, that activate happiness, or dread, or a wish to attack. Autobiographical memory is built out of such events; this is the basis for the organization of the self in the interpersonal world.
>
> (Bucci, 2011, p. 49).

We connect together our inner patterns through the rhythmic movement of difference; with this movement we create something new, which we in turn anchor within ourselves as emotional experience. These movements can also be given different names, they can be called "crescendos, decrescendos, pauses, accents, rhythmic patterning of both matching and mismatching" (Knoblauch, 2018, p. 144). The language of the physical unfolds in a rhythm outside of thought: it can be represented with metaphors of music and jazz improvisation. Resonance takes place primarily on the sub-symbolic level; reflection, which is put into words, is a secondary process of thinking. The emotional schemas described by Bucci form the basis for our experience of human interaction, unfolding as patterns with varying dynamics:

> The emotion schemas develop in an interpersonal context; the baby who laughs and smiles and has feelings of joy can see and hear the other person also smiling and laughing and making the corresponding sounds; the expressions of the other become incorporated into the schema of joy. When the child who cries hears sympathetic sounds and sees a particular facial expression, along with a soothing feeling touch, the child's schemas of pain or fear will develop to incorporate responses of turning to others and expectations that others can help. If the caretaker typically responds to the child's cries with annoyance or withdrawal, schemas of negative expectations and associated responses will develop.
>
> (Bucci, 2011, p. 49).

Every image summons up these patterns or schemas within us: they are what enables us to put order into what we see, and into the world around us more generally. The intensity of this expression leads us to speak of an enactment, which we can then formulate as a thought and understand as a memory. "Patterns emerged as both a product of our capacity for thinking and representing – the symbolic – and in our forms of relating – the sub-symbolic" (Knoblauch, 2018, p. 151). Memory is embedded in attention to the sub-symbolic flow of vitality and rhythmicity. Without being framed in a categorizing form of attentiveness, a space of meaning and knowledge unfolds which relates to a mode of registering with the emotions (D.B. Stern 1999, 2016). We refer to this awareness as our *feelings*, which we now experience and to which we assign categorical meaning. We associate feelings with our experience, in this way going beyond interpersonal perception, instead creating a kind of intersubjective perception. "This kind of attention can help link what is going on between (the intersubjective) to what is going on within (the subjective)" (Knoblauch, 2018, p. 151). Inhibitions – as well as other forms of expression which we would call pathological – are reflected in the impossibility of linking together these perceptions. The sub-symbolic attempts at expression find no connection to other symbolic systems (Bucci, 1997, 2011). Many relational psychoanalysts here will use the concept of *dissociation*, in which there is a blanking out of any registration of the emotions. Changes to the rhythmicity of non-awareness will give us a reference point for repeating patterns from our past: these changes enable us to recognize these patterns, and link them to a new emotional experience, which can act as a catalyst for us.

Evaluating reports in terms of resonance, complementarity and sensitivity

> In the reception area for daytime clients – that's what we call visitors to the day centre – it was terribly hectic, like it always is, so much that I didn't really see when a tall man with a full head of long hair came through the door into the dining room, slumped over his rollator.

In her observation report, the student describes a process of not seeing, the disappearance behind the phrase "daytime clients", and mentions her concern with "really seeing". The complementarity to this thought is not false perception, but rather non-perception.

> It wasn't until early afternoon that I sat down at his table; he was sunk deep in conversation with a carer. Sunk, in the truest sense of the word. This man would probably have been around 1.90m tall if he stood or sat upright, but that no longer seems possible for him. His pelvis looks like it has been shifted to the left, and so his entire upper body tilts to the right when he is sitting down.

The student's response reflects what is not visible, being "sunk", something she associates with the body. The non-visible is formulated in the contradiction: "Probably around 1.90m tall". Here the reference is unfolded; the impossibility of standing up is formulated as a thought.

Sensitivity develops through the pain of the body.

> What also struck me was his gait, it didn't matter whether he had a rollator or not, he walked with his knees very bent, as if his upper body alone weighed 150kg. I thought to myself that if he got up from his chair, he would definitely straighten his legs. That was a misconception: he grabbed the rollator and walked away using it, in almost the same position he had been when sitting down.

Seeing becomes the focus of observation. "When he speaks, he looks directly at the supervisor; as soon as he finishes his sentences, he turns his gaze away from her, and his look sinks into a certain emptiness". The use of emptiness as a metaphor is an expression of what the images have caused to resonate within the student. She looks at the scene and experiences a sinking into herself. The next thought represents a countermovement to emptiness, developing an idea about the eyes, about looking. "His eyes are dark, almost black, but don't seem lively, they are cloudy instead, even when he talks about his life..." Here again is a mental movement between the idea of intensity – through "black" and "dark" – which appears in a back-and-forth movement with metaphors of "not alive" and "cloudy instead". Between these images we perceive an idea of pain, the complementarity of the movement making something visible.

The colour black and the idea of "length" express admiration, a loving look towards observation, care expressed through sensitivity.

> What else catches my eye is that everything about him is supernaturally long. His fingers, his arms, his hair, and his legs.
>
> His long, full, slightly curly hair, which reaches approximately to his shoulder, is mostly black, partly streaked with threads of silver; he wears it with a slight side parting. This is on the left side of his head, and from there emerges, towards the right, a striking strand of hair, almost white and maybe five centimetres wide, which extends over his entire forehead, as far as his right ear.

Something that catches the eye, the long look at the patient: these acknowledge his emptiness, they express a seeing of his pain, something which remains invisible in the patient's everyday life. The observation which absorbs the images, allowing them to penetrate and catch the eye, is a recognition of the pain of disappearance on the part of the patient. The inner resonant space opens up through the rhythmic motion between emptiness and recognition, holding on to individuated images of the patient's hair. The student's resonant sounding board is based on the idea of loneliness and emptiness and the counter-movement towards the hair, in stark contrast to the hairlessness of the observer. This back-and-forth movement towards recognizing individuality in and around the patient, through the pain of emptiness and the wealth of his "threads of silver [hair]". Empathy is a shared growth beyond these pendulum movements: it is about recognizing one's own pain as something different to the desire for this head of hair and the idea of growing older, expressed gracefully in the silver metaphor. Here recognition unfolds between the emptiness of one's own idea of loneliness, as identification and differentiation, a recognition that she does not have this head of hair. "We are the same and yet different", would be the summarized realization in this movement, which goes from the rigidity of non-perception "it was terribly hectic, like it always is, so much that I didn't really see when a tall man with long full hair, came through the door into the dining room, slumped over his rollator" – touching on his individuality – "when I looked at him go, I noticed how far his spine had shifted and that a large 'hump' had formed in the sacral area, which was clearly visible through his blue, faded sweatshirt". Via observation, the patient gains a self in which individuation can unfold.

The following report deals with turning off phenomena like resonance, sensitivity, rhythmicity, and recognition.

> I'm sitting in the duty room. A resident comes in. He had just changed his clothes because he was out and about and it was raining heavily. He asks if he can have the remote control for the television in the common room because he would like to watch television. The carer who sits with

> me in the office gives it to him, and the resident thanks him and immediately asks if he could have something to nibble. The supervisor says no.

The images here are not linked to ideas; it is not possible to read any individuation from these lines. The student cannot assign an identity to herself or to the scene. The pain of the report lies in the superficial view, which can develop no space of dimensionality. It's like a child's drawing full of stick figures. The student remains in the event, but without individuality or meaning; it seems as if she were not there. The world remains concrete: only the "visible" is reflected in these lines.

"The carer asked if he could help me, he had just written a lot and was in the mood to write. I say no. We're still talking about political and philosophical topics". Seeing and recognition are reflected in the ability to attribute needs to myself and others and, thus, by the ability to become dependent. I give meaning to the other when I allow myself to be helped, recognizing mutual dependence in the encounter.

These two reports represent a back-and-forth movement, reflecting on the one hand the dimensionality of a triangle, and on the other, the concreteness of one-dimensionality, in which there is only a single "truth" of observation.

Another report begins by observing an intake situation: "She has very thin arms and legs, her lips are pale. Her dark blonde hair is tied up in a braid ... now she is sitting here with her parents. They look helpless, don't know what to do, Maria has been [eating?] less and less since Christmas". The scene is also about the disappearance and helplessness of a family. Resonance is based on the idea of "looking helpless" and their associated pain of Maria unravelling.

"When food comes, she repeatedly gets very stressed. Thoughts of self-harming occur. Hannah cut herself for about two months". Here we see a countermovement in the description of the scene; Maria is depicted without emotions, not conveying what happens as a psychological event. The student's own feelings are not interwoven into the scene, the report remains a distanced description, so as not to be flooded by feelings. The helplessness expressed in the image of the family is held back and "lived" in the description as dissociation. "She describes her mood as anxious, sad, not happy": this is the girl's mood, not the mood of the shared scene, as it was at the beginning of the report. The student re-approaches the scene by directly quoting Maria: "Now I'm here, it has to work here, it didn't work at home anymore". The significance of the sentence lies in the resonance it sets up within the student, who already has a good understanding of changing place and function.

At this point, the description again takes on a great deal of three-dimensionality: "As the nutrition plan is explained to her, her voice becomes quieter and quieter, she smiles hesitantly. When it comes to portion sizes, she can barely hold back her tears. Her eyes become sadder and she stares into space. She bites her lip, fights back tears". Maria has now gone deep into the student, offering a resonant sounding board for the tears, emptiness and struggles. In the subsequent lines there is both countermovement and recognition of Mary's individuation.

> The way I perceived Maria in the last minutes of the intake interview is how she appears at subsequent meals. A blank stare while eating, she puts her food in her mouth as if she is disgusted or revolted. The potato is halved, quartered, and mashed until it is the size of a grain of rice. Or yoghurt is pushed back and forth, so that the edges of it are barely touching her fingers: the main thing is that it doesn't go into her mouth. And she cries after eating, after every meal.

The difference of helplessness is marked by anger, which is also a form of recognition: it serves as a resonant sounding board. The student feels powerless with regard to the patient and counteracts these feelings by concluding the report with questions of comprehension: "What must have happened that she can't eat? Why is it so difficult for her? There is a complete lack of enjoyment of food, the joy of life is lost…" Loss and control permeate the observation, with helplessness emerging as a central underlying feeling.

The reports are related to the group's own resonant sounding board; they enable the group to more deeply understand sensitivity and recognition. Here, too, we reflect on our individual life story and draw conclusions about the material so as to understand the scene through our own reaction, and in this way also to achieve a differentiation between myself and you.

6 Ideas of "Third" and "Thirdness"

The idea of a third party within the triangular constellation and its psychological meaning are already very firmly present in Freud's idea of Oedipality.

> In boys the situation of the Oedipus complex is the first stage that can be recognized with certainty. It is easy to understand, because at that stage a child retains the same object which he previously cathected with his libido – not as yet a genital one – during the preceding period while he was being suckled and nursed. The fact, too, that in this situation he regards his father as a distributing rival and would like to get rid of him and take his place is a straightforward consequence of the actual state of affairs.
>
> (S. Freud, 1927).

Freud refers here to element of reality in the development of the Oedipal triangle and the psychological significance of processing the triangular situation for the child's development. The Oedipus complex represents a core element of Freud's psychoanalytic teaching. For Freud, difference has an elementary personality-structuring power, whether that goes through narcissistic processing or displacement, etc. As he sees it, recognizing difference is an important building block for developmental significance. He goes on to say that recognition and non-recognition develop on the basis of the observation of anatomical difference, to which he attaches great importance. From the perspective of the little girl, he writes: "They notice the penis of a brother or playmate, strikingly visible and of large proportions, at once recognize it as the superior counterpart of their own small and inconspicuous organ, and from that time forward fall a victim to envy for the penis" (S. Freud, 1927).

Freud's thoughts go immediately to the idea of the little girl's interpretation and not to the meaning of difference, nor to any possible recognition of it. When depicting psychological development, Freud's protagonists are children or patients who desire their analyst. His developmental psychology portrays parents and analysts very passively. The child develops based on rigid ideas about their parents, in this way experiencing a variety of emotional aspects which he now has to process. No psychological significance is attributed to the "brother or playmate" who shows his penis; Freud strips out people's affective and intentional involvement from his conception of psychological development, omitting the influence on the scene associated with them.

Freud's conception of the psychological is also based on the fact that the girl already has an idea of having and not having, and she now needs feelings of envy in order to form an inner psychological constellation.

> When a little boy first catches sight of a girl's genital region, he begins by showing irresolution and lack of interest; he sees nothing or disavows [12] what he has seen, he softens it down or looks about for expedients for bringing it into line with his expectations. It is not until later, when some threat of castration has obtained a hold upon him, that the observation becomes important to him: if he then recollects or repeats it, it arouses a terrible storm of emotion in him and forces him to believe in the reality of the threat which he has hitherto laughed at. This combination of circumstances leads to two reactions, which may become fixed and will in that case, whether separately or together or in conjunction with other factors, permanently determine the boy's relations to women: horror of the mutilated creature or triumphant contempt for her.
>
> (S. Freud, 1927)

For Freud, the threat or idea of castration is something unavoidable, but these are not linked to real people. They are either articulated because they are generally valid, or because of some actual event which can only be understood in terms of removing or cutting off, etc.

The text, Freud goes on to explain, is in the intended sense the product of a third party or a co-construction which requires a counterpart.

> In the following pages I bring forward some findings of analytic research which would be of great importance if they could be proved to apply

> universally. Why do I not postpone publication of them until further experience has given me the necessary proof, if such proof is obtainable? Because the conditions under which I work have undergone a change, with implications which I cannot disguise. ... In those days I had unlimited time before me, 'oceans of time'; as an amiable author puts it and material poured in upon me in such quantities that fresh experiences were hardly to be escaped. Moreover, I was the only worker in a new field, so that my reticence involved no danger to myself and no loss to others.
>
> (S. Freud, 1927)

Freud's thoughts are not as plentiful as they once were, competition appears to becoming increasingly important, and with it the danger associated with keeping something back, with failing to publish. He also begins his reflections: "In my own writings and in those of my followers more and more stress is laid on the necessity that ..."

The aspiration to remain at the top of the psychoanalytic community and maintain its hierarchical structures requires great personal effort, including the production of basic texts, in order to be able to support one's claims. Analytic texts are shaped by ideas about patricide and the sons' competing upward trajectories. If we regard this text as an emerging third party, along with Freud's students, it can also be viewed through the current situation in the community: it was created under time pressure and thus embedded to a greater degree in affective moments of the here and now. What losses could Freud have meant here, which might result from keeping his work back? Could it be that his students' texts, now more public, could damage him, or even surpass him? Does this text represent his triumph over his students? Passivity, as he puts it in his initial thoughts, involves a risk of harm. For Freud, passive and active have emphatic meanings in describing gender difference and its development. He starts to use the metaphor of the ocean again, as an idea of happiness and infinity, which stands opposed to any physical experience of transience.

His greatest wish is for his thoughts to be universal. Behind this lies the idea that science can only develop meaning by the subtraction of the soul and the body: that no people with individual feelings, needs, wishes, etc. are ever involved. In the Oedipal context, the third is perhaps to be found in descriptions of triumph, mutilation, and contempt as universal emotions, formulated through an idea of danger and the fear associated with it. The more promptly a text is written, the fewer hermeneutic circles of thought it will have gone through; in these circumstances, it comes very close to being a shared construction and thus embedded in the here and now.

The language with which Freud feels his way towards a description of his observations seems very much based on archaic, Christian imagery. The idea of universality is subject to an upward striving, in the sense of striving for heaven, as concretized in Gothic buildings (Vitz, 1988; Whitebook, 2018).

Freud's thought here encompasses the form of "Jewish interpretation" along with the Christian ideal of striving upwards, towards a summit, seeking to elevate it to omnipotence.

Published in 1974, Andre Green's *De la tiercèitè* offered some contemporary formulations of concepts of "the third"; Thomas Ogden developed these in *The Analytic Third* (Coelho, 2017). Ideas of the third include imagining the triangle as a psychic space, thinking of it as an emergent property in shared interaction, and as a shared accomplishment needed for reflexive awareness and mentalization (Aron, 2018).

The version of the concept we will explore here is taken from the writings of Jessica Benjamin: "The term third is used to designate a position or principal to mean the representation of a potential relationship that we use to break out of the reciprocal lock of complementarity" (Benjamin, 2016b).

The concept of "thirdness" is based on the structural idea of complementarity. The structural representation of complementarity can best be seen as a straight line in which both end points complement or enable each other in their one-dimensionality. Both are interdependent and complement each other in their actions. Benjamin developed her idea of "Doer and Done" for this purpose, so as to clothe the idea of dependency in the metaphorical image of a seesaw, where one is at the top and the other at the bottom. (Benjamin, 2018).

If it is possible to leave this seesaw, the idea of a third is formed, with a new conceptualization of a psychic space, and the dissolution of duality.

> Because communicative speech establishes a space of dialogue potentially outside the mental control of either or both participants, it is a site of mediation, the 'third term'.
>
> (Benjamin, 1998, p. 28).

A three-dimensional psychological space includes many possible combinations of complementarity and thus there is also a variety of physical events which can develop. In three-dimensional space, neither of the two participants feels trapped or dependent in the sense of submission. The structural arrangement is heavily influenced by the attitude I develop: whether I regard it as multidimensional or as a situation with only one winner and one loser. "Rather than following the rigid and predictable back and forth movement of a seesaw, transference can begin to serve as a 'strange attractor', allowing the emergence of surprisingly new configurations and unpredictable interpersonal adjustments" (Aron, 2018, p. 129). Unpredictability is an excellent basic predictor for the design of a Third, and thus for the development of something new.

Benjamin subsequently came up with the concept of *The One in the Third and the Third in the One*, outlined in the book of that name (Benjamin, 2018). "One in the Third" refers to Sander's studies and their idea of rhythmicity as a harmonious unity, which she describes in terms of musical improvisation. This represents a sharing of rhythm, something which first develops in the mother-child relationship. "In sum, the early two-body experience is seen as crucial to the way that representation emerges intersubjectively" (Benjamin, 1998, p. 27). Representation is what is created together in "the one in the third", and both are influenced by the mutual rhythm, with both thus being termed "the third in the one". Aron refers to this as "mutual accommodation" (Aron, 2018, p. 130). For Benjamin, the rhythm is now thirdness, which only arises from the dyad, which she also refers to as the *moral third* or *symbolic third*. This moral third can now be distinguished from *Oneness* and is based on the concepts of "marking" and "congruence" developed by György Gergely in his theory of social biofeedback in affect reflection (Fonagy et al., 2002). Mirroring in the sense of congruent marking is a dyadic system that creates something new between infant and mother. Both figures know that the reflection is not the mother and not the infant. This creates the knowledge of an independent self and of the idea of an other. "The one-in-the-third and the third-in-the-one are interconnected. Rhythmicity and markedness go together, with the former emphasizing connectedness, and the latter emphasizing difference; each is necessary" (Aron, 2018, p. 132). The idea of the Third offers the possibility of conceptualizing reflection and symbolization, and enables a theory of thought which is different to that of the isolated mind. The third is formed through noticing an internal process, particularly internal conflicts or inconsistencies in the observation of a scene. Through your own reaction, a space of thirdness will open up in the observation, generating a different understanding, with new insights. Only this psychic space allows for reflective consciousness and offers an opportunity for mentalization. In a fluid process, this space of thirdness is constructed, lost, destroyed, and repaired. Intersubjectivity is a process of negotiating differences and togetherness.

"Intersubjective space, I suggested (Benjamin, 1988) more broadly could be understood in terms of the dialogue as creating a third, something like the dance that is distinct from the dancers yet co-created by them" (Benjamin, 1998, p. 28).

The Third is not a form of objectivity; thus, it is not free from desires, distortions, and affective involvement. It is a fluid, dynamic process which takes place in the field of tension between, on the one hand, complementarity, and, on the other, the opening of a psychological space in which reflective thinking can unfold. "Intersubjectivity consists of a dialectic process of mutual recognition and breakdown into complementarity" (Aron, 2018, p. 137).

The rhythms of observation can lead to a dead end of dualistic imagination. If I can imagine a third position with regard to the observed scene, then I go beyond binary imprisonment in my own affects, as in sadomasochistic thinking. In the symbolic space of thirdness and intersubjectivity we find the possibility of a congruent, protective marking for my regulation.

By acknowledging the influence on every dynamic interaction between every person involved, a moral third position comes into being. Morality is defined as taking responsibility for the co-creation of a scene and for the feelings of everyone involved. This assumption of responsibility can create a feeling of self-efficacy and in this way change the positions of perpetrator and victim.

Recognition means the ability to undertake observation with an inherent capacity for reflection, in which subjectivity can be attributed to the other. Observation, in the sense of the moral third, means granting everyone involved their own reality.

Observing and developing a new way of seeing, in this sense of thirdness, is based on a recognition of one's own feelings, conferring of pity on the other, and acknowledging the possibility of hurt, within an "objective" description. In an observation, hurt occurs when I cannot ascribe feelings to myself, usually out of fear of being flooded by them. Being able to attribute feelings and reflective understanding to myself means taking responsibility for my own observation and in this way creating a moral third position. If I am overwhelmed by fear, guilt, or shame, I cannot take responsibility for my observation and cannot acknowledge my feelings. The recognition of feelings and the inevitability of my subjective observation leads to a recognition of the inevitable: this enables me to "surrender" (in Ghent's sense) to the observation. When I acknowledge my feelings, I can now take responsibility for my own part in the observation, something which also creates feelings of effectiveness and meaning.

The experience of images opens up through the formation of rhythmic interchange between the observation and my reflection on my feelings: the rhythm here thus reflects the mother-child interaction, in the sense of representing a common third element within me. Sub-symbolic communication begins as resonance and reflection within me: it is not about the "objective" images, but rather a capacity to attribute meaning to images. We do not absorb representations of individuals – our mother, for example – but rather representations of the interaction which develops in this particular rhythmic pattern. If I cannot create an experience of these images, I will remain on a concrete level in perceptual terms, and thus remain blind to psychological events, and I will develop no capacity for mentalization. I enter the space of the moral third when I am able to accept my fallibility and be tolerant of my ignorance, while acknowledging my shameful feelings (Benjamin, 2018, 2004a).

Dissociative processes are also often reflected in the reports written by students, where it is impossible to express one's own reflections and feelings since they are often associated with shame. To avoid destabilization, the observer withdraws from the scene and cannot provide a reflective-resonant sounding board. Dissociation brings about withdrawal because the observing person can no longer regulate the scenes they perceive; it is no longer possible to bring them to life with emotions – the mechanism of affective regulation – because of the looming danger of being emotionally flooded. Self-regulation is the ability to allow a rhythm to be set up within oneself but without harming oneself in the sense of "doer and done to" (Schore, 2009).

Dissociation should only be introduced as a mechanism if there is no longer movement back, with rigidity occurring. Above all, we need movement and "slight" dissociation in order to be able to create difference, rather than simple identification. This requires rhythm: a rhythm of seeing, permitting, breaking off, dissociating, and recognizing the difference between myself and the other.

The result of this process is *compassion*, as the momentum of understanding, which allows us to recognize the other as an individual, including all of their needs and feelings.

Evaluating Reports with Regard to "the Third"

> I was also allowed to take part, along with the psychologist, in the DBG (the depression management group). In the end, everyone there seemed to me to be stressed and overwhelmed. After the two-hour session, we spoke about the 'severity' of the meeting's topics, and I organized the institution's skill box. It struck me that one woman, despite playing with the rubber band, did not seem more relaxed or less stressed; rather, it seemed as if the rubber band was just another annoying obligation, a torment in her current condition.

The "third" in the observation unfolds through the description's idea of "stressed and overwhelmed". The student can provide a resonant sounding board with which to reflect on how she expresses being "stressed and overwhelmed". She can also observe that "one woman ... did not seem more relaxed or less stressed". Seeing and knowing can only develop through the reflective experience of being relaxed and less stressed. This also suggests the helplessness of everyone involved in terms of externalizing their moods and coping with them – the "institution's skill box". The patient is experienced as lonely and abandoned. "Obligation and torment" dominate the scene, suggesting that both staff and patients in inpatient treatment are overwhelmed.

Recognizing others is always a moral act and thus a "moral third" (Benjamin, 2018). The other comes into existence through my own perception of my feelings and my ability to attribute them to the other person, always with the prerequisite that these are something created together, a co-creation.

Here is another scene described in a report, one involving physical intimacy:

> In the toilet, I ask him how he normally moves from the wheelchair to the toilet. I quickly realize that he is not able to give me clear, direct answers.
>
> So I try to give instructions, and he appears to understand them all.
>
> Pay attention to the position of the legs, make firm contact with the floor, hold onto the handles on the right and the left, then move your upper body forward and stand up. That went relatively well, now he's standing up in a stable position.

> I start to pull down his trousers, which are soaked with urine, and I open his incontinence pants. The urine condom had come loose and they had forgotten to put the incontinence pants on properly the last time he went to the toilet. Double protection, I think, how terribly uncomfortable it must be to be restricted in movement for 24 hours, with such a big nappy around your legs, I think.
>
> Reach with your left hand to the right handle, then turn and sit down. Ok, that's done.
>
> As soon as he sits down, the first loud farts begin. He starts talking, I think in order to alleviate the situation, which is awkward for both of us. He talks about a trade fair in S. [a town in Austria], later on his wife tells me that he often went there for work. He speaks as if it were the most normal thing ever to have a conversation in the toilet. I sometimes imagine that this is how things used to work in old-fashioned bathhouses. Except in our situation, I'm dressed and he's sitting at the toilet. It's kind of funny too.
>
> By now I just want to give him the bell and get out of there. But I am afraid he will fall and this makes me continue to endure the situation. And our conversation skips from one topic to another. He doesn't seem to find the situation as unpleasant as I do.

Awareness of a feeling of shame comes into play here, influencing the conversation with the search for other topics to speak about. The patient offers a solution to distract from shameful feelings. He begins to describe himself in a previous work role, so as to present himself in some other way than just this intimate situation.

Shame also has a cultural background, as the student explains. In "old-fashioned bath houses", this would be a "normal" situation if both people were unclothed. "Fear" is a motive for staying with the situation: the concern that the patient might hurt himself, and the student would be hurt by any punishment that might happen.

The intimate situation only unfolds in the shared third which is created here. Without witnessing, there would be no intimacy; only with witnessing does intimacy become present, requiring the negotiation of a moral third party, concerning who feels ashamed and what is the meaning of helplessness and fear in the scene. The body's nakedness is also perceived as powerlessness; the clothed body is suggested to be superior. The naked body expresses great vulnerability through its transient quality; a badly-applied condom allows urine to escape and in this way is removed from sexual activity. The student now becomes aware of how awareness arises: "How often have I had exactly this, or a very similar situation, in my years in this profession? And I've never thought about it so consciously, let alone written about it".

Typically, most intimate care acts are performed in a state of dissociation, as a mechanical act in the visible world, in order to keep at bay feelings of shame, vulnerability, sexuality, death, and fear. This intimate action of cleaning someone else is one of the most psychologically complex encounters with which people can be challenged: the task is to manage physical and linguistic intimacy in an asymmetrical relationship of dependence.

A report on the subject of intimate care and dissociation:

> Specifically, I accompanied a colleague who was changing a pair of incontinence pants. When the colleague opened the pants, there was quite a foul smell of urine, which smelled a lot like older, dried urine. My colleague obviously did not expect the smell or did not notice it when entering the room. So he reacted without constraint, feeling the urge to vomit, and letting out a loud cry of 'wah!' In itself, this is not forbidden: on the contrary: it should happen and does.

This example can really help us to understand about the dissociation of feelings. Although it "should happen and does", there is little sense of the feelings of those involved. This is not an intimate situation; rather, it is a scene where smell triggers a reflex that appears without psychological involvement. What remains is a concrete world, in which the scene's own significance is not revealed, and the self, i.e. the student's own identity, is not permitted to be present. Although the words seem to present a kind of moral respite, using a dichotomy to express linguistic permission: "In itself, this is not forbidden". Nonetheless, the scene still seems to contain a judgment of superiority. The student "borrows" an identity by allowing the colleague to feel intense nausea, but is unable to introduce the colleague as a witness in the encounter described. Likewise, the patient also remains without identity: these lines of the report present the patient as an other, in the disappearance of his identity. Neither the student nor the patient have value in the scene, they remain of lesser importance; what is produced is an idea about what it means to not be present.

The student goes on to attempt to identify the essential thing about the scene for her:

> The most important thing for me was the colleague's continuing or subsequent behaviour. It seemed as if he was ashamed and annoyed by his reaction: because as soon as he did it, he began to justify himself and to go red.
>
> When I talked to him about it, our conversation revealed that he had simply reacted emotionally, before he could deal with the situation.

Feelings of disgust, shame, and physical impermanence are very hard to cope with and require complex and stable emotional experience. The description is characterized by dissociation and a lack of recognition of being a witness (Benjamin, 2018). The psychological complexity of care activity is usually not perceived, and thus goes unrecognized. Empathy is based on the recognition of my complex and psychological experience, and thus so too is the possibility of having a reflective resonant space for patients, or of designing the encounter.

> A second situation arose a little later with another colleague. He had removed incontinence pants from a patient and disposed of them without gloves, although they were covered in faeces.
>
> After this nursing procedure was completed, we were actually able to discuss the scene without judgment. I was concerned about the incident: not primarily because of disgust, but rather his attitude towards self-protection and his lazy neglect of this.
>
> He justified his approach with the argument 'When you have children, it will never bother you and you will understand.' I pointed out the difference between doing this for your own child and doing it for other patients. It turned out that, regardless of the argument he made, this colleague also accepted the lack of self-protection and was able to cope with laziness in this situation and everything that went with it.

These lines express the level of anger about being left alone, and how this is connected with the feelings prompted by disgust. "Self-protection" is a strategy for psychological survival and the projection of the question of value in close proximity, this transpires as normality. Intellectualization supports dissociation and thus also re-traumatization connected to one's own past history.

Extract from a report, on the subject of tenderness and recognition:

> Ms M. looks very elegant and well-groomed today, with her pink lipstick. I like pink on the lips, with her Snow White complexion, she is a real feast for the eyes, despite the Rapunzel hair. She was certainly very beautiful at one time, and still is. The cool blonde, Dr. M. The whole ward is afraid of her. She was also the one who showed me the ropes. Somehow I really like this woman.

These words allow a person to slip into something quite specific, a recognition of individuality, which, for the readers of these lines, creates an interest in this person. Desire develops through individuality, and thus our ability to love develops through a desire for recognition. If we look at love as involving a complex of different facets, then the external world of the body is only a part of desire, and we only become capable of love because of psychological love, in the desire for the specificity of being seen and thus the significance of being considered as a psychological being.

> She seems to have had a very eventful professional life, first studying for fun and then doing something more serious that you could earn a living from, yes, that's how she put it. Then she must have made it a long way within the male ranks of company management. A kind of Iron Lady,

> that's how she appears, she also looks a little bit like her [Margaret Thatcher]. This kind of woman is certainly well able to assert herself in a man's world and to break through the glass ceiling. Factual, cool, and undoubtedly competent. Between her allure and her complaints, she smiles at you, a really, really affected, calculating smile, you might even say a fake smile, but at least she smiles at me and doesn't just scold me like she does with all the other nursing staff. She offers me a sweet which comes from her brother's company, who I had thought was her husband. A tough gnarly coffee bean, coated in chocolate. After she had been fired, the staff asked: what kind of a thing to do is it is to give the staff a box of chocolates which is almost empty? It is chocolate coins and Mozart sweets by Mirabell. I'm amused by this, and I think it's kind of generous, right? Maybe I'm just dazzled by her courtly etiquette, and somehow this person appealed to me. Behind her façade, there is a lot of experience and knowledge, and probably also loneliness and disappointment. How does she live? And what happens when she lets go all her strength and reveals her true nature, to someone she trusts?
>
> A sincere tyranny with good arguments seems more likeable than some of the 'games' played by other patients. One of her nightgowns, that's almost what you'd have to call them, is in a strong but not overpowering shade of rosé. There is nice lace at the arms and neckline, I'm guessing Palmers or maybe Triumph, it's something good anyway. If you had a lot of time – and she did too – you could get through to her core, ask her for her advice, appeal to her expertise, this would definitely impress her. Outside her window, the leaves of the birch trees are blowing in the wind. A slight rustling, silver-green, I have always really liked these trees.

Isn't this how we also want to be seen? To receive a self, transported on this tenderness, suspended in the space of the other, embedded in meaning? This connection is also expressed in the desire to "impress" the other person: to feel recognized by the other person through one's own desire to be desired, to acquire psychological significance for them and thus to be liberated from one's own selflessness. This report underlines the meaning of our capacity to love and of the diversity of desire.

7 Summary

These reports were explicitly written after observation. Kächele and Buchholz refer to this kind of reporting as "great inaccuracy of primary data", because they are merely selective memories and "dishonest retrospectives" (Bucholz, 2013c, p. 28f.; Kächele, 2010). If case histories are regarded as lies, there is a truth that is concealed in this manner of speaking. Kächele's dissatisfaction probably lies more with written interpretations and the significance attributed to them. From an intersubjective point of view, the phenomenological observation of material written down later is also cognitively significant, if both writer and reader are taken into account at the moment of reading. Many case descriptions say more about the writers and their fears than they do about the patients described. The material comes to life when the writers are ascribed meaning and identity in terms of understanding what they have read. If a competitive situation develops between transcripts, observations, and case histories, all that remains is dichotomization.

As a solution to this one-dimensionality, we would suggest a paradigm shift in the consideration of all these documents, one which would mean adopting an attitude of subjectivity and a common constructed reality, in this way situating knowledge acquisition as a cyclical event. Case histories and reports remain devoid of psychological meaning if only their content is granted significance, with writer and reader dissolving (Atwood & Stolorow, 1979).

Intersubjectivity is a process that unfolds in the form of resonance, sensitivity, rhythmicity, complementarity, and recognition.

11 Conclusion

> Do we not first become aware of ourselves in the gaze of another person? In your gaze, as that of the second person who speaks to me as a first person, I become aware of myself not only as a conscious subject but also as a unique *individual*. The subjectifying gaze of others possesses an individuating power.
>
> Jürgen Habermas (2008, p. 15)

As this wander through the text comes to its end, there is an apparent tension between a linguistic grasp of attitude, dynamics, relationality, etc. and the rigidity of casting these as representations in thought. Words transform thought into language; when in dichotomizing mode, words become thoughts, and in this way are subject to particular rhythms: "Words also have an embodied dimension expressed through rhythm" (Knoblauch, 2018, p. 143).

Words give us a structure by which our thoughts may be grasped. In verbal expression, they are underpinned by our voices and facial expressions. Our emotional experiences are revealed in every expression, allowing our past and present to flow together. Without experiences we would be unable to grasp the moment; we would have no words, not even for the new, which is embedded in a structure via an experience of astonishment.

Timely encounters between students and teachers allow both to develop and experience the mutual creation of meaning, each for the other. To lend form to the other means recognizing sameness and difference, embedded in the endurance of the loneliness of the thirdness unfolding between them. To be recognized is to be understood and to be seen. It also means being different from one another: this contour is fraught with the grief of difference. The vitality of life, its "vitality affects", are reflected in these tensions: they form a fluid dimension of mobility (D.N. Stern, 1991, p. 157). This mobility leads in turn to a struggle for recognition: it cannot be experienced as a goal, but rather as an attitude whereby movement can unfold. Recognition is a dynamic process: it means staying in meaningful contact with one's own emotions and underlying experiences, in the context of emotional experience with others.

This project should allow students to experience a sense of connection with patients and to recognize the underlying structures. When they recognize these

DOI: 10.4324/9781003483441-11

patterns, they can connect emotional scenes with their own past and now give meaning to this emotional experience.

Students get an idea of meaning when experience it in their encounter with the people training them, where they will have experienced growth through warmth and generosity.

> The people whose manners we genuinely admire and enjoy are those who, without it being obvious, skilfully enhance our sense of significance and worth. All contact, whether conversational or silent, is accompanied by an atmosphere of warmth and generosity; this promotes trust and openness.
>
> (Coltart, 1992, p. 137).

We want to offer this kind of growth to our students, giving them a framework of openness and trust in which to develop. Growth requires that we can maintain a certain tension in which opportunities to generate new perspectives will arise. Through their own acceptance of being a resonant sounding board, group leaders can lead students to the possibility of recognizing the other person; this recognition takes form through our capacity for self-recognition amidst all this differentiation. The recognition of difference must take place within ourselves: "In order to find the patient (student), we must look for him within ourselves" (Bollas, 2017, p. 202).

Empathy involves a mutual calling-forth of emotion; the recognition of this emotion, through the understanding created, leads to difference and a sense of uniqueness. Students and group leaders find themselves in a shared world of blending and recognition. Understanding the other means creating difference and creates a loneliness towards them, which in turn makes closeness possible, since there is no fear of symbiosis or fusion and thus no fear of abandonment of the self. Within these tensions, growth occurs in a circular process! At the end of the training process, leaders realize that generosity means losing; they must recognize their own smallness, accepting that they are outdone by their own students. Growth means putting on fertilizer and then giving in to their own process of shrinkage, enjoying the development of the next generation of students, feeling their own place in history. Students' psychological growth reflects the rawness of their trainers. Accepting the zenith of their development, they are thus freed from narcissistic feelings of grandiosity. Maybe students will take us part of the way: receiving recognition from young people makes growth possible in group leaders. In turn, young people gain recognition from the group leaders through their participation in teachers' own experience of transience.

If each passing generation develops in an increasingly psychologically differentiated way, the continent's traumatization can heal a little, after all of the catastrophes of the last century.

1 The History of the ART Project

The ART project has existed since the winter semester of 2010, based at the training centre for psychiatric nursing at the Otto Wagner Hospital in Vienna, Austria. The project's basic concept is subject to an ongoing process of testing, evaluation, and redesign. The more experience we get, the less noticeable adjustments to the project become: our fine-tuning becomes ever finer. The project is continually developed by our students, through our shared experience; their energy and their reflected experiences are the framework for our actions and for our existence.

At the outset of this journey was a desire to give our students a new learning experience and to convey this experience in terms of its learnability. While searching for ways of practical implementation, the author came across Esther Bick's ideas and the way she made observation usable in training child psychoanalysts. In terms of thought, the underlying concepts came from psychoanalysis and generally developed in the direction of attachment theory. The question of whether empathy could be learned prompted us to turn to the idea of mentalization, which opened up the world of relational thinking and intersubjectivity. These modes of thinking led us to make the importance of group leaders the focus of the project. The starting point here was our framework of mentalization-based pedagogy, a course which covers two full semesters. During these two semesters, we set up this new kind of observation and reflection, a novelty in training in the nursing professions. Among the leadership group, there quickly developed a desire to evaluate the project. We developed a questionnaire, later abandoned because of the lack of any international reference point for results; this made it difficult to compare our results with other institutions. For this reason, the Giessen test was selected: it is a test with quite a long tradition, meaning we could draw on a variety of results. In terms of qualitative material for evaluation, since the beginning of the project we have had student reports available to evaluate in depth, using a hermeneutic method. When small group sessions began, in the third and fourth semesters of training, a student recorded group sessions so as to establish an emotional connection the following week. It soon became clear that the meta-position occupied by the note-taker was a special kind of external position in the small group. It was more important to us to have all students really be "in" the group, so we abandoned this role. Limitations on time and associated costs also had an impact on the project. We were always of the opinion that the training time available was not enough to stimulate the student development. A desire to spend more time together was shared by most students and group leaders.

As a next step, we looked closely at the first two semesters of training, during which time we sought to establish self-awareness and self-perception in our students. The project was meant to be a training program which would promote awareness of feelings. The basis for this came from Marshall B. Rosenberg's ideas of nonviolent communication, specifically adapted for our training purposes (Schossmaier, 2018, 2019b; Zemann, 2019; Zemann et al. 2015; Zemann et al., 2017; Rosenberg, 2009). For Rosenberg, the most important application of non-violent communication is the development of self-empathy. Self-care is the beginning of the training project.

To integrate this aspect of training and to emphasize the "newness" of our overall concept, we agreed on a new name, "Affect Resonance Training" (ART).

ART III was the next element to be developed: this is in a fluid phase. It is currently the responsibility of a single group leader: the next step is to build this phase into the process of group leader training and teaching.

The project group in ART consists of a stable core group, which in turn is influenced and developed by the various trainers who go part of the way with us. The management of the project is currently divided into three. ART I is currently being independently developed by two members of the research group. ART II and III were developed and established by the author, who continues to teach the modules himself. Another colleague largely takes charge of public relations, implementation of training at the various outside facilities, and supervising quantitative research.

This kind of observation and self-reflection had its first test as part of two field research trips to West Papua in 2009 and 2010: this involved participatory observation, in which those participating allowed themselves to drift through, being shaped by and in the roles on offer. In this way, they gained an understanding of the here and now. "Floating" is what Gerhard Kubik called this kind of field research (Kubik, 1987, 2003, 2004, 2007; Reichmayer, 2013), drawing on the idea of "evenly suspended" attention, as well as techniques of ethno-psychoanalysis as a way of understanding the "other" in and around us.

Here there is a blending of "techniques" drawn from psychoanalysis and ethnology, in a kind of cultural and social understanding. The field research project saw ethno-psychoanalysis develop as a form of participant observation within a relational space. At this point, psychoanalytic "techniques" gave way to intersubjective ideas of a constructed understanding. Working with Fritz Morgenthaler in Papua in 1984, Florence Weiss, the Swiss-born ethno-psychoanalyst, had used the classic application of psychoanalytic explanatory models, but later developed relational understandings in the descriptions in her 2001 book *Before the Volcanic Eruption* (*Vor dem Vulkanausbruch*; Morgenthaler et al., 1986; Weiss, 2001). The aim of the research trips was to use ethno-psychoanalysis to gain new insights via relational understanding.

The insights gained here about ego constitution, about understanding the self in a foreign country, formed one key basis for the development of the ART project.

In 2012, we presented our project to a larger audience for the first time, at the AHA conference "Learning Shapes the Future" in Vienna (April 13–14, 2012). Using our observations of small children, we developed a subsidiary project, moving towards "mentalization in elementary education". We

Figure 11.1 First research trip to West Papua; encounter with inhabitants of a Lani village (2009).

designed a workshop to address how to train people in reflection and empathy, especially in controlling affects and violence. Later, we presented the overall concept and held workshops on it at international events (Hamburg, 2013; Weimar, 2014; Berlin, 2014, 2015).

ART I was designed as an independent teaching module from 2014 on and integrated into the overall training program.

2 ART I to III

Affect Resonance Training has by now developed into a three-stage training concept. In the first stage, the focus is on self-awareness, specifically on perceiving one's own needs and emotional reactions in a variety of life situations and associated life narratives.

ART I (affect resonance-oriented, needs-focused self-empathy) draws on concepts of non-violent communication (NVC) developed by Marshall B. Rosenberg. It is a training program which develops self-awareness and self-empathy. NVC is based on humanistic psychology and client-centred talk therapy developed by Carl Rogers; its basic assumption states that people, consciously or unconsciously, strive to fulfil their needs, which leads to a wide variety of dynamic communicational constellations. Underlying the entire ART I training programme is the intention to become aware of one's needs, in a sense of self-empathy. The NVC model focuses on orienting feelings and needs within a communication context; it tries to foster conscious perception of needs and feelings in the context of encounters (Hajek, 2019; Zöchling, 2019; Zemann, 2019; Zemann et al., 2015, 2017; Sieberth & Steinberger, 2013; Steinberger et al., 2013; Stiefmaier, 2017, 2018, 2019a). Affects are converted into meaning; they are then named as needs: "This part of the training is intended to make it easier to deal with (reaction=resonance) intense, and even violent emotional states (=affects). It does this by focusing on the needs underlying these affects" (Schoßmaier, 2017, p. 5).

The training in ART I is based on various exercises which focus on perceptions of the "self", allowing students to reflect on "pre-judgments" and "evaluation". Needs are considered in the light of shared action and respect for others, solutions are sought out. ART should began a process which can never be regarded as over: it should unfold as a lifelong process of development, structuring the personality on a profoundly individual level. The basic model of non-violent communication (NVC) has four stages: perception, feeling, need, and request. These are discussed in a number of exercises. In the ART I phase, groups have around ten to twelve students, including the group leader: its composition should remain unchanged. After an introductory lecture, the program extends for a period of two to three weeks: this forms the foundation for the two subsequent levels of ART. To qualify to lead the group, leaders must have been trained in Rosenberg's non-violent communication; they must have a repertoire of at least ten exercises which can be deployed (Schoßmaier, 2017; 2019b).

ART II focuses on shared, intersubjective, relational, mentalizing understanding, and construction of realities, as a way of developing competence in empathy.

The content of ART III includes developing an ability to use intersubjective, relational supervision and demonstrating self-reflective behaviour towards patients and colleagues.

3 Empathy and Enactment

Enactment should no longer be seen as a conflict that unfolds in the encounter, nor as a problem to be resolved. Rather it should be seen as an existing, fluid, ongoing phenomenon that takes place with a wide variety of energy levels.

The basis of empathy is formed by enactment, or the scene as it proceeds. Empathy is developed through mirror neurons in neural circuits: these now can become a form of explicit knowledge, or else can give rise to implicit reactions: these can then be subject to description, for example, framed in terms of attachment behaviour. In this view, conflict is explained as the need to create difference to be a basis for perception. In this kind of representation, enactment does not have to be unconscious per se, rather it represents a form of expression, the appearance of which can be subjected to interpretation. Conscious or unconscious, it can be defined by attributing meaning to an action or enactment. The basis for attributing meaning or interpretation lies in the possibility of thinking up alternatives or metaphors, which allow for new distinctions to be made. In this way, enactment becomes more ambiguous in its meaning: it can offer greater freedom in decision-making, but at the same time loses the absolutism of its power of action.

Enactment makes available my inner resonance, something which is in turn based on my affective experiences. It is only possible to create a self through the possibility of creating difference and the recognition associated with this. We create the here and now from the past, and we experience it as the present, which can only be represented through another person, or to put it another way, the other creates an image of themselves within me, via the affective experiences of my past. We create the new through past emotional experiences; every relationship is characterized by rupture and repair, which complement each other, allowing us to share experiences. Our experiences of relationships are encompassed by rupture and repair; these two things are what make relationships possible, as well as the encounters inherent to them. Rupture creates difference, going to form an idea of an ego, or feelings of identity. We experience this difference as a rupture which arises from our past emotional experiences: this allows us to experience ourselves as identical to ourselves. In the intersection of difference and rupture we experience a conception of the self as a separate person. These intersections – as here between rupture and difference – are based on the permanent process of enactment and the development of those enactments, which we fix in place as implicit experiences. These experiences in turn form both a resonant sounding board for our experiences and an enactment involving the other. But we can only perceive this other person as other by making our own past resonances available, while acknowledging something new (the third) in the encounter. The dynamic of rupture creates the ability to know-through-difference: it allows us to know. The Boston Change Process Study Group describes this dynamic of rupture "not as the return of a dissociated memory but as the threshold for the introduction of emergent ways of being that bring forth new relational possibilities in the dyad" (Boston Change Process Study Group, 2013, p. 730).

Enactments have been described as a disruptive element within the therapeutic encounter. Here we aim to argue that the term should be reinterpreted and given a new use, in this way alleviating fears of enactment and allowing us to recognize its effect. Enactment does not represent conflict by producing a description of it; instead, the energy of difference and non-recognition leads to a kind of tension, which we view as conflict and thus experience in terms of emotional strain. However, if there is too great a tension between the flood of feelings prompted and the experience of difference as non-recognition, no insight will be gained from it: the emotion will remain trapped on the level of action and experience.

The term "enactment" was first publicly coined in 1983 by Theodore J. Jacobs at the IPA Congress in Amsterdam in his paper "The analyst and the patient's object world: Notes on an aspect of countertransference". In a later essay, he explained the term in more detail (Jacobs, 1983, 1986). The term is rooted in a variety of psychoanalytic concepts; only in recent years has it begun to emerge as a more autonomous term, but it has done so in two quite divergent directions. On the one hand is the clinical view that enactment is to be avoided; on the other, the view that it is an absolute necessity for a clinical situation. A further split in the term's meaning can be seen in controversy around the role of the analyst in enactment, i.e. his or her active participation in the emergence of a situation of enactment (Bohleber et al., 2013).

Bohleber et al. put it like this: "We can easily prove that not everything that happens in an analysis is an enactment. For example, one could describe an appropriate and helpful interpretation given at the right time as being the opposite of an enactment" (Bohleber et al., 2013, p. 1231).

For Karen Maroda, enactment represents the complex relation between transference and countertransference. For her, it means opening a transitional space in which the emotions of the analysand and the therapist can meet. In contrast to most authors, she considers enactments to be conscious experiences, especially where they are expressed as painful emotions (Maroda, 1998, 2010, 2018).

Hirsch considers enactment to be "a living out of affective experience, usually by both parties in the analytic dyad, within the strict boundaries of the analytic frame". He describes enactment as an "acting out" by both participants in an encounter and "a violation of the frame" (Hirsch, 1994, p. 172). Like most authors, he regards it as a disruption to the treatment process, but one which occurs on both sides and thus does not only come from the patient. Enactment is distinguished from projective identification by its stimulation and expression of strong unconscious affects. A willingness to act and a high level of emotionality can be associated with the concept of enactment (Maroda, 1998).

In stark contrast to this view is the belief that enactment can take any kind of expression, from silence to action. Its expression remains an unconscious one, which only later gains validity through a process of reflection. However, discussion continues on enactment's negative connotations within psychoanalytic discourse (Richards et al., 1997). Discussion in the scientific literature has focussed on the question: to what degree are those involved in the encounter partaking in an enactment? And does enactment thus raise questions of responsibility, given that this behaviour is still viewed negatively?

For Maroda, enactment is "motivated by the mutual stimulation of strong affect, with both persons usually stating that they felt out of control, or at least felt something come over them that was mysterious and powerful" (Maroda, 1998, p. 519). She regards it as a loss of control on the part of both patient and analyst, in which something "mysterious" happens. However, I would argue that the concept of enactment should be reformulated, to make it available for a phenomenon which primarily expresses encounter and can be described as a dynamic, fluid event.

Maroda goes on: "Enactment is an affectively driven repetition of converging emotional scenarios from the patient's and the analyst's lives. It is not merely an affectively driven set of behaviours, it is necessarily a repetition of past events …" (Maroda, 1998, p. 520). One can only agree with her formulation. But I am not in agreement with the exaggerated idea of repeating unprocessed emotions, which are held to represent affects anchored in the unconscious.

Enactment is not simply a repetition of unresolved feelings from the respective pasts of both participants, rather it is the basis of an encounter between two people. We can only begin from our experiences, bringing that into the encounter. Only the new, which unfolds as a mystery, serves to differentiate my past, allowing me to create or feel something new. By this definition, enactment describes a permanent process which unfolds in every encounter. Levenson writes: "[E]nactment is a continuous and ubiquitous process, being the behavioural component of what is being talked about. In other words, what is being said is simultaneously being shown" (Levenson, 2006, p. 322). Here Levenson is describing the basis of our ability to empathize, as well as expression and recognition of my counterpart, and the idea of being our own physical person. In a therapeutic encounter, change unfolds through this rhythmic process: I bring my past experience into play, creating new reality with the other person, detaching from the past and thus permitting the new or allowing me to acknowledge myself and the other person. If the process can be embedded in reflected insights, new and vital experience will unfold. As Mitchell puts it:

> The analyst discovers himself a co-actor in a passionate drama involving love and hate, sexuality and murder, intrusion and abandonment, victims and executioners. Whichever path he chooses, he falls into one of the patient's predesigned categories and is experienced by the patient in that way. The struggle is towards a new way of experiencing both himself and the patient, a different way of being with the analysand …
>
> (Mitchell, 1988, p. 295).

The drama can only be performed together: it incorporates the vitality of life. Whether a way out will be chosen depends on the "new way", which only appears in the form of new experience, felt through an idea of "being with".

Enactment does not represent drama emerging out of the depths; it is the necessary prerequisite for creating an encounter, which unfolds in the here and now. The dramatic momentum is experienced through the force of feelings and not through a "staging" of the enactment.

"Too little enactment leads to stagnation; too much leads to premature termination, impasse, or unacceptable acting out" (Maroda, 1998, p. 521).

Without enactment, therapy becomes stagnant, with chronic behaviour emerging in sessions. Maroda continues: "Enactment is a dynamic, naturally occurring manifestation of the transference and counter-transference merging into a living entity, making the past alive in the present. This mix will always include some element of re-creating the analyst's past" (Maroda, 1998, p. 530). She views enactment as a naturally occurring phenomenon, part of a living being. I am in complete agreement on this but do not regard it as having negative or disturbing connotations. Rather, it is an absolute necessity in order to develop an ability to empathize and thus is also the foundation for the encounter and the basis for any capacity to mentalize.

The Boston Change Process Study Group has also addressed the question of enactment, attempting to reconceive the phenomenon. The group's researchers interrogated the meaning of enactment within the dyadic treatment process, the therapist's reaction to it, and the relationship between change and enactment. They formulate enactment as a threshold phenomenon which opens the possibility of a new relational experience: "We understand that moment not as the return of a dissociated memory but as the threshold for the introduction of emergent ways of being that bring forth new relational possibilities in the dyad" (Boston Change Process Study Group, 2013, p. 730).

I agree with this, but do not regard enactment as something which is embedded in the encounter dyad, but rather as a kind of brace, which arches over the dyad. We thus need a more precise formulation of what takes place inside this encounter. Enactments are not events embedded in the process, as the Boston Change Process Study Group claims. Rather, enactments describe the process of encounter, in all its loud and quiet tones, within a non-linear treatment process. Interruptions, ruptures, and adjustments are constantly occurring, forming a rhythmic process which takes place on different implicit and explicit levels. In literature, enactment is usually used when the threshold from implicit to explicit experience is crossed.

The Boston Change Process Study Group also assumes that small, manageable, circumscribed events can prove to dramatically amplify change processes. I would argue that dramatic events can only be conceived when explicit recognition is transcended and that enactment-type processes are always present within a fluid process; in fact enactments are what make such overall processes possible. It is not that dissociative processes unfold in enactment; in fact, these processes are necessary for encounters to be possible at all. As a phenomenon, dissociation is necessary to create a structure of difference and thus an idea of separateness and of two different living beings. If this fluid process of fragile regulation between rupture/dissociation and equality is severely disrupted, one side can come to predominate: we experience this as a dramatic representation and regard it as an enactment. To experience closeness in encounters or empathic understanding, we need our past, including the experiences and stored relationship patterns which are embedded in it. Next, we must create an experience of dissociation so as to locate it in a rupture and thus create difference between myself and the other person. In my view, the energy levels of the drama of encounter, and the possible flooding of emotions, are so strong that energy presents at a recognizable level of action or else it bursts out impulsively. The physical level is always embedded within our communications, ranging from implicit facial gestures to dramatic actions (Streeck, 2009).

In our dreams, we experience these encounter scenes, but we need no other person, since our involvement in it is as a kind of relationship experience within us; we have this available as possible fantasies regarding future encounters. This process takes place below a threshold and if this is broken, we will bind the enactment to images experienced in dreams, or there is some kind of discontinuity or rupture which causes us to wake: "From a nonlinear dynamics perspective, these exchanges may have been occurring beneath a threshold of organizational complexity at which small quantitative increases eventuate in qualitative discontinuities and the development of new levels" (Boston Change Process Study Group, 2013, p. 734).

The Boston researchers here argue in favour of a quantitative perspective, which takes things across a threshold into the perceivable. Freud said: "The voice of the intellect is a soft one, but it does not rest till it has gained a hearing" (S. Freud, 1961a, p. 53). If we juxtapose listening to something quiet to listening to something dramatic, we realize that the important thing is not making the unconscious conscious. Rather, what is important is achieving a sensitivity as a therapist which allows a move from dramatic perception to sensitive perception, in this way transforming more of the implicit into the explicit. If we do not transform our past, it will remain in the here and now, in the form of non-recognition. The more sensitively we experience ourselves, the richer we experience ourselves in our encounters with other people, and the more explicit things can be gained from the difference. The movement towards difference generates ideas of autonomy and feelings of identity. Many developmental psychologists report disorganization in a child's behaviour before developmental spurts occur (Boston Change Process Study Group, 2013; Brazelton, 2006). This disorganization is an event of difference: it activates an autonomously-experienced sense of a new ability, and thus the child's own new sense of itself; the child thus now locates, from within the disorganization, a new capacity that is its own.

Enactment can be represented as a process in which many phenomena take place. It can be understood as a basic element of our being-together, or else as a short, briefly emergent sequence in a complex mechanism of encounter.

To be able to experience empathy, we need access to many representations of relationships, which are available to us in the encounter, and which we use to differentiate between ourselves and the other person, via rupture or difference (Reis, 2010; Sander, 2009). These relational representations are not available to us as explicit experience, "memory takes an implicit form that is expressed non-consciously as an embodied tendency toward patterned activity" (Boston Change Process Study Group, 2013, p. 738). This is

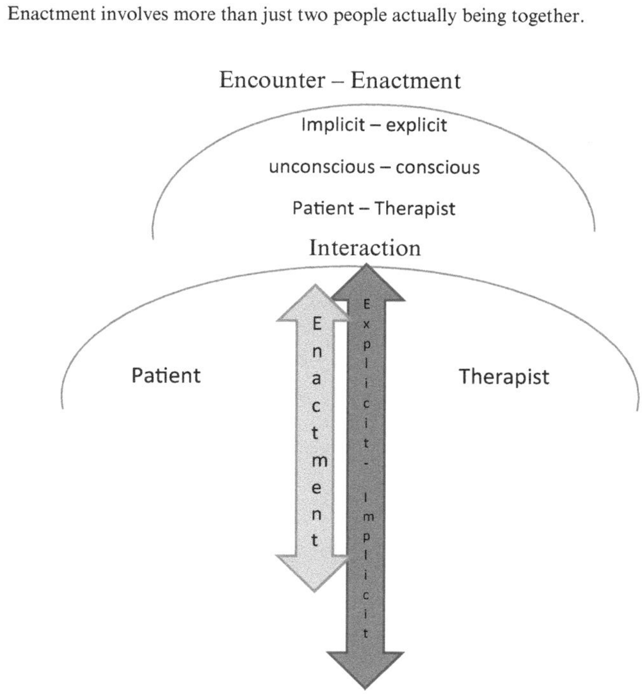

Figure 11.2 Enactment runs along a quantitative line of expression and refers to a crossing of the threshold from implicit to explicit perception (own representation).

not a mental phenomenon but rather represents "the dyadic history of an individual in relationship" (Boston Change Process Study Group, 2013).

These implicit body memories are fluid and can be re-formed with every encounter, in the manner of a Gadamerian hermeneutic circle. For this reason, they take the form of a cyclical event, a permanent transformation in "present moments" (D.N. Stern, 2004) and experiences of re-formation which thus become possible. These enactive relational representations not only play a significant role in dealing with others, they are also the prerequisite for my own self-perception and perception of others. They likewise underlie the particular forms of empathy I derive, and my resulting interpretations of experiences and actions. These physically situated representations are the interpretative sounding board for my "world" and their place within it. In other words: "[W]e think dyadically and systemically about the self as an intersubjectively open system continually in the process of forming larger and more complex systems in interaction with others" (Boston Change Process Study Group, 2013, p. 739).

The psyche is an inherently relational system: it is always in a relationship with itself and with others. It encompasses a permanent process of exchange, between the rhythmic formation of adaptations, comparisons, and differences, embedded in a system of explicit and implicit perception, from which knowledge unfolds. Dissociation – in the sense of splitting off – as conceived within relational psychoanalysis, is based on the phenomenon of flooding and on holding back between an explicit and an implicit boundary. The concept of structure also takes place at the interface between implicit and explicit expression and their visible forms. Explicit and implicit can also be thought of as different forms of expression, with thinking developing on the explicit level, while physical resonances unfold on an implicit level. These physical resonances are expressed in a back-and-forth movement: the term psychological structure refers to the affectivity or drama of this experience. Consciousness does not in this way acquire any significance in terms of changing structures. Rather, it serves as the linguistic embodiment of the form of knowledge gained from the change. We generate change through differentiation from old experiences: this happens on different levels, both physical and mental. Observations in attachment research fit together well with these ideas of difference and connection. The exploratory phase can be regarded as a phase of difference, and vice versa. The concept of mentalization can also be easily classified within this overall structure: it will be seen as a phenomenon whereby knowledge is gained through the cognitive ability to generate meaning by recognizing differentiation. In this way, we can recognize different "minds".

4 Enactment and Conflict

Many analysts suggest that enactment is simply another name for conflict, whereby conflict, rather than being dealt with, slips out of control for both parties. Enactment is primarily experienced as a burden on the analyst and is seen as an overflowing of unconscious, long-standing conflict within a relationship. The roots of this conflict stem from existing differences in the relationship. Maroda describes the conflict's origin as follows: "[D]ifferences emerge due to the asymmetry and power relations between analyst and patient; in sexual tension; in differing values based on culture, sexual orientation, socioeconomic status, age and gender; in integrational competition, or in some perceived slight or insensitivity" (Maroda, 2018, p. 159). We agree with her in conceiving of difference as a form of enactment, as the second side of a fluid system. Conflict arises from an inability to tolerate a difference between both parties, which is connoted with negative feelings. The question which arises here is which kind of limit has been exceeded, such that difference can no longer be maintained and it thus then appears in the form of conflict.

Perhaps precisely what is lost here is the counterweight of holding, in a sense of symbiosis and equality, and thus the idea of autonomy swings too strongly in a single direction. Conflict is perceived differently, everyone experiences friction as marking the possibility of expressing something in language, but they experience it at different levels. A level of tension must also be exceeded for someone to reveal themselves on an explicit level. The idea of a dualistic system of sadomasochistic phenomena fits together well into this pendulum movement; the sexual element also emerges in the form of excessive excitement (Bader, 1993).

5 Enactment and Students

The significance of a person's career choice can be understood by looking at their past. Many students bring with them implicit modes of regulating relationships, learned in personal experience in their family of origin, which then develop in their encounter with patients. This represents a possible basis for resonance and for the rhythmic, fluid movements that go with it.

> For many colleagues the experiences in childhood and adolescence of being an empathic listener to parents or other family members has played a role of importance in their choice of vocation. It is not a rare occurrence for the memories of these experiences to be evoked in the analytic situation. Then silently, outside of awareness, the analyst's usually valuable empathic responses may contain enactments of those memories – enactments which, subtly, can alter and distort his perceptions and understanding.
>
> (Jacobs, 1986, p. 297).

People in the social professions are often seen as empathetic and have very often been assigned a conflict-avoiding role in their family of origin. People who go into a social profession know how to regulate enactments within their family, how to regulate strong emotional surges, and how to protect themselves from the emotions of others in the family, so as not to be taken over and dominated by a false self (Maroda, 2010, 2018). The conflict-avoidance strategies which they used in their families of origin represent the first step towards becoming a lay helper. When an encounter with a patient involves strong emotions, there is often a reenactment of the fear of being overwhelmed by emotions. In this sense, helping means confronting the repetitions of the past and healing by surviving a conflict. We are looking for knowledge of our own past, which we bring to the encounter as potential for change. Helping involves repeating our experiences, as a building block in understanding and influencing the other person, but also in recognizing that we are creating something new. When we are abandoned by patients and relive experiences of loss, we often perceive this as defeat and experience a sense of having failed. To undertake helping behaviour not only involves a re-enactment of our past, but the maintenance of a fluid, dynamic psychological state which can evolve and allow us to have new experiences with patients (Klein et al., 2011; Rønnestad & Skovholt, 2013).

Here I have embedded my idea of the meaning of "enactment" within the metaphor of "grasping". To grasp something, to put it in our mouths, to feel it, can lead us to an understanding of a large picture, and we are touched if, along our common path of knowledge, we can feel included or understood.

6 The Importance of ART in Learning and Teaching Empathy in the Social Professions

At the endpoint of our journey is the ability to attach value to ourselves and to others. In other words: to love ourselves and love others. There are few examples in the scientific literature which deal with the importance of tender affection towards patients. The main things discussed in this context are factors like aggressive behaviour or sexual feelings in the encounter. If therapists do have those kind of feelings towards patients, these emotions seem easier to work with and to reflect on in the context of the relationship with the patient. Warmth, openness, and affection, on the other hand, seem to be feelings that should not be permitted and are only marginally discussed in the literature. Archaic feelings can be more easily dissociated from a person's significance in the encounter. By contrast, feelings of warmth and affection are experienced as threatening and are immediately written off as the therapist's narcissistic need-satisfaction directed towards the patient. These feelings seem to encompass more than aggression and sexuality; this is a question of recognition and of being able to attribute meaning to the other person. It is also feeling a kind of tenderness through providing the other person with resonance and in this way absorbing them into myself.

> No one can cure another if he has not a genuine desire to help him; and no one can have the desire to help unless he loves, in the deepest sense of the word. I certainly do not wish to fall into psycho-analytic pseudo-evangelism.
>
> (Nacht, 1962, p. 210).

Sacha Nacht contrasts love with a feeling which he regards as inauthentic. Freud vehemently advocated for a rule of honesty on the part of analysts and, along with this, a sense of authenticity in encounters with patients.

Authenticity is a basic attitude, and flows into the development and the suffering of patients, ultimately determining, through attitude, the success or failure of healing (Shaw, 2018; Nacht, 1962). Empathy also means an ability to represent a relationship experience to the other person, and in this way set off a process of change (Fosshage, 1992). This representation requires love and respect for the individual and for their individual development (Loewald, 1986). Understanding is based on one's own implicit experience of being a loved person: "In seeking to understand the person before me, I assume that experiences of loving and being loved are either figure or ground at any given point in the analytic process" (Shaw, 2018, p. 211).

For Shaw, understanding the other person begins with a conception of their ability to love and their capacity to be loved, which is crucial for a feeling of vitality and authentic self-esteem (Shaw, 2018; Mitchell, 1993). It turns out to be difficult to define love in a nursing, therapeutic, analytical context, if we do not immediately do so in terms of transferential love, which is not categorized as "real" love at all.

Loewald characterizes the form of love in analytical treatment as differing from an exploitative, abusive satisfaction of needs. He defines it as marked by a prevailing sense of respect, which guides both parties involved. Individuality develops so as to recognize the other as an independent being, and not to use them for a narcissistic expansion of one's own self (Miller, 2008; Loewald, 1986).

"Loewald's phrase 'love and respect' implies a sense of awe and reverence for human potential" (Shaw, 2018, p. 211). For Loewald, love means, within the encounter, attributing to oneself and the other an inner attitude of potential development. This is capacity to engage together in a process of change.

The ability to convey security is another important aspect in our attempt to characterize love within the encounter. This can mean, within an asymmetry, a security in respecting boundaries as a form of abstinence. Or it can be an awareness of knowing one's own needs as a practitioner and in this way exuding an attitude of insurmountable difference (Aron, 2016). An attitude of difference opens up a willingness for empathy and feelings based on respect: "I would hope that our predominant feelings would include respect, understanding, acceptance, empathy, admiration, caring, the sincere wish for the other's happiness and fulfilment, and love" (Shaw, 2018, p. 212).

Being able to encounter the other with this form of respect and acceptance is a kind of experience which unfolds in the encounter with others. Experiences can be internalized as meaningful – as the making of meaning – and can lead to trauma or to development. Respect within the encounter is based on conveying authenticity and thus an ability to a kind of empathetic tuning in: "I contend that any authentic analytic engagement will necessarily include a fluid, oscillating, often simultaneous use of the analyst's capacity for empathic attunement, as well as his skill in negotiating intersubjective difference as a means of reaching mutual recognition" (Shaw, 2003, p. 274). For Shaw, the basis for mutual recognition is the negotiating of degrees of difference, embedded within a flowing, oscillating process.

Roy Barseness works through a number of aspects of this in his work on relational competencies. He and his research team sum up the core skill of relational psychoanalytic treatment as "core competency: love". He also confirmed that many participants in the study were uncomfortable with the word *love*, but despite these concerns, his interviews with experienced therapists came up with no other definition for what they were attempting to describe: an essential emotional element within treatment (Barsness, 2018).

7 Research Results and Summary

Looking over the results of the quantitative and qualitative research, we can conclude that attitude, as a phenomenon, is important. Moreover, the formation of an attitude, as seen in the quantitative results, is something which goes beyond the individual: this is shown in the results regarding the diversity of training institutions and their lived "cultures". Moreover, the results reflect the importance of a sense of community: this is a central leitmotif in the formation of a psychological world. If there is a community in which there is an appreciation for a non-visible world, set apart from a concretizing worldview, then students can experience their own development within a world of psychological and mentalizing understanding of themselves and of others. Empathy and attitude are closely linked: they develop beyond the individual person, acquiring meaning within an intersubjective structure.

We may presume that other influences, expressed either on an institutional or a societal level, will influence our understandings of reflection, self-awareness, and empathy.

Our qualitative research results underline in a very impressive way how empathy, reflection, and attitude develop within us as meaningful elements of our development, and also how intersubjectivity is represented by inner psychological events which themselves can only develop through that intersubjectivity.

Reports and their interpretation process raise new questions about recognizing concepts around attitude, existence, hearing, empathy, sensitivity, resonance, complementarity, and thirdness.

Can phenomena only be seen if there are words for them? Do we need words to describe a theory of the psyche in metaphoric terms, or do we need vision in order to then formulate a theory from it?

8 Outlook for Research and Training

The ART program is meant to give students impetus for further development; they should receive a solid concept of how they encounter themselves and others. They also gain a sense of security about what they do and the actions they take, leading them to a sense of autonomy and self-efficacy. They should develop an interest in their own and others' psychological worlds and better access to ideas about themselves. Students should learn to be tolerant of feelings of shame and fallibility, and in this way develop joy in taking responsibility; they should be capable of relating meaningfully to others, and be able to develop a shared understanding of the significance of change; they should have a sense of their ability to love and should understand how this permits them to be generous towards themselves and others.

New perspectives are needed in the education of upcoming generations, moving away from cognitive meaning and towards developing psychological meanings and new forms of psychological understanding. We attach great importance to technical progress and the pursuit of change in cognitive experience. We attach less importance to our psychological development and thus stick with outdated development models. Our explanations of violent phenomena and of gender roles and their meaning still await further development. The creative basis for future generations will be found in attitude and in psychological understanding. We must go beyond the current generation that determines society, we must face this development with generosity and accept with humility our own psychological rawness. If we can do so, then we will release ourselves from controlling of our next generations; instead, we can place ourselves in the transitory, in what lies in the future. Through our letting go, we may experience the effectiveness of life. Life unfolds in a mutual interdependence in an intersubjective field, across generations.

The paradigm shift in interpretive social research should lead to greater recognition of the importance of jointly-created research results. If we take writers of texts and their background into account, we can achieve a different understanding of reality; in this way, our scientific self-understanding can get away from Cartesian modes of thought. Realities are created through the construction of an intersubjective world, under a different self-conception, and thereby will include writers of texts as real people in their work. Generalizations are also based on the cultural and psychological background of the writers. Our current understanding of science detaches itself from the actual person, attempting to present their thoughts and theories as something independent of time and place. In order to understand a text intersubjectively, it is important to think about oneself as a reader and about one's condition. One must understand oneself as a fluid being, in the sense that every new engagement with a text generates new thoughts and thus a new understanding of the text. In this understanding of science there is no truth, but rather a kind of possible knowledge through interpretation, one which is embedded in perception and consciousness (Müller, 1996).

Finally, let's allow a student to sum up the importance of the ART project for their training:

> I take out my things and try to be very present with the patients. At the school, I had really vented my anger about ART, because I was simply so ready for vacation, so I very consciously prepare myself for the last shift and really have a wonderful, very warm, and attentive last day at work. The deputy ward sister says she can easily imagine me in the team and that you can tell that I get along very well with people. I'm still thinking about *'being moved'* in nursing which we discussed in ART and I wonder if that isn't what it's all about. Maybe so much anger built up in me because we didn't have the opportunity to talk about our fears and experiences, about what we had gone through. Maybe I also noticed that my batteries were running low and I needed to recharge, but I still wanted to do my work with total attention and appreciation, so I almost

> ran out of breath. Then I get hugs and kisses and suddenly I think to myself, maybe orthopaedics would be a good place for me and maybe I don't belong on a psychiatric ward after all. Maybe I belong somewhere else entirely. Somehow everything on the outside is OK if you're OK on the inside. If you are honest and authentic with yourself and the world around you, and you stay like that.

These lines give our project meaning, I feel very moved by them and regard myself as embedded in a meaningful experience, I feel a self whose meaning goes beyond my own conception. The most enriching thing for me about this project has been the progress which students have made possible for me: for me, every encounter with them is a journey, in which new things are always revealed to me and every encounter, every moment proves to be unique, not to be exchanged with any other.

Bibliography

Adler, Alfred & Ringel, Erwin (Eds.). (1977). *Ein Österreicher namens Alfred Adler. Seine Individualpsychologie*. Vienna: Österreichischer Bundesverlag für Unterricht Wissenschaft und Kunst.

Ainsworth, Mary D. Salter, Blehar, Mary C., Waters, Everett, & Wall, Sally (1978). *Patterns of Attachment: A Psychological Study of the Strange Situation*. Hillsdale, NJ: Erlbaum.

Aisenstein, Marilia (2008). Die psychoanalytische Behandlung einer Patientin mit Kolonkarzinom. In Katharina Leithner-Dziubas, Peter Schuster, & Marianne Springer-Kremser (Eds.), *Borderline-Störungen* (pp. 35–57). Vienna: Facultas.

Al-Ani, Ayad (2013). *Widerstand in Organisationen. Organisationen im Widerstand: Virtuelle Plattformen, Edupunks und der nachfolgende Staat*. Wiesbaden: Springer VS.

Alder, Marie-Luise, Brakemeier, Eva-Lotta, Dittmann, Michael, Dreyer, Florian, & Buchholz, Michael B. (2016). Fehlleistungen als Empathie-Chance – die Gegenläufigkeit von 'Projekten' der Patientin und der Therapeutin. *Psychotherapie Forum*, 21(1), 2–10. doi:10.1007/s00729-015-0056-1.

Allen, Jon G. (Ed.). (2009). *Mentalisierungsgestützte Therapie. Das MBT-Handbuch – Konzepte und Praxis*. Stuttgart: Klett-Cotta.

Allen, Jon G., Fonagy, Peter, & Bateman, Anthony (2011). *Mentalisieren in der psychotherapeutischen Praxis*. 1st ed. Stuttgart: Klett-Cotta.

Althoff, Marie-Luise (2017). *Macht und Ohnmacht mentalisieren*. Berlin, Heidelberg: Springer.

Althusser, Louis (2010). *Ideologie und ideologische Staatsapparate*. Hamburg: VSA-Verlag.

Altman, Neil (2010). *The Analyst in the Inner City: Race, Class, and Culture through a Psychoanalytic Lens*. 2nd ed. New York: Routledge.

Altmeyer, Martin (2004). Affekt und Selbst. Affect and self. *Selbstpsychologie. Europäische Zeitschrift für Psychoanalytische Therapie und Forschung*, 3–4/2004(17/18), 275–288.

Altmeyer, Martin (2003). *Im Spiegel des Anderen. Anwendungen einer relationalen Psychoanalyse*. Giessen: Psychosozial-Verlag.

Altmeyer, Martin & Ogden, Thomas (Eds.). (2010). *Die vernetzte Seele. Die intersubjektive Wende in der Psychoanalyse*. 2nd ed. Stuttgart: Klett-Cotta.

Anastasopoulos, Dēmētrēs & Papanicolaou, Evagelos (Eds.). (2004). *The Therapist at Work: Personal Factors Affecting the Analytic Process*. London: Karnac.

Anderson, Frances Sommer (Ed.). (2008). *Bodies in Treatment. The Unspoken Dimension*. New York, London: Analytic Press.

Antons-Volmerg, Klaus, Amann, Andreas, Clausen, Gisela, König, Oliver, & Schattenhofer, Karl (2001). *Gruppenprozesse verstehen. Gruppendynamische Forschung und Praxis*. Wiesbaden: VS Verlag für Sozialwissenschaften.

Aragno, Anna (2008). The Language of Empathy: An Analysis of its Constitution, Development, and Role in Psychoanalytic Listening. *Journal of the American Psychoanalytic Association*, 56 (3), 713–740.

Aragno, Anna (2014). The Roots of Evil: A Psychoanalytic Inquiry. *Psychoanalytic Review*, 101 (2), 249–288.

Arefjord, Nina, Morken, Katharina, & Lossius, Kari. (2019). Comorbid Substance Use Disorder and Personality Disorder. In Anthony W.Bateman & Peter Fonagy (Eds.), *Handbook of Mentalizing* (pp. 403–416). Washington, DC: American Psychiatric Publishing.

Aron, Lewis (1992). Interpretation as Expression of the Analyst's Subjectivity. *Psychoanalytic Dialogues*, 2(4), 475–507. doi:10.1080/10481889209538947.

Aron, Lewis (2003). The Paradoxical Place of Enactment in Psychoanalysis: Introduction. *Psychoanalytic Dialogues*, 13(5), 623–631. doi:10.1080/10481881309348760.

Aron, Lewis (2016). *A Meeting of Minds. Mutuality in Psychoanalysis*. London: Routledge.

Aron, Lewis (2018). Core Competency Four: Relational Dynamic. The There and Then and the Here and Now. In Roy E.Barsness (Ed.), *Core Competencies of Relational Psychoanalysis: A Guide to Practice, Study and Research* (pp. 121–141). New York: Routledge.

Aron, Lewis & Harris, Adrienne (Eds.). (1993). *The Legacy of Sandor Ferenczi*. New York: Routledge.

Aron, Lewis & Harris, Adrienne (2010). In Beziehungen denken – in Beziehungen handeln. Neuere Entwicklungen der relationalen Psychoanalyse. In Martin Altmeyer & Thomas Ogden (Eds.), *Die vernetzte Seele. Die intersubjektive Wende in der Psychoanalyse* (pp. 108–121). 2nd ed. Stuttgart: Klett-Cotta.

Aron, Lewis & Harris, Adrienne (Eds.). (2012). *Relational Psychoanalysis, Volume 5. Evolution of Process*. Hoboken: Taylor & Francis.

Aron, Lewis & Henik, Libby (Eds.) (2015). *Answering a Question with a Question: Contemporary Psychoanalysis and Jewish Thought*. Brighton, USA: Academic Studies Press.

Aron, Lewis & Starr, Karen (2013). *A Psychotherapy for the People: Toward a Progressive Psychoanalysis*. New York.

Asen, Eia & Nick Midgley (2019). Working With Families. In Anthony W.Bateman & Fonagy, Peter (Eds.), *Handbook of Mentalizing* (pp. 135–157). Washington, DC: American Psychiatric Publishing.

Astington, Janet W. & Baird, Jodie Alison (Eds.). (2005). *Why Language Matters for Theory of Mind*. Oxford: Oxford University Press.

Astington, Janet Wilde & Reiss, Matthias (2000). *Wie Kinder das Denken entdecken*. Munich: Reinhardt.

Atwood, George E. (2017). *Der Abgrund des Wahnsinns. Psychoanalytische Erkundungen von Erfahrungen seelischer Zerstörung*. Giessen: Psychosozial-Verlag.

Atwood, George E. & Stolorow, Robert D. (1979). *Faces in a Cloud: Intersubjectivity in Personality Theory*. Northvale, NJ: Aronson.

Atwood, George E. & Stolorow, Robert D. (2014). *Structures of Subjectivity. Explorations in Psychoanalytic Phenomenology and Contextualism*. 2nd ed. London: Routledge.

Aulbert, Petra, Enriquez de Salamanca, Cecilia, & Treier, Ulrike (2015). Säuglingsbeobachtung nach der Methode von Esther Bick. Über die Schwierigkeit, einen guten Ort emotionaler Nähe und Distanz zu finden. In Gabriele Häussler & Petra Aulbert (Eds.), *Psychoanalytische Säuglingsbeobachtung und Säuglings-Kleinkind-Eltern-Psychotherapie* (pp. 65–86) Frankfurt: Brandes & Apsel.

Ayad, Al-Ani (2013). *Widerstand in Organisationen. Organisationen im Widerstand. Virtuelle Plattformen, Edupunks und der nachfolgende Staat*. Wiesbaden: Springer VS.

Bader, Michael J. (1993). Adaptive Sadomasochism and Psychological Growth. *Psychoanalytic Dialogues*, 3(2), pp. 279–300. doi:10.1080/10481889309538974.

Badura, H.O. & Steinmeyer, E.M. (1978). Objektivierung des Behandlungserfolges einer analytischen Gruppentherapie mit dem Giessen-Test. *Psychother Psychosom*, 29(1–4), 118–124. doi:10.1159/000287111.

Bales, Dawn. (2019). Partial Hospitalization Settings. In Anthony W. Bateman & Peter Fonagy (Eds.), *Handbook of Mentalizing* (pp. 197–210). Washington, DC: American Psychiatric Publishing.

Balint, Michael (1957). *The Doctor, his Patient and the Illness*. New York: International Universities Press.

Bantelmann, Jürgen Michael (2005). *Die Integrativen Verlaufsskalen (IVS-39). Ein Instrument zur Veränderungsmessung und Diagnostik tiefenpsychologisch und integrativ orientierter Psychotherapie*. 1st ed. Münster: LIT. Previously: Dissertation, Oldenburg University, 2004.

Baranger, Madeleine & Baranger, Willy (2018). Die analytische Situation als dynamisches Feld. *Psyche*, 72(09), 734–738. doi:10.21706/ps-72-9-734.

Baron-Cohen, Simon (2011). *Zero Degrees of Empathy: A New Theory of Human Cruelty*. London: Allen Lane.

Baron-Cohen, Simon & Bolton, Patrick (2006). *Autism: The Facts*. Oxford: Oxford University Press.

Barone, Carole (2005). The New Academy. In Diana G. Oblinger & James L. Oblinger (Eds.), *Educating the Net Generation* (pp. 212–227). Educause e-book. https://www.educause.edu/research-and-publications/books/educating-net-generation.

Barrett-Lennard, Godfrey T. (1981). The Empathy Cycle: Refinement of a Nuclear Concept. *Journal of Counseling Psychology*, 28(2), 91–100. doi:10.1037/0022-0167.28.2.91.

Barsness, Roy E. (Ed.). (2018). *Core Competencies of Relational Psychoanalysis: A Guide to Practice, Study and Research*. New York: Routledge.

Barsness, Roy E. (2003). A Review of The Supervisory Relationship: A Contemporary Psychodynamic Approach by Mary Gail Frawley-O'Dea, Ph.D. and Joan Sarnat Ph.D. New York: Guilford Press. *Contemporary Psychoanalysis*, 39(4), 711–717.

Bartsch, Karen & Wellman, Henry M. (1995). *Children Talk About the Mind*. New York: Oxford University Press.

Bass, Anthony (1999). When the Frame Doesn't Fit the Picture. In Stephen A. Mitchell, Lewis Aron, Adrienne Harris, & Melanie Suchet (Eds.), *Relational Psychoanalysis* (pp. 241–264). New York: Routledge.

Bass, Anthony (2007). When the Frame Doesn't Fit the Picture. *Psychoanalytic Dialogues*, 17(1), 1–27. doi:10.1080/10481880701301022.

Bass, Anthony (2014a). Supervision and Analysis at a Crossroad: The Development of the Analytic Therapist: Discussion of Papers by Joan Sarnat and Emanuel Berman. *Psychoanalytic Dialogues*, 24(5), 540–548. doi:10.1080/10481885.2014.94948.
Bass, Anthony (2014b). Three Pleas for a Measure of Uncertainty, Reverie, and Private Contemplation in the Chaotic, Interactive, Nonlinear Dynamic Field of Interpersonal/Intersubjective Relational Psychoanalysis. *Psychoanalytic Dialogues*, 24 (6), 663–675. doi:10.1080/10481885.2014.970967.
Bass, Anthony (2018). Emmanuel Ghent and the origins of relational psychoanalysis. In Emmanuel Ghent, Victoria Demos, & Adrienne Harris (Eds.), *The Collected Papers of Emmanuel Ghent: Heart Melts Forward* (pp. 21–27). New York: Routledge.
Bateman, Anthony W. & Fonagy, Peter (2006). *Mentalization-based Treatment for Borderline Personality Disorder: A Practical Guide*. Oxford: Oxford University Press.
Bateman, Anthony W. & Fonagy, Peter (2013). Mentalisierungsbasierte Therapie und Borderline-Persönlichkeitsstörung. In John F. Clarkin & Elizabeth Allison (Eds.), *Psychodynamische Psychotherapie der Persönlichkeitsstörungen. Handbuch für die klinische Praxis* (pp. 184–205). Stuttgart: Schattauer.
Bateman, Anthony W. & Fonagy, Peter (Eds.). (2019a). *Handbook of Mentalizing in Mental Health Practice, 2nd edition*. Washington, DC: American Psychiatric Publishing.
Bateman, Anthony W. & Fonagy, Peter (2019b). Borderline Personality Disorder. In Anthony W. Bateman & Peter Fonagy (Eds.), *Handbook of Mentalizing* (pp. 323–334). Washington, DC: American Psychiatric Publishing.
Bateman, Anthony, Kongerslev, Mickey, & Hansen, Sune Bo. (2019). Group Therapy for Adults and Adolescents. In Anthony W. Bateman & Peter Fonagy (Eds.), *Handbook of Mentalizing* (pp. 117–134). Washington, DC: American Psychiatric Publishing.
Bateman, Anthony, Motz, Anna, & Yakeley, Jessica. (2019). Antisocial Personality Disorder in Community and Prison Settings. In Anthony W. Bateman & Peter Fonagy (Eds.), *Handbook of Mentalizing* (pp. 335–350). Washington, DC: American Psychiatric Publishing.
Bauer, Joachim (2009). *Warum ich fühle, was du fühlst: Intuitive Kommunikation und das Geheimnis der Spiegelneurone*. 13th ed. Munich: Heyne.
Baumgärtel, Knut & Stockert, Marianne (1977). Die Erziehungsberatungsstellen. In Alfred Adler & Erwin Ringel (Eds.), *Ein Österreicher namens Alfred Adler: Seine Individualpsychologie* (pp. 201–211). Vienna: Österreichischer Bundesverlag für Unterricht Wissenschaft und Kunst.
Beckmann, Dieter (Ed.). (1979). *Erfahrungen mit dem Giessen-Test (GT): Praxis, Forschung u. Tabellen*. Berne, Vienna: Huber.
Beckmann, Dieter, Brähler, Elmar, & Richter, Horst-Eberhard (Eds.). (2012a). *GT-II: Der Giessen-Test-II*. Berne: Hans Huber/Hogrefe.
Beckmann, Dieter, Brähler, Elmar, & Richter, Horst-Eberhard (2012b). *Der Giessen-Test II: GT-II, Manual*. Berne: Huber.
Beckmann, Dieter & Richter, Horst-Eberhard (1972). *Giessen-Test (GT) Ein Test für Individual- und Gruppendiagnostik*. Berne: Huber.
Beebe, Beatrice (2006). Co-constructing mother-infant distress in face-to-face interactions: Contributions of microanalysis. *Infant Observation*, 9 (2), 151–164. doi:10.1080/13698030600810409.
Beebe, Beatrice, Jaffe, Joseph, Lachmann, Frank, Feldstein, Stanly, Crown, Cynthia, & Jasnow, Michael (2015). Koordination von Sprachrhythmus und Bindung:

Systemtheoretische Modelle. In Karl Heinz Brisch (Ed.), *Bindung und seelische Entwicklungswege. Grundlagen, Prävention und klinische Praxis* (pp. 47–85) 3rd ed. Stuttgart: Klett-Cotta.

Beebe, Beatrice & Lachmann, Frank (2010). Die relationale Wende in der Psychoanalyse: Ein dyadischer Systemansatz aus Sicht der Säuglingsforschung. In Martin Altmeyer & Thomas Ogden (Eds.), *Die vernetzte Seele. Die intersubjektive Wende in der Psychoanalyse* (pp. 122–159). 2nd ed. Stuttgart: Klett-Cotta.

Beebe, Beatrice, Lachmann, Frank, & Jaffe, Joseph (1997). Mother-infant Interaction Structures and Pre-Symbolic Self- and Object Representations. *Psychoanalytic Dialogues*, 7(2), 133–182. doi:10.1080/10481889709539172.

Belardi, Nando (2003). Hans Jürgen Wirth. Narzissmus und Macht. Zur Psychoanalyse seelischer Störungen in der Politik. *OSC*, 10(1), 94. doi:10.1007/s11613-003-0050-2.

Belardi, Nando (2013). *Supervision: Grundlagen, Techniken, Perspektiven*. 4th updated ed., Munich: Beck.

Benjamin, Jessica (1988). *The Bonds of Love. Psychoanalysis, Feminism and the Problem of Domination*. New York: Pantheon.

Benjamin, Jessica (1995a). *Like Subjects, Love Objects: Essays on Recognition and Sexual Difference*. New Haven: Yale University Press.

Benjamin, Jessica (1995b). Introduction. In Jessica Benjamin (Ed.), *Unbestimmte Grenzen: Beiträge zur Psychoanalyse der Geschlechter* (pp. 7–17). Frankfurt: Fischer.

Benjamin, Jessica (1999a). Afterword. In Aron Mitchell (Ed.), *Relational Psychoanalysis* (pp. 201–210). London: The Analytic Press.

Benjamin, Jessica (1998). *Shadow of the Other: Intersubjectivity and Gender in Psychoanalysis*. London: Routledge.

Benjamin, Jessica (2004a). Beyond Doer and Done to: An Intersubjective View of Thirdness. *Psychoanalytic Quarterly*, 73(1), 5–46. doi:10.1002/j.2167-4086.2004.tb00151.x.

Benjamin, Jessica (2004b). The Relationship of Doer and Done To and Its Dissolution through the Intersubjective Third. Lecture: Macht und Ohnmacht. DGPT conference, Berlin, November 5, 2004.

Benjamin, Jessica (2010). Tue ich oder wird mir angetan? Ein intersubjektives Triangulierungskonzept. In Martin Altmeyer & Thomas Ogden (Eds.), *Die vernetzte Seele: Die intersubjektive Wende in der Psychoanalyse* (pp. 65–107). 2nd ed. Stuttgart: Klett-Cotta.

Benjamin, Jessica (2016a). *Anerkennung, Zeugenschaft und Moral Soziale Traumata in psychoanalytischer Perspektive. Hans-Kilian-Preis 2015*. Giessen: Psychosozial-Verlag.

Benjamin, Jessica (2016b). The Concept of the Third. [Film]. Jane Ryan (Dir.). https://www.youtube.com/watch?v=HO5pJR9EWWE (December 17, 2018).

Benjamin, Jessica (2018). *Beyond Doer and Done To: Recognition Theory, Intersubjectivity and the Third*. London: Routledge.

Benjamin, Jessica & Atlas, Galita (2015). The 'too muchness' of excitement: Sexuality in light of excess, attachment and affect regulation. *International Journal of Psychoanalysis*, 96(1), 39–63.

Bennis, Warren G. (2009). *On Becoming a Leader*. New York: Basic Books.

Bennis, Warren G. & Shepard, Herbert A. (1956). A Theory of Group Development. *Human Relations*, 9 (4), 415–437. doi:10.1177/001872675600900403.

Bergin, Allen E. & Garfield, Sol L. (Eds.). (1994). *Handbook of Psychotherapy and Behavior Change*. 4th ed. New York: Wiley.

Berman, Emanuel (2004). *Impossible Training: A Relational View of Psychoanalytic Education*. Hillsdale, New York: The Analytic Press.
Berman, Emanuel (2005). Psychoanalytic Supervision: The Intersubjective Development (2000). In Lewis Aron & Adrienne Harris (Eds.), *Relational Psychoanalysis. vol. 2. Innovation and Expansion* (pp. 145–173). New York: The Analytic Press.
Beywl, Wolfgang (2012). *Stärkung der Professionalität des Lehrberufs durch selbstverantwortliche Qualitätsarbeit*. Schulisches Evaluationsvermögen durch unterrichtsintegrierte Selbst-Evaluation. Fachhochschule Nordwestschweiz. Delegiertenversammlung des LCH. St. Gallen, June 16, 2012. http://www.lch.ch/fileadmin/files/documents/Positionspapiere/120616_Referat_Prof_Beywl.pdf (March 21, 2015).
Beywl, Wolfgang, Bestvater, Hanne, & Friedrich, Verena (2011). *Selbstevaluation in der Lehre: Ein Wegweiser für sichtbares Lernen und besseres Lehren*. Münster: Waxmann.
Beywl, Wolfgang, Speer, Sandra, & Kehr, Jochen (2004). Wirkungsorientierte Evaluation im Rahmen der Armuts- und Berichterstattung Perspektivstudie. https://www.univation.org/publikation/wirkungsorientierte-evaluation-rahmen-armuts-reichtumsberichterstattung (March 21, 2015).
Bick, Esther (2009a). Bemerkungen zur Säuglingsbeobachtung in der psychoanalytischen Ausbildung. In Gertraud Diem-Wille (Ed.), *Ein-Blicke in die Tiefe: Die Methode der psychoanalytischen Säuglingsbeobachtung und ihre Anwendungen* (pp. 19–36). Stuttgart: Klett-Cotta.
Bick, Esther (2009b). Das Hauterleben in frühen Objektbeziehungen. In Gertraud Diem-Wille (Ed.), *Ein-Blicke in die Tiefe: Die Methode der psychoanalytischen Säuglingsbeobachtung und ihre Anwendungen* (pp. 37–40). Stuttgart: Klett-Cotta.
Bielefeld, Claus-Ulrich (2016). In Auschwitz hat sich die Wirklichkeit entlarvt. https://www.welt.de/kultur/literarischewelt/article158365767/In-Auschwitz-hat-sich-die-Wirklichkeit-entlarvt.html (January 22, 2019).
Bion, Wilfred R. (1992). *Lernen durch Erfahrung*. 1st ed. Frankfurt: Suhrkamp.
Bion, Wilfred R. (2001). *Erfahrungen in Gruppen und andere Schriften*. 3rd ed. Stuttgart: Klett-Cotta.
Black, Margaret J. & Mitchell, Stephen A. (2016). *Freud and Beyond – a History of Modern Psychoanalytic Thought*. New York: The Perseus Books Group.
Blessing, Deborah (2012). Beyond the borders of 'ordinary': Difficult observations and their implications. *Infant Observation International Journal of Infant Observation and Its Applications*, 15(1), 33–48.
BMUKK Zahlenspiegel (2013). https://www.bmbwf.gv.at/Themen/schule/schulsystem/gd/stat_tb.html (November 21, 2020).
Böck, Andrea (2011). Mentalisierung und soziale Kompetenz. BA thesis, Universität Vienna: (Pädagogisches Institut). http://www.academia.edu/1577085/Mentalisierung_und_soziale_Kompetenz (April 8, 2014).
Bohleber, Werner (1999). Psychoanalyse, Adoleszenz und das Problem der Identität. *Psyche – Z Psychoanal*, 53(6), 507–529.
Bohleber, Werner, Fonagy, Peter, Jimenez, Juan Pablo, Scarfone, Dominique, Varvin, Sverre & Zysman, Samuel (2013). Für einen besseren Umgang mit psychoanalytischen Konzepten, modellhaft illustriert am Konzept 'Enactment'. *Psyche – Z Psychoanal*, 67(12), 1212–1250.
Böker, Heinz (1999). *Selbstbild und Objektbeziehungen bei Depressionen: Untersuchungen mit der Repertory Grid-Technik und dem Giessen-Test an 139 PatientInnen mit depressiven Erkrankungen*. Heidelberg: Steinkopff.

Bollas, Christopher (2018) [1987]. *The Shadow of the Object. Psychoanalysis of the Unthought Known*. London: Routledge.
Bolm, Thomas (2009). *Mentalisierungsbasierte Therapie (MBT): Für Borderline-Störungen und chronifizierte Traumafolgen*. Cologne: Deutscher Ärzteverlag.
Bolm, Thomas (2010). Mentalisierungsdefizite und ihre Behandlung bei verschiedenen psychischen Störungen. What works for whom? *Psychodynamische Psychotherapie, Forum der tiefenpsychologisch fundierten Psychotherapie*, 9(4), 205–215.
Bolm, Thomas (2015). *Mentalisierungsbasierte Therapie*. 1st ed. Munich: Ernst Reinhardt Verlag.
Bolm, Thomas, Schöps, Axel, Robertz, Anke, & Herzog, Thomas (2007). Psychosomatisch-psychotherapeutische Fachkliniken und -abteilungen in der Versorgung schwerer Persönlichkeitsstörungen. *Persönlichkeitsstörungen: Theorie und Therapie*, 11(3), 181–186.
Boston Change Process Study Group (2013). Enactment and the emergence of new relational organization. *Journal of the American Psychoanalytic Association*, 61(4), 727–749. doi:10.1177/0003065113496636.
Boulanger, Ghislaine (2002). Wounded by Reality. *Contemporary Psychoanalysis*, 38 (1), 45–76. doi:10.1080/00107530.2002.10745806.
Boulanger, Ghislaine (2014). *Wounded by Reality: Understanding and Treating Adult Onset Trauma*. New York: Routledge.
Bowlby, John (1973). *Separation: Anxiety and Anger, Attachment and Loss vol. II*. London: Penguin.
Boynton, Robert S. (2002). Return of the Repressed: The strange case of Masud Khan. *Boston Review*, December 1, 2002. http://bostonreview.net/books-ideas/robert-s-boynton-return-repressed (October 28, 2018).
Bradley, Jonathan (2008). The work discussion seminar: a learning enviroment. In Margaret Rustin, Jonathan Bradley, & Trudy Klauber (Eds.), *Work Discussion: Learning from Reflective Practice in Work with Children and Families* (pp. 22–37). London: Karnac.
Brähler, Elmar (1989). Giessen-Test. *Psychotherapia*, 3(70), 21–31.
Brähler, Elmar, Holling, Heinz, Leutner, Detlev, & Petermann, Franz (Eds.). (2002). *Brickenkamp Handbuch psychologischer und pädagogischer Tests. vol. 1*. 3rd ed. Göttingen: Hogrefe.
Brandchaft, Bernard, Doctors, Shelley R., & Sorter, Dorienne (2015). *Emanzipatorische Psychoanalyse: Systeme pathologischer Anpassung – Brandchafts Konzept der Intersubjektivität*. Frankfurt: Brandes & Apsel.
Brazelton, T. Berry (2006). *Touchpoints: Birth to 3 – Your Child's Emotional and Behavioral Development*. 2nd ed. Cambridge, Mass.: Perseus Books.
Breithaupt, Fritz (2017). *Die dunklen Seiten der Empathie*. 2nd ed. Berlin: Suhrkamp.
Breyer, Thiemo (Ed.). (2013). *Grenzen der Empathie: Philosophische, psychologische und anthropologische Perspektiven*. Munich: Wilhelm Fink.
Breyer, Thiemo, Buchholz, Michael B., Hamburger, Andreas, Pfänder, Stefan, & Schumann, Elke (Eds.). (2017). *Resonanz – Rhythmus – Synchronisierung. Interaktionen in Alltag, Therapie und Kunst*. Bielefeld: transcript.
Breyer, Thiemo & Pfänder, Stefan (2017). Resonanz, Rhythmus und Synchronisierung. In Thiemo Breyer, Michael B. Buchholz, Andreas Hamburger, Stefan Pfänder, & Elke Schumann (Eds.), *Resonanz – Rhythmus – Synchronisierung. Interaktionen in Alltag, Therapie und Kunst* (pp. 9–29). Bielefeld: transcript.

Brisch, Karl Heinz (2011). *Bindung und frühe Störungen der Entwicklung*. Stuttgart: Klett-Cotta.

Brisch, Karl Heinz (Ed.). (2015). *Bindung und seelische Entwicklungswege: Grundlagen, Prävention und klinische Praxis*. 3rd ed. Stuttgart: Klett-Cotta.

Bromberg, Philip M. (2003). Something wicked this way comes: Trauma, dissociation, and conflict –The space where psychoanalysis, cognitive science, and neuroscience overlap. *Psychoanalytic Psychology*, 20(3), 558–574. doi:10.1037/0736-9735.20.3.558.

Browning, Christopher R. (1992). *Ordinary Men: Reserve Police Battalion 101 and the Final Solution in Poland*. New York: Harper Collins.

Buber, Martin (1970). *I and Thou*. Translated by Walter Kaufmann. New York: Scribner.

Bucci, Wilma (1997). *Psychoanalysis and Cognitive Science: A Multiple Code Theory*. New York: Guilford Press.

Bucci, Wilma (2011). The Interplay of Subsymbolic and Symbolic Processes in Psychoanalytic Treatment: It Takes Two to Tango – But Who Knows the Steps, Who's The Leader? The Choreography of the Psychoanalytic Interchange. *Psychoanalytic Dialogues*, 21(1), 45–54. doi:10.1080/10481885.2011.545326.

Buchholz, Michael B. (1999). *Psychotherapie als Profession*. Giessen: Psychosozial-Verlag.

Buchholz, Michael B. (2003). *Metaphern der 'Kur': Eine qualitative Studie zum psychotherapeutischen Prozess*. Giessen: Psychosozial-Verlag.

Buchholz, Michael B. (2004). Für eine relationale Psychoanalyse: Stephen Mitchell. *psychosozial*, 97(3), 29–41.

Buchholz, Michael B. (2008). Kompetenzkompetenz. *Psycho-Newsletter*, 72, 1–14. http://dgpt.de/fileadmin/download/psychonewsletters/PNL-72.pdf (May 31, 2014).

Buchholz, Michael B. (2012). Heilen durch Sprechen: Warum es so schwierig ist, Psychotherapie zu definieren. *Psychologische Medizin*, 23(2), 36–47.

Buchholz, Michael B. (2013a). Die Herausbildung psychotherapeutischer Kompetenz in der Supervision – unterwegs zur Analyse supervisorischer Konversation. Vorschlag zur Definition von Psychotherapie und für ein praktisches Modell der Supervision. In Stefan Busse (Ed.), *Supervisions- und Coachingprozesse erforschen. Theoretische und methodische Zugänge* (pp. 77–108). Göttingen: Vandenhoeck & Ruprecht.

Buchholz, Michael B. (2013b). Supervision ist eine Beobachtung, wie Therapeuten (sich) bei der Arbeit beobachten – oder: Etwas Empirie ist manchmal Salz in der Suppe organisierter Anarchie. In Reinhard Hörster, Stefan Köngeter, & Burkhard Müller (Eds.), *Grenzobjekte: Soziale Welten und ihre Übergänge* (pp. 137–160). Wiesbaden: Springer VS.

Buchholz, Michael B. (2013c). Wie sich implizites Wissen bei Therapeuten entwickelt. Eine Skizze. In Peter Geißler, André J. Sassenfeld, & Michael B. Buchholz (Eds.), *Jenseits von Sprache und Denken: Implizite Dimensionen im psychotherapeutischen Geschehen* (pp. 25–55). Giessen: Psychosozial-Verlag.

Buchholz, Michael B. (2014a). Peter Fonagy und die Mentalisierung. In Günter Gödde & Jörg Zirfas (Eds.), *Lebenskunst im 20. Jahrhundert: Stimmen von Philosophen, Künstlern und Therapeuten* (pp. 353–372). Paderborn: Fink.

Buchholz, Michael B. (2014b). Neues zu Kultur und Praxis. *Psycho-News-Letter*, (97), pp. 1–15. http://dgpt.de/fileadmin/download/psychonewsletters/PNL-97.pdf (September 21, 2014).

Buchholz, Michael B. (2017a). Empathie und 'Typische Problem-Situationen' (TPS): Plädoyer für einen psychoanalytischen Situationismus. *Psyche*, 71(1), 28–58.

Buchholz, Michael B. (2017b). Wie Therapeuten sich bei der Arbeit beobachten – ein prozessforschungsbasiertes Modell der Supervision. In Wolfgang Mertens & Andreas Hamburger (Eds.), *Supervision in der Ausbildung* (pp. 83–99). 1st ed. Stuttgart: Kohlhammer.

Buchholz, Michael B., Bergmann, Jörg, Alder, Marie-Luise, Dittmann, Michael M., Dreyer, Florian, & Kächele, Horst (2017). The Building of Empathy: Conceptual 'Pillars' and Conversational Practices in Psychotherapy. In Makiko Kondo (Ed.), *Empathy – An Evidence-based Interdisciplinary Perspective* (pp. 95–128). Croatia: National and University Library in Zagreb.

Buchholz, Michael B., Lamott, Franziska, & Mörtl, Kathrin (2011). *Tat-Sachen: Narrative von Sexualstraftätern*. 2nd ed. Giessen: Psychosozial-Verlag.

Bugnyar, Thomas & Heinrich, Bernd (2005). Ravens, Corvus corax, differentiate between knowledgeable and ignorant competitors. *Proceedings of the Royal Society B: Biological Sciences*, 272(1573), 1641–1646 doi:10.1098/rspb.2005.3144.

Bühl, Achim (2012). *SPSS 20. Einführung in die moderne Datenanalyse*. 13th ed. Munich: Pearson.

Buirski, Peter & Haglund, Pamela (2001). *Making Sense Together: The Intersubjective Approach to Psychotherapy*. Northvale, NJ: Jason Aronson.

Burian, Wilhelm (1972). *Psychoanalyse und Marxismus: Eine intellektuelle Biographie Wilhelm Reichs*. Frankfurt: Makol-Verlag.

Burian, Wilhelm (Ed.) (1998). *Der beobachtete und der rekonstruierte Säugling*. Göttingen: Vandenhoeck & Ruprecht.

Busse, Stefan & Hausinger, Brigitte (Eds.). (2013). *Supervisions- und Coachingprozesse erforschen: Theoretische und methodische Zugänge*. Göttingen: Vandenhoeck & Ruprecht.

Butler, Judith (1993). *Bodies That Matter: On the Discursive Limits of Sex*. New York: Routledge.

Cardenal, Monica (1998). A psycho-analytically informed approach to clinically ill babies. *Infant Observation International Journal of Infant Observation and Its Applications*, 2(1), 90–100.

Carvalho, Paula Teresa (2010). Die Container-Funktion der Gruppenanalyse: Wie kann ich dich lieben, wenn ich nicht wütend auf dich sein kann? In Mathias Hirsch (Ed.), *Die Gruppe als Container: Mentalisierung und Symbolisierung in der analytischen Gruppenpsychotherapie* (pp. 25–33). 2nd ed. Göttingen: Vandenhoeck & Ruprecht.

Casement, Patrick (1993). Psychoanalyse – Verfahren oder Prozess? *Psyche – Z Psychoanal*, 47(11), 1013–1026.

Caspi, Avshalom, Houts, Renate M., Belsky, Daniel W., Goldman-Mellor, Sidra J., Harrington, HonLee, Israel, Salomon, Meier, Madeline H., Ramrakha, Sandhya, Shalev, Idan, Poulton, Richie, Moffitt, & Terrie E. (2014). The p factor: One general psychopathology factor in the structure of psychiatric disorders? *Clinical Psychological Science*, 2(2), 119–137 doi:10.1177/2167702613497473.

Chodorow, Nancy (1979). *The Reproduction of Mothering: Psychoanalysis and the Sociology of Gender*. Berkeley: University of California Press.

Chodorow, Nancy (1992). Heterosexuality as a Compromise Formation: Reflections on the Psychoanalytic Theory of Sexual Development. *Psychoanalysis & Contemporary Thought*, 15(3), 267–304.

Clarkin, John F. & Allison, Elizabeth (Eds.). (2013). *Psychodynamische Psychotherapie der Persönlichkeitsstörungen. Handbuch für die klinische Praxis*. Stuttgart: Schattauer.

Clarkin, John F., Yeomans, Frank E., & Kernberg, Otto F. (2008). *Psychotherapie der Borderline-Persönlichkeit: Manual zur psychodynamischen Therapie, mit einem Anhang zur Praxis der TFP im deutschsprachigen Raum*. 2nd ed., Stuttgart: Schattauer.
Clough, Patricia Ticineto (1995). Femininities, Masculinities, Sexualities. Freud and Beyond. Nancy J. Chodorow. *American Journal of Sociology*, 100(4), 1073–1074. doi:10.1086/230620.
Coelho, Nelson E. Jr. (2017). Ursprünge und Entwicklungsgeschichte des Dritten in der zeitgenössischen Psychoanalyse. In Karsten Münch (Ed.) *Neues zu vertrauten Konzepten: Ausgewählte Beiträge aus dem international journal of psychoanalysis* (pp. 43–71). Giessen: Psychosozial-Verlag.
Coelho, Nelson E. Jr. (2016). The origins and destinies of the idea of thirdness in contemporary psychoanalysis. *International Journal of Psychoanalysis*, 97 (4), 1105–1127.
Coltart, Nina (1992). *Slouching towards Bethlehem, and Further Psychoanalytic Explorations*. London: Free Association.
Cooper, Steven H. (2010). *A Disturbance in the Field: Essays in Transference-Countertransference Engagement*. New York: Routledge.
Corbett, Ken (2009a). Boyhood Femininity, Gender Identity Disorder, Masculine Presuppositions, and the Anxiety of Regulation. *Psychoanalytic Dialogues*, 19 (4), 353–370. doi:10.1080/10481880903088484.
Corbett, Ken (2009b). *Boyhoods: Rethinking Masculinities*. New Haven: Yale University Press.
Corbett, Ken (2014). The Analyst's Private Space: Spontaneity, Ritual, Psychotherapeutic Action, and Self-Care. *Psychoanalytic Dialogues*, 24(6), 637–647. doi:10.1080/10481885.2014.970964.
Corpt, Elizabeth A. (2011). Clinical generosity: An attitude deeply embedded in the contemporary self-psychology. Presentation at the Annual Conference. International Association for Psychoanalytic Self Psychology. Los Angeles, CA.
Critchfield, Adam R. & Pula, Jack (2015). On Psychotherapy, LGBT Identity, and Cultural Visibility. In Conversation with Alison Bechdel. *Journal of Gay & Lesbian Mental Health*, 19(4), 397–412. doi:10.1080/19359705.2015.1046202.
Cushman, Philip (1995). *Constructing the Self, Constructing America: A Cultural History of Psychotherapy*. Cambridge, Mass.: Da Capo Press.
Cushman, Philip (2015). Relational Psychoanalysis as Political Resistance. *Contemporary Psychoanalysis*, 51(3), 423–459. doi:10.1080/00107530.2015.1056076.
Datler, Wilfried (2003). Erleben, Beschreiben und Verstehen: Vom Nachdenken über Gefühle im Dienst der Entfaltung von pädagogischer Professionalität. In Margret Dörr & Rolf Göppel (Eds.), *Bildung der Gefühle: Innovation?, Illusion?, Intrusion?* (pp. 241–264) Giessen: Psychosozial-Verlag.
Datler, Wilfried (2004). Die heilpädagogische Beziehung als Gegenstand der Reflexion und Ort der Veränderung: Über das Ringen um Verstehen, die Erarbeitung von Handlungsspielräumen und das Konzept der 'work discussion'. In Sybille Kannewischer, Bettina Kolb, & Gabriela Hopfinger (Eds.), *Verhalten als subjektiv-sinnhafte Ausdrucksform* (pp. 116–126). [Festschrift für Konrad Bundschuh zum 60. Geburtstag]. Bad Heilbrunn: Klinkhardt.
Datler, Wilfried (2006). Geistig behinderte Menschen an-sprechen: Über Mentalisierungsprozesse und die Bedeutung der Thematisierung von Innerpsychischem. In Johannes Gruntz-Stoll (Ed.), *Verwahrlost, beziehungsgestört, verhaltensoriginell. Zum Sprachwandel in der Heil- und Sonderpädagogik* (pp. 69–91). 1st ed. Berne: Haupt.

Datler, Wilfried (2009). Von der akademischen Entwicklungspsychologie zur psychoanalytischen Säuglingsbeobachtung: Über Esther Bick, die Methode der Infant Observation und die Entwicklung von psychosozialer Kompetenz. In Gertraud Diem-Wille (Ed.), *Ein-Blicke in die Tiefe: Die Methode der psychoanalytischen Säuglingsbeobachtung und ihre Anwendungen* (pp. 41–66). Stuttgart: Klett-Cotta.

Datler, Wilfried, Lazar, Ross A., & Trunkenpolz, Karin (2012). Lust und Leid im Erkunden der inneren Welt von Organisationen: Über Organisationsbeobachtung, institutionalisierte Abwehr und den Alltag im Pflegeheim. In Gertraud Diem-Wille & Agnes Turner (Eds.), *Die Methode der psychoanalystischen Beobachtung: Über die Bedeutung von Containment, Übertragung, Abwehr und anderen Phänomenen in der psychoanalytischen Beobachtung* (pp. 94–114). Vienna: Facultas.

Datler, Wilfried, Lazar, Ross A., & Trunkenpolz, Karin (2012). Observing in Nursing Homes: The Use of Single Case Studies and Organisational Observation as a Research Tool. In Cathy Urwin & Janine Sternberg (Eds.), *Infant Observation and Research: Emotional Processes in Everyday Lives* (pp. 160–170). London: Routledge.

Datler, Wilfried & Trunkenpolz, Karin (2009). Observation nach dem Tavistock-Konzept: Deutschsprachige Veröffentlichungen über Infant Observation und damit verbundene Varianten des psychoanalytischen Beobachtens. Eine kommentierte Bibliographie. In Gertraud Diem-Wille (Ed.), *Ein-Blicke in die Tiefe: Die Methode der psychoanalytischen Säuglingsbeobachtung und ihre Anwendungen* (pp. 233–253). Stuttgart: Klett-Cotta.

Davies, Jody Messier (1994). Love in the afternoon: A relational reconsideration of desire and dread in the countertransference. *Psychoanalytic Dialogues*, 4(2), 153–170. doi:10.1080/10481889409539011.

Davies, Jody Messler (2008). Falling in Love with Love: Oedipal and Post-oedipal Manifestations of Idealization, Mourning, and Erotic Masochism. *Psychoanalytic Dialogues*, 13(1), 1–27. doi:10.1080/10481881309348718.

Davies, Jody Messler & Frawley-O'Dea, Mary Gail (1994). *Treating the Adult Survivor of Childhood Sexual Abuse: A Psychoanalytic Perspective*. New York: Basic Books.

Davoine, Françoise & Gaudillière, Jean-Max (2015). Stoppage of time in schizophrenia: Similarities to the field of war trauma. *International Forum of Psychoanalysis*, 25(2), 104–109. doi:10.1080/0803706X.2016.1143565.

Dennett, D.C. (1987). Beliefs About Beliefs. *Behav Brain Scienc The Intentional Stance*, 4(1), 568–570.

Devereux, George (1973). *Angst und Methode in den Verhaltenswissenschaften*. 1st ed. Frankfurt: Suhrkamp.

Diem-Wille, Gertraud (Ed.). (2009a). *Ein-Blicke in die Tiefe: Die Methode der psychoanalytischen Säuglingsbeobachtung und ihre Anwendungen*. Stuttgart: Klett-Cotta.

Diem-Wille, Gertraud (2009b). Psychoanalytische Säuglingsbeobachtung als Ausbildungsmethode – ihre Wurzeln und ihre Anwendung in der Eltern-Kleinkind-Therapie. In Gertraud Diem-Wille (Ed.), *Ein-Blicke in die Tiefe: Die Methode der psychoanalytischen Säuglingsbeobachtung und ihre Anwendungen* (pp. 67–100). Stuttgart: Klett-Cotta.

Diem-Wille, Gertraud & Turner, Agnes (Eds.). (2012). *Die Methode der psychoanalytischen Beobachtung: Über die Bedeutung von Containment, Übertragung, Abwehr und anderen Phänomenen in der psychoanalytischen Beobachtung*. Vienna: Facultas.

Dimen, Muriel (2005). Sexuality and Suffering, Or the Eew! Factor. *Studies in Gender and Sexuality*, 6(1), 1–18. doi:10.1080/15240650609349262.

Dimen, Muriel (2011). Lapsus Linguae, or A Slip of the Tongue? *Contemporary Psychoanalysis*, 47(1), 35–79. doi:10.1080/00107530.2011.10746441.

Dimen, Muriel (2014). *Sexuality, Intimacy, Power*. Abingdon: Routledge.

Dimen, Muriel & Goldner, Virginia (2010). *Gender in Psychoanalytic Space: Between Clinic and Culture*. 2nd ed. New York: Other Press.

Dimen-Schein, Muriel (1977). *The Anthropological Imagination*. New York: McGraw-Hill.

Disler, Werner A. (2017). *Intersubjektivität – persönlichkeitsspezifische Therapieformen: Lehrbuch der analytisch-selbstpsychologischen Imaginationstherapie Ich, Selbst, innere und äußere Objekte. vol. 2*. 1st ed. Berlin: Pro Business digital.

Doering, Stephan & Hörz, Susanne (Eds.). (2011). *Handbuch der Strukturdiagnostik: Konzepte, Instrumente, Praxis*. 1st ed., Stuttgart: Schattauer.

Döring, Peter (2013). Mentalisierungsbasiertes Management. In Ulrich Schultz-Venrath (Ed.), *Lehrbuch Mentalisieren: Psychotherapien wirksam gestalten* (pp. 351–382). 1st ed. Stuttgart: Klett-Cotta.

Dornes, Martin (2004). Mentalisierung, psychische Realität und die Genese des Handlungs- und Affektverständnisses in der frühen Kindheit. In Christa Rohde-Dachser & Franz Wellendorf (Eds.), *Inszenierungen des Unmöglichen: Theorie und Therapie schwerer Persönlichkeitsstörungen* (pp. 297–338). Stuttgart: Klett-Cotta.

Dörr, Margret & Göppel, Rolf (Eds.). (2003). *Bildung der Gefühle: Innovation? Illusion? Intrusion?*Giessen: Psychosozial-Verlag.

Dulz, Birger, Briken, Peer, Kernberg, Otto F., & Rauchfleisch, Udo (Eds.). (2017). *Handbuch der antisozialen Persönlichkeitsstörung*. Stuttgart: Schattauer.

Dulz, Birger, Herpertz, Sabine, Kernberg, Otto F., & Sachsse, Ulrich (Eds.). (2011). *Handbuch der Borderline-Störungen*. 2nd ed. Stuttgart: Schattauer.

Dürr, Hans-Peter (2016). *Es gibt keine Materie! Revolutionäre Gedanken über Physik und Mystik*. 5th ed. Amerang: Crotona.

Eckert, Jochen & Biermann-Ratjen, Eva-Maria, (1985). *Stationäre Gruppenpsychotherapie: Prozesse, Effekte, Vergleiche*. Berlin: Springer.

Edlhaimb-Hrubec, Christiana Maria (2004). Etymologische Fragmente zu Wort und Begriff Supervision: Im Fokus der Integrativen Supervision. Dissertation. Donau-Universität Krems an der Donau.

Ekman, Paul (2010). *Gefühle lesen: Wie Sie Emotionen erkennen und richtig interpretieren*. 2nd ed. Heidelberg: Spektrum.

Ekman, Paul (2011). *Ich weiß, dass du lügst: Was Gesichter verraten*. Reinbek bei Hamburg: Rowohlt.

Elliott, Rober, Filipovich, Howard, Harrigan, Linda, Gaynor, James, Reimschuessel, Cora, & Zapadka, Judith K. (1982). Measuring response empathy: The development of a multicomponent rating scale. *Journal of Counseling Psychology*, 29(4), 379–387. doi:10.1037/0022-0167.29.4.379.

Elsass, Peter (2003). *Håndbog i kulturpsykologi. Et fag på tværs*. Copenhagen: Gyldendal.

Emery, Nathan J. & Clayton, Nicola S. (2004). Comparing the Complex Cognition of Birds and Primates. In Lesley Rogers & Gisela Kaplan Gisela (Eds.), *Comparative Vertebrate Cognition: Are Primates Superior to Non-Primates?* (pp. 3–55). New York: Kluwer Academic/Plenum Publishers.

Enfield, N.J. (Ed.) (2006). *Roots of Human Sociality: Culture, Cognition and Interaction*. Oxford: Berg.

Erikson, Erik H. & Hügel, Käte (1998). *Identität und Lebenszyklus. Drei Aufsätze*. Frankfurt: Suhrkamp.

Ermann, Michael (1987). *Die Persönlichkeit bei psychovegetativen Störungen. Klinische und empirische Ergebnisse*. Berlin: Springer.

Ermann, Michael & Körner, Jürgen (2014). Persönliche Stile in der Beziehung zur Psychoanalyse. *Forum Psychoanal*, 30(1), 9–10. doi:10.1007/s00451-014-0173-4.

Ernstson, Sven & Meyer, Christine (Eds.). (2013). *Praxis geschlechtersensibler und interkultureller Bildung*. 1st ed. Wiesbaden: Springer VS.

European Commission (2011). Global Europe 2050. https://ec.europa.eu/research/social-sciences/pdf/global-europe-2050-summary-report_en.pdf (June 16, 2014).

Fachhochschule Nordwestschweiz (n.d.). Die Standards für Programmevaluation des Joint Committee on Standards for Educational Evaluation. Fachhochschule Nordwestschweiz Pädagogische Hochschule. www.fhnw.ch/ph/weiterbildung (March 21, 2015).

Fanon, Frantz (1981). *Die Verdammten dieser Erde*. 1st ed. Frankfurt: Suhrkamp.

Felsberger, Helga (2014). Foreword: Gruppenanalyse und die Entwicklung von Intersubjektivität. In Wolfgang Martin Roth, Helga Felsberger, & Josef Shaked (Eds.), *Gruppenanalyse und die Entwicklung von Intersubjektivität* (pp. 5–10). 1st ed. Vienna: Facultas.

Ferenczi, Sándor, Dupont, Judith, Balint, Michael, & Sabourin, Pierre (2013). *Das klinische Tagebuch*. Giessen: Psychosozial-Verlag.

Fernández Mínguez, Gorka (2019). *Aprende y Disfruta*. Spanien: Editorial Libros.

Ferro, Antonino (2003). *Das bipersonale Feld: Konstruktivismus und Feldtheorie in der Kinderanalyse*. Giessen: Psychosozial-Verlag.

Fiala, E. (1986). Salzburger Sozialisationsstudien: Supervision als systematische Reflexion beruflichen Handelns in psychosozialen Praxisfeldern. Dissertation. Universität Salzburg (Natural Science).

Fiegl, Jutta (2016). *Empirische Untersuchung zum Direktstudium Psychotherapie: Forschungsergebnisse zur Eignung und zum Ausbildungsverlauf aus der Perspektive von Studierenden und Experten*. Münster: Waxmann.

Fiegl, Jutta & Sindelar, Brigitte (2014). Zur Frage der Eignung für die Psychotherapieausbildung. *Forschungsbulletin Research Bulletin*, 2(2), 27–44. doi:10.15135/14.2.2.27-44.

Fischer, Gottfried & Eichernberg, Christiane (2011). *Psychotherapiewissenschaft: Einführung in eine neue humanwissenschaftliche Disziplin*. Giessen: Psychosozial-Verlag.

Fischer-Kern, Melitta & Fonagy, Peter (2012). Die Reflective Functioning Scale. In Stephan Doering & Susanne Hörz (Eds.), *Handbuch der Strukturdiagnostik. Konzepte, Instrumente, Praxis* (pp. 225–255). 1st ed., Stuttgart: Schattauer.

Flick, Uwe (1995). *Qualitative Forschung: Theorie, Methoden, Anwendung in Psychologie und Sozialwissenschaften*. Reinbek bei Hamburg: Rowohlt.

Fodor, J.A. (1992). Discussion: A Theory of the Child's Theory of Mind. *Cognition*, 44 (3), 283–296. doi:10.1016/0010-0277(92)90004-2.

Fonagy, Peter (1989). On Tolerating Mental States: Theory of Mind in Borderline Personality – A Child's Understanding of Others. *Bulletin Anna Freud Centre*, 12 (2), 91–115.

Fonagy, Peter (1991). Thinking about thinking: Some clinical and theoretical considerations in the treatment of a borderline patient. *The International Journal of Psycho-analysis*, 72(4), 639–656.

Fonagy, Peter (1997). Can we use observations of infant-caregiver interactions as the basis for a model of the representational world? Commentary on paper by Beebe, Ilchmann, and Jaffe. *Psychoanalytic Dialogues*, 7(2), 207–213. doi:10.1080/10481889709539176.

Fonagy, Peter (1998). Die Bedeutung der Entwicklung metakognitiver Kontrolle der mentalen Repräsentanzen für die Betreuung und das Wachstum des Kindes. *Psyche – Z Psychoanal*, 52(4), 349–368.

Fonagy, Peter (2008). Persönlichkeitsstörung und Gewalt – Ein psychoanalytisch-bindungstheoretischer Ansatz. In Fritz Lackinger & Wolfgang Berner (Eds.), *Psychodynamische Psychotherapie bei Delinquenz: Praxis der übertragungsfokussierten Psychotherapie* (pp. 326–365). Stuttgart: Schattauer.

Fonagy, Peter (2009). *Bindungstheorie und Psychoanalyse*. 3rd ed. Stuttgart: Klett-Cotta.

Fonagy, Peter & Bateman, Anthony W. (2017). Mentalisierungsbasierte Therapie der Antisozialen Persönlichkeitsstörung. In Birger Dulz, Peer Briken, Otto F. Kernberg, & Udo Rauchfleisch (Eds.), *Handbuch der antisozialen Persönlichkeitsstörung* (pp. 428–441). Stuttgart: Schattauer.

Fonagy, Peter & Anthony Bateman. (2019). Introduction. In Anthony W. Bateman & Peter Fonagy (Eds.), *Handbook of Mentalizing* (pp. 3–20). Washington, DC: American Psychiatric Publishing.

Fonagy, Ivan & Fonagy, Peter (1995). Communication with pretend actions in language, literature and psychoanalysis in language, literature and psychoanalysis. *Psychoanalysis and Contemporary Thought*, 18, 363–418.

Fonagy, Peter, Gergely, György, Jurist, Elliot L., & Target, Mary (2002). *Affect Regulation, Mentalization and the Development of the Self*. 1st ed. London: Routledge.

Fonagy, Peter & Luyten, Patrick (2011). Die entwicklungspsychologischen Wurzeln der Borderline-Persönlichkeitsstörung in Kindheit und Adoleszenz: Ein Forschungsbericht unter dem Blickwinkel der Mentalisierungstheorie. *Psyche – Z Psychoanal*, 65(9/10), 900–952.

Fonagy, Peter, Luyten, Patrick, Bateman, Anthony W., Gergely, György, Strathearn, Lane, Target, Mary, & Allison, Elizabeth (2013). Bindung und Persönlichkeitsstörung. In John F. Clarkin & Elizabeth Allison (Eds.), *Psychodynamische Psychotherapie der Persönlichkeitsstörungen. Handbuch für die klinische Praxis* (pp. 35–84). Stuttgart: Schattauer.

Fonagy, Peter, Luyten, Patrick, Allison, Elizabeth, & Campbell, Chloe (2017). What we have changed our minds about. Part 1: Borderline personality disorder as a limitation of resilience. *Borderline personality disorder and emotion dysregulation*, 4(11). doi:10.1186/s40479-017-0061-9.

Fonagy, Peter, Steele, Miriam, Steele, Howard, Moran, Georg S., & Higgitt, Anna C. (1991). The Capacity for Understanding Mental States: The Reflective Self in Parent and Child and Its Significance for Security of Attachment. *Infant Mental Health Journal*, 12(3), 201–218.

Fonagy, Peter & Target, Mary (1995). Playing With Reality: The Development Of Psychic Reality And Its Malfunction In Borderline Personalities. *International Journal of Psycho-Analysis*, 76:39–44.

Fonagy, Peter & Target, Mary (2002). Neubewertung der Entwicklung der Affektregulation vor dem Hintergrund von Winnicotts Konzept des 'falschen Selbst'. *Psyche – Z Psychoanal*, 56(9/10), 839–862.

Fonagy, Peter & Target, Mary (2003). *Frühe Bindung und psychische Entwicklung: Beiträge aus Psychoanalyse und Bindungsforschung*. 1st ed. Giessen: Psychosozial-Verlag.

Fonagy, Peter & Target, Mary (2011). *Psychoanalyse und die Psychopathologie der Entwicklung*. 3rd ed. Stuttgart: Klett-Cotta.

Fosshage, James, L. (1992). Self-Psychology: The Self and its Vicissitudes within a Relational Matrix. In Neil J. Skolnick & Susan C. Warshaw (Eds.), *Relational Perspectives in Psychoanalysis* (pp. 21–42). Hillsdale, NJ: Analytic Press.

Fosshage, James L. (1997). Toward a Model of Psychoanalytic Supervision from a Self Psychological/Intersubjective Perspective. In M.H. Rock (Ed.), *Psychodynamic Supervision* (pp. 189–212). Northvale, NJ: Jason Aronson.

Foulkes, S.H. (2007). *Praxis der gruppenanalytischen Psychotherapie*. 2nd ed. Eschborn bei Frankfurt: Klotz.

Foulkes, S.H. (2017). *Gruppenanalytische Psychotherapie*. 4th ed. Hohenwarsleben: Westarp Verlagsservicegesellschaft mbH.

Franke, Guido (Ed.). (2008). *Komplexität und Kompetenz: Ausgewählte Fragen der Kompetenzforschung*. Bundesinstitut für Berufsbildung. Bielefeld: Bertelsmann.

Franke, Renate (2004). Wirth, H.-J. (2002). Narzissmus und Macht: Zur Psychoanalyse seelischer Störungen in der Politik. *Gruppendynamik*, 35(1), 105–109. doi:10.1007/s11612-004-0009-6.

Frawley-O'Dea, Mary Gail (1997). Who's Doing What To Whom? *Contemporary Psychoanalysis*, 33(1), 5–18.

Frawley-O'Dea, Mary Gail & Sarnat, Joan E. (2001). *The Supervisory Relationship: A contemporary psychodynamic approach*. New York: Guilford Press.

Freud, Anna (1951). Observations on Child Development. *The Psychoanalytic Study of the Child*, 6(1), 18–30.

Freud, Ernest W. (1976). Beobachtung frühkindlicher Entwicklungen. *Psyche*, 30(8), 723–743.

Freud, Sigmund (1927) [1925]. Some Psychological Consequences of the Anatomical Distinction between the Sexes. Translated by James Strachey. *International Journal of Psychoanalysis*, 8, pp. 133–142.

Freud, Sigmund (1933) [1910]. *"The Future Prospects of Psycho-Analytic Therapy" Sigmund Freud: Collected Papers, vol. II: Clinical Papers, Papers on Technique*. Transl. James Strachey. London: Hogarth.

Freud, Sigmund (1940a) [1938]. An Outline Of Psycho-Analysis. *International Journal of Psychoanalysis*, 21, 27–84.

Freud, Sigmund (1961a) [1927]. *The Future of an Illusion*. Translated by James Strachey. New York: W.W. Norton.

Freud, Sigmund (1961b) [1920g]. *Beyond the Pleasure Principle*. Translated by James Strachey. New York: Norton.

Freud, Sigmund (1962a) [1905e]. Fragment of an Analysis of a Case of Hysteria. In *The Standard Edition of the Complete Psychological Works of Sigmund Freud, Volume VII (1901–1905)*. Translated by James Strachey (pp. 1–122). London: Hogarth.

Freud, Sigmund (1962b) [1914]. Observations on Transference Love. In *The Standard Edition of the Complete Psychological Works of Sigmund Freud, Volume XII (1911–1913)*. Transl. James Strachey (pp. 157–171). London: Hogarth.

Freud, Sigmund (1962c) [1912]. Recommendations to Physicians Practising Psycho-Analysis. In *The Standard Edition of the Complete Psychological Works of Sigmund Freud, Volume XII (1911–1913): The Case of Schreber, Papers on Technique and Other Works* (pp. 109–120). London: Hogarth.

Freud, Sigmund (1997) [1914]. The Moses of Michelangelo. In *Writings on Art and Literature*. Translated by James Strachey (pp. 122–150). Stanford: Stanford University Press.

Freud, Sigmund (2004) [1930]. *Civilization and Its Discontents*. Translated by David McLintock. London: Penguin.

Frie, Roger (2015). Post-Cartesian Psychoanalysis and the Sociocultural Turn: From Cultural Contests to Hermeneutic Understanding. *Psychoanalytic Inquiry, Postmodernism and Psychoanalysis*, 35(6), 597–608.

Frie, Roger (2017). *Not in My Family: German Memory and Responsibility After the Holocaust*. Oxford: Oxford University Press.

Friedman, Robi (2015). Gruppenanalyse heute – Entwicklungen in der Intersubjektivität. In Wolfgang Martin Roth, Helga Felsberger, & Josef Shaked (Eds.), *Gruppenanalyse und die Entwicklung von Intersubjektivität* (pp. 15–22). 1st ed. Vienna: Facultas.

Fromm, Erich (1996). *Anatomie der menschlichen Destruktivität*. Reinbek bei Hamburg: Rowohlt.

Fromm, Erich (2005). *Haben oder Sein: Die seelischen Grundlagen einer neuen Gesellschaft*. 33rd ed. Munich: Deutscher Taschenbuch Verlag.

Fürst-Pfeifer, Gabriele (2013). *Biographie und (un)bewusste Berufswahlmotive von Psychotherapeuten*. Psychoanalytiker und systemische Familientherapeuten erzählen aus ihrem Leben. Münster: Waxmann. Zugl.: Vienna, Univ., Diss., 2012.

Gadamer, Hans-Georg (1990). *Hermeneutik I und II. Band I: Wahrheit und Methode. Grundzüge einer philosophischen Hermeneutik. Band II: Wahrheit und Methode. Ergänzungen, Register*. 6th ed. Tübingen: J.C.B Mohr – Paul Siebeck.

Gadamer, Hans-Georg (2010). *Gesammelte Werke. Band 1: Hermeneutik I: Wahrheit und Methode: Grundzüge einer philosophischen Hermeneutik*. 7th revised ed. Tübingen: Mohr Siebeck.

Gallese, Vittorio (2009). Mirror Neurons, Embodied Simulation, and the Neural Basis of Social Identification. *Psychoanalytic Dialogues*, 19(5), 519–536. doi:10.1080/10481880903231910.

Gallese, Vittorio, Eagle, Morris N., & Migone, Paolo (2007). Intentional Attunement: Mirror Neurons and the Neural Underpinnings of Interpersonal Relations. *Journal of the American Psychoanalytic Association*, 55(1), 131–176. doi:10.1177/00030651070550010601.

Gambaroff, Maria (2012). Zur Dynamik der Intersubjektivität im Supervisionsprozess. In Wolfgang Weigand & Michael B. Buchholz (Eds.), *Philosophie und Handwerk der Supervision* (pp. 35–52). Giessen: Psychosozial-Verlag.

Gazzaniga, Michael S. & Bizzi, Emilio (Eds.). (2000). *The New Cognitive Neurosciences*. 2nd ed. Cambridge, Mass.: MIT Press.

Geißler, Peter (2012). Prolog. In Peter Geißler (Ed.), *Stimme und Suggestion: Die 'musikalische Dimension' und ihre suggestive Kraft im psychotherapeutischen Geschehen* (pp. 11–57). Giessen: Psychosozial-Verlag.

Geißler, Peter, Sassenfeld, André J., & Buchholz, Michael B. (Eds.). (2013). *Jenseits von Sprache und Denken. Implizite Dimensionen im psychotherapeutischen Geschehen*. Giessen: Psychosozial-Verlag.

Gelernter, David (2012). Hausfrauen, Polizisten – jeder ist als Lehrer geeignet. *FAZ – Frankfurter allgemeine Zeitung*, Nr. 33, February 8, 2012, p. 5.
Gelo, Omar Carlo Gioacchino & Mergenthaler, Erhard (2012). Unconventional metaphors and emotional-cognitive regulation in a metacognitive interpersonal therapy. *Psychotherapy Research*, 22(2), 159–175. doi:10.1080/10503307.2011.629636.
Gelso, Charles J. (2009). The real relationship in a postmodern world: Theoretical and empirical explorations. *Psychotherapy Research*, 19(3), 253–264. doi:10.1080/10503300802389242.
Gergely, György (1998). Margaret Mahlers Entwicklungstheorie im Licht der jüngsten empirischen Erforschung der kindlichen Entwicklung. In Wilhelm Burian (Ed.), *Der beobachtete und der rekonstruierte Säugling* (pp. 91–118). Göttingen: Vandenhoeck & Ruprecht.
Gergely, György & Unoka, Zsolt (2011). Bindung und Mentalisierung beim Menschen. Die Entwicklung des affektiven Selbst. *Psyche – Z Psychoanal*, 65(09/10), 862–899.
Gergely, G. & Watson, John S. (1996) The social biofeedback theory of parental affect-mirroring: the development of emotional self-awareness and self-control in infancy. *International Journal of Psychoanalysis*, 77 (Pt 6):1181–1212. PMID: 9119582.
Ghent, Emmanuel (1989). Credo – The Dialectics of One-Person and Two-Person Psychologies. *Contemporary Psychoanalysis*, 25(2), 169–211.
Ghent, Emmanuel (1990). Masochism, Submission, Surrender – Masochism as a Peversion of Surrender. *Contemporary Psychoanalysis*, 26(1), 108–136.
Ghent, Emmanuel, Demos, Victoria, & Harris, Adrienne (Eds.). (2018). *The Collected Papers of Emmanuel Ghent: Heart Melts Forward*. London: Routledge.
Gill, Merton M. & Hoffman, Irwin Z. (1982). *Theory and Technique, vol 1*. New York: International University Press.
Glotz, Peter (1998). Bildungsziele für die Informationsgesellschaft. Heinrich-Böll-Stiftung. http://www. http://www.forschungsnetzwerk.at/downloadpub/1998_glotz_peter_bildungsziele.pdf (October 31, 2020).
Gödde, Günter & Zirfas, Jörg (Eds.). (2014). *Lebenskunst im 20. Jahrhundert: Stimmen von Philosophen, Künstlern und Therapeuten*. Paderborn: Fink.
Goffman, Erving (1961). *Asylums: Essays on the Social Situation of Mental Patients and Other Inmates*. Garden City, NY: Anchor Books Doubleday.
Goffman, Erving (1978). Response Cries. *Language*, 54(4), 787–815.
Goldner, Virginia (2011). Trans: Gender in Free Fall. *Psychoanalytic Dialogues*, 21(2), 159–171. doi:10.1080/10481885.2011.562836.
Goldner, Virginia (2014). Romantic Bonds, Binds, and Ruptures: Couples on the Brink. *Psychoanalytic Dialogues*, 24(4), 402–418. doi:10.1080/10481885.2014.932209.
Görnitz, Thomas & Görnitz, Brigitte (2016). *Von der Quantenphysik zum Bewusstsein: Kosmos, Geist und Materie*. Berlin: Springer.
Graf-Nold, Angela (1988). *Der Fall Hermine Hug-Hellmuth: eine Geschichte der frühen Kinder-Psychoanalyse*. Munich: Verlag Int. Psychoanalyse.
Grand, Sue (2018). The Other Within: White Shame, Native-American Genocide. *Contemporary Psychoanalysis*, 54(1), 84–102. doi:10.1080/00107530.2017.1415106.
Greenberg, Jay R. & Mitchell, Stephen A. (1983). *Object Relations in Psychoanalytic Theory*. Cambridge, Mass.: Harvard University Press.
Grossmann, Klaus E., Grossmann, Karin, Winter, Monika, & Zimmermann, Peter (2015). Bindungsbeziehungen und Bewertung von Partnerschaften. In Karl Heinz

Brisch (Ed.), *Bindung und seelische Entwicklungswege: Grundlagen, Prävention und klinische Praxis* (pp. 125–164). 3rd ed. Stuttgart: Klett-Cotta.
Grunenberg, Antonia (2016). König im Reich des Denkens – oder Fürst der Finsternis? Wie Hanna Arendt das Denken Martin Heideggers auseinandernahm. In Walter Homolka & Arnulf Heidegger (Eds.), *Heidegger und der Antisemitismus* (pp. 242–256). Freiburg: Herder.
Gruntz-Stoll, Johannes (Ed.). (2006). *Verwahrlost, beziehungsgestört, verhaltensoriginell. Zum Sprachwandel in der Heil- und Sonderpädagogik*. 1st ed. Berne: Haupt.
Guba, Egon G. & Lincoln, Yvonna S. (1989). *Fourth Generation Evaluation*. Newbury Park, Ca.: Sage Publications.
Günther, Johann & Hüffel, Clemens (1999). Massenmedien in unserer Gesellschaft: Zahlen – Daten – Fakten. Edition Donau-Universität Krems. http://www.eduhi.at/dl/03tel_01.pdf (June 17, 2014).
Gysling, Andrea (2009). *Die analytische Antwort: Eine Geschichte der Gegenübertragung in Form von Autorenportraits*. Giessen: Psychosozial-Verlag.
Habermas, Jürgen (2008). *Between Naturalism and Religion: Philosophical Essays: Philosophical Essays*. London: Polity.
Hajek, Gisela (2019). Persönliches wird beruflich: Selbsterfahrung in der Pflege. *Pflege Professionell – Das Fachmagazin*, 27/2019, 53–62.
Ham, Jacob & Tronick, Ed (2009). Relational psychophysiology: lessons from mother-infant physiology research on dyadically expanded states of consciousness. *Psychotherapy Research*, 19(6), 619–632. doi:10.1080/10503300802609672.
Hansbury, Griffin (2005). The Middle Men: An Introduction to the Transmasculine Identities. *Studies in Gender and Sexuality*, 6(3), 241–264. doi:10.1080/15240650609349276.
Hansbury, Griffin (2011). King Kong & Goldilocks: Imagining Transmasculinities Through the Trans–Trans Dyad. *Psychoanalytic Dialogues*, 21(2), 210–220. doi:10.1080/10481885.2011.562846.
Hansbury, Griffin (2017). King Kong und die Goldglöckchen: Transmännlichkeiten vor dem Hintergrund der Trans-Trans-Dyade. In Esther Hutfless & Barbara Zach (Eds.), *Queering psychoanalysis. Psychoanalyse und Queer Theory: transdisziplinäre Verschränkungen* (pp. 559–587). 1st ed. Vienna: Zaglossus.
Hare, Brian, Call, Josep, & Tomasello, Michael (2001). Do chimpanzees know what conspecifics know? *Animal Behavior*, 61(1), 139–151. doi:10.1006/anbe.2000.1518.
Harris, Adrienne (2000). Gender as a Soft Assembly: Tomboys' Stories. *Studies in Gender and Sexuality*, 1(3), 223–250.
Harris, Adrienne (2004). *Gender as a Soft Assembly*. Hoboken: Taylor & Francis.
Harris, Adrienne (2009). 'You Must Remember This'. *Psychoanalytic Dialogues*, 19(1), 2–21. doi:10.1080/10481880802634537.
Harris, Adrienne (2012). The House of Difference, or White Silence. *Studies in Gender and Sexuality*, 13(3), 197–216.
Harris, Adrienne (2018). The Relational Tradition: Landscape and Canon. In Roy E. Barsness (Ed.), *Core Competencies of Relational Psychoanalysis: A Guide to Practice, Study and Research* (pp. 43–64). New York: Routledge.
Harris, Adrienne & Sinsheimer, Kathy (2008). The Analyst's Vulnerability: Preserving and Fine-Tuning Analytic Bodies. In Frances Sommer Anderson (Ed.), *Bodies in Treatment: The Unspoken Dimension* (pp. 255–274). London: Analytic Press.

Harris, Martha (1977). The Tavistock Training and Philosophy. In Martha Harris & Esther Bick (1987). *Collected Papers of Martha Harris and Esther Bick* (259–282). Perthshire: Cluni Press for Roland Harris Trust.

Harris, Martha & Bick, Esther (1987). *Collected Papers of Martha Harris and Esther Bick*. Perthshire: Cluni Press for Roland Harris Trust.

Harris, Martha & Bick, Esther (2011). *The Tavistock Model: Papers on Child Development and Psychoanalytic Training*. Edited by Meg Harris Williams. London: Karnac Books.

Hartland-Rowe, Lydia (2005). Teaching and observing in work discussion. *Infant Observation International Journal of Infant Observation and Its Applications*, 8(1), 93–102.

Haslam-Hopwood, G. Tobias G., Allen, Jon G., Stein, April, & Bleiberg, Efrain (2009). Verbesserung des Mentalisierens durch Psychoedukation. In Jon G. Allen (Ed.), *Mentalisierungsgestützte Therapie. Das MBT-Handbuch – Konzepte und Praxis* (pp. 347–372). Stuttgart: Klett-Cotta.

Hattie, John A.C. (2009). *Visible Learning: a Synthesis of Meta-Analyses Relating to Achievement*. London: Routledge.

Haubl, Rolf & Hausinger, Brigitte (Eds.). (2009). *Supervisionsforschung: Einblicke und Ausblicke*. Göttingen: Vandenhoeck & Ruprecht.

Häussler, Gabriele & Aulbert, Petra (Eds.). (2015). *Psychoanalytische Säuglingsbeobachtung und Säuglings-Kleinkind-Eltern-Psychotherapie*. Frankfurt a.M: Brandes & Apsel.

Hayes, Jeffrey A. (2004). The inner world of the psychotherapist: A program of research on countertransference. *Psychotherapy Research*, 14(1), 21–36. doi:10.1093/ptr/kph002.

Hayes, Jeffrey A., Gelso, Charles J., & Hummel, Ann M. (2011). Managing countertransference. *Psychotherapy*, 48(1), 88–97. doi:10.1037/a0022182.

Heidegger, Martin (2018). *Zollikoner Seminare: Gesamtausgabe. IV. Abteilung: Hinweise und Aufzeichnungen. Band 89*. Edited by Peter Trawny. Frankfurt: Vittorio Klostermann.

Heisenberg, Werner (2011). *Physik und Philosophie*. 8th ed. Stuttgart: Hirzel.

Hell, Daniel (1982). The spouses of depressive and schizophrenic patients. A controlled study. *Archiv für Psychiatrie und Nervenkrankheiten*, 232(2), 167–178.

Hill, Clara E. & Knox, Sarah (2013). Training in Psychotherapy. In Michael J. Lambert (Ed.), *Bergin and Garfield's Handbook of Psychotherapy and Behavior Change* (pp. 775–812). 6th ed. Hoboken, New Jersey: Wiley.

Hinshelwood, Robert D. & Skogstad, Wilhelm (2006). Zur psychosozialen Dynamik in Einrichtungen des Gesundheitswesens. *Freie Assoziation*, 9(2), 29–45.

Hirblinger, Heiner (2011). *Unterrichtskultur*. Giessen: Psychosozial-Verlag.

Hirsch, Mathias (Ed.). (2010). *Die Gruppe als Container: Mentalisierung und Symbolisierung in der analytischen Gruppenpsychotherapie*. 2nd ed. Göttingen: Vandenhoeck & Ruprecht.

Hirsch, Irwin (1994). Countertransference love and theoretical model. *Psychoanalytic Dialogues*, 4(2), 171–192. doi:10.1080/10481889409539012.

Hirschmüller, Barbara (2015). Von der Säuglingsbeobachtung zur analytischen Psychotherapie von Müttern mit Säuglingen und sehr kleinen Kindern. In Gabriele Häussler & Petra Aulbert (Eds.), *Psychoanalytische Säuglingsbeobachtung und Säuglings-Kleinkind-Eltern-Psychotherapie*. Frankfurt: Brandes & Apsel.

Hochschulrektorenkonferenz (Ed.). (1999). Viel Lärm um nichts? Evaluation von Studium und Lehre und ihre Folgen. Beiträge zur Tagung an der Universität Rostock vom 6. bis 8. September 1998. https://arbeitsblaetter.stangl-taller.at/FEEDBACK/FEEDBACK-MATERIAL/1999-04_Viel_Laerm_um__nichts.pdf (March 21, 2015).

Hofer, Peter (2014). *Krisenbewältigung und Ressourcenentwicklung*. Wiesbaden: Springer VS.

Hoffman, Irwin Z. (1994). Dialectical thinking and therapeutic action in the psychoanalytic process. *Psychoanalytic Quarterly*, 63(2), 187–218.

Hoffman, Irwin Z. (1998). *Ritual and Spontaneity in the Psychoanalytic Process: A Dialectical-Constructivist View*. Hoboken: Taylor & Francis.

Hoffman, Irwin Z. (2009). Therapeutic passion in the countertransference. *Psychoanalytic Dialogues*, 19(5), 617–637.

Hollmann, Laurie (2010). The impact of observation on the evolution of a relationship between an at-risk mother and infant. *Infant Observation International Journal of Infant Observation and Its Applications*, 13(3), 325–338.

Holmes, Jeremy (2005). Notes on Mentalizing – Old Hat, or New Wine? *Britisch Journal of Psychiatry*, 22(2), 179–198. doi:10.1111/j.1752-0118.2005.tb00275.x.

Hörster, Reinhard, Köngeter, Stefan, & Müller, Burkhard (Eds.). (2013). *Grenzobjekte: Soziale Welten und ihre Übergänge*. Wiesbaden: Springer VS.

Huber, Wolfgang (1977). *Psychoanalyse in Österreich seit 1933*. Vienna: Geyer-Edition.

Hug, Theo, Poscheschnik, Gerald, & Lederer, Bernd (2010). *Empirisch forschen: Die Planung und Umsetzung von Projekten im Studium*. 1st ed. Konstanz: UVK-Verlagsgesellschaft.

Hug-Hellmuth, Hermine (1919). *Tagebuch eines halbwüchsigen Mädchens*. Leipzig: Internationaler Psychoanalytischer Verlag.

Hutfless, Esther & Zach, Barbara (Eds.). (2017). *Queering psychoanalysis: Psychoanalyse und Queer Theory: transdisziplinäre Verschränkungen*. 1st ed. Vienna: Zaglossus.

Iacoboni, Marco (2009). *Woher wir wissen, was andere denken und fühlen: Die neue Wissenschaft der Spiegelneuronen*. 1st ed. Munich: Deutsche Verlags-Anstalt.

Israel, Agathe (2007). Der Einfluss der Säuglingsbeobachtung nach Esther Bick auf die Grundhaltung des Therapeuten und die psychoanalytische Säuglings-Kleinkind-Eltern-Psychotherapie. In Agathe Israel (Ed.), *Der Säugling und seine Eltern. Die psychoanalytische Behandlung frühester Entwicklungsstörungen* (pp. 37–42). 1st ed. Frankfurt: Brandes & Apsel.

Israel, Agathe (2015). Das Besondere in der psychoanalytischen Säuglings-Kleinkind-Eltern-Psychotherapie. In Gabriele Häußler (Ed.), *Psychoanalytische Säuglingsbeobachtung und Säuglings-Kleinkind-Eltern-Psychotherapie* (pp. 187–202). Frankfurt: Brandes & Apsel.

Israel, Agathe & Reißmann, Björn (2008). *Früh in der Welt: Das Erleben des Frühgeborenen und seiner Eltern auf der neonatologischen Intensivstation*. 1st ed. Frankfurt a.M: Brandes & Apsel.

Jacobs, Theodore J. (1983). The analyst and the patient's object world: Notes on an aspect of countertransference. *Journal of the American Psychoanalytic Association*, 31(3), 619–642. doi:10.1177/000306518303100303.

Jacobs, Theodore J. (1986). On Countertransference Enactments. *Journal of the American Psychoanalytic Association*, 34(2), 289–307.

Jaenicke, Chris (2006). *Das Risiko der Verbundenheit – Intersubjektivitätstheorie in der Praxis*. Stuttgart: Klett-Cotta.

Jaenicke, Chris (2010). *Veränderung in der Psychoanalyse: Selbstreflexionen des Analytikers in der therapeutischen Beziehung*. Stuttgart: Klett-Cotta.

Jaenicke, Chris (2014). *Die Suche nach Bezogenheit: Eine intersubjektiv-systemische Sicht*. Frankfurt: Brandes & Apsel.

Juen, Florian & Fizke, Ella (2010). Mentalisierung in der Kindheit: Entwicklung und klinische Erfassung in frühen Lebensjahren. *Psychodynamische Psychotherapie*, 9 (4), 223–234.

Jurist, Elliot (2020). *Minding Emotions: Cultivating Mentalization in Psychotherapy*. New York: Guilford Press.

Kabadayi, Can & Osvath, Mathias (2017). Ravens parallel great apes in flexible planning for tool-use and bartering. *Science* 357(6347), 202–204. doi:10.1126/science.aam8138.

Kächele, Horst (2010). Klinische Überzeugung und empirische Belege. In Karsten Münch & Michael B. Buchholz (Eds.), *Die Psychoanalyse im Pluralismus der Wissenschaften* (pp. 13–32). Giessen: Psychosozial-Verlag.

Kahl-Popp, Jutta (2001). Familienbeobachtung in der psychoanalytischen Ausbildung: Das Kieler Modell. *Forum der Psychoanalyse*, 17, 175–193.

Kahl-Popp, Jutta (2004). Lernziel – Kontextbezogene psychotherapeutische Kompetenz: Einige Gedanken zur psychoanalytischen Ausbildung. *Forum der Psychoanalyse*, 20(4), 403–418.

Kahl-Popp, Jutta (2007). *Lernen und Lehren psychotherapeutischer Kompetenz am Beispiel der psychoanalytischen Ausbildung*. Würzburg: Ergon-Verlag. Zugl.: Kiel, Univ., Diss., 2006.

Kahl-Popp Jutta (2009). Die interne Seite psychotherapeutischer Kompetenz. *Psychodynamische Psychotherapie, Forum der tiefenpsychologisch fundierten Psychotherapie*, 8(3), 115–123.

Kahl-Popp, Jutta (2011). Forschen – Lernen – Heilen: Zur Entwicklung psychotherapeutischer Kompetenz, Implikationen für die Ausbildung. *Analytische Kinder- und Jugendlichen Psychotherapie (AKJP)*, 1/2011, 116–133.

Kahl-Popp, Jutta (2015). *Das Gefühl, Gestalt anzunehmen: Zur Subjektivität in der Psychotherapieausbildung*. 1st ed. Frankfurt: Brandes & Apsel.

Kamenetz, Anya (2009). How Web-Savvy Edupunks are Transforming American Higher Education. http://www.fastcompany.com/1325728/how-web-savvy-edupunks-are-transforming-american-higher-education (May 17, 2014).

Kamenetz, Anya (2011). The Edupunks' Guide to a DIY Credential. http://www.google.at/url?sa=t&rct=j&q=&esrc=s&source=web&cd=3&ved=0CC4QFjAC&url=http%3A%2F%2Fwww.smashwords.com%2Fbooks%2Fdownload%2F77938%2F1%2Flatest%2F0%2F0%2Fthe-edupunks-guide-to-a-diy-credential.pdf&ei=-CWYU4K0A4b8OeeNgYAO&usg=AFQjCNGu97P2dlOSubPlzBHbIUTWVUWRAw, (June 11, 2014).

Kaminski, Juliane, Neumann, Martina, Bräuer, Juliane, Call, Josep, & Tomasello, Michael (2011). Dogs, Canis familiaris, communicate with humans to request but not to inform. *Animal Behaviour*, 82, 651–658 doi:10.1016/j.anbehave.2011.06.015.

Kannewischer, Sybille, Kolb, Bettina, & Hopfinger, Gabriela (Eds.). (2004). *Verhalten als subjektiv-sinnhafte Ausdrucksform*. Bad Heilbrunn: Klinkhardt.

Kantrowitz, Judy L. (1997). A Different Perspective on the Therapeutic Process: The Impact Of The Patient on the Analyst. *Journal of the American Psychoanalytic Association*, 45(1), 127–153.

Kantrowitz, Judy L. (2004). A different perspective on the therapeutic process: the impact of the patient on the analyst. In Dēmētrēs Anastasopoulos & Evagelos Papanicolaou (Eds.), *The Therapist at Work: Personal Factors Affecting the Analytic Process* (pp. 17–42). London: Karnac.

Keats, John (1795–1821). http://www.keatsian.co.uk/negative-capability.php (May 10, 2020).

Kellermann, Nathan P.F. (2010). Christian Pross, Verletzte Helfer. Umgang mit dem Trauma: Risiken und Möglichkeiten sich zu schützen. Leben Lernen – Klett-Cotta, Stuttgart 2009. 288p. ISBN: 978-3-608-89090-7. *Intervention,* 8(3), 280–284. doi:10.1097/WTF.0b013e328341342b.

Kernberg, Otto Friedmann (1996). Thirty methods to destroy the creativity of psychoanalytic candidates. *The International Journal of Psycho-analysis,* 77(5), 1031–1040.

Kernberg, Otto Friedmann (2000). *Ideologie, Konflikt und Führung: Psychoanalyse von Gruppenprozessen und Persönlichkeitsstruktur*. 1st ed. Stuttgart: Klett-Cotta.

Kernberg, Otto Friedmann (Ed.). (2009). *WIR: Psychotherapeuten über sich und ihren 'unmöglichen' Beruf.*

Kernberg, Otto Friedmann (2011a). Divergent contemporary trends in psychoanalytic theory. *Psychoanalytic Review,* 98(5), 633–664. doi:10.1521/prev.2011.98.6.633.

Kernberg, Otto Friedmann (2011b). Mentalisierung, Empathie, Achtsamkeit und Introspektion – ein Vergleich. In Birger Dulz, Sabine Herpertz, Otto F. Kernberg & Ulrich Sachsse (Eds.), *Handbuch der Borderline-Störungen* (pp. 825–835). 2nd ed. Stuttgart: Schattauer.

Kernberg, Otto Friedmann (2014). *Liebe und Aggression: Eine unzertrennliche Beziehung*. 1st ed. Schattauer.

Kernberg, Otto Friedmann (2016). *Psychoanalytic Education at the Crossroads: Reformation, Change and the Future of Psychoanalytic Training*. London: Routledge.

Kernberg, Otto Friedmann (2017). Psychoanalytic Supervision: The Supervisor's Tasks. *The Psychoanalytic Quarterly,* 79(3), 603–627. doi:10.1002/j.2167-4086.2010.tb00459.x.

Kiefer, Ferenc (2005). https://www.universalis.fr/encyclopedie/ivan-fonagy (January 2, 2018).

Kirsch, Holger, Brockmann, Josef, Taubner, Svenja, & Bateman, Anthony W. (2016). *Praxis des Mentalisierens*. Stuttgart: Klett-Cotta.

Klauber, Trudy (2008). Foreword. In Margaret Rustin, Jonathan Bradley, & Trudy Klauber (Eds.), *Work Discussion: Learning from Reflective Practice in Work with Children and Families* (pp. ixi–xxii). London: Karnac.

Kleemann, Frank, Krähnke, Uwe, & Matuschek, Ingo (2013). *Interpretative Sozialforschung: Eine Einführung in die Praxis des Interpretierens*. 2nd ed. Wiesbaden: Springer.

Klein, Robert H., Bernard, Harold S., & Schermer, Victor L. (Eds.). (2011). *On Becoming a Psychotherapist: The Personal and Professional Journey*. Oxford: Oxford University Press.

Kleinschnitger, J. & Meyer, A. (1977). *Selbstbewertung und soziale Situation Giessener Obdachloser*. Dissertation (Psychology). Justus-Liebig-Universität Giessen.

Klöpper, Michael (2014). *Reifung und Konflikt: Säuglingsforschung, Bindungstheorie und Mentalisierungskonzept in der tiefenpsychologischen Psychotherapie*. 2nd ed. Stuttgart: Klett-Cotta.

Knoblauch, Steven (2018). Core Competency Five: Patterning and Linking. In Roy E. Barsness (Ed.), *Core Competencies of Relational Psychoanalysis: A Guide to Practice, Study and Research* (pp. 142–157). New York: Routledge.

Knott, Maria (2017). Alle denken an das Baby. *Psyche*, 71(2), 151–154. doi:10.21706/ps-71-2-151.

Köhler-Weisker, Angela (1980). Teilnehmende Beobachtung der frühen Kindheit in der psychoanalytischen Ausbildung. *Psyche*, 34(7), 625–651.

Kohut, Heinz (1984). *How Does Analysis Cure?*2nd ed. Chicago: University of Chicago Press.

Kondo, Makiko (Ed.). (2017). *Empathy – An Evidence-based Interdisciplinary Perspective*. Rijeka, Croatia: InTechOpen.

Kop, Rita (2007). Blogs and wikis as disruptive technologies. Is it time for a new pedagogy? In Michael Osborne, Muir Houston, & Nuala Toman (Eds.), *The Pedagogy of Lifelong Learning: Understanding Effective Teaching and Learning in Diverse Contexts* (pp. 192–202). London: Routledge.

Krause, Rainer (2005). Das Gegenwartsbewusste als kleinster gemeinsamer Nenner aller Techniken – Integration und Differenzierung als Zukunft der Pychotherapie. In Gerald Poscheschnik (Ed.), *Empirische Forschung in der Psychoanalyse: Grundlagen – Anwendungen – Ergebnisse* (pp. 239–256). Giessen: Psychosozial-Verlag.

Krüger, Reinhard T. (2015). *Störungsspezifische Psychodramatherapie: Theorie und Praxis*. Göttingen: Vandenhoeck & Ruprecht.

Kubik, Gerhard (1987). *Nyau: Maskenbünde im südl. Mala⊠i*. Vienna: Verlag der Österreichischen Akademie der Wissenschaften.

Kubik, Gerhard (2003). *Zur ontogenetischen Basis der Inzestscheu: Ein kulturvergleichender Ansatz*. Münster: LIT.

Kubik, Gerhard (2004). *Totemismus: Ethnopsychologische Forschungsmaterialien und Interpretationen aus Ost- und Zentralafrika 1962–2002*. Hamburg: LIT.

Kubik, Gerhard (2007). *Tabu: Erkundungen transkultureller Psychoanalyse in Afrika, Europa und anderen Kulturgebieten*. Vienna: LIT.

Küchenhoff, Joachim (2004). The analyst's clinical theory and its impact on the analytic process in psychoanalytic psychotherapy. In Dēmētrēs Anastasopoulos & Evagelos Papanicolaou (Eds.), *The Therapist at Work: Personal Factors Affecting the Analytic Process* (pp. 1–16). London: Karnac.

Kunzke, Dieter (2011). Grundlegende Merkmale interpersonaler, intersubjektiver und relationaler Ansätze als Ausdruck aktueller Entwicklungstendenzen in der Psychoanalyse. *Psyche – Z Psychoanal*, 65(7), 577–616.

Kuriloff, Emily A. (2014). *Contemporary Psychoanalysis and the Legacy of the Third Reich: History, Memory, Tradition*. New York: Routledge.

Lachmann, Frank M. (2003). Supervision: The Devil Is in the Details. *Psychoanalytic Dialogues*, 13(3), 341–353. doi:10.1080/10481881309348738.

Lachmann, Frank M. (2004). *Aggression verstehen und verändern: Psychotherapeutischer Umgang mit destruktiven Selbstzuständen*. Stuttgart: Pfeiffer bei Klett-Cotta.

Lackinger, Fritz (2008). Zur Dynamik von Perversion und Übertragung. In Fritz Lackinger & Wolfgang Berner (Eds.), *Psychodynamische Psychotherapie bei Delinquenz: Praxis der übertragungsfokussierten Psychotherapie* (pp. 197–217). Stuttgart: Schattauer.

Lackinger, Fritz & Berner, Wolfgang (Eds.). (2008). *Psychodynamische Psychotherapie bei Delinquenz: Praxis der übertragungsfokussierten Psychotherapie*. Stuttgart: Schattauer.

Lakoff, George & Johnson, Mark (2003). *Metaphors We Live By*. Chicago: University of Chicago Press.
Lakoff, George & Johnson, Mark (2014). *Leben in Metaphern: Konstruktion und Gebrauch von Sprachbildern*. 8th ed. Heidelberg: Carl-Auer Verlag.
Lambert, Michael J. (Ed.). (2013). *Bergin and Garfield's Handbook of Psychotherapy and Behavior Change*. 6th ed. Wiley.
Laplanche, Jean (1991). *New Foundations for Psychoanalysis*. London: Blackwell.
Layton, Lynne (2006). Racial Identities, Racial Enactments, and Normative Unconscious Processes. *The Psychoanalytic Quarterly*, 75(1), 237–269.
Lazar, Ross A. (2000). Erforschen und Erfahren: Teilnehmende Säuglingsbeobachtung 'Empathietraining' oder empirische Forschungsmethode? *Analytische Kinder- und Jugendlichen-Psychotherapie (AKJP) Zeitschrift für Theorie und Praxis der Kinder- und Jugendlichen-Psychoanalyse*, 31(108), 399–417.
Lazar, Ross A. (2009). Vom Kinderzimmer zum Konferenzraum. Die Beobachtungsmethode von Esther Bick und ihre Anwendungen. In Gertraud Diem-Wille (Ed.), *Ein-Blicke in die Tiefe: Die Methode der psychoanalytischen Säuglingsbeobachtung und ihre Anwendungen* (pp. 201–214). Stuttgart: Klett-Cotta.
Lazar, Ross A., Lehmann, Nora, & Häußlinger, Gabriele (1986). Die psychoanalytische Beobachtung von Babys innerhalb der Familie. In Jochen Stork (Ed.), *Zur Psychologie und Psychopathologie des Säuglings – neue Ergebnisse in der psychoanalytischen Reflexion. 3. Symposium in der Poliklinik für Kinder- und Jugendpsychotherapie der Technischen Universität Munich* (pp. 185–211). Stuttgart: Frommann-holzboog.
Lear, Jonathan (2003). *Therapeutic Action: An Earnest Plea for Irony*. London: Other Press.
Lehner, Barbara & Sengschmied, Irmtraud (2009). 'Oliver wendet sich von seiner Mutter ab': Lernerfahrungen einer Babybeobachterin vom Wegschauen bis hin zur Reflexion von bedrohlichen Erlebnisinhalten. In Gertraud Diem-Wille (Ed.), *Ein-Blicke in die Tiefe: Die Methode der psychoanalytischen Säuglingsbeobachtung und ihre Anwendungen* (pp. 119–135). Stuttgart: Klett-Cotta.
Leithner-Dziubas, Katharina, Schuster, Peter, & Springer-Kremser, Marianne (Eds.). (2008). *Borderline-Störungen*. Vienna: Facultas.
Leonhardt, Henrike, (2017). 9. September 1924 – Kinderpsychologin Hugh-Hellmuth ermordet [Radio essay] http://www.br.de/radio/bayern2/wissen/kalenderblatt/hug-hellmuth100.html (April 13, 2017).
Leslie, Alan M. (1987). Pretense and representation. The origins of 'theory of mind'. *Psychological Review*, 94(4), 412–426. doi:10.1037/0033-295X.94.4.412.
Leslie, Alan M. (2000). "Theory of Mind" as a Mechanism of Selective Attention. In Michael S. Gazzaniga & Emilio Bizzi (Eds.), *The New Cognitive Neurosciences* (pp. 1235–1248). 2nd ed. Cambridge, Mass.: The MIT Press.
Levenson, Edgar A. (2006). Response to John Steiner. *International Journal of Psychoanalysis*, 87(2), 321–324.
Lévinas, Emmanuel (Ed.). (2012). *Die Spur des Anderen. Untersuchungen zur Phänomenologie und Sozialphilosophie*. 6th ed. Freiburg i.Br.: Alber.
Lévinas, Emmanuel (1969). *Totality and Infinity: An Essay on Exteriority*. Pittsburgh: Duquesne University Press.
Levinson, S. (2006). Cognition at the heart of human interaction. *Discourse Studies*, 8 (1), 85–93. doi:10.1177/1461445606059557.
Levold, Tom (2004). Therapeutenpersönlichkeit zwischen Rolle und Identität. *Systemagazin*, 18(1), 41–51.

Lewis, Paul (2003). Emmanuel Ghent, 77, Composer, Innovator and Psychoanalyst. *The New York Times*, April 13, Section A, p. 36.

Lichtenberg, Joseph D. (1990). Einige Parallelen zwischen den Ergebnissen der Säuglingsbeobachtung und klinischen Beobachtungen an Erwachsenen, besonders Borderline-Patienten und Patienten mit narzißtischen Persönlichkeitsstörung. *Psyche*, 44(10), 871–901.

Lichtenberg, Joseph D., Lachmann, Frank M., & Fosshage, James L. (2017). *Das Selbst und die motivationalen Systeme: Zu einer Theorie psychoanalytischer Technik*. 2nd revised ed. Frankfurt: Brandes & Apsel.

Lieberman, Matthew D. (2007). Social Cognitive Neuroscience: A Review of Core Processes. *Ann Rev Psychol*, 58, 259–289.

Loewald, Hans W. (1986). *Psychoanalyse: Aufsätze aus den Jahren 1951–1979*. Stuttgart: Klett-Cotta.

Loganbill, Carol, Hardy, Emily, & Delworth, Ursula (1982). Supervision: A Conceptual Model. *The Counseling Psychologist*, 10(1), 3–42. doi:10.1177/001100008210100 2.

Lohmer, Mathias (2004). *Psychodynamische Organisationsberatung: Konflikte und Potentiale in Veränderungsprozessen*. 2nd ed. Stuttgart: Klett-Cotta.

Lohmer, Mathias (2017). Ein Wirkmodell der Supervision. In Heide Möller & Mathias Lohmer (Eds.), *Supervision in der Psychotherapie: Grundlagen – Forschung – Praxis* (pp. 21–33). Stuttgart: Kohlhammer.

Lorenz, Konrad (1935). Der Kumpan in der Umwelt des Vogels: Der Artgenosse als auslösendes Moment sozialer Verhaltensweisen. *Journal für Ornithologie*, 83(2), 137–213.

Löwer-Hirsch, Marga (2001). Intersubjektivität und Supervision. In Bernd Oberhoff & Ullrich Beumer (Eds.), *Theorie und Praxis psychoanalytischer Supervision* (pp. 16–45). Münster: Votum.

Ludwig-Körner, Christiane (2008). Psychoanalyse und Frühpädagogik. *Psyche*, 62(2), 171–181.

Ludwig-Körner, Christine (2012–2013). Kindergruppen beforschen in Kindertagesstätten. IPU. www.ipu-berlin.de/hochschule/forschung/projekt/foerderung-der-eltern-kind-beziehung (April 12, 2014).

Ludwig-Körner, Christiane (2015). Und wer denkt an das Baby? Überlegungen zur Methodik der Säuglingsbeobachtung. *Psyche*, 69(12), 1162–1184.

Ludwig-Körner, Christiane (2017). Infant Observation nutzt dem Beobachter, nicht dem Säugling. *Psyche*, 71(3), 260–262. doi:10.21706/ps-71-3-260.

Luif, Ingeborg (Ed.). (1997). *Supervision: Tradition, Ansätze und Perspektiven in Österreich*. Vienna: Orac.

Luyten, Patrick & Fonagy, Peter. (2019). Mentalizing and Trauma. In Anthony W. Bateman & Peter Fonagy (Eds.), *Handbook of Mentalizing* (pp. 79–102). Washington, DC: American Psychiatric Publishing.

Luyten, Patrick, Malcorps, Saskia, Fonagy, Peter, & Ensink, Karin. (2019). Assessment of Mentalizing. In Anthony W. Bateman & Peter Fonagy (Eds.). *Handbook of Mentalizing* (pp. 37–62). Washington, DC: American Psychiatric Publishing.

Maiello, Suzanne (2015). Säuglingsbeobachtung als Lernerfahrung in der psychoanalytischen Ausbildung: Der Beobachter in der Position des Dritten und die Begegnung mit dem inneren Kind. In Gabriele Häussler & Petra Aulbert (Eds.), *Psychoanalytische Säuglingsbeobachtung und Säuglings-Kleinkind-Eltern-Psychotherapie* (pp. 51–64). Frankfurt: Brandes & Apsel.

Majce-Egger, Maria (Ed.). (1999). *Gruppentherapie und Gruppendynamik – dynamische Gruppenpsychotherapie: Theoretische Grundlagen, Entwicklungen und Methoden*. Vienna: Facultas.

Makari, George (2010). *Revolution in Mind: The Creation of Psychoanalysis*. London: Duckworth Overlook.

Markowitsch, Jörg, Messerer, Karin, & Prokopp, Monika (Eds.). (2004). *Handbuch praxisorientierter Hochschulbildung*. Vienna: WUV-Univ.-Verl.

Maroda, Karen J. (1998). Enactment: When the patient's and analyst's pasts converge. *Psychoanalytic Psychology*, 15(4), 517–535. doi:10.1037//0736-9735.15.4.517.

Maroda, Karen J. (2010). *Psychodynamic Techniques: Working with Emotion in the Therapeutic Relationship*. New York, NY: Guildford Press.

Maroda, Karen J. (2018). Core Competency Six: Repetition and Working Through. In Roy E. Barsness (Ed.), *Core Competencies of Relational Psychoanalysis: A Guide to Practice, Study and Research* (pp. 158–178). New York: Routledge.

Marty, Pierre (1968). A Major Process of Somatization: The Progressive Disorganization. *The International Journal of Psychoanalysis*, 49, 246–249.

Marty, Pierre (1980). *L'ordre psychosomatique*. Paris: Payot.

Marty, Pierre (1990). *Mentalisation et psychosomatique*. 6th ed. Paris: Laboratoires Delagrange Presses Universitaires de France.

Mauz, A. (2005). Neukom, M. Robert Walsers Mikrogramm 'Beiden klopfte das Herz'. Eine pychoanalytisch orientierte Erzähltextanalyse. Giessen: Imago Psychosozial, 2003, 274 pp. *Zeitschrift für psychoanalytische Theorie und Praxis*, 20(1–2),162–172. doi:10.15534/ZPTP/2005/1-2/15.

McWilliams, Nancy (2004). *Psychoanalytic Psychotherapy: A Practitioner's Guide*. New York: Guilford Publications.

McWilliams, Nancy (2018). Core Competency Two: Therapeutic Stance/Attitude. In Roy E. Barsness (Ed.), *Core Competencies of Relational Psychoanalysis: A Guide to Practice, Study and Research* (pp. 87–103). New York: Routledge.

Merkator, Nadine & Welger, Andrea (2013). Neue Formen der Qualitätssicherung – dialogische Evaluation in Lehre und Studium. *Zeitschrift für Hochschulentwicklung*, 8(2), 167–174.

Mertens, Wolfgang (2011). *Psychoanalytische Schulen im Gespräch, vol 2: Selbstpsychologie, Post-Selbstpsychologie, relationale und intersubjektive Kritik*. 1st ed. Berne: Huber.

Mertens, Wolfgang & Hamburger, Andreas (Eds.). (2017). *Supervision in der Ausbildung*. 1st ed. Stuttgart: Kohlhammer.

Merzenich, Michael M. (2013). *Soft-Wired: How the New Science of Brain Plasticity Can Change your Life*. San Francisco: Parnassus.

Messerer, Karin (2004). Work paper discussion (work discussion, work-study seminar). In Jörg Markowitsch, Karin Messerer, & Monika Prokopp (Eds.), *Handbuch praxisorientierter Hochschulbildung* (pp. 141–148). Vienna: WUV.

Messerer, Karin (2008). Erwerb heilpädagogischer Kompetenz durch Beobachtung und Reflexion: Ein Beispiel aus der Ausbildung von Frühförderinnen. *Heilpädagogik – Fachzeitschrift der Heilpädagogischen Gesellschaft Österreich*, 51(5), 2–7.

Meyer, John W. & Ramirez, Francisco O. (2005). Die globale Institutionalisierung der Bildung. In Georg Krücken (Ed.), *Weltkultur: Wie die westlichen Prinzipien die Welt durchdringen* (pp. 212–234). Frankfurt: Suhrkamp.

Midgley, Nick, Muller, Nicole, Malberg, Norka, Lindqvist, Karin, & Ensink, Karin (2019). Children. In Anthony W. Bateman & Peter Fonagy (Eds.), *Handbook of Mentalizing* (pp. 247–264). Washington, DC: American Psychiatric Publishing.

Miller, Alice (2008). *The Drama of the Gifted Child: The Search for the True Self*. New York: Basic Books.

Mills, Jon (2018a). Challenging Relational Psychoanalysis: A Reply to My Critics. *Psychoanalytic Perspectives*, 15(1), 2–9. doi:10.1080/1551806X.2018.1396114.

Mills, Jon (2018b). Critique of Relational Psychoanalysis. In Roy E. Barsness (Ed.), *Core Competencies of Relational Psychoanalysis: A Guide to Practice, Study and Research* (pp. 321–341). New York: Routledge.

Mitchell, Stephen A. (1981a). The psychoanalytic treatment of homosexuality: Some technical considerations. *International Review of Psychoanalysis*, 8, 63–80.

Mitchell, Stephen A. (1981b). Psychodynamics, homosexuality, and the question of pathology. *Journal of Interpersonal Process*, 41, 254–263.

Mitchell, Stephen A. (1988). *Relational Concepts in Psychoanalysis: An Integration*. 5th ed. Cambridge, Mass.: Harvard University Press.

Mitchell, Stephen A. (1993). *Hope and Dread in Psychoanalysis*. New York: Basic Books.

Mitchell, Stephen A. (1997). *Influence and Autonomy in Psychoanalysis*. London: Routledge.

Mitchell, Stephen A. (2000). *Relationality: From attachment to intersubjectivity*. Hillsdale, NJ: Analytic Press.

Mitchell, Stephen A. (2003a). *Can Love Last? The Fate of Romance over Time*. 1st ed. New York: W.W. Norton.

Mitchell, Stephen (2003b). *Bindung und Beziehung: Auf dem Weg zu einer relationalen Psychoanalyse*. Giessen: Psychosozial-Verlag.

Mitchell, Stephen A. & Aron, Lewis (Eds.). (1999). *Relational Psychoanalysis, vol. 1: The Emergence of a Tradition*. Hoboken: Taylor & Francis.

Mitchell, Stephen A., Aron, Lewis, Harris, Adrienne, & Suchet, Melanie (Eds.). (1999). *Relational Psychoanalysis*. New York: Routledge.

Mitchell, Stephen A. & Black, Margaret J. (2016). *Freud and Beyond: A History of Modern Psychoanalytic Thought*. New York, NY: Basic Books.

Mitchell, Stephen A. & Harris, Adrienne (2004). What's American about American psychoanalysis? *Psychoanalytic Dialogues*, 14(2), 165–192.

Möller, Heidi, Lohmer, Mathias, Freyberger, Harald, Rosner, Rita, Seidler, Günter H., Stieglitz, Rolf-Dieter, & Strauß, Bernhard (2017). *Supervision in der Psychotherapie: Grundlagen – Forschung – Praxis*. Stuttgart: Kohlhammer.

Morgenthaler, Fritz, Weiss, Florence, & Morgenthaler, Marco (1986). *Gespräche am sterbenden Fluß: Ethnopsychoanalyse bei den Iatmul in Papua Neuguinea*. Frankfurt: Fischer.

Mottron, Laurent (2016). *L'intervention précoce pour enfants autistes: Nouveaux principes pour soutenir une autre intelligence*. Brussels: Mardaga.

Mühlleitner, Elke & Reichmayr, Johannes (1992). *Biographisches Lexikon der Psychoanalyse: Die Mitglieder der psychologischen Mittwoch-Gesellschaft und der Wiener psychoanalytischen Vereinigung 1902–1938*. Tübingen: Edition Diskord.

Müller, Brit (1996). *Strukturen der Wahrnehmung und des Bewusstseins: Ein Vergleich zwischen Leopold von Andrians 'Der Garten der Erkenntnis' und Robert Musils 'Die Verwirrungen des Zöglings Törleß'*. MA thesis (Modern German Literature). Berlin: Freie Universität Berlin.

Münch, Karsten (Ed.). (2017). *Neues zu vertrauten Konzepten: Ausgewählte Beiträge aus dem International Journal of Psychoanalysis*. Giessen: Psychosozial-Verlag.

Münch, Karsten & Buchholz, Michael B. (Eds.). (2010). *Die Psychoanalyse im Pluralismus der Wissenschaften*. Giessen: Psychosozial-Verlag.

Nacht, Sacha (1962). The Curative Factors in Psycho-Analysis. *Int. J. Psychoanal*, 43, 206–211.

Nagenkögel, Petra (2012). *Anagramme: Da die Bäume, die Sprache, ein Schlaf*. Salzburg: Otto Müller.

Nentwich, Michael (2004). *Cyberscience: Research in the Age of the Internet*. Vienna: Austrian Acad. of Sciences Press.

Neuweg, Georg Hans (2004). *Könnerschaft und implizites Wissen: Zur lehr-lern-theoretischen Bedeutung der Erkenntnis- und Wissenstheorie Michael Polanyis*. 3rd ed. Münster: Waxmann. Also as: Linz University, Habilitation, 1998.

Norman, Johan (2015). Der Psychoanalytiker und der Säugling: Eine neue Sicht der Arbeit mit Babys. In Gabriele Häussler & Petra Aulbert (Eds.), *Psychoanalytische Säuglingsbeobachtung und Säuglings-Kleinkind-Eltern-Psychotherapie* (pp. 217–244). Frankfurt: Brandes & Apsel.

Nowak, Martin A. & Highfield, Roger (2013). *Kooperative Intelligenz: Das Erfolgsgeheimnis der Evolution*. Munich: Beck.

O'Brien, Kymberlee M., Afzal, Karim, & Tronick, Edward (2013). Relational Psychophysiology and Mutual Regulation During Dyadic Therapeutic and Developmental Relating. In J.H.D. Cornelius-White, R. Motschnig-Pitrik, & M. Lux (Eds.), *Interdisciplinary Handbook of the Pperson-Centered Approach: Research and Theory* (pp. 183–197). Springer Science + Business Media. doi:10.1007/978-1-4614-7141-7_13.

Obholzer, Anton (2009). Interview mit Anton Obholzer: Zu den Anfängen der psychoanalytischen Organisationsbeobachtung. In Gertraud Diem-Wille (Ed.), *Ein-Blicke in die Tiefe: Die Methode der psychoanalytischen Säuglingsbeobachtung und ihre Anwendungen* (pp. 215–229). Stuttgart: Klett-Cotta.

Oevermann, Ulrich (2002). Klinische Soziologie auf der Basis der Methodologie der objektiven Hermeneutik – Manifest der objektiv hermeneutischen Sozialforschung. http://www.ihsk.de/publikationen/Ulrich_Oevermann-Manifest_der_objektiv_hermeneutischen_Sozialforschung.pdf (May 31, 2014).

Oevermann, Ulrich, Allert, Tilman, Konau, Elisabeth, & Krambeck, Jürgen (1979). Die Methodologie einer 'objektiven Hermeneutik' und ihre allgemeine forschungslogische Bedeutung in den Sozialwissenschaften. In Hans-Georg Soeffner (Ed.), *Interpretative Verfahren in den Sozial- und Textwissenschaften* (pp. 352–434). Stuttgart: Metzler.

Ogden, Thomas H. (1994). *Subjects of Analysis*. Northvale, NJ: Aronson.

Ogden, Thomas H. (2004). The Analytic Third: Implications for Psychoanalytic Theory and Technique. *Psychoanalytic Quarterly*, LXXIII, 2004. 167–195.

Orange, Donna M. (2000). Psychische Struktur: Transl. Erwin Bartosch & Christine Pawlowsky. In Gerhard Stumm, Alfred Pritz & Martin Voracek (Eds.), *Wörterbuch der Psychotherapie* (pp. 543). Vienna: Springer.

Orange, Donna M. (2011). *The Suffering Stranger: Hermeneutics for Everyday Clinical Practice*. New York: Routledge/Taylor & Francis.

Orange, Donna M. (2015). *Nourishing the Inner Life of Clinicians and Humanitarians*. New York: Routledge/Taylor & Francis.

Orange, Donna M. (2018). American Relationale Psychoanalysis. UNI Lectures 2018. Lecture. University of Vienna: ÖVIP – Österr. Verein für Individualpsychologie, April 12.

Orange, Donna M. (2020). *Psychoanalysis, History, and Radical Ethics, Learning to Hear*. New York: Routledge/Taylor & Francis.

Orange, Donna M., Atwood, George E., & Stolorow, Robert D. (2001). *Intersubjektivität in der Psychoanalyse: Kontextualismus in der psychoanalytischen Praxis*. 1st ed. Frankfurt: Brandes & Apsel.

Orange, Donna M. & Ross, Wolfgang F. (2004). *Emotionales Verständnis und Intersubjektivität: Beiträge zu einer psychoanalytischen Epistemologie*. 1st ed. Frankfurt: Brandes & Apsel.

Orlinsky, David (2018). Betrachtungen zur Würde als Wort und Handlung: Ergebnisse aus der psychotherapeutischen Forschung. In Hinrich Bents & Annette Kämmerer (Eds.), *Psychotherapie und Würde: Herausforderung in der psychotherapeutischen Praxis* (pp. 21–34). Berlin, Heidelber: Springer.

Orlinsky, David E., Grawe, Klaus, & Parks, Barbara K. (1994). Process and Outcome in Psychotherapy. In Allen E. Bergin & Sol L. Garfield (Eds.), *Handbook of Psychotherapy and Behavior Change* (pp. 270–376). 4th ed. New York: Wiley.

Orlinsky, David Elliot, Rønnestad, Michael Helge, & Ambühl, Hansruedi (2005). *How Psychotherapists Develop. A Study of Therapeutic Work and Professional Growth*. 1st ed. Washington, DC: American Psychological Association.

Osborne, Michael, Houston, M. & Toman, Nuala (eds.). (2007). *The Pedagogy of Lifelong Learning. Understanding Effective Teaching and Learning in Diverse Contexts*. London: Routledge.

Pap, Gabriela (2017). *Das Gemeinschaftsgefühl aus der Sicht der Intersubjektivität: Philosophische, psychoanalytische und entwicklungspsychologische Wurzeln*. Wiesbaden: Springer.

Paschotta, H.D. (1972). *Krankheitsverhalten bei Myasthenia gravis pseudoparalytica*. Inaugural-Dissertation. Justus-Liebig-Universität Giessen.

Perner, Josef (1993). *Understanding the Representational Mind*. Cambridge, Mass.: MIT Press.

Peters, Uwe Henrik (1977). *Übertragung, Gegenübertragung. Geschichte und Formen der Beziehungen zwischen Psychotherapeut und Patient*. Munich: Kindler.

Petzold, Hilarion G., Schigl, Brigitte, Fischer, Martin, & Höfner, Claudia (2003). *Supervision auf dem Prüfstand: Wirksamkeit, Forschung, Anwendungsfelder, Innovation*. Wiesbaden: VS Verlag für Sozialwissenschaften.

Pillow, Bradford H. (2012). *Children's Discovery of the Active Mind: Phenomenological Awareness, Social Experience, and Knowledge About Cognition*. New York, NY: Bradford H. Pillow.

Pizer, Stuart A. (1992). The negotiation of paradox in the analytic process. *Psychoanalytic Dialogues*, 2(2), 215–240. doi:10.1080/10481889209538930.

Pizer, Stuart (2018). Core Comptency Three: Deep Listening/Affective Attunment. In Roy E. Barsness (Ed.), *Core Competencies of Relational Psychoanalysis: A Guide to Practice, Study and Research* (pp. 104–120). New York: Routledge.

Plenker, Franz Peter (2015). Behandlungskrisen und die Rolle des Analytikers. *Psyche*, 69(1), 25–46.

Pohlmann, Werner (2013). 'Intersubjektivität' – ein neues Paradigma der Psychoanalyse? *Psyche*, 67(3), 251–275.

Poland, Warren S. (2016). The Analyst's Witnessing and Otherness. *J Am Psychoanal Assoc*, 48(1), 17–34. doi:10.1177/00030651000480011301.

Polanyi, Michael (1958). *Personal Knowledge: Towards a Post-Critical Philosophy*. Chicago: University of Chicago Press.

Polanyi, Michael (1985). *Implizites Wissen*. 1st ed. Frankfurt: Suhrkamp.
Pollmann, Armin (1985). Die Zulassung zur psychoanalytischen Ausbildung. Eine historische und empirische Studie. Göttingen: Verlag für Med. Psychologie im Verl. Vandenhoeck & Ruprecht. Also: Freie Universität Berlin, Dissertation., 1983 under the title.: Untersuchung über die Auswahl von Bewerbern zur psychoanalytischen Weiterbildung.
Poscheschnik, Gerald (Ed.). (2005). *Empirische Forschung in der Psychoanalyse: Grundlagen – Anwendungen – Ergebnisse*. Giessen: Psychosozial-Verlag.
Potthof, Peter (2015). Foulkes: ein Pionier in unvermessenen Territorien. In Wolfgang Martin Roth, Helga Felsberger, & Josef Shaked (Eds.), *Gruppenanalyse und die Entwicklung von Intersubjektivität. Österreichisches Jahrbuch für Gruppenanalyse. Band 7* (pp. 103–123). Vienna: Facultas.
Potthoff, Peter & Wollnik, Sabine (2003). Fairbairn, W.R.D.: Das Selbst und die inneren Objektbeziehungen – Eine psychoanalytische Objektbeziehungstheorie. *Zeitschrift für psychoanalytische Theorie und Praxis,* 18(3–4), 407–417. doi:10.15534/ZPTP/2003/3-4/12.
Prange, Klaus (2012). *Die Zeigestruktur der Erziehung: Grundriss der operativen Pädagogik*. 2nd revised ed. Paderborn, Vienna: Schöningh.
Prat, Règine (2013). Shaping and misshaping (French: 'Formation et deformation') during clinical training: some reflections on the impact of infant observation on the clinical paradigm. *Infant Observation International Journal of Infant Observation and Its Applications,* 16(3), 244–256.
Proske, Sarah (2014). *Der Giessen-Test: Funktion und Möglichkeiten seiner Verwendung im Kontext der Sozialen Arbeit*. Munich: GRIN Verlag GmbH.
Raab-Steiner, Elisabeth & Benesch, Michael (2012). *Der Fragebogen: Von der Forschungsidee zur SPSS-Auswertung*. 3rd ed. Vienna: Facultas.
Ramseyer, Fabian (2008). *Synchronisation nonverbaler Interaktion in der Psychotherapie*. Dissertation. University of Berne.
Reichmayr, Johannes (2013). *Ethnopsychoanalyse: Geschichte, Konzepte, Anwendungen*. 3rd corrected ed. Giessen: Psychosozial-Verlag.
Reis, Bruce (2010). Enactive Fields: An Approach to Interaction in the Kleinian-Bionian Model: Commentary on Paper by Lawrence J. Brown. *Psychoanalytic Dialogues,* 20(6), 695–703. doi:10.1080/10481885.2010.532405.
Reis, Bruce & Grossmark, Robert (Eds.). (2009). *Heterosexual Masculinities: Contemporary perspectives from Psychoanalytic Gender Theory*. New York: Routledge.
Renik, Owen (1995). The ideal of the anonymous analyst and the problem of self-disclosure. *Psychoanalytic Quarterly,* 64(3), 466–495.
Renik, Owen (1999). Playing one's cards face up in analysis: An approach to the problem of self-disclosure. *Psychoanalytic Quarterly,* 68(4), 521–539.
Rhode, Maria (2009). Sensorische Aspekte der Sprachentwicklung in Beziehung mit frühen Ängsten. In Gertraud Diem-Wille (Ed.), *Ein-Blicke in die Tiefe: Die Methode der psychoanalytischen Säuglingsbeobachtung und ihre Anwendungen* (pp. 103–118). Stuttgart: Klett-Cotta.
Richards, Arnold, Bachant, Janet L., & Lynch, Arthur A. (1997). Interaction in the transference/countertransference continuum. Lecture. International Psychoanalytic Association. Barcelona, July.
Riecken, Bernd (2006). 'Die ganze Welt ist eine Bühne ...': Kulturgeschichtliche und anthropologische Einflüsse auf Adlers Nervösen Charakter. *Zeitschrift für Individualpsychologie,* 31(3), 192–209.

Riegler, Sabine (2012). *Ein Überblick über die aktuelle Evaluierungspraxis an Hochschulen in Europa*. Munich: GRIN Verlag für akademische Texte.
Rieken, Bernd, Sindelar, Brigitte, & Stephenson, Thomas (2011). *Psychoanalytische Individualpsychologie in Theorie und Praxis: Psychotherapie, Pädagogik, Gesellschaft*. Vienna: Springer.
Rifkin, Jeremy (2011). *The Third Industrial Revolution: How Lateral Power is Transforming Energy, the Economy, and the World*. New York: Macmillan Education.
Ringstrom, Philip A. (2014). *A Relational Psychoanalytic Approach to Couples Psychotherapy*. London: Routledge.
Rizzolatti, Giacomo, Griese, Friedrich, & Sinigaglia, Corrado (2008). *Empathie und Spiegelneurone: Die biologische Basis des Mitgefühls*. 1st ed. Frankfurt: Suhrkamp.
Robinson, Paul & Skårderud, Finn. (2019). Eating Disorders. In Anthony W. Bateman & Peter Fonagy (Eds.), *Handbook of Mentalizing* (pp. 369–386). Washington, DC: American Psychiatric Publishing.
Rogers, Carl R. (1957). The necessary and sufficient conditions of therapeutic personality change. *Journal of Consulting Psychology*, 21(2), 95–103. doi:10.1037/h0045357.
Rogers, Carl R. (1996). *Die klientenzentrierte Gesprächspsychotherapie: Client-Centered Therapy*. Frankfurt: Fischer.
Rohde-Dachser, Christa & Wellendorf, Franz (Eds.). (2004). *Inszenierungen des Unmöglichen: Theorie und Therapie schwerer Persönlichkeitsstörungen*. Stuttgart: Klett-Cotta.
Rollwagen, Ingo (2013). Exkurs: Kreative Zerstörung oder kreative Gestaltung durch aktiven, intelligenten, techniknutzenden Widerstand. In Ayad Al-Ani (Ed.), *Widerstand in Organisationen. Organisationen im Widerstand. Virtuelle Plattformen, Edupunks und der nachfolgende Staat* (pp. 201–205). Wiesbaden: Springer VS.
Rønnestad, Michael Helge & Skovholt, Thomas M. (1997). Berufliche Entwicklung und Supervision von Psychotherapeuten. *Psychotherapeut*, 42(5), 299–306.
Rønnestad, Michael Helge & Skovholt, Thomas M. (2013). *The Developing Practitioner: Growth and Stagnation of Therapists and Counselors*. New York: Routledge.
Rosenberg, Marshall B. (2009). *Kinder einfühlend unterrichten: Wie SchülerInnen und LehrerInnen durch gegenseitiges Verständnis Erfolg haben können*. 2nd ed. Paderborn: Junfermann.
Roth, Wolfgang Martin, Felsberger, Helga, & Shaked, Josef (Eds.). (2014). *Gruppenanalyse und die Entwicklung von Intersubjektivität*. [Österreichisches Jahrbuch für Gruppenanalyse, 7]. 1st ed. Vienna: Facultas.
Rustin, Margaret (2008). Work discussion: some historical and theoretical observations. In Margaret Rustin, Jonathan Bradley, & Trudy Klauber (eds.), *Work Discussion: Learning from Reflective Practice in Work with Children and Families* (pp. 3–21). London: Karnac.
Rustin, Margaret (2009). Esther Bick's legacy of infant observation at the Tavistock – some reflections 60 years on. *Infant Observation*, 12(1), 29–41. doi:10.1080/13698030902731691.
Sadler, Lois S., Sladle, Arietta, & Mayes, Linda C. (2009). Das Baby bedenken: mentalisierungsgestützte Erziehungsberatung. In Jon G. Allen (Ed.), *Mentalisierungsgestützte Therapie: Das MBT-Handbuch – Konzepte und Praxis* (pp. 375–398). Stuttgart: Klett-Cotta.
Salzberger-Wittenberg, Isca (2002). *Psychoanalytisches Verstehen von Beziehungen: Ein Kleinianischer Ansatz*. Vienna: Facultas.

Salzberger-Wittenberg, Isca, Williams, Gianna Polacco, & Osborne, Elsie (1997). *Die Pädagogik der Gefühle: Emotionale Erfahrungen beim Lernen und Lehren*. Vienna: WUV.
Sander, Louis W. (2009). *Die Entwicklung des Säuglings, das Werden der Person und die Entstehung des Bewusstseins*. 1st ed. Stuttgart: Klett-Cotta.
Sarnat, Joan E. (1992). Supervision in Relationship: Resolving the teach-treat controversy in psychoanalytic supervision. *Psychoanalytic Psychology*, 9(3), 387–403. doi:10.1037/h0079388.
Sassenfeld, André J. & Jordan, Juan Francisco (2015). *Relationale Psychotherapie: Grundlagen und klinische Prinzipien*. Giessen: Psychosozial-Verlag.
Sauer, Joachim (1997). Zur Geschichte und Tradition der Supervision in Österreich. In Ingeborg Luif (Ed.), *Supervision. Tradition, Ansätze und Perspektiven in Österreich* (pp. 27–42). Vienna: Orac.
Savoy, Nick (2009). *Magic Bullets*. 2nd ed. Hamburg: Classic Books.
Scaife, Joyce (2013). *Supervision in Clinical Practice: A Practitioner's Guide*. 2nd ed. Hoboken: Taylor & Francis.
Scaife, Joyce (2014). *Supervising the Reflective Practitioner: An Essential Guide to Theory and Practice*. Hoboken: Taylor & Francis.
Scharff, David (2014). Five Things Western Therapists Need to Know for Working with Chinese Therapists and Patients. *Int. J. Appl. Psychoanal. Studies*, 11(1), 48–59. doi:10.1002/aps.1343.
Scharff, Jill Savege & Scharff, David (2000). *Tuning the Therapeutic Instrument: Affective learning of psychotherapy*. Northvale, NJ: Aronson.
Scharff, Jill Savege & Scharff, David (2014). Das affektbasierte Modell für die Ausbildung in psychoanalytischer Theorie und klinischer Praxis der psychoanalytischen Psychotherapie und Psychoanalyse. *Psyche*, 68(11), 1132–1163.
Scharff, Jill Savege & Scharff, David E. (2017). Group affective learning in training for psychotherapy and psychoanalysis. *The International Journal of Psycho-analysis*, 98 (6), 1619–1639. doi:10.1111/1745-8315.12638.
Scheer, Jörn W. (1979). Ein faktorenanalytisches Verfahren zur Untersuchung von Gruppenstrukturen mit dem Giessen-Test. In Dieter Beckmann & Horst-Eberhard Richter (Eds.), *Erfahrungen mit dem Giessen-Test (GT): Praxis, Forschung und Tabellen* (pp. 117–154). Berne: Huber.
Schindler, Raoul (2016). *Das lebendige Gefüge der Gruppe. Ausgewählte Schriften*. Edited by Christina Spaller, Konrad Wirnschimmel, Andrea Tippe, Judith Lamatsch, Ursula Margreiter, Ingrid Krafft-Ebing, & Michael Ertl. Giessen: Psychosozial-Verlag.
Schlicht, Tobias (2013). Mittendrin statt nur dabei. Wie funktioniert soziale Kognition? In Thiemo Breyer (Ed.), *Grenzen der Empathie. Philosophische, psychologische und anthropologische Perspektiven* (pp. 45–91). Munich: Fink.
Schmidt-Hellerau, Cordelia (n.d.) Das Ich, der Analytiker und die analytische Beziehung: Überlegungen zur gegenwärtigen amerikanischen Psychoanalyse. https://www.psyche.de/article/pdf/57912475546f88d21c8b52b7/ps_2002_07_0657-0686_0657_01 (April 19, 2018).
Schore, Allan N. (2009). *Affektregulation und die Reorganisation des Selbst*. 2nd ed. Stuttgart: Klett-Cotta.
Schoßmaier, Gerhard (2017). *ART Modul 1. Affektresonanzorientierte bedürfnisfokussierte Selbstempathie: Schule für psychiatrische Gesundheits- und Krankenpflege am Otto Wagner Spital Vienna*. Unpublished manuscript.

Schoßmaier, Gerhard (2018). Lehrpersonen als Unterstützer, Begleiter und Partner: Nähe und Distanz aus pflege-pädagogischer Sicht. *Psychiatriesche Pflege*, 3(6), 1–6. doi:10.1024/2297-6965/a000215.

Schoßmaier, Gerhard (2019a). Bedürfniswahrnehmung in der Pflegeausbildung. *Pflege Professionell – Das Fachmagazin*, 27/2019, 33–40.

Schoßmaier, Gerhard (2019b). *Psychosoziale Pflege: Grundlagen – Modelle – Interventionen*. Vienna: Facultas.

Schultz-Venrath, Ulrich (Ed.). (2013). *Lehrbuch Mentalisieren: Psychotherapien wirksam gestalten*. 1st ed. Stuttgart: Klett-Cotta.

Schultz-Venrath, Ulrich (2017). Therapie von Persönlichkeitsstörungen aus Sicht der Mentalisierungsbasierten Therapien. *PTT – Persönlichkeitsstörungen: Theorie und Therapie*, 21(1), 25–38.

Schultz-Venrath, Ulrich & Felsberger, Helga (2016). *Mentalisieren in Gruppen*. [Mentalisieren in Klinik und Praxis, vol. 1]. Stuttgart: Klett-Cotta.

Searles, Harold F. (1974). *Der psychoanalytische Beitrag zur Schizophrenieforschung: Collected Papers on Schizophrenia and Related sSbjects*. Munich: Kindler.

Seligman, Stephen (2003). The Developmental Perspective in Relational Psychoanalysis. *Contemporary Psychoanalysis*, 39(3), 477–508. doi:10.1080/00107530.2003.10747216.

Shaw, Daniel (2003). On the Therapeutic Action of Analytic Love. *Contemporary Psychoanalysis*, 39(2), 251–278.

Shaw, Daniel (2018). Core Competency: Love. In Roy E. Barsness (Ed.), *Core Competencies of Relational Psychoanalysis: A Guide to Practice, Study and Research* (pp. 201–217). New York: Routledge.

Sieberth, Wolfgang & Steinberger, Johann (2013). Beobachtung: Ein mentalisierungsgestütztes Pädagogikkonzept. In Sven Ernstson & Christine Meyer (Eds.), *Praxis geschlechtersensibler und interkultureller Bildung* (pp. 183–194). 1st ed. Wiesbaden: Springer VS.

Siegler, Robert S., DeLoache, Judy S., & Eisenberg, Nancy (2005). *Entwicklungspsychologie im Kindes- und Jugendalter*. 1st ed. Munich: Elsevier, Spektrum.

Sies, Claudia & West-Leuer, Beate (2003). *Coaching – ein Kursbuch für die psychodynamische Beratung. Zur Bedeutung zentraler Beziehungswünsche*. Stuttgart: Klett-Cotta.

Skogstad, Wilhelm (2004). Psychoanalytic Observation – The mind as Research Instrument. *Organisational & Social Dynamics*, 4(1), 67–87.

Skolnick, Neil J. & Warshaw, Susan C. (Eds.). (1992). *Relational Perspectives in Psychoanalysis*. Hillsdale, NJ: Analytic Press.

Skovholt, Thomas M. & Rønnestad, Michael Helge (1997). *The Evolving Professional Self: Stages and Themes in Therapist and Counselor Development*. Chichester: Wiley.

Slavin, Jonathan H. (1997). Models of learning and psychoanalytic traditions can reform be sustained in psychoanalytic training? *Psychoanalytic Dialogues*, 7(6), 803–817. doi:10.1080/10481889709539221.

Slavin, Jonathan H. (2010). Becoming an Individual: Technically Subversive Thoughts on the Role of the Analyst's Influence. *Psychoanalytic Dialogues*, 20(3), 308–324. doi:10.1080/10481885.2010.483957.

Slavin, Jonathan H. & Rahmani, Miki (2016). Slow Dancing. Mind, Body, and Sexuality in a New Relational Psychoanalysis. *Psychoanalytic Perspectives*, 13(2), 152–167. doi:10.1080/1551806X.2016.1156430.

Slochower, Joyce (2011). Holding, Collaborating, Colliding. A Cross Theoretical Conversation. *Psychoanalytic Inquiry*, 31(5), 501–512. doi:10.1080/07351690.2011.552053.
Soeffner, Hans-Georg (Ed.). (1979). *Interpretative Verfahren in den Sozial- und Textwissenschaften*. Stuttgart: Metzler.
Solano, Luigi (2010). Some thoughts between body and mind in the light of Wilma Bucci's multiple code theory. *The International journal of psycho-analysis*, 91(6), 1445–1464. doi:10.1111/j.1745-8315.2010.00359.x.
Somaini, Paola (2013). The eyes to see. *Infant Observation International Journal of Infant Observation and Its Applications*, 16(2), 157–169.
Spangenberg, Lena & Brähler, Elmar (2011). Bevölkerungsrepräsentative Neunormierung des Giessen-Tests (14–92 Jahre). *Psychotherapie, Psychosomatik, medizinische Psychologie*, 61(5), e15–18. doi:10.1055/s-0031-1271639.
Spezzano, Charles (1998). Listening and interpreting – how relational analysts kill time between disclosures and enactments. Commentary on papers by Bromberg and by Greenberg. *Psychoanalytic Dialogues*, 8(2), 237–246. doi:10.1080/10481889809539245.
Spitz, René A. (1957). *Die Entstehung der ersten Objektbeziehungen*. Stuttgart: Klett.
Stadler, Thomas (2017). Supervision in der Ausbildung zum Analytischen Kinder- und Jugendlichentherapeuten. In Wolfgang Mertens & Andreas Hamburger (Eds.), *Supervision in der Ausbildung* (pp. 44–57). 1st ed. Stuttgart: Kohlhammer.
Stadler, Christian & Kern, Sabine (2010). *Psychodrama: Eine Einführung*. 1st ed. Wiesbaden: Springer VS.
Staemmler, Frank M. (2009). *Das Geheimnis des Anderen – Empathie in der Psychotherapie. Wie Therapeuten und Klienten einander verstehen*. Stuttgart: Klett-Cotta.
Statistik Austria (2013a). Lehramt-Studierende an Pädagogischen Hochschulen 2012/13. https://www.bmbwf.gv.at/Themen/schule/schulsystem/gd/stat_tb.html (June 11, 2014).
Statistik Austria (2013b). Studierende in Österreich 2010/11–2012/13. https://www.bmbwf.gv.at/Themen/schule/schulsystem/gd/stat_tb.html (June 11, 2014).
Statistik Austria (2014). Studierende an Privatuniversitaeten 2013/14 nach Universität. https://www.bmbwf.gv.at/Themen/schule/schul system/gd/stat_tb.html (June 11, 2014).
Stattler, Manfred (2017). Ja Peperl, bist des du? Supervision im ländlichen Kontext. Masterarbeit. Universität Vienna. Postgraduate Center.
Stattler, Manfred (2018). Ja Peperl, bist des du? Supervision im ländlichen Kontext. Ein Forscchungsbericht von Manfred Stattler, Supervisor im Waldviertel. *ÖVS news*, 1/2018, 8–10.
Staun, Lenka (2017). *Mentalisieren bei Depressionen*. [Mentalisieren in Klinik und Praxis, 2. Band]. Stuttgart: Klett-Cotta.
Steinberger, Johann (2010). Kommunikation statt Kommando? Arbeitsbilder im Postfordismus. Weitere Beteiligte: Ö1 Radiokolleg. Armin Medosch (Regie). Radio Österreich 1 June 28–August 1, 2010.
Steinberger, Johann (2016). *Borderline-Kommunikation. Eine konversationsanalytische Studie*. Giessen: Psychosozial-Verlag.
Steinberger, Johann (2019). Schwierige Herausforderungen – Auswahlverfahren im Bereich der Krankenpflegeausbildung. *Psychiatrische Pflege*, 4(3), 29–33. Berne: Hogrefe.
Steinberger, Johann, Sieberth, Wolfgang & Zemann, Ewa (2013). P2. Ein mentalisierungsgestütztes Pädagogik-Konzept in der Ausbildung für Krankenpflegepersonal. *HBScience*, 4(S2), 30. doi:10.1007/s16024-013-0189-5.

Steinhardt, Kornelia & Reiter, Helga (2009). 'Work-Discussion' Lernen durch Beobachtung und Reflexion von Arbeitsprozessen. In Gertraud Diem-Wille (Ed.), *Ein-Blicke in die Tiefe: Die Methode der psychoanalytischen Säuglingsbeobachtung und ihre Anwendungen* (pp. 136–156). Stuttgart: Klett-Cotta.

Stephenson, Thomas (2014). Gemeinschaftsgefühl reloaded: Communityorientierung und Schlüsselkompetenzen Vom individualpsychologischen Grundbegriff zum Organisator pädagogischer Innovationen. *Zeitschrift für freie psychoanalytische Forschung und Individualpsychologie*, 1(1), 16–37.

Stephenson, Thomas (2017). Relationalität in der Hochschuldidaktik: Das fokus:bildung-Konzept. *Zeitschrift für freie psychoanalytische Forschung und Individualpsychologie*, 4(2), 55–56.

Stern, Daniel N. (1991). *The Interpersonal World of the Infant. A View from Psychoanalysis and Developmental Psychology*. 14th ed. New York, NY: Basic Books.

Stern, Daniel N. (2000). *The Interpersonal World of the Infant: A View from Psychoanalysis and Developmental Psychology*. New York: Basic Books.

Stern, Daniel N. (2003). *Die Lebenserfahrung des Säuglings*. 8th ed. Stuttgart: Klett-Cotta.

Stern, Daniel N. (2004). *The Present Moment in Psychotherapy and Everyday Life*. New York: Norton.

Stern, Daniel N. (2005). *Der Gegenwartsmoment: Veränderungsprozesse in Psychoanalyse, Psychotherapie und Alltag*. 1st ed. Frankfurt: Brandes & Apsel

Stern, Daniel N. (2014). *Der Gegenwartsmoment: Veränderungsprozesse in Psychoanalyse, Psychotherapie und Alltag*. 4th ed. Frankfurt: Brandes & Apsel.

Stern, Daniel N. (2016). *Die Lebenserfahrung des Säuglings*. 11th ed. Stuttgart: Klett-Cotta.

Stern, Daniel N., Sander, Louis W., Nahum, Jeremy P., Harrison, Alexandra M., Lyons-Ruth, Karlen, Morgan, Alexander C., & Bruschweiler-Stern, Nadia (2012). *Veränderungsprozesse: Ein integratives Paradigma*. 1st ed. Frankfurt: Brandes & Apsel.

Stern, Daniel N., Sander, Louis W., Nahum, Jeremy P., Harrison, Alexandra M., Lyons-Ruth, Karlen, Morgan, Alexander C., Bruschweiler-Stern, Nadia, & Tronick, E. Z. (1998). Non-interpretive mechanisms in psychoanalytic therapy. The 'something more' than interpretation. The Process of Change Study Group. *The International Journal of Psycho-analysis*, 79(5), 903–921.

Stern, Donnel B. (1999). Unformulated experience: From dissociation to imagination in psychoanalysis. *Psychoanalytic Psychology*, 16(3), 481–486. doi:10.1037//0736-9735.16.3.481.

Stern, Donnel B. (2003). *Unformulated Experience. From Dissociation to Imagination in Psychoanalysis*. New York, NY: Psychology Press.

Stern, Donnel B. (2010). *Partners in Thought: Working with Unformulated Experience, Dissociation, and Enactment*. London: Routledge.

Stern, Donnel B. (2014). Partners in Thought. A Clinical Process Theory of Narrative. In Lewis Aron & Adrienne Harris (Eds.), *Relational Psychoanalysis, Volume 5. Evolution of Process* (pp. 381–406). Hoboken: Taylor & Francis.

Stern, Donnel B. (2015a). *Relational Freedom: Emergent Properties of the Interpersonal Field*. London: Routledge.

Stern, Donnel B. (2015b). *Unformulated experience: From Dissociation to Imagination in Psychoanalysis*. London: Routledge.

Stern, Donnel B. (2019). *The Infinity of the Unsaid: Unformulated Experience, Language, and the Nonverbal*. London: Routledge.

Stevens, Holly & Stevens, Wallace (1990). *The Palm at the End of the Mind: Selected Poems and a Play*. New York: Random House, Vintage Books.
Stifter, Ruth (2012). Psychodrama und Mentalisieren: Psychoanalytisch-pädagogische Bildungsaspekte. Dissertation, Pedagogy, Universität Vienna. https://core.ac.uk/download/pdf/11598840.pdf (April 8, 2014).
Stolorow, Robert D. & Atwood, George E. (1996). The Intersubjective Perspective. *Psychoanalytic Review*, 83, 181–194. http://icpla.edu/wp-content/uploads/2012/10/Stolorow-Atwood-The-Intersubjective-Perspective-Psychoa.-Review-1996.pdf (May 3, 2018).
Stolorow, Robert D. & Atwood, George E. (2002). *Contexts of Being: The Intersubjective Foundations of Psychological Life*. Hillsdale, NJ: The Analytic Press.
Stolorow, Robert D., Brandchaft, Bernard, & Atwood, George E. (1996). *Psychoanalytische Behandlung: Ein intersubjektiver Ansatz*. Deutsche Erstausgabe. Frankfurt: Fischer.
Stolorow, Robert D., Brandchaft, Bernard, & Atwood, George E. (2014). *Structures of Subjectivity. Explorations in Psychoanalytic Phenomenology and Contextualism*. 2nd ed. London: Routledge/Taylor & Francis.
Stowasser, Josef M., Petschenig, Michael, & Skutsch, Franz (1998). *Stowasser: Lateinisch-deutsches Schulwörterbuch*. Edited by Alexander Christ. Vienna: Verlag Hölder-Pichler-Tempsky; Munich: R. Oldenbourg Verlag.
Streeck, Ulrich (2009). *Gestik und die therapeutische Beziehung: Über nichtsprachliches Verhalten in der Psychotherapie*. Stuttgart: Kohlhammer.
Strupp, Hans H. (1996). The tripartite model and the Consumer Reports study. *American Psychologist*, 51(10), 1017–1024. doi:10.1037/0003-066X.51.10.1017.
Stumm, Gerhard, Pritz, Alfred, & Voracek, Martin (Eds.). (2000). *Wörterbuch der Psychotherapie*. Vienna: Springer.
Suchet, Melanie (2007). Unraveling Whiteness. *Psychoanalytic Dialogues*, 17(6), 867–886. doi:10.1080/10481880701703730.
Sullivan, Harry Stack (1983). *Die interpersonale Theorie der Psychiatrie*. Frankfurt: Fischer.
Sullivan, Kate & Winner, Ellen (1993). Three-Year-Olds' Understanding of Mental States: The Influence of Trickery. *Journal of Experimental Child Psychology*, 56(2), 135–148.
Sünkel, Wolfgang (2002). *Phänomenologie des Unterrichts: Grundriss der theoretischen Didaktik*. 2nd ed. Weinheim: Juventa.
Szecsödy, Imre (2004). How Does Psychoanalysis Work? In Dēmētrēs Anastasopoulos & Evagelos Papanicolaou (Eds.), *The Therapist at Work: Personal Factors Affecting the Analytic Process* (pp. 53–62). London: Karnac.
Szecsödy, Imre (2017). Supervision – ein komplexes Mittel der psychoanalytischen Ausbildung. In Wolfgang Mertens & Andreas Hamburger (Eds.), *Supervision in der Ausbildung* (pp. 157–169). 1st ed. Stuttgart: Kohlhammer.
Taubner, Svenja (2015). *Konzept Mentalisieren: Eine Einführung in Forschung und Praxis*. Giessen: Psychosozial-Verlag.
Taubner, Svenja & Juen, Florian (2010). Gewalt in der Spätadoleszenz: Perspektiven der Bindungsforschung. *Psychotherapie & Sozialwissenschaft. Zeitschrift für qualitative Forschung und klinische Praxis*, 12(2), 59–77.
Taubner, Svenja, Munder, Thomas, Möller, Heidi, Hanke, Wiebke, & Klasen, Jennifer (2014). Selbstselektionsprozesse bei der Wahl des therapeutischen Ausbildungsverfahrens: Unterschiede in therapeutischen Haltungen, Persönlichkeitseigenschaften

und dem Mentalisierungsinteresse. *Psychotherapie, Psychosomatik, medizinische Psychologie*, 64(6), 214–223. doi:10.1055/s-0033-1358720.

Taubner, Svenja, Nolte, Tobias, Luyten, Patrick, & Fonagy, Peter (2010). Mentalisierung und das Selbst. *Persönlichkeitsstörungen*, 14(4), 243–258.

Thomä, Helmut (2001). Ferenczis 'mutuelle Analyse' im Lichte der modernen Psychoanalyse. *Forum der Psychoanalyse*, 17(3), 263–270. doi:10.1007/s004510100098.

Tomasello, Michael (2011). *Die Ursprünge der menschlichen Kommunikation*. 1st ed. Frankfurt: Suhrkamp.

Trevarthen, Colwyn (2009). The Intersubjective Psychobiology of Human Meaning. Learning of Culture Depends on Interest for Co-Operative Practical Work–and Affection for the Joyful Art of Good Company. *Psychoanalytic Dialogues*, 19(5), 507–518. doi:10.1080/10481880903231894.

Tronick, Edward (2007). *The Neurobehavioral and Social-emotional Development of Infants and Children*. New York: Norton.

Tronick, Ed & Beeghly, Marjorie (2011). Infants' meaning-making and the development of mental health problems. *The American Psychologist*, 66(2), 107–119. doi:10.1037/a0021631.

Truax, Charles B. & Carkhuff, Robert R. (1973). *Toward Effective Counseling and Psychotherapy: Training and Practice*. Chicago: Aldine.

Trunkenpolz, Kathrin (2008). Überlegungen zur Beziehungsgestaltung zwischen alten und pflegebedürftigen Menschen und deren Betreuungspersonen – basierend auf psychodynamischen Einzelbeobachtungen nach dem Tavistock-Konzept. *Heilpädagogik*, 51(5), 8–18.

Trunkenpolz, Kathrin, Datler, Wilfried, Funder, Antonia, & Hover-Reisner, Nina (2009). Von der Infant Observation zur Altersforschung: Die psychoanalytische Methode des Beobachtens nach dem Tavistock-Konzept im Kontext von Forschung. *Zeitschrift für Individualpsychologie*, 34(3), 331–350.

Tublin, Steven (2018). Core Competency One. Therapeutic Intent. In Roy E. Barsness (Ed.), *Core Competencies of Relational Psychoanalysis: A Guide to Practice, Study and Research* (pp. 66–85). New York: Routledge.

Tuckett, David (2011). Inside and Outside the window: Some Fundamental Elements in the Theory of Psychoanalytic Technique. *The International Journal of psychoanalysis*, 92(6), 1367–1390. doi:10.1111/j.1745-8315.2011.00471.x.

Tuckett, David (2017). Does Anything Go? Towards a Framework for the More Transparent Assessment of Psychoanalytic Competence. *The International Journal of Psychoanalysis*, 86(1), 31–49. doi:10.1516/R2U5-XJ37-7DFJ-DD18.

Turner, Agnes & Ingrisch, Doris (2009). Erfahrungslernen durch die psychoanalytische Beobachtungsmethode – Auf dem Weg zu einer neuen Lernkultur? Über das Verstehen der eigenen Emotionen und der von SchülerInnen aus der Perspektive von LehrerInnen. In Gertraud Diem-Wille (Ed.), *Ein-Blicke in die Tiefe: Die Methode der psychoanalytischen Säuglingsbeobachtung und ihre Anwendungen* (pp. 157–181). Stuttgart: Klett-Cotta.

Twemlow, Stuart W. & Fonagy, Peter (2009). Vom gewalterfüllten sozialen System zum mentalisierenden System: Ein Experiment in Schulen. In Jon G. Allen (Ed.), *Mentalisierungsgestützte Therapie. Das MBT-Handbuch – Konzepte und Praxis* (pp. 399–421). Stuttgart: Klett-Cotta.

Uddin, Lucina Q., Iacoboni, Marco, Lange, Claudia, & Keenan, Julian Paul (2007). The self and social cognition. The role of cortical midline structures and mirror neurons. *Trends in Cognitive Sciences*, 11(4), 153–157. doi:10.1016/j.tics.2007.01.001.

Urwin, Cathy & Sternberg, Janine (Eds.). (2012). *Infant Observation and Research: Emotional processes in everyday lives*. East Sussex: Routledge.

Vitz, Paul C. (1988). *Sigmund Freud's Christian Unconscious*. New York: Guildford.

Volkan, Vamik D. (1997). *Bloodlines: From Ethnic Pride to Ethnic Terrorism*. New York: Farrar Straus and Giroux.

Volkan, Vamik D. (2003). *Das Versagen der Diplomatie. Zur Psychoanalyse nationaler, ethnischer und religiöser Konflikte*. 3rd ed. Giessen: Psychosozial-Verlag.

Wander, Esther (1935). *Gruppenbildung im zweiten Lebensjahr*. Dissertation. Vienna: Universität Vienna, Philosophische Fakultät.

Watillon, Annette (2015). Die Dynamik psychoanalytischer Therapien der frühen Eltern-Kind-Beziehung. In Gabriele Häussler & Petra Aulbert (Eds.), *Psychoanalytische Säuglingsbeobachtung und Säuglings-Kleinkind-Eltern-Psychotherapie* (pp. 167–186). Frankfurt: Brandes & Apsel.

Watson John S. (1972). Smiling, Cooing, and 'the game'. *Merril-Palmer Quarterly*, 18 (4), 323–339.

Weigand, Wolfgang & Buchholz, Michael B. (Eds.). (2012). *Philosophie und Handwerk der Supervision*. Giessen: Psychosozial-Verlag.

Weinberg, Haim (2007). So What is this Social Unconscious Anyway? *Group Analysis*, 40(3), pp. 307–322. doi:10.1177/0533316407076114.

Weinberg, Haim (2015). From the Individual Unconscious Through the Relational Unconscious to the Social Unconscious. *Canadian Journal of Psychoanalysis*, 23(1), 195–201.

Weiss, Florence (2001). *Vor dem Vulkanausbruch. Meine Freundinnen in Rabaul*. Frankfurt: Fischer.

Weiste, Elina & Peräkylä, Anssi (2014). Prosody and empathic communication in psychotherapy interaction. *Psychotherapy Research*, 24(6), 687–701.

Wellman, Henry M. (1992). *The Child's Theory of Mind*. Cambridge, Mass.: MIT Press.

Wellman, Henry M. (2014). *Making Minds: How Theory of Mind Develops*. Oxford: Oxford University Press.

Wellman, Henry M. & Gelman, Susan A. (1992). Cognitive Development: Foundational theories of core domains. *Annual Review of Psychology*, 57, 337–375.

Wellman, H.M. & Woolley, J.D. (1990). From Simple Desires to Ordinary Beliefs: The Early Development of Everyday Psychology. *Cognition*, 35(3), 245–275.

West, G.B., Brown, J.H., & Enquist, B.J. (1997). A General Model for the Origin of Allometric Scaling Laws in Biology. *Science*, 276(5309), 122–126.

West-Leuer, Beate (2007). *Coaching an Schulen: Psychodynamische Beratung zur Stärkung professioneller Beziehungskompetenz*. Giessen: Psychosozial-Verlag.

West-Leuer, Beate (2011). Von der Angst, Supervisorin zu sein. Psychoanalytisch-intersubjektive Supervision in der Suchttherapie. In Elisabeth Möller & Stefani Träupmann (Eds.), *Aspekte der psychodynamischen Supervision* (pp.86–107). Kassel: University Press.

Whitebook, Joel (2018). *Freud: Sein Leben und Denken*. Stuttgart: Klett-Cotta.

Wikipedia (2018a). Emmanuel Ghent – Wikipedia. https://en.wikipedia.org/w/index.php?oldid=837545315 (April 26, 2018).

Wikipedia (2018b). Lewis Aron – Wikipedia. https://en.wikipedia.org/w/index.php?oldid=835263261 (April 29, 2018).

Will, Herbert (2010). *Psychoanalytische Kompetenzen. Standards und Ziele für die psychotherapeutische Ausbildung und Praxis*. Stuttgart: Kohlhammer.

Williams, Laurel L., Fonagy, Peter, Target, Mary, Fearon, Pasco, Sargent, John, Bleiberg, Efrain, & McGregor, Jacqueline (2009). Die Ausbildung von psychiatrischen Assistenzärzten in mentalisierungsgestützter Behandlung. In Jon G. Allen (Ed.), *Mentalisierungsgestützte Therapie. Das MBT-Handbuch – Konzepte und Praxis* (pp. 314–325). Stuttgart: Klett-Cotta.

Winnicott, Donald W. (1989). Transitional Objects and Transitional Phenomena. In Donald W. Winnicott (Ed.), *Playing and Reality*. London: Routledge.

Winnicott, Donald W. (1989). *Vom Spiel zur Kreativität*. 5th ed. Stuttgart: Klett-Cotta.

Winnicott, Donald W. (1997). *Von der Kinderheilkunde zur Psychoanalyse: Aus den 'Collected Papers'*. Frankfurt: Fischer.

Winnicott, Donald W. (2017). *The Collected works of D.W. Winnicott*. Volume 6. Edited by Lesley Caldwell & Helen Taylor Robinson. Oxford: Oxford University Press.

Wolf, R. (1976). Das Selbstkonzept (Selbstbild, Idealbild und normatives Bild) bei depressiven und psychopathischen Zustandsbildern. Diplomarbeit, Justus-Liebig-Universität Giessen.

Yalom, Irvin D. (2016). *Theorie und Praxis der Gruppenpsychotherapie: Ein Lehrbuch*. 12th ed. Stuttgart: Klett-Cotta.

Yarbrough, Donald B., Caruthers, Flora A., Shulha, Lyn M., & Hopson, Rodney K. (2011). *The Program Evaluation Standards: A Guide for Evaluators and Evaluation Users*. 3rd ed. Thousand Oaks, Calif.: SAGE.

Zabini, Christian (2009). Die Psychodynamik des Abschiednehmens – Eine Betrachtung von Beendigungs-Prozessen in der Schule. In Gertraud Diem-Wille (Ed.), *Ein-Blicke in die Tiefe: Die Methode der psychoanalytischen Säuglingsbeobachtung und ihre Anwendungen* (pp. 182–200). Stuttgart: Klett-Cotta.

Zelazo, Philip David, Argitis, Gina, & Carlson, Stephanie M. (2003). *The Development of Executive Function in Early Childhood*. Boston, Mass.: Blackwell.

Zemann, Ewa (2019). ART-Affektresonanztraining in der Pflegeausbildung. *Pflege Professionell – Das Fachmagazin*, 27/2019, 23–32.

Zemann, Ewa, Gundacker, Claudia, Schoßmaier, Gerhard, Steinberger, Johann, & Totzauer, Georg (2017). Affektresonanztraining ART© in der speziellen Grundausbildung in der psychiatrischen Gesundheits- und Krankenpflege am Otto-Wagner-Spital der Stadt Wien. *Österreichische Pflegezeitschrift ÖPZ*, 1/2017, 26–28.

Zemann, Ewa, Steinberger, Johann, Schoßmaier, Gerhard, & Gundacker, Claudia (2015). Empathische Kommunikation – ist sie erlernbar? Theorie und Praxis – Praxisprojekt. In Susanne Schoppmann, Harald Stefan, Anna Hegedüs, Udo Finklerburg, Ian Needham, Michael Schulz, Caroline Gurtner & Sabine Hahn (Eds.), *'Sprachen': Eine Herausforderung für die psychiatrische Pflege in Praxis – Management – Ausbildung – Forschung*. Kongressband 12, Dreiländerkongress Pflege in der Psychiatrie in Wien. Verlag Berner Fachhochschule.

Žižek, Slavoj & Gilmer, Eva (2010). *Die Tücke des Subjekts*. 1st ed. Berlin: Suhrkamp.

Zöchling, Gerlinde (2019). Achtsamkeit und Selbsterfahrung in der Ausbildung. *Pflege Professionell – Das Fachmagazin 27/2019*, 77–85.

Index

Page numbers in *italics* refer to figures.

FSC
www.fsc.org
MIX
Papier | Fördert gute Waldnutzung
FSC® C083411

Kolibri 360 GmbH
Ferdinand-Jühlke-Straße 7
99095 Erfurt, Deutschland
produktsicherheit@kolibri360.de